American College of Physicians

MKSAP® 15

Medical Knowledge Self-Assessment Program®

Gastroenterology and Hepatology

Gastroenterology and Hepatology

Contributors

Steven K. Herrine, MD, FACP, Book Editor[2]
Professor of Medicine
Division of Gastroenterology and Hepatology
Thomas Jefferson University
Philadelphia, Pennsylvania

Thomas Fekete, MD, FACP, Associate Editor[1]
Professor of Medicine
Associate Professor of Microbiology
Temple University Medical School
Philadelphia, Pennsylvania

Brian P. Bosworth, MD[2]
Assistant Professor of Medicine
Weill Medical College of Cornell University
New York, New York

Patricia Kozuch, MD[2]
Assistant Professor of Medicine
Division of Gastroenterology and Hepatology
Thomas Jefferson University
Philadelphia, Pennsylvania

David E. Loren, MD[2]
Assistant Professor of Medicine
Division of Gastroenterology and Hepatology
Thomas Jefferson University
Philadelphia, Pennsylvania

Victor J. Navarro, MD[2]
Professor of Medicine, Pharmacology and Experimental
  Therapeutics
Hepatology and Liver Transplantation
Thomas Jefferson University
Philadelphia, Pennsylvania

Amy S. Oxentenko, MD, FACP[2]
Assistant Professor of Medicine
College of Medicine, Mayo Clinic
Rochester, Minnesota

Patrick R. Pfau, MD[1]
Associate Professor of Medicine
University of Wisconsin
Madison, Wisconsin

Simona Rossi, MD[2]
Assistant Professor of Medicine
Division of Gastroenterology and Hepatology
Thomas Jefferson University
Philadelphia, Pennsylvania

Editor-in-Chief

Patrick C. Alguire, MD, FACP[1]
Director, Education and Career Development
American College of Physicians
Philadelphia, Pennsylvania

Gastroenterology and Hepatology Reviewers

Amindra S. Arora, MD[1]
Raymond F. Bianchi, MD, FACP[1]
Douglas Einstadter, MD, MPH, FACP[2]
Asad Khan Mohmand, MD[1]
Darrell S. Pardi, MD[2]
Amir Qaseem, MD, PhD, MHA, FACP[2]
Darius A. Rastegar, MD, FACP[1]
Joel E. Richter, MD, FACP[2]
Ingram M. Roberts, MD, FACP[1]
Suzanne Rose, MD, MSEd, FACP[2]

Gastroenterology and Hepatology ACP Editorial Staff

Charles Rossi, Senior Associate of Clinical Content
  Development
Sean McKinney, Director, Self-Assessment Programs
Margaret Wells, Managing Editor
Katie Idell, Production Administrator/Editor

ACP Principal Staff

Steven E. Weinberger, MD, FACP[2]
Deputy Executive Vice President
Senior Vice President, Medical Education and Publishing

D. Theresa Kanya, MBA[1]
Vice President, Medical Education and Publishing

Sean McKinney[1]
Director, Self-Assessment Programs

Margaret Wells[1]
Managing Editor

Charles Rossi[1]
Senior Associate of Clinical Content Development

Becky Krumm[1]
Senior Staff Editor

Ellen McDonald, PhD[1]
Senior Staff Editor

Amanda Neiley[1]
Staff Editor

Katie Idell[1]
Production Administrator/Editor

Valerie Dangovetsky[1]
Program Administrator

John Murray[1]
Editorial Coordinator

Shannon O'Sullivan[1]
Editorial Coordinator

Developed by the American College of Physicians

1. Has no relationships with any entity producing, marketing, re-selling, or distributing health care goods or services consumed by, or used on, patients.

2. Has disclosed relationships with entities producing, marketing, re-selling, or distributing health care goods or services consumed by, or used on, patients. See below.

Conflicts of Interest

The following contributors and ACP staff members have disclosed relationships with commercial companies:

Brian P. Bosworth, MD
Stock Options/Holdings
Schering-Plough
Research Grants/Contracts
Abbott, Centocor, Cerimon, PDL Biopharma, Salix, UCB, Procter & Gamble

Douglas Einstadter, MD, MPH, FACP
Consultantship
Medical Mutual of Ohio

Steven K. Herrine, MD, FACP
Research Grants/Contracts
Human Genome Sciences, Roche, Schering-Plough, Bristol-Myers Squibb, McNeil Consumer Products, Sanofi-Aventis
Speakers Bureau
Roche, Schering-Plough

Patricia Kozuch, MD
Consultantship
UCB, Abbott
Speakers Bureau
Scientific American Frontiers
Research Grants/Contracts
Sub investigator: Abbott, Ocera, Celltech, Berlex, Otsuka, Prometheus, Given Imaging, Alba Therapeutics, AstraZeneca, Salix, PDL Biopharma; Primary investigator: Abbott, Centocor
Other (Educational Speaking, Ad Board)
UCB, Centocor, Abbott, Elan

David E. Loren, MD
Speakers Bureau
Olympus America, Boston Scientific
Research Grants/Contracts
Boston Scientific, Protherics

Victor J. Navarro, MD
Consultantship
Merck, Alza, Amgen, Bristol-Myers Squibb, Theravance, Metabasis, Janssen, Viropharma, Johnson & Johnson
Research Grants/Contracts
Alza, Biotrin, Bristol-Myers Squibb, Janssen, McNeil Consumer Products, Madaus Pharma, Merck, Metabasis, Roche, Sanofi-Aventis, Theravance

Amy S. Oxentenko, MD, FACP
Research Grants/Contracts
PDL Biopharma

Darrell S. Pardi, MD
Research Grants/Contracts
Salix, AstraZeneca, Procter & Gamble
Consultantship
Biobalance Corporation, Lonza, Salix, Elan

Amir Qaseem, MD, PhD, MHA, FACP
Employment
American College of Physicians
Honoraria
NovoNordisk

Joel E. Richter, MD, FACP
Honoraria
AstraZeneca, TAP
Speakers Bureau
AstraZeneca, TAP

Suzanne Rose, MD, MSEd, FACP
Royalties
Hayes-Barton Press
Consultantship
Takeda, Novartis
Speakers Bureau
Takeda, TAP

Simona Rossi, MD
Research Grants/Contracts
Bristol-Myers Squibb, Human Genome Sciences, McNeil
  Consumer Products, Novartis Pharmaceuticals, Roche,
  Sanofi-Aventis, Schering-Plough, Gilead Sciences, Inc.
Honoraria
Gilead

Steven E. Weinberger, MD, FACP
Stock Options/Holdings
Abbott, GlaxoSmithKline

Acknowledgments

The American College of Physicians (ACP) gratefully
acknowledges the special contributions to the development
and production of the 15th edition of the Medical
Knowledge Self-Assessment Program® (MKSAP 15) of Scott
Thomas Hurd (Senior Systems Analyst/Developer), Ricki Jo
Kauffman (Manager, Systems Development), Michael Ripca
(Technical Administrator/Graphics Designer), and Lisa
Torrieri (Graphic Designer). The Digital version (CD-ROM
and Online components) was developed within the ACP's
Interactive Product Development Department by Steven
Spadt (Director), Christopher Forrest (Senior Software
Developer), Ryan Hinkel (Senior Software Developer), John
McKnight (Software Developer), Sean O'Donnell (Senior
Software Developer), and Brian Sweigard (Senior Software
Developer). Computer scoring and reporting are being per-
formed by ACT, Inc., Iowa City, Iowa. The College also
wishes to acknowledge that many other persons, too numer-
ous to mention, have contributed to the production of this
program. Without their dedicated efforts, this program
would not have been possible.

Continuing Medical Education

The American College of Physicians is accredited by the
Accreditation Council for Continuing Medical Education
(ACCME) to provide continuing medical education for
physicians.

The American College of Physicians designates this educational activity for a maximum of 166 *AMA PRA Category 1
Credits*™. Physicians should only claim credit commensurate with the extent of their participation in the activity.

AMA PRA Category 1 Credit™ is available from July 31,
2009, to July 31, 2012.

Learning Objectives

The learning objectives of MKSAP 15 are to:
• Close gaps between actual care in your practice and pre-
  ferred standards of care, based on best evidence
• Diagnose disease states that are less common and some-
  times overlooked and confusing
• Improve management of comorbidities that can compli-
  cate patient care
• Determine when to refer patients for surgery or care by
  subspecialists
• Pass the ABIM certification examination
• Pass the ABIM maintenance of certification examination

Target Audience

• General internists and primary care physicians
• Subspecialists who need to remain up-to-date in internal
  medicine
• Residents preparing for the certifying examination in
  internal medicine
• Physicians preparing for maintenance of certification in
  internal medicine (recertification)

How to Submit for CME Credits

To earn CME credits, complete a MKSAP 15 answer sheet.
Use the enclosed, self-addressed envelope to mail your completed answer sheet(s) to the MKSAP Processing Center for
scoring. Remember to provide your MKSAP 15 order and
ACP ID numbers in the appropriate spaces on the answer
sheet. The order and ACP ID numbers are printed on your
mailing label. If you have not received these numbers with
your MKSAP 15 purchase, you will need to acquire them to
earn CME credits. E-mail ACP's customer service center at
custserv@acponline.org. In the subject line, write "MKSAP
15 order/ACP ID numbers." In the body of the e-mail, make
sure you include your e-mail address as well as your full name,
address, city, state, ZIP code, country, and telephone number.
Also identify where you have made your MKSAP 15 purchase. You will receive your MKSAP 15 order and ACP ID
numbers by e-mail within 72 business hours.

Disclosure Policy

It is the policy of the American College of Physicians (ACP)
to ensure balance, independence, objectivity, and scientific
rigor in all its educational activities. To this end, and consistent with the policies of the ACP and the Accreditation
Council for Continuing Medical Education (ACCME), contributors to all ACP continuing medical education activities
are required to disclose all relevant financial relationships with
any entity producing, marketing, re-selling, or distributing
health care goods or services consumed by, or used on,
patients. Contributors are required to use generic names in
the discussion of therapeutic options and are required to
identify any unapproved, off-label, or investigative use of
commercial products or devices. Where a trade name is used,
all available trade names for the same product type are also

included. If trade-name products manufactured by companies with whom contributors have relationships are discussed, contributors are asked to provide evidence-based citations in support of the discussion. The information is reviewed by the committee responsible for producing this text. If necessary, adjustments to topics or contributors' roles in content development are made to balance the discussion. Further, all readers of this text are asked to evaluate the content for evidence of commercial bias so that future decisions about content and contributors can be made in light of this information.

Resolution of Conflicts

To resolve all conflicts of interest and influences of vested interests, the ACP precluded members of the content-creation committee from deciding on any content issues that involved generic or trade-name products associated with proprietary entities with which these committee members had relationships. Contributors' disclosure information can be found with the list of contributors' names and those of ACP principal staff listed in the beginning of this book.

Educational Disclaimer

The editors and publisher of MKSAP 15 recognize that the development of new material offers many opportunities for error. Despite our best efforts, some errors may persist in print. Drug dosage schedules are, we believe, accurate and in accordance with current standards. Readers are advised, however, to ensure that the recommended dosages in MKSAP 15 concur with the information provided in the product information material. This is especially important in cases of new, infrequently used, or highly toxic drugs. Application of the information in MKSAP 15 remains the professional responsibility of the practitioner.

The primary purpose of MKSAP 15 is educational. Information presented, as well as publications, technologies, products, and/or services discussed, is intended to inform subscribers about the knowledge, techniques, and experiences of the contributors. A diversity of professional opinion exists, and the views of the contributors are their own and not those of the ACP. Inclusion of any material in the program does not constitute endorsement or recommendation by the ACP. The ACP does not warrant the safety, reliability, accuracy, completeness, or usefulness of and disclaims any and all liability for damages and claims that may result from the use of information, publications, technologies, products, and/or services discussed in this program.

Publisher's Information

Unauthorized Use of This Book Is Against the Law

MKSAP 15 ISBN: 978-1-934465-25-7
Gastroenterology and Hepatology ISBN: 978-1-934465-29-5

Printed in the United States of America.

For order information in the U.S. or Canada call 800-523-1546, extension 2600. All other countries call 215-351-2600. Fax inquiries to 215-351-2799 or e-mail to custserv@acponline.org.

Errata and Norm Tables

Errata for MKSAP 15 will be posted at http://mksap.acponline.org/errata as new information becomes known to the editors.

MKSAP 15 Performance Interpretation Guidelines with Norm Tables, available December 31, 2010, will reflect the knowledge of physicians who have completed the self-assessment tests before the program was published. These physicians took the tests without being able to refer to the syllabus, answers, and critiques. For your convenience, the tables are available in a printable PDF file at http://mksap.acponline.org/normtables.

Table of Contents

Gastroenterology and Hepatology

Disorders of the Esophagus

Symptoms of Esophageal Disorders

Dysphagia

Dysphagia, or difficulty swallowing, is a symptom whose prevalence increases with age, affecting up to 15% of persons older than 65 years and up to 50% of persons in chronic care facilities. Recurrent, frequent, or persistent dysphagia can be an alarm symptom and requires investigation. Dysphagia is classified as either oropharyngeal dysphagia (also called transfer dysphagia) or esophageal dysphagia. Each of the two kinds of dysphagia has distinct epidemiology, pathophysiology, and management implications.

Oropharyngeal Dysphagia

Oropharyngeal dysphagia usually occurs immediately with deglutition and is often associated with a neuromuscular disorder; it usually consists of difficulty initiating a swallow, often associated with coughing or choking sensations. Other manifestations include recurrent pulmonary infections and regurgitation; associated symptoms include dysarthria and dysphonia. Although structural lesions of the esophagus are more common in esophageal dysphagia, high lesions such as pharyngoesophageal (Zenker) diverticulum, thyromegaly, large cervical osteophytes, and carcinomas can present as oropharyngeal dysphagia. The most common neuromuscular disorders associated with oropharyngeal dysphagia include stroke, Parkinson disease, amyotrophic lateral sclerosis, myasthenia gravis, and muscular dystrophy (**Table 1**). The diagnosis of oropharyngeal dysphagia is best accomplished by videofluoroscopy, which may lead to the need for endoscopy if a structural lesion is detected.

Esophageal Dysphagia

Esophageal dysphagia usually occurs after the initiation of a swallow, which suggests a mechanical interference with swallowing. It frequently presents as a feeling of food "sticking" in the chest, often localized to the lower sternum, but occasionally as high as the suprasternal notch. The causes of esophageal dysphagia can often be distinguished by the history of the patient's swallowing difficulty. Important distinctions include whether the symptom occurs with swallowing liquids, solid food, or both; the duration of the symptoms and whether they are progressive; and whether heartburn is present. Dysphagia for solids is usually caused by structural lesions, such as a Schatzki ring (**Figure 1**),

TABLE 1 Medical Conditions Associated with Dysphagia
Oropharyngeal Dysphagia
Structural Disorders
Cervical osteophytes
Cricoid webs
Pharyngoesophageal (Zenker) diverticulum (aspiration, neck mass, and regurgitation of food)
Thyromegaly
Neurologic/Myogenic Disorders
Amyotrophic lateral sclerosis (upper and lower motor neuron signs; fasciculations)
Central nervous system tumor
Stroke
Muscular dystrophy
Myasthenia gravis
Parkinson disease
Sicca syndrome
Esophageal Dysphagia
Structural Disorders
Dysphagia lusoria (vascular dysphagia)
Epiphrenic/traction diverticulum
Esophageal strictures (intermittent dysphagia–especially for solids–history of reflux)
Esophageal webs (usually incidental finding, may be associated with iron deficiency anemia)
Neoplasms (rapidly progressive dysphagia for solids then liquids; anorexia and weight loss)
Motility Disorders
Achalasia

stricture, or cancer. Esophageal dysphagia for both solids and liquids is usually the result of a motility disorder, especially achalasia, scleroderma, or diffuse esophageal spasm. Diagnosis of esophageal dysphagia often entails endoscopic visualization, a procedure that can provide therapy as well as diagnosis.

Heartburn

Heartburn, also known as pyrosis, is a feeling of burning or warmth that begins in the lower esophagus, tends to rise toward the neck, and occurs in waves most commonly postprandially. Heartburn is one of the most common gastrointestinal symptoms, affecting an estimated 20% of the U.S. population at least once a week. Heartburn is usually associated with gastroesophageal reflux disease (GERD), although the severity of the heartburn does not correlate with the severity of the esophageal disorder. Heartburn is often experienced

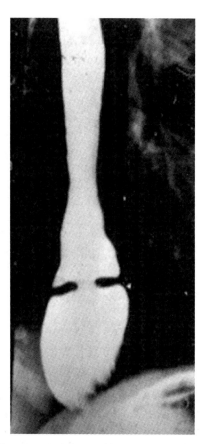

FIGURE 1.
Barium esophagography showing a Schatzki ring.

TABLE 2 Factors Aggravating Heartburn
Cigarette smoking
Eating habits
Eating large meals
Eating late at night
Foods/beverages
Alcohol
Chocolate
Citrus fruits and juices
Coffee
Fatty and fried foods
Onions
Peppermint
Medications
Anticholinergic agents
Aspirin and other NSAIDs
Calcium channel blockers
Nitrates
Progesterone
Body position
Bending over
Exercising

within an hour of eating a large meal, especially when foods that decrease lower esophageal sphincter pressure or irritate an already inflamed esophagus are ingested (**Table 2**).

Noncardiac Chest Pain

Esophageal disorders are second only to cardiac disease as a cause of chest pain. The two types of discomfort can be clinically indistinguishable because they have a common innervation and anatomic location. Esophageal chest pain is more likely than cardiac chest pain to be nonexertional, long lasting, disturbing of sleep, and associated with meals. Esophageal chest pain is frequently associated with GERD, and most authorities recommend an empiric trial of acid suppression therapy with a proton pump inhibitor as the first diagnostic test for this disorder. In the presence of ongoing symptoms, the addition of a low-dose tricyclic antidepressant can be helpful by decreasing visceral sensitivity. If cardiac causes of chest pain have been ruled out and the patient's symptoms do not resolve with medical therapy, referral for ambulatory pH monitoring and/or esophageal manometry is indicated.

Odynophagia and Globus Sensation

Odynophagia, or painful swallowing, is most frequently related to esophageal ulceration. The most common causes are pill esophagitis, infectious (especially viral) esophagitis, and severe peptic ulcer disease. The clinical setting in which the episode of odynophagia takes place–the presence of an offending medication, the presence of immunosuppression, or a history of GERD–can help elucidate the cause. Globus sensation is a feeling of a lump or tightness in the throat that is unrelated to meals but that may be associated with emotional stress. Psychological factors have traditionally been thought to account for most cases of globus sensation, but GERD can be detected in many affected patients.

KEY POINTS

- Oropharyngeal dysphagia occurs immediately with deglutition and often has a neuromuscular origin.
- Esophageal dysphagia usually occurs after the initiation of a swallow and is often caused by a mechanical interference with swallowing.
- Dysphagia for solids is usually caused by a structural lesion; dysphagia for both solids and liquids is usually caused by a motility disorder.
- Odynophagia is usually caused by esophageal ulceration.

Gastroesophageal Reflux Disease

Gastroesophageal reflux disease (GERD) is caused by an insufficiency of physiologic antireflux barriers at the gastroesophageal junction, resulting in reflux of gastric contents into the esophagus. GERD is one of the most common conditions leading to the need for health care in the United States. Although the incidence of peptic ulcer disease has decreased greatly in the United States over the past several decades, the incidence of GERD is rising rapidly. GERD imposes the greatest financial burden of any gastrointestinal disease in the United States, with an estimated total cost of nearly $10 billion annually, of which more than half is spent on drugs.

Pathogenesis

Maintenance of the mucosal integrity of the esophagus involves (1) anatomic antireflux barriers, (2) mechanisms of esophageal acid clearance, and (3) gastric acidity and acid volume. Although the presence of acidic gastric material is central to the pathogenesis of GERD, most patients with the disorder are not hypersecretors. The most important etiologic factor appears to be inappropriate transient relaxations of the lower esophageal sphincter.

Anatomic reflux barriers include the lower esophageal sphincter and other structures near the gastroesophageal junction. Transient relaxations of the sphincter, which are not associated with a swallow, are thought to be the pathophysiologic mechanism of most episodes of reflux. The minority of patients with GERD, usually those with severe disease, develop reflux because of a low resting lower esophageal sphincter pressure. Hiatal hernia is a common anatomic condition in which the gastroesophageal junction and part of the stomach are located above the diaphragmatic hiatus. The prevalence of hiatal hernia in patients with reflux is significantly higher than in the normal population.

Esophageal acid is cleared by peristalsis, gravity, and neutralization from saliva and alkaline esophageal secretions. Failure of these mechanisms (which may be caused by xerostomia, cigarette smoking, medications, and esophageal motility disorders [for example, scleroderma]) can increase esophageal acid exposure. The presence of gastric acid is necessary for this process, although the amount of gastric acid produced does not correlate with the severity of GERD. For example, *Helicobacter pylori* decreases gastric acidity, whereas eradication of the organism may increase acid production. Poor gastric emptying, such as in gastroparesis, can increase esophageal acid exposure.

Diagnosis

Patients with heartburn and regurgitation, the classic symptoms of GERD, should be given empiric antisecretory therapy with a proton pump inhibitor. Response to a 4-week empiric trial of a proton pump inhibitor has 75% sensitivity and 55% specificity for the diagnosis of GERD when compared to the gold standard of ambulatory pH monitoring. Patients with such symptoms as weight loss, dysphagia, odynophagia, and bleeding or anemia, and patients with long-standing symptoms or symptoms that are refractory to

acid-suppression therapy should undergo further evaluation, including gastrointestinal endoscopy.

During upper endoscopy the esophageal mucosa can be visualized. Endoscopy is more accurate than barium studies in making the diagnosis of esophagitis, especially in milder cases. The presence of refluxed barium material at the time of radiologic study is neither sensitive nor specific for the diagnosis of GERD and should not be used for this purpose.

Ambulatory esophageal pH monitoring, which consists of inserting a pH monitor into the distal esophagus and recording the results over a period of usually 24 hours, is the most accurate means to confirm the diagnosis of GERD. The technique also allows determination of an association between symptoms and the amount and pattern of esophageal acid exposure. Newer technologies include impedance monitoring, which can detect nonacidic reflux, and wireless ambulatory pH monitoring, which provides a longer monitoring time than previous techniques and is more comfortable for the patient.

Treatment

Medical Therapy

The traditional, conservative approach to therapy for GERD includes lifestyle modifications such as elevation of the head of the bed, smoking cessation, weight loss, and avoiding lying down after meals. These measures have all been reported to decrease esophageal acid exposure, although their superiority to placebo has not been established. Self-directed therapies for GERD include antacids, alginic acid, histamine$_2$-receptor antagonists (H2RAs), and proton pump inhibitors (PPIs). Antacids and alginic acid, also available in combination, provide short-term relief of reflux symptoms in about 20% of patients. Over-the-counter H2RAs also have a short onset of action, but a longer duration of efficacy. These agents are especially effective when taken in anticipation of a reflux-inducing event such as eating certain foods. PPIs are also available over the counter, but the product information recommends self-directed use for only 2 weeks after which time a physician should be consulted.

The standard of care for the medical treatment of GERD is PPI therapy. Although H2RA therapy relieves symptoms and heals esophagitis in 50% to 60% of patients, PPI therapy provides results in the 80% range. There are five PPIs available in the United States: omeprazole, esomeprazole, lansoprazole, pantoprazole, and rabeprazole; they all have similar efficacy. PPI therapy is usually given once a day before meals, usually before breakfast. In patients who require twice-daily dosing (for example, patients with noncardiac chest pain, extraesophageal manifestations, incomplete response to standard therapy, or Barrett esophagus), the second dose should be administered before dinner. GERD symptoms often recur after acid suppression therapy is stopped, and, therefore, many patients with reflux require maintenance therapy. Maintenance therapy reduces the risk of recurrent peptic strictures but has not been shown to prevent progression of Barrett esophagus. Long-term PPI therapy is considered generally safe for patients who require ongoing acid suppression. The risks and benefits of long-term PPI therapy need to be considered in light of case-controlled studies that suggest an increased risk of enteric infections, pneumonia, and hip fractures with such use. Despite concern that long-term PPI therapy in patients infected with *H. pylori* increases the risk of atrophic gastritis and gastric cancer, current guidelines do not recommend routine *H. pylori* testing.

Antireflux Surgery

Because of the efficacy of medical therapy for GERD, surgical approaches are used with caution. The best outcomes are observed in patients whose symptoms are well controlled with medical therapy and who have few comorbidities. Early reports of surgical superiority were conducted using inadequately aggressive medical therapy. Relief of symptoms with surgery is significant but not always long-lasting; more than half of patients who have surgery for GERD resume regular PPI therapy within 10 to 15 years after surgery. Side effects of surgery, which include dysphagia, gas-bloat syndrome, and diarrhea, occur in approximately 25% of patients. Antireflux surgery is most effective if done by an experienced surgeon in a high-volume center.

Endoscopic Therapy

Initial enthusiasm for endoscopic management of GERD has given way to cautious recommendations. There are three major types of endoscopic interventions: radiofrequency application to the lower esophageal sphincter, endoscopic sewing devices, and injection of polymers into the lower esophageal sphincter. All have been shown to decrease GERD symptoms for the first 6 to 12 months, but none have demonstrated a durable decrease in the use of PPIs, increase of lower esophageal sphincter pressure, or decrease in stricture frequency. The American Gastroenterological Association position statement on endoscopic therapy for GERD concludes that there are no definite indications for endoscopic therapy for GERD.

Extraesophageal Manifestations of Gastroesophageal Reflux Disease

Up to one third of patients evaluated for heartburn have evidence of extraesophageal reflux disease. Empiric PPI therapy can aid in the diagnosis of such extraesophageal manifestations, but they do not respond to PPI therapy as well as traditional reflux-type symptoms.

Asthma

GERD is thought to cause asthma through microaspiration of refluxate and/or vagally mediated esophagobronchial reflex.

Because of the frequency of both GERD and asthma in the population, causality is difficult to determine, but population-based studies have suggested an epidemiologic association. An estimated 30% to 90% of patients with asthma have either GERD or GERD-like symptoms. Clinical trials assessing the efficacy of PPI therapy for GERD-induced asthma have yet to show a convincing or reproducible benefit, although a number of reports of small cohorts suggest symptomatic benefit.

Cough

Chronic cough, defined as cough lasting 3 to 8 weeks, has been associated with GERD in up to 40% of patients. The pathophysiology of GERD-related chronic cough involves, as in GERD-related asthma, both microaspiration and vagal reflex. Only three small studies with varying methodologies have been published regarding PPI therapy and chronic cough, none of which show convincing benefit.

Laryngitis

Due to difficulty in establishing a consistent definition of laryngitis, estimates of the prevalence of GERD-related laryngitis are unreliable. It has been estimated, however, that up to 10% of patients evaluated by ear, nose, and throat physicians have GERD-like symptoms. The pathogenesis of GERD-induced laryngitis may involve direct laryngeal injury or may be due to vagally induced throat clearing and cough, leading to laryngeal irritation. There have been multiple trials of PPI therapy in patients with GERD-related laryngitis, but the majority of these trials and meta-analyses failed to show convincing benefit. The use of PPI therapy for chronic laryngitis remains empiric and based on clinical judgment.

KEY POINTS

- Transient relaxation of the lower esophageal sphincter is an important cause of gastroesophageal reflux disease.
- Ambulatory pH monitoring is the gold standard for the diagnosis of gastroesophageal reflux disease.
- Empiric therapy with a proton pump inhibitor has an acceptable sensitivity and specificity for diagnosing gastroesophageal reflux disease.
- The standard of care for the medical treatment of gastroesophageal reflux disease is proton pump inhibitor therapy.
- Lifestyle modifications and surgical and endoscopic approaches are of unclear long-term benefit for gastroesophageal reflux disease.
- Up to one third of patients with gastroesophageal reflux disease have extraesophageal manifestations, such as asthma, noncardiac chest pain, chronic cough, and laryngitis.

Barrett Esophagus

Barrett esophagus is a complication of GERD in which the normal squamous epithelium of the distal esophagus is replaced by specialized columnar epithelium (**Figure 2**). The disorder is most common in patients with long-standing and severe GERD and in patients with large hiatal hernias, low lower esophageal sphincter pressure, and abnormal esophageal motility. The pathophysiology of Barrett esophagus is unclear.

Barrett esophagus is uncommon, but the incidence is increasing, perhaps due to higher detection rates. Approximately 10% of patients who undergo upper endoscopy for symptomatic GERD are found to have Barrett esophagus, whereas up to 2% of unselected patients who undergo upper endoscopy have the characteristic mucosal changes of the disorder. The results of autopsy series suggest that most cases of Barrett esophagus are undetected. Barrett esophagus is a premalignant condition; affected patients have an estimated 30-fold increased risk of esophageal adenocarcinoma compared to those without Barrett esophagus and an annual incidence of esophageal adenocarcinoma of 0.5%.

Screening and Diagnosis

The diagnosis of Barrett esophagus is suspected by endoscopic features and made histologically by detection of specialized intestinal metaplasia with acid-mucin containing goblet cells (**Figure 3**). Long-segment Barrett esophagus, defined as greater than 3 cm of columnar-lined esophagus, appears to be associated with a higher risk of esophageal adenocarcinoma. This increased risk has led to screening and surveillance programs for Barrett esophagus, although there is no evidence that screening improves survival. Current standards for endoscopic screening in patients with GERD are controversial, but most authorities agree that upper endoscopy should be performed on patients who have had symptomatic GERD for at least 5 years. If Barrett esophagus is determined by histology, surveillance endoscopy with multiple biopsies should be performed at diagnosis and at 1 year (**Table 3**). If no dysplasia is found, further surveillance can be deferred for 5 years. The presence of low-grade or high-grade dysplasia requires further intensive management, including the possibility of esophagectomy. Molecular markers for premalignant conditions of the

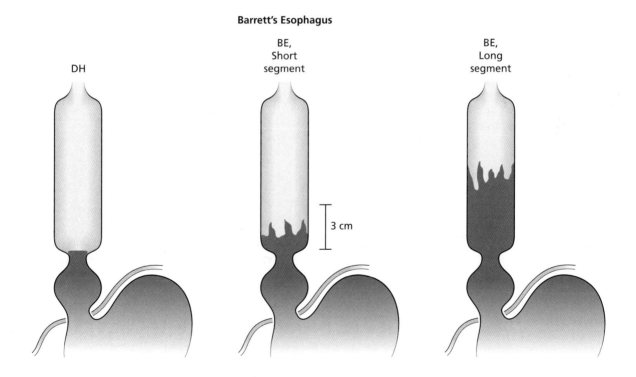

Barrett's Esophagus

DH

BE, Short segment

3 cm

BE, Long segment

FIGURE 2.
Barrett esophagus.
Diagram of the esophageal and gastric junction showing replacement of normal esophageal squamous mucosa by specialized intestinal mucosa (shown in red).
Courtesy of Dr. Alan Cameron.

BE = Barrett esophagus; DH = diaphragmatic (hiatal) hernia.

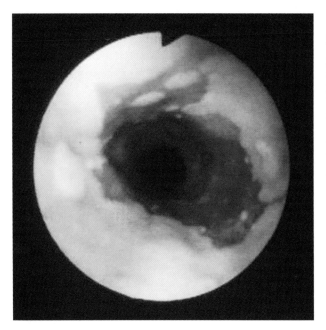

FIGURE 3.
Barrett mucosa.
Upper endoscopic view of Barrett mucosa. Note the salmon-colored mucosa representing Barrett mucosa compared with the normal pearl-colored squamous mucosa.

esophagus are under development but have not displaced histologic grading of dysplasia.

Treatment

Therapy with PPIs has not been shown to slow progression of Barrett esophagus or lead to regression of the abnormal esophageal mucosa. Surgical fundoplication has also not been shown to decrease cancer risk in affected patients. Ablative therapies that consist of removal of metaplastic epithelium can, when combined with intensive acid suppression therapy, lead to the regeneration of squamous mucosa. Photodynamic therapy is an ablative therapy approved by the FDA for use in patients with high-grade dysplasia to reduce cancer risk. Concerns remain that areas of abnormal mucosa below the normal-appearing regenerated epithelium may still harbor

cancer risk. Esophagectomy is reserved for those patients with Barrett esophagus and a confirmed diagnosis of dysplasia. Epidemiologic data suggest that chemoprevention with aspirin, NSAIDs, and cyclooxygenase-2 inhibitors may reduce cancer risk in patients with Barrett esophagus. Epidemiologic evidence suggests that lifestyle modifications such as smoking cessation, weight control, and diets rich in fruits and vegetables may also be effective.

Esophageal Carcinoma

The overwhelming majority of esophageal malignancies are primary carcinomas, with roughly equal numbers of squamous cell carcinoma and adenocarcinoma. Approximately 14,000 new cases of esophageal carcinoma are diagnosed in the United States annually, with 13,000 deaths resulting. Adenocarcinoma is the most rapidly increasing histologic tumor type, with a 300% increase since about 1970. Esophageal cancer, which is more common in men than in women, is the seventh leading cause of cancer death among U.S. men, with black men having a higher risk than other groups. Risk factors for squamous cell carcinoma include long-term exposure to alcohol and tobacco, nitrosamine exposure, corrosive injury to the esophagus, vitamin deficiencies, achalasia, tylosis (keratosis of the palms and soles), and human papillomavirus infection. Besides Barrett esophagus, risk factors for the development of adenocarcinoma include tobacco use, obesity, and GERD.

Diagnosis and Staging

Squamous cell carcinoma often arises in the upper portions of the esophagus, whereas adenocarcinoma arises more distally; however, the presentation of the two variants is similar. Dysphagia for solids is the most common presenting symptom (70%); odynophagia is less common and often is associated with ulceration of the lesion. Chest pain, anorexia, weight loss, gastrointestinal bleeding, and regurgitation are other presenting complaints. The diagnosis is often made with direct endoscopic visualization and biopsy. Staging of the tumor is useful in determining prognosis and guiding therapy (**Table 4**).

TABLE 3 Practice Guidelines for Endoscopic Surveillance of Barrett Esophagus	
Dysplasia Grade	**Recommendation**
None	Repeat surveillance 1 year after baseline screening; if negative, every 5 years Discontinue surveillance if life expectancy <1 year or patient unable to tolerate therapeutic measures
Low-grade	Surveillance every 6 months for 1 year, then yearly until age 80, depending on health status
High-grade	If confirmed by two experienced pathologists, definitive surgical or endoscopic management If patient declines, consider continued surveillance: Focal high-grade dysplasia: continue surveillance every 3 months for 2 years then every 6 months Multifocal high-grade dysplasia: definitive intervention Mucosal irregularity: endoscopic ultrasonography and mucosal resection, if available

Adapted from: Wang KK, Wongkeesong M, Buttar NS; American Gastroenterological Association. American Gastroenterological Association technical review on the role of the gastroenterologist in the management of esophageal carcinoma. Gastroenterology. 128;(5):1468-70. [PMID: 15887129]. Copyright 2005, with permission from Elsevier.

TABLE 4 Staging of Esophageal Carcinoma According to the American Joint Commission on Cancer		
Stage	**Histologic Description**	**5-Year Mortality Rate (%)**
0	Carcinoma in situ	>90
I	Tumor confined to lamina propria or submucosa	>50
II	Tumor extends to adventitia without lymph node involvement or to muscularis with lymph node involvement	10-30

Accurate staging may incorporate cross-sectional imaging, endoscopic ultrasonography, positron emission tomography, laparoscopy, and video-assisted thoracoscopy. The choice of these modalities depends on their availability and the expertise of the team caring for the patient.

Treatment

Curative treatment for esophageal carcinoma is surgical. Early-stage esophageal cancers usually do not cause symptoms and are usually detected incidentally or as part of a surveillance program. Most esophageal cancers are detected at later stages and are treated with combined-modality therapy consisting of surgery and radiation therapy and/or chemotherapy. Neoadjuvant therapy (that is, therapy given before the primary therapy usually to reduce tumor size) has been advocated to allow tumor downstaging, but the current evidence does not support its regular use. Overall survival in patients with esophageal cancer is strongly correlated with stage at diagnosis. In patients with advanced disease, various forms of palliative approaches are used, including enteral feeding tubes for nutrition support, expandable esophageal stents and ablative techniques to reduce tumor mass and thereby relieve dysphagia, adequate analgesic therapy, and the employment of team-based palliative care.

KEY POINTS

- Upper endoscopy with biopsies is necessary to diagnose Barrett esophagus.
- Barrett esophagus is associated with a 30-fold increased risk of esophageal adenocarcinoma.
- Surveillance endoscopy with biopsy is recommended in patients with Barrett esophagus.
- Early detection and surgical resection of esophageal cancer offers the best chance for good outcome.
- Most esophageal cancers are detected at later stages and are treated with combined-modality therapy consisting of surgery and radiation therapy and/or chemotherapy.

Esophageal Motility Disorders

The esophagus is an active organ whose function depends on a complex interrelationship of mechanical and neurohumoral functions. The upper esophagus is composed of striated muscle under central neurologic control from the nucleus ambiguus in the medulla. The lower two thirds of the esophagus is composed of smooth muscle and is under the control of the vagal and myenteric nervous systems. Two areas of the esophagus are normally contracted: the upper esophageal sphincter and the lower esophageal sphincter, which prevent retrograde flow of gastric contents. With initiation of swallowing, both sphincters must relax to allow passage of the ingested bolus (**Figure 4**). Dysregulation of this function in motility disorders can lead to dysphagia, aspiration, chest pain, and various other symptoms. These motility disorders are generally classified into hypertonic (or spastic) disorders and hypotonic disorders.

Hypertonic (Spastic) Motility Disorders

Achalasia and Pseudoachalasia

Achalasia, the best characterized of the esophageal motility disorders, consists of the failure of the lower esophageal sphincter to relax with swallowing. The resulting functional obstruction of the distal esophagus leads to dysphagia, chest pain, regurgitation of food, and weight loss. Achalasia is thought to be caused by degeneration of the myenteric plexus with resulting loss of inhibitory neurons in the lower esophageal sphincter, which remains tonically contracted. The disorder affects both sexes equally and usually presents insidiously in the third to fifth decade of life. Diagnosis is suggested by a typical history of dysphagia and regurgitation, often with some relief afforded by postural maneuvers, such as raising the arms above the head. Plain chest radiographs may reveal a dilated esophagus with an air/fluid level. Barium radiography is the primary screening test, and esophageal dilatation with the classic "bird's beak" appearance distally and the to-and-fro movement of barium (loss of peristalsis) suggest the diagnosis (**Figure 5**).

Diagnosis of achalasia is confirmed by esophageal manometry, which shows lack of relaxation of the lower esophageal sphincter with swallowing and aperistalsis of the esophageal body (**Figure 6**). Upper endoscopy is often performed to evaluate for mechanical obstruction of the esophagus in the region of the lower sphincter. If obstruction is caused by a malignant lesion, the disorder is designated "pseudoachalasia."

Treatment of achalasia consists of pharmacologic or mechanical disruption of the lower esophageal sphincter tone (**Table 5**). Smooth muscle relaxants such as nitrates

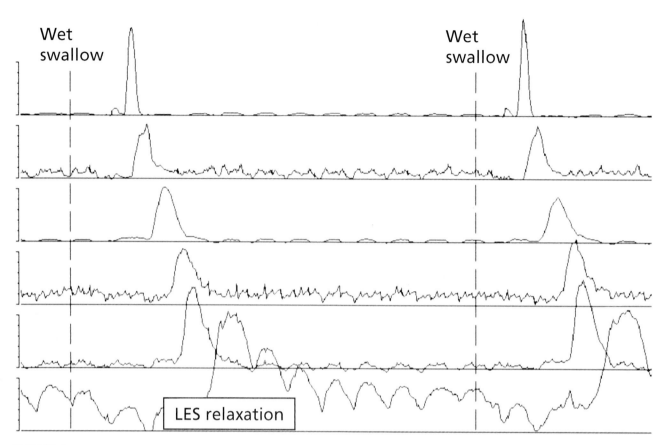

Wet swallow

Wet swallow

LES relaxation

FIGURE 4.
Normal esophageal manometric tracing.
The lower esophageal sphincter (LES) pressure relaxes to the baseline during the wet swallow, and peristaltic waves are seen. (The scale for the esophageal leads is 100 mm Hg.)

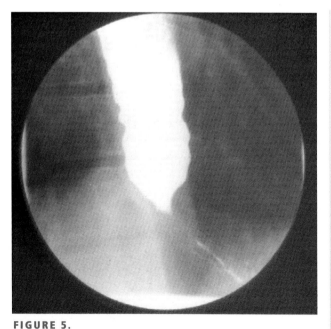

FIGURE 5.
Barium esophagography in a patient with achalasia.
The typical "bird's beak" appearance of the distal esophagus in a patient with achalasia is shown.

and calcium channel blockers may provide temporary relief for some patients, but do not appear to retard progression of disease. Injection of botulinum toxin into the sphincter provides symptomatic relief in up to three quarters of patients, but the effect is not usually durable; this therapy is now rarely used as first line in patients with acceptable risk for dilatation. Endoscopic pneumatic balloon dilatation provides long-lasting improvement in most patients but is associated with an approximately 5% risk of esophageal perforation. Surgical disruption of the lower esophageal sphincter can now be performed laparoscopically through the abdomen and, though often complicated by secondary GERD, is considered a first-line therapy. The choice of therapy usually depends on the expertise available at a given medical setting.

Diffuse Esophageal Spasm and Nutcracker Esophagus

Many hypertonic motility disorders of varying severity have been defined manometrically; most of these syndromes are now classified as nonspecific motility disorders. A subset of hypertonic disorders with specific manometric findings called "diffuse esophageal spasm" is characterized by intermittent nonperistaltic contractions in response to swallowing. Some

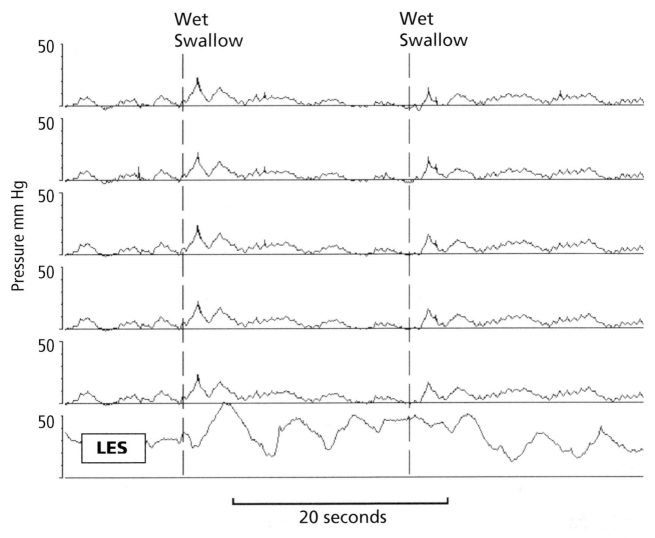

FIGURE 6.
Esophageal manometric tracing in a patient with achalasia.
The vertical scale is set in increments of 10 mm Hg (to a maximum of 50 mm Hg). The elevated lower esophageal sphincter (LES) pressure does not relax during the wet swallow. In addition, there is no esophageal body peristalsis (the waves seen are superimposable).

patients with this disorder are diagnosed with nutcracker esophagus because of the high amplitude of these ineffective contractions. Severity of manometric findings does not correlate well with clinical presentation. Diagnosis is made by clinical presentation and manometry, with exclusion of other disorders, especially cardiac disease and GERD. Because these disorders are not usually progressive or life threatening, treatment is symptomatic. Therapy with nitrates and calcium channel blockers has had some success. Antidepressants, including trazodone and imipramine, have been shown to alleviate pain associated with these disorders.

Hypotonic Motility Disorders
Syndromes of esophageal hypomotility are far less common than those of hypermotility. Most are classified manometrically

as "ineffective esophageal motility," which is most frequently encountered in the setting of GERD. Severe hypomotility may increase the risk of dysphagia after antireflux surgery. Hypomotility syndromes also occur in association with systemic diseases, especially systemic sclerosis (scleroderma). Symptoms of reflux are not uniformly present in such patients, and their onset may occur years after the recognition of the connective tissue disorder, presumably due to esophageal hyposensitivity along with hypomotility. The combination of manometrically determined aperistalsis of the esophageal body and a hypotensive lower esophageal sphincter has been termed "scleroderma esophagus"; however, less than half the patients with these manometric abnormalities have evidence of connective tissue disease. Treatment is largely aimed at controlling acid reflux, which may reduce the incidence of stricturing.

TABLE 5 Treatments for Achalasia

	Smooth Muscle Relaxants	Botulinum Toxin Injection	Pneumatic Dilatation	Open Surgical Myotomy	Minimally Invasive Surgical Myotomy
Response					
Initial	50%-70%	90% at 1 month	60%-90% at 1 year	>90% at 1 year	>90% at 1 year
Subsequent	<50% at 1 year	60% at 1 year	60% at 5 years	75% at 20 years	85% at 5 years
Morbidity					
Minor	30% (headache, hypotension)	20% (rash, transient chest pain)	Rare technique-related complications	<10% at 1 year (symptomatic reflux)	10% (symptomatic reflux)
Serious	Not reported	Not reported	3%-5% (perforation)	10% dysphagia, <2% mortality	Not available
Advantages					
	Rapidly initiated; well accepted	Low morbidity; modest response durability; well accepted	Good response durability	Best response rate and durability	Avoids thoracotomy
Disadvantages					
	Inconvenient side effects, tachyphylaxis; poor effect on esophageal emptying	Repeat injection often required within 1 year; fibrinoinflammatory reaction at lower esophageal sphincter	Risk of perforation	Thoracotomy required; severe reflux may develop	Long-term outcome unknown; small chance of thoracotomy

Adapted with permission from: Feldman M, Friedman LS, Brandt LJ. *Sleisenger and Fordtran's Gastrointestinal and Liver Disease: Pathophysiology, Diagnosis, Management.* 8th ed. Philadelphia, PA: Saunders. Copyright Elsevier (2006).

KEY POINTS

- All patients with achalasia require esophagogastroduodenoscopy and biopsy to rule out cancer-related pseudoachalasia.

- Most esophageal motility disorders are hypertonic (spastic), of which the best characterized is achalasia.

- Pseudoachalasia mimics the manometric findings of achalasia but is caused by obstruction by an underlying malignancy.

- Patients with achalasia present with dysphagia and can be treated by disruption of the malfunctioning lower esophageal sphincter tone.

Infectious, Pill-induced, and Eosinophilic Esophagitis

Infectious Esophagitis

Esophageal infections can occur in both immunosuppressed and immunocompetent patients. With increasingly successful therapy for HIV infection and the use of various prophylactic antimicrobial agents in immunosuppressed persons, the incidence of such infections has greatly decreased. Esophageal infections in immunocompetent persons are most common in patients who use inhaled corticosteroids or in patients with disorders that cause stasis of esophageal contents. *Candida albicans* is the most common organism causing esophagitis in immunocompetent patients (**Figure 7**). Less frequently encountered pathogens include herpesviruses, cytomegalovirus, human papillomavirus, *Trypanosoma cruzi*, *Mycobacterium tuberculosis*, and *Treponema pallidum*.

Patients with esophageal infection usually present with odynophagia, although bleeding from esophageal ulceration may also occur. Concomitant oral thrush occurs in up to two thirds of patients with candidal esophagitis, but oral lesions are rare in patients with viral esophagitis. Empiric fluconazole therapy is indicated in patients with typical symptoms of infectious esophagitis in the presence of oral thrush. In the absence of oral thrush, definitive diagnosis of infectious esophagitis can be made by endoscopy with brush cytology or mucosal biopsy of affected regions. Barium esophagography findings are too nonspecific to be used for diagnosis.

Pill-induced Esophagitis

Medication-induced esophageal injury is an underrecognized disorder. Recognition of the syndrome can preclude unnecessary testing, facilitate treatment, and allow preventive measures to be taken. Most patients present with the sudden onset of odynophagia with or without chest pain. The injury can occur with a medication that the patient has taken for some time, and it may not therefore be recognized as pill-related.

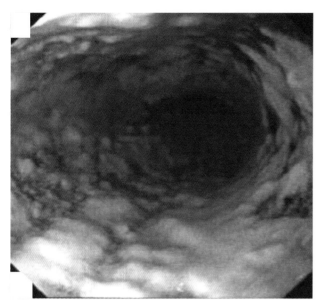

FIGURE 7.
Upper endoscopy showing *Candida* esophagitis.

The medications most commonly implicated are tetracycline, iron sulfate, bisphosphonates, potassium, NSAIDs, and quinidine. Although the diagnosis of pill-induced esophagitis can often be made by clinical history alone, upper endoscopy can be useful in evaluating for the presence of other lesions. The cornerstone of prevention of pill-induced esophagitis is avoidance of the offending agent or alteration of the method of administration, including taking a large fluid bolus prior to swallowing pills or remaining upright for 30 minutes after taking medication.

Eosinophilic Esophagitis

Originally considered primarily a pediatric disease, eosinophilic esophagitis has recently been recognized with increasing frequency in adults. This increased incidence parallels that of allergic disease and asthma in the population. Although the pathogenesis is unclear, recent data suggest sensitization of the esophagus to respiratory or oral antigens, with recruitment of peripheral eosinophils to the esophagus. The differentiation of eosinophilic esophagitis from GERD is therapeutically important. Patients with eosinophilic esophagitis can present with symptoms similar to those of GERD, but young adults frequently present with extreme dysphagia and food impaction. Diagnosis is made endoscopically, with mucosal biopsies showing marked infiltration with eosinophils. Macroscopic findings at endoscopy are nonspecific and insensitive, but mucosal furrowing, white specks, and mucosal friability have been consistently described. Treatment with oral topical corticosteroids (that is, taking inhaled corticosteroid preparations by mouth) or systemic corticosteroids provides excellent short-term relief, whereas avoidance of dietary allergens based on allergy testing has been advocated for long-term control in children.

KEY POINTS

- Infectious esophagitis occurs in immunosuppressed patients and in persons with abnormal esophageal stasis.
- Odynophagia is the most common presenting symptom in infectious esophagitis, which is most frequently caused by *Candida albicans*.
- Pill-induced esophagitis is most frequently caused by tetracycline, iron sulfate, potassium, bisphosphonates, NSAIDs, and quinidine.
- Eosinophilic esophagitis is rapidly increasing in incidence and is associated with atopy.

Bibliography

El-Serag HB. Time trends of gastroesophageal reflux disease: a systematic review. Clin Gastroenterol Hepatol. 2007;5:17-26. [PMID: 17142109]

Falk GW, Fennerty MB, Rothstein RI. AGA Institute technical review on the use of endoscopic therapy for gastroesophageal reflux disease. Gastroenterology. 2006;131:1315-36. [PMID: 17030199]

Grochenig HP, Tilg H, Vogetseder W. Clinical challenges and images in GI. Pill esophagitis. Gastroenterology. 2006;131:996, 1365. [PMID: 17030168]

Jafri NS, Hornung CA, Howden CW. Meta-analysis: Sequential therapy appears superior to standard therapy for Helicobacter pylori infection in patients naive to treatment. [erratum in Ann Intern Med. 2008;149:439]. Ann Intern Med. 2008:148:923-31. [PMID: 18490667]

Katzka DA. Eosinophilic esophagitis. Curr Opin Gastroenterol. 2006; 22:429-32. [PMID: 16760762]

Kahrilas PJ, Shaheen NJ, Vaezi MF, et al; and American Gastroenterological Association. American Gastroenterological Association Medical Position Statement on the management of gastroesophageal reflux disease. Gastroenterology. 2008;135:1383-91. [PMID: 18789939]

Pandolfino JE, Kahrilas PJ; American Gastroenterological Association. AGA technical review on the clinical use of esophageal manometry. Gastroenterology. 2005;128:209-24. [PMID: 15633138]

Park W, Vaezi MF. Etiology and pathogenesis of achalasia: the current understanding. Am J Gastroenterol. 2005;100:1404-14. [PMID: 15929777]

Tran T, Lowry AM, El-Serag HB. Meta-analysis: the efficacy of over-the-counter gastro-oesophageal reflux disease therapies. Aliment Pharmacol Ther. 2007;25:143-53. [PMID: 17229239]

Wang KK, Wongkeesong M, Buttar NS. American Gastroenterological Association technical review on the role of the gastroenterologist in the management of esophageal carcinoma. Gastroenterology. 2005; 128:1471-505. [PMID: 15887129]

Disorders of the Stomach and Duodenum

Peptic Ulcer Disease

A peptic ulcer is an ulcer of the mucous membrane of the alimentary tract caused by gastric acid. Peptic ulcer disease accounts for many hospitalizations and deaths each year despite recognition of risk factors for the disorder and the widespread use of acid suppression therapy. In the proximal gastrointestinal tract, mucosal insults and mucosal defenses are usually in balance; interruption of this balance results in peptic ulcer disease. Gastric acid is made by parietal cells in the stomach; these cells have three stimulant receptors for gastric acid production, namely gastrin, acetylcholine, and histamine. Gastric acid production is inhibited by somatostatin and prostaglandins. Excessive gastric acid can cause peptic ulceration, esophagitis (in patients predisposed to reflux), and steatorrhea; steatorrhea results from acid's inactivation of pancreatic lipase which aids in fat digestion. Gastric defenses include a mucous and bicarbonate layer, epithelial barrier function, and adequate blood flow. Gastric acid aids in absorption of various nutrients (iron, vitamin B_{12}), defends against food-borne illnesses, and prevents small intestinal bacterial overgrowth.

The most common causes of peptic ulcer disease are *Helicobacter pylori* infection and NSAIDs, which together account for more than 90% of ulcers; other causes include Crohn disease, acid hypersecretion states (Zollinger-Ellison syndrome), malignancy, viral infections (cytomegalovirus), and drugs (cocaine).

Clinical Features, Diagnosis, and Complications

Most patients with peptic ulcer disease do not have pain at diagnosis; the ulcers are usually detected during an evaluation for potential ulcer-related complications such as overt or obscure bleeding. When symptoms are present, they include dyspepsia or a nonspecific, gnawing epigastric pain. Other presentations include bleeding, perforation (sometimes with penetration into adjacent organs), and gastric outlet obstruction. Upper endoscopy is the diagnostic test of choice.

The most common complication of peptic ulcer disease is gastrointestinal bleeding, which occurs in approximately 15% of cases. Bleeding may manifest as hematemesis, melena, or hematochezia; occult bleeding manifested as iron deficiency anemia is less common. Bleeding tends to be more frequent and more severe in patients older than 60 years because of their increased use of NSAIDs and presence of comorbidities.

Patients with perforation from peptic ulcer disease often present with sudden, severe abdominal pain and hemodynamic compromise. Affected patients may be febrile, hypotensive, and tachycardic; bowel sounds may be absent, and abdominal examination may show guarding and rebound tenderness. The ulcer may penetrate into the pancreas, manifesting additionally with acute pancreatitis. Imaging often reveals free intraperitoneal air. Upper endoscopy is contraindicated in patients with perforation, and emergent surgical consultation is indicated. Nearly all patients with perforated peptic ulcers require emergent surgical intervention; however, if the perforation is small and contained, the patient can be managed with fasting, nasogastric tube decompression, and acid suppression.

Gastric outlet obstruction is a rare complication of peptic ulcer disease, typically from ulceration in the prepyloric region or pyloric channel. Patients with obstruction present with progressive nausea, vomiting, early satiety, and weight loss. Upper endoscopy often shows retained food within the stomach with ulceration distally, often precluding passage of the endoscope. Patients with gastric outlet obstruction should undergo nasogastric decompression and receive intravenous proton pump inhibitor (PPI) therapy for several days. If the obstruction has not resolved after a trial of conservative therapy, surgical consultation is needed.

Management

If a patient with peptic ulcer disease is taking an NSAID, the therapy should ideally be discontinued; if the patient requires long-term analgesia, safer alternatives should be considered (see Complications of NSAIDs). Patients with documented ulcer disease should also be evaluated for *H. pylori* infection and treated accordingly (see *Helicobacter pylori* Infection). PPI therapy is essential to heal peptic ulcers, and long-term therapy may be needed in patients who require ongoing NSAID therapy. Follow-up endoscopy is only required for gastric ulcers if adequate biopsies were not originally obtained or if worrisome endoscopic features were noted.

Surgery for peptic ulcer disease is typically reserved for patients whose disease fails to respond to medical therapy or who have life-threatening complications. The surgery typically involves a vagotomy with a drainage procedure but depends on the urgency, indication, and baseline anatomy. Although only 1% of ulcers recur after surgery, postoperative complications are not uncommon (see Complications of Gastric Surgical Procedures).

Dyspepsia

Clinical Features

Dyspepsia is chronic or recurrent discomfort in the upper mid-abdomen. The prevalence of dyspepsia is not well known because of the vagueness of its description by both patients and physicians. In addition to discomfort, affected patients may have mild nausea or bloating. Clinically, dyspepsia needs to be distinguished from GERD in patients who have features of acid regurgitation and heartburn and from irritable bowel syndrome in patients whose pain correlates with bowel movements. The following structural conditions have been found in patients undergoing upper endoscopy for dyspepsia: peptic ulcer disease (5% to 15%), reflux esophagitis (5% to 15%), and malignancy (2%). Up to 60% of patients with dyspepsia have functional dyspepsia, which consists of a 3-month history of dyspepsia in patients who do not have peptic ulcer disease, reflux disease, or malignancy. Patients with features of dyspepsia who have not had testing to exclude other conditions are said to have uninvestigated dyspepsia.

Neither the physician's clinical impression nor the patient's characteristics can accurately distinguish organic from functional dyspepsia. The patient's medications should be reviewed because various drugs may cause dyspepsia, including NSAIDs, antibiotics, bisphosphonates, and potassium supplements; up to 20% of patients taking NSAIDs have dyspeptic symptoms. The presence of epigastric tenderness has a sensitivity of 64% and specificity of only 30% for detecting structural abnormalities; the presence of alarm features (**Table 6**) should prompt further evaluation.

Management

For patients younger than 55 years with uninvestigated new-onset dyspepsia, a "test and treat" approach for *H. pylori* infection is recommended. For patients from an area of low *H. pylori* prevalence (<10%), therapy with a PPI is the recommended initial treatment. Although the yield of upper endoscopy is low in the evaluation of dyspepsia, it is recommended in patients older than 55 years because of their increased incidence of gastrointestinal malignancy and in patients with alarm features. In patients who undergo upper endoscopy, biopsy specimens should be taken to evaluate for the presence of *H. pylori*. A management approach to dyspepsia is presented in **Figure 8**. Up to 40% of patients with functional dyspepsia may have impaired gastric emptying or accommodation; however, evaluation for these disorders is not usually required because they do not alter management.

KEY POINTS

- *Helicobacter pylori* infection and NSAIDs are responsible for more than 90% of peptic ulcers.
- Patients with peptic ulcers are commonly asymptomatic at diagnosis; the ulcers are often detected during evaluation for ulcer-related complications such as overt or obscure bleeding.
- Gastrointestinal bleeding is the most common complication of peptic ulcer disease, present in approximately 15% of cases.
- The management of peptic ulcer disease includes acid suppression, testing for *Helicobacter pylori* infection, and assessing the use of NSAIDs.
- For patients younger than 55 years with uninvestigated new-onset dyspepsia without alarm features, a "test and treat" approach for *Helicobacter pylori* infection is recommended.

Helicobacter pylori Infection

Helicobacter pylori infection is one of the most common infections worldwide. The prevalence of infection is inversely related to socioeconomic status: in developing countries, the prevalence may be as high as 80%; an estimated 40% of persons living in the United States are infected. The infection is most commonly acquired through oral ingestion of the organism, which is transmitted among family members.

TABLE 6 Alarm Features in Dyspepsia

Age >55 years with new-onset symptoms

Family history of proximal gastrointestinal cancer

Unintentional weight loss

Gastrointestinal bleeding

Progressive dysphagia

Odynophagia

Unexplained iron-deficiency anemia

Persistent vomiting

Palpable mass or lymphadenopathy

Jaundice

Reprinted with permission from: Talley NJ, Vakil NB, Moayyedi P. American Gastroenterological Association technical review on the evaluation of dyspepsia. Gastroenterology. 2005;129(5): 1756-80. Copyright 2005, Elsevier.

Clinical Features

The clinical features of *H. pylori* infection range from asymptomatic gastritis to gastrointestinal malignancy. An antral-based gastritis occurs in nearly 95% of infected patients. This form of gastritis predisposes patients to duodenal ulcers, whereas the less common corpus-predominant gastritis is a risk factor for gastric ulcers (**Figure 9**). Up to 80% of duodenal ulcers and 50% of gastric ulcers are associated with *H. pylori* infection; eradication of the organism significantly reduces the risk of ulcer recurrence.

H. pylori is a group I carcinogen (that is, an agent that is definitely carcinogenic to humans); it is the leading cause of gastric cancer worldwide. Mucosa-associated lymphoid tissue (MALT) lymphoma is a low-grade B-cell marginal zone lymphoma that arises from lymphoid tissue within the lamina propria. *H. pylori* has been detected in more than 75% of patients with MALT lymphoma; eradication of the organism causes varying degrees of tumor regression in 70% to 80% of patients. Patients with early-stage disease are most likely to have complete remission with *H. pylori* treatment. Patients with more extensive disease—as demonstrated by ulceration, nodular submucosal mass lesions, invasion throughout the wall of the stomach, or lymphadenopathy—are more likely to require standard lymphoma therapy.

Gastric adenocarcinoma from *H. pylori* infection develops through a sequence of gastritis, atrophy, intestinal metaplasia, dysplasia, and carcinoma. Patients who undergo endoscopic resection for early-stage gastric cancer with remaining gastric mucosa should be considered for testing and eradication of *H. pylori* because of the risk of metachronous neoplasia. Patients with intestinal metaplasia on routine gastric biopsy should be tested and treated for *H. pylori* because intestinal metaplasia is an independent risk factor for gastric malignancy, although the extent to which there is regression of metaplasia with eradication of the organism is not known.

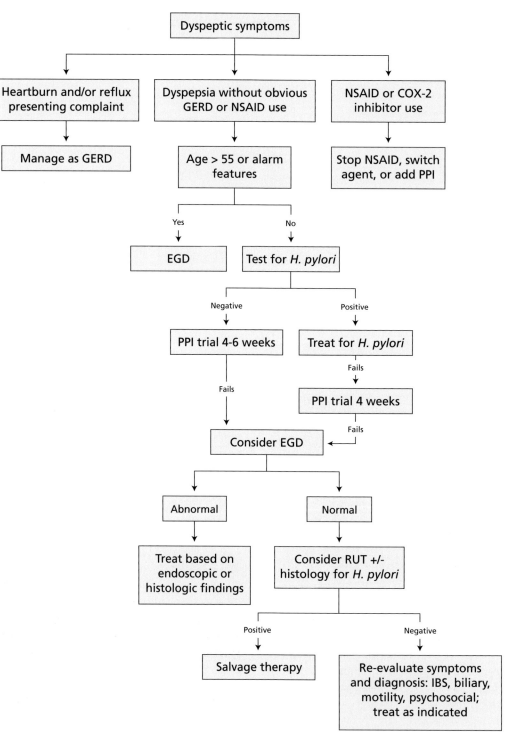

FIGURE 8.
Evaluation of the patient with dyspepsia.

COX-2 = cyclooxygenase-2; EGD = esophagogastroduodenoscopy; GERD = gastroesophageal reflux disease; IBS = irritable bowel syndrome; PPI = proton pump inhibitor; RUT = rapid urease test.

Adapted from Talley NJ; American Gastroenterological Association. American Gastroenterological Association medical position statement: evaluation of dyspepsia. Gastroenterology. 2005;129:1754. [PMID: 16285970] Copyright 2005, Elsevier.

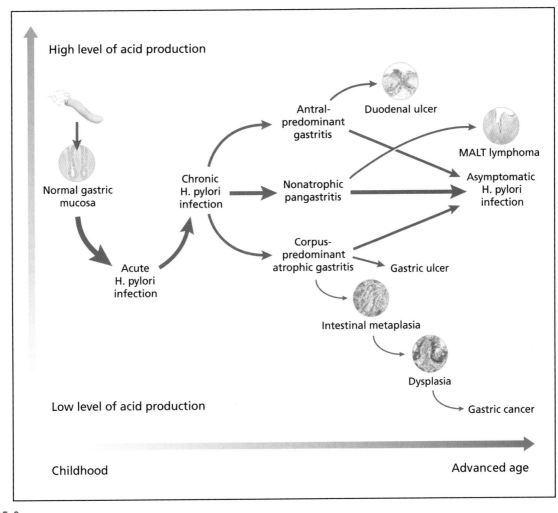

FIGURE 9.
Natural history *of Helicobacter pylori* **infection.**

MALT = mucosa-associated lymphoid tissue.

Reproduced with permission from Suerbaum S, Michetti P. *Helicobacter pylori* infection. N Engl J Med. 2002;347:1180. [PMID: 12374879] Copyright 2002, Massachusetts Medical Society. All rights reserved.

It has been reported that 20% to 60% of patients with functional dyspepsia have evidence of *H. pylori* gastritis and that eradication of the organism results in symptomatic benefit in a small number (10%) of these patients. Therefore, as mentioned above in the discussion of dyspepsia, patients younger than 55 years who have new-onset dyspepsia without alarm features should undergo *H. pylori* testing and treatment if infection is confirmed. Another option in uninvestigated dyspepsia in the absence of alarm symptoms is the use of acid suppression therapy with monitoring for clinical response given the relative equivalence in terms of cost effectiveness compared with a test-and-treat approach.

There has been long-standing concern about the relationship of *H. pylori* infection and GERD, including the development of new GERD-related symptoms after eradication of *H. pylori*. However, the current evidence does not allow definitive conclusions on whether patients with *H. pylori* infection have more, less, or equal rates of GERD-related symptoms compared with uninfected patients. Similarly, studies have not supported the conjecture that treating *H. pylori* infection will worsen GERD. Therefore, therapy for *H. pylori* infection should not be withheld because of concerns of worsening GERD.

Diagnostic Tests

Testing for *H. pylori* is indicated in patients with active peptic ulcer disease (duodenal or gastric), in patients with a history of peptic ulcer disease who have not been previously treated for *H. pylori,* in patients with low-grade gastric MALT lymphoma, in patients who have undergone endoscopic resection of early gastric cancer, and in patients younger than 55 years with uninvestigated dyspepsia without alarm symptoms. The diagnostic tests for *H. pylori* are shown in **Table 7**. The most commonly used endoscopic tests include histologic assessment and the rapid urease test. The sensitivity of the rapid urease test can be reduced up to 25% in patients who have taken a PPI within 2 weeks or bismuth or antibiotic therapy within 4 weeks of the endoscopy; histology is the endoscopic test of choice in such patients. Histologic examination that shows an antral-based gastritis, pangastric atrophy, or gastric intestinal metaplasia (which may be surrogate markers of infection) without identification of the organism should be followed by an additional test for the organism. The sensitivity of urea breath testing, like that of the rapid urease test, is reduced by medications that affect urease production; therefore, PPI therapy, bismuth and antibiotic therapy should be held for the intervals previously noted.

Testing all patients with *H. pylori* infection after therapy to confirm eradication of the organism is not practical or cost-effective; however, with the declining efficacy of treatment regimens, eradication testing may become more common. Confirmation of eradication is recommended in patients with *H. pylori*–associated ulcer, persistent dyspepsia despite a test-and-treat approach, *H. pylori*–associated MALT lymphoma, and previous treatment for early-stage gastric cancer. The urea breath test and stool antigen test can be used to confirm eradication; confirmatory tests should be done at least 4 weeks after completion of therapy.

Treatment

Treatment regimens for *H. pylori* are shown in **Table 8**. Triple therapy consisting of a PPI, amoxicillin, and clarithromycin is the most commonly used initial treatment. If the patient is from an area with increased clarithromycin resistance, metronidazole is used in place of clarithromycin. Bismuth-based regimens have the advantage of low cost and effectiveness in areas of high clarithromycin resistance. Sequential therapy has shown promising results, with eradication rates of >90%; in addition, eradication rates were approximately three times higher in patients with clarithromycin-resistant strains. However, sequential therapy has not been validated in the United States.

Treatment failure is usually the result of noncompliance with medical therapy or of antimicrobial resistance, given the low reinfection rate (<2% of patients/year). For retreatment, clarithromycin should be avoided if it was included in the initial therapy. If both clarithromycin- and metronidazole-resistance is suspected, salvage therapy should be considered (**Figure 10**). In the United States, failed PPI–based triple therapy would preferably be followed by 7 to 14 days of bismuth-based quadruple therapy. Salvage therapy with a levofloxacin-based regimen may be better tolerated and more effective than bismuth-based quadruple therapy, but further validation is required.

TABLE 7 Characteristics of Commonly Used Tests for Detection of *Helicobacter pylori* Infection			
Test	**Sensitivity**	**Specificity**	**Comments**
Nonendoscopic Tests			
Antibody test (serum)	88%–94%	74%–88%	Inexpensive; good negative predictive value; positive predictive value depends on prevalence; not recommended after therapy to document eradication
Antibody test (whole blood)	67%–85%	75%–91%	
Enzyme-linked immunosorbent assay (serum)	86%–94%	78%–95%	
Stool antigen test	94%	92%	Good positive and negative predictive value irrespective of prevalence; can be used before and after therapy
Urea breath test	90%–96%	88%–98%	Good positive and negative predictive value irrespective of prevalence; can be used before and after therapy; sensitivity affected by use of PPI, bismuth, antibiotics
Endoscopic Tests			
Urease test (biopsy)	88%–95%	95%–100%	Inexpensive; sensitivity affected by use of PPI, bismuth, antibiotics
Histology	93%–96%	98%–99%	Provides tissue diagnosis; expensive
Culture	80%–98%	100%	Expensive, not widely available
Polymerase chain reaction	>95%	>95%	Not widely available or standardized; not practical for routine diagnosis

TABLE 8 First-Line Regimens for *Helicobacter pylori* Eradication

Regimen	Duration (days)	Eradication Rates (%)
PPI, BID Clarithromycin, 500 mg BID Amoxicillin, 1000 mg BID	10-14	70-85
PPI, BID Clarithromycin, 500 mg BID Metronidazole, 500 mg BID	10-14	70-85
PPI, BID Bismuth subsalicylate, 525 mg QID Metronidazole, 250 mg QID Tetracycline, 500 mg QID	10-14	75-90
Sequential Therapy[a]		>90

Standard-dose PPI BID
  Amoxicillin 1000 mg BID,
  followed by:
	5	

PPI, BIDClarithromycin, 500 mg BID Tinidazole, 500 mg BID	5	

PPI=proton pump inhibitor; BID=twice daily; QID=four times daily.

[a] Sequential therapy has not been validated in the United States.

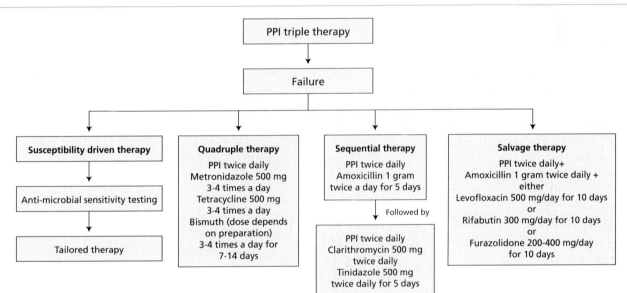

FIGURE 10.

Treatment strategies for the patient who fails initial *Helicobacter pylori* therapy.

PPI = proton pump inhibitor.

Reprinted from Vakil N, Megraud F. Eradication therapy for *Helicobacter pylori*. Gastroenterology 2007;133:990. [PMID: 17854602] Copyright 2007, with permission from Elsevier.

KEY POINTS

- Manifestations of *Helicobacter pylori* infection include gastritis, ulcer disease, mucosa-associated lymphoid tissue (MALT) lymphoma, and gastric adenocarcinoma.

- The urea breath test and fecal antigen test detect active *Helicobacter pylori* infection and can be used before therapy to confirm infection and at least 4 weeks after therapy to confirm eradication.

- Triple therapy consisting of a proton pump inhibitor, amoxicillin, and clarithromycin is the most commonly used initial treatment for *Helicobacter pylori* infection.

- Testing all treated patients for *Helicobacter pylori* eradication is neither practical nor cost-effective; such testing should be performed in patients with associated peptic ulcer disease, persistent dyspepsia despite a test-and-treat approach, MALT lymphoma, or a history of early-stage gastric cancer.

Complications of Nonsteroidal Anti-Inflammatory Drugs

NSAIDs are one of the most widely used classes of drugs in the world. In the United States, 5% to 10% of the population takes NSAIDs regularly, with higher rates of use in the elderly. Gastrointestinal complications from NSAIDs include dyspepsia, peptic ulcer disease, and strictures or web formation. More than 16,000 patients die annually from NSAID-induced gastrointestinal injury.

NSAIDs cause topical injury to the gastric mucosa on contact, but many of the toxic effects of these agents are the result of their mechanism of action, that is, the inhibition of prostaglandin synthesis, which results in decreased surface mucus, bicarbonate secretion, and epithelial proliferation, all of which make the mucosa more susceptible to injury. Because of the systemic effects of prostaglandin inhibition, enteric-coated NSAIDs and NSAIDs given by intravenous or rectal routes of administration also cause gastrointestinal toxic effects.

Factors related to an increased risk for NSAID-induced complications include age >60 years, history of peptic ulcer disease or hemorrhage, escalating doses of NSAIDs, combination of two or more NSAIDs (including low-dose aspirin), concurrent use of anticoagulants or corticosteroids, or significant medical comorbidities.

Prevention of NSAID-Induced Injury

For patients who require long-term NSAID therapy, the use of alternative analgesics such as acetaminophen should be considered. If NSAID therapy is required, the lowest therapeutic dose should be given. Additionally, NSAIDs with safer side effect profiles (etodolac, nabumetone, meloxicam or selective cyclooxygenase-2 [COX-2] inhibitors) should be considered. The risk of gastrointestinal injury with COX-2 inhibitors is significantly lower than that of traditional NSAIDs; however, the risk is not affected if COX-2 inhibitors are combined with low-dose aspirin therapy. COX-2 inhibitor therapy has been associated with the development of ischemic cardiovascular disease. Celecoxib is a COX-2 inhibitor that is still in clinical use, whereas rofecoxib and valdecoxib have been withdrawn from the market.

Patients taking long-term NSAID therapy who need prophylaxis for peptic ulcer disease include the elderly, those with previous NSAID-related gastrointestinal complications, and those taking anticoagulation or corticosteroid therapy. The most common prophylaxis is PPI therapy. High-dose famotidine has also been found to significantly prevent ulcers but is not considered first-line therapy. The prostaglandin-E1 analogue misoprostol also effectively reduces NSAID-related ulcers; however, the side effects of misoprostol, including dose-related diarrhea (>20% of patients) and its role as an abortifacient, limit its use.

Treatment of NSAID-Induced Injury

For patients with NSAID-induced gastrointestinal injuries, consideration should be given to eliminating or reducing the dose of the NSAID. Even in the setting of NSAID use, the patient with peptic ulcer disease should be evaluated for *H. pylori* infection. For ulcer healing, antisecretory therapy should be initiated. Therapy with a PPI heals peptic ulcers whether or not NSAID therapy is discontinued; H_2-receptor antagonists heal ulcers if the NSAID is discontinued, but healing is significantly delayed if NSAID therapy is continued.

KEY POINTS

- All NSAIDs inhibit prostaglandin synthesis, and therefore, different formulations (enteric-coated) and routes (intravenous, rectal) of NSAIDs share the toxicity of oral NSAIDs.

- Factors related to an increased risk for NSAID-induced complications include age >60 years, previous peptic ulcer disease or hemorrhage, higher doses or the combination of two or more NSAIDs, concurrent use of anticoagulants or corticosteroids, and significant medical comorbidities.

- Proton pump inhibitors more effectively heal peptic ulcerations than H_2-receptor antagonists, whether or not NSAID therapy is ongoing.

Gastric Polyps, Subepithelial Lesions, and Adenocarcinoma

Gastric Polyps

Gastric polyps, which are often incidentally found during upper endoscopy, have a prevalence of approximately 1%. Synchronous polyps are found in approximately 25% of patients. Although most patients with gastric polyps are asymptomatic, some patients may present with obstruction or bleeding.

Fundic gland polyps are the most common form of gastric polyps, accounting for approximately 50% of all cases; they are small (often 1 to 5 mm) and occur exclusively in the body and fundus. Most fundic polyps are sporadic, may be multiple (often <10), with a 1% likelihood of dysplasia and no defined cancer risk. Fundic gland polyps are more common in patients with familial adenomatous polyposis; polyps in these patients may be numerous, have a 25% likelihood of dysplasia, and a low cancer risk. Endoscopic surveillance is recommended in these patients. Hyperplastic polyps average 1 cm in diameter, may be multiple, and often occur in the setting of chronic gastritis. Malignant potential is very small. The polyps may regress in size with eradication of *H. pylori* in infected patients.

Gastric adenomatous polyps vary in size, occur most commonly in the gastric antrum, and may also occur in the setting of chronic gastritis. There can be varying grades of dysplasia, with risk of malignant transformation. Gastric adenomas should be removed with endoscopic polypectomy. There are no guidelines for endoscopic surveillance for patients with gastric adenomas; however, follow-up endoscopy should be strongly considered in patients with gastric adenomas and other risk factors for gastric cancer, such as a family history of gastric cancer, personal history of intestinal metaplasia, and familial cancer syndromes.

Gastric Subepithelial Lesions

Gastric subepithelial lesions (or submucosal lesions) appear as a protrusion into the lumen of the stomach, with normal overlying mucosa; they are either extra- or intramural and may be benign or malignant. The detection rate of subepithelial lesions during upper endoscopy is less than 0.5%. Endoscopic ultrasonography can be used to differentiate these lesions and to obtain specimens for histopathology if needed. CT or MRI scans can determine spread of malignant lesions.

Gastrointestinal stromal tumors are the most common intramural subepithelial lesion in the stomach, with up to a 30% rate of malignancy. These tumors express CD117, a c-kit protein with tyrosine kinase activity. Features that may help predict malignant behavior include tumor size, irregularity, and mitotic count. Surgery is the standard of care for most gastrointestinal stromal tumors.

Gastric Adenocarcinoma

In 2008 in the United States, an estimated 21,260 patients will be diagnosed with gastric cancer and 11,210 will die of it, with an incidence rate for all races of 11.4/100,000 men and 5.6/100,000 women. The incidence of gastric cancer is decreasing significantly, but it remains one of the most common malignancies worldwide. The falling incidence may be related to increased recognition and modification of risk factors, including treatment of *H. pylori* infection.

There are various environmental, host, and familial risk factors for gastric cancer. Environmental risk factors include diets high in nitrates (cured meats, pickled items), fried foods, processed meats and fish, and salt; diets low in vegetables and citrus fruits are associated with the disease. Tobacco use is thought to increase the risk of gastric cancer, but alcohol consumption has not been consistently related. Host-related risk factors include blood group A; whether this is related to the actual blood group antigens or nearby genes is not clear. In addition, patients with chronic atrophic gastritis, pernicious anemia, *H. pylori* infection, premalignant gastric polyps, and past gastric resections are also at risk. Familial cancer syndromes such as hereditary nonpolyposis colorectal cancer or familial adenomatous polyposis are associated with increased risk for gastric cancer, as are germline mutations of the E-cadherin gene *CDH1*, an autosomal dominant condition with a greatly increased lifetime cumulative risk of gastric cancer.

Weight loss and abdominal pain are the most common clinical manifestations of gastric cancer, with other symptoms including nausea, early satiety, gastric outlet obstruction, or occult bleeding. Most symptomatic patients have advanced disease at presentation, with only 50% of patients being candidates for curative resection. Upper endoscopy is often the first test performed to establish the diagnosis. CT scanning is often the next step to evaluate for metastatic involvement, but it cannot accurately assess the depth of disease in early lesions. Conversely, endoscopic ultrasonography is the most reliable preoperative test for assessing depth of invasion, but it is poor at determining distant metastases. Positron emission tomography may be used preoperatively to follow-up suspicious but nondiagnostic abnormalities detected on CT scan. A chest radiograph should be done in all patients preoperatively; chest CT imaging should be considered in those with proximal gastric lesions to evaluate for intrathoracic disease. If ascites is present, paracentesis should be done to evaluate for peritoneal carcinomatosis. (The management of gastric cancer is addressed in the MKSAP 15 Hematology and Oncology section.)

KEY POINTS

- Fundic gland polyps, the most common form of gastric polyps, are small, often multiple, and, if sporadic, have no defined cancer risk.

- Most symptomatic patients with gastric cancer have advanced disease at presentation, with only 50% of patients being candidates for curative resection.

Gastric Motility Disorders

Gastroparesis is delayed gastric emptying in the absence of mechanical obstruction. The prevalence of the disorder is not known, but it is estimated to occur in 20% to 40% of patients with type 1 diabetes mellitus and 25% to 40% of patients with functional dyspepsia. Most patients with gastroparesis are women.

Diagnosis

The evaluation for gastroparesis is based on the patient having compatible clinical features and requires objective confirmation of delayed gastric emptying and the absence of mechanical obstruction. Clinical features of gastroparesis include nausea, vomiting, bloating, and postprandial fullness with early satiety. Weight loss may ensue because of inadequate nutritional intake. Abdominal discomfort is present in 50% to 90% of affected patients, and it may be the predominant symptom in patients with gastroparesis and functional dyspepsia. The abdominal examination may show epigastric distention or tenderness, and there may be a succussion splash. However, epigastric distention or a succussion splash does not distinguish obstruction from gastroparesis.

An upper endoscopy or barium radiograph should be performed to rule out mechanical obstruction before tests are done to assess gastric motility. Retained food in the stomach after an overnight fast is suggestive of delayed gastric emptying, and in the absence of mechanical obstruction detected endoscopically, may indicate gastroparesis. A stepwise approach to the patient suspected to have gastroparesis is shown in **Table 9**.

Testing

Delayed gastric emptying is confirmed by gastric scintigraphy of a radiolabeled solid meal. Many medications can affect gastric emptying (notably opioid analgesics, anticholinergic agents, metoclopramide, and erythromycin) and should be discontinued before scintigraphy based on the medication half-life.

Many centers test for 2 hours after the ingested meal, but testing for 4 hours increases the yield of the scintigraphic test and is recommended. Retention of more than 10% of the ingested meal at 4 hours is abnormal. Disadvantages of this test include exposure to radioactive material, cost, and variability

---

TABLE 9 Evaluation of the Patient Suspected to Have Gastroparesis

Initial Evaluation

History and examination

Laboratory studies
  CBC, glucose, electrolytes, protein, albumin, calcium
  Pregnancy test (if applicable)

Flat and upright abdominal radiograph
  Consider if vomiting or pain is acute and/or severe

Evaluate for Organic Disorders

EGD or upper gastrointestinal barium series
  Rule out obstruction or mucosal lesions

Biliary ultrasound
  Consider if pain a predominant feature

Evaluate for Delayed Gastric Emptying

Solid-phase gastric emptying study (scintigraphy)

Evaluate for secondary causes of gastroparesis
  TSH, ANA, anti-Scl-70, HbA$_{1c}$

Treatment Trial with Prokinetic +/- Antiemetic

See text for options

If No Response, Consider Further Studies

Electrogastrography

Antroduodenal manometry

Small bowel imaging
  Barium follow-through or enteroclysis

Further laboratory studies
  Paraneoplastic antibodies (ANNA), tTG

CBC = complete blood count; EGD = esophagogastroduodenoscopy; TSH = thyroid-stimulating hormone; ANA = antinuclear antibody; anti-Scl-70 = scleroderma antibody; HbA$_{1c}$ = hemoglobin A$_{1c}$; ANNA = antineuronal nuclear antibody; tTG = tissue transglutaminase antibody.

---

in test performance. Gastric emptying can also be indirectly assessed by breath testing in which a meal containing ^{13}C-labeled isotope is ingested, and breath samples are analyzed for the presence of isotope in exhaled carbon dioxide, thus determining the rate of gastric emptying. Breath testing offers the advantage of using a nonradioactive isotope, with a sensitivity of 86% and specificity of 80% compared to scintigraphy; however, there may be lack of standardization among various centers. After gastroparesis is confirmed, antroduodenal manometry may be used to differentiate a myopathic from a neurologic cause; this procedure can also differentiate mechanical obstruction from pseudo-obstruction if not apparent.

The predominant causes of gastroparesis include idiopathic (33%), diabetes mellitus (25%), and postoperative states (20%). Other causes include eating disorders, renal failure, neurologic disorders (such as Parkinson disease), paraneoplastic syndromes, rheumatologic conditions (such as scleroderma), previous lung or heart-lung transplantation, and viral infections. A viral cause is suggested by rapid onset of gastroparesis after a presumed viral infection. Medications can also contribute to gastroparesis from any of these disorders. The diabetic patient with gastroparesis often has had diabetes mellitus for more than 10 years and has other end-organ involvement. However, hyperglycemia alone may account for delayed gastric emptying given its effect on reducing antral contractions, increasing pyloric contractions, and modulating fundic relaxation.

Management

The management for gastroparesis includes dietary manipulation, medical therapy for symptomatic relief, and modifying risk factors that may improve motility. Patients with gastroparesis should be placed on a low-fat, low-fiber diet. Roughage should be avoided to decrease bezoar formation. Smaller, more frequent meals are recommended. Because liquids empty from the stomach more rapidly than solids, patients with severe symptoms may need to replace solid foods with nutrient drinks. Electrolyte abnormalities should be corrected and glycemic control tightened in diabetic patients. Exacerbating medications should be discontinued.

Medical therapy for gastroparesis may include a combination of antiemetic therapy and promotility agents. Prokinetic agents available in the United States include metoclopramide and erythromycin (**Table 10**).

Metoclopramide has prokinetic and antiemetic properties and can be used for short-term treatment of gastroparesis. Tardive dyskinesia is a serious complication of metoclopramide therapy, is more common in women, occurs with increased frequency with prolonged use, and may be irreversible. Erythromycin is most useful in hospitalized patients with acute gastroparesis because long-term use leads to tachyphylaxis. Both metoclopramide and erythromycin are available in a liquid formulation. Domperidone is a dopamine receptor

TABLE 10 Prokinetic Agents for Gastroparesis

Agent	Dosing Route	Side Effects	Availability
Metoclopramide	10 mg QID before meals and bed Can increase to 20 mg as needed PO, SQ, IV, suppository	Acute dystonic reactions Drowsiness, fatigue Breast engorgement, galactorrhea, menstrual irregularities Parkinsonian-like tardive dyskinesia	Yes
Erythromycin	125-250 mg PO TID before meals 3 mg/kg IV every 8 hoursPO, IV	Gastrointestinal side effects Consider cytochrome P450 drug interactions Tachyphylaxis with chronic use	Yes
Cisapride	NA	QT interval prolonged, torsades de pointes Death	Withdrawn from market 2000; available for compassionate use only
Domperidone	NA	Near lack of extrapyramidal effects Breast engorgement, galactorrhea, menstrual irregularities	Available in Canada, Mexico, Europe but not in the United States
Tegaserod	NA	Cardiovascular events Death	Withdrawn from market 2007

QID = four times daily; PO = orally; SQ = subcutaneously; IV = intravenously; TID = three times daily; NA = not available.

Adapted with permission from: Parkman HP, Hasler WL, Fisher RS. American Gastroenterological Association technical review on the diagnosis and treatment of gastroparesis. Gastroenterology. 2004;127(5):1592-622. [PMID: 15521026] Copyright 2004, Elsevier.

antagonist that may cause fewer extrapyramidal side effects than metoclopramide, but it is not FDA-approved. Tegaserod and cisapride were previously FDA-approved for gastrointestinal motility disorders, but both agents have been withdrawn from the market because of serious cardiovascular side effects associated with their use. Cisapride is available to a limited degree on a compassionate use basis for select patients with serious motility problems that exceed the cardiotoxic risk of the medication. Botulinum toxin injected into the pyloric sphincter can decrease pyloric pressure to ease gastric emptying, with long-term relief not expected. Gastric electrical stimulation is FDA-approved for humanitarian use in patients with refractory symptoms.

A feeding jejunostomy tube with or without a venting gastrostomy may be needed for nutritional support for patients with gastroparesis who have not met their nutritional needs and access for medication therapy. Total parenteral nutrition should be reserved for the patient who cannot tolerate enteral feeding given the risks associated with long-term parenteral nutrition.

KEY POINTS

- Before gastroparesis can be diagnosed, mechanical obstruction needs to be excluded.
- The test of choice to document delayed gastric emptying is a 4-hour gastric scintigraphy of a radiolabeled solid meal.
- Management of gastroparesis includes a combination of diet modification, antiemetic agents, and prokinetic therapy.

Complications of Gastric Surgical Procedures

Bariatric Surgery Complications

Because of the increasing use of bariatric surgery, clinicians need to be aware of the complications of the procedures. There are two forms of bariatric surgery: restrictive procedures limit caloric intake by reducing the stomach's capacity; malabsorptive procedures decrease the effectiveness of nutrient absorption by shortening the functional small intestine. The most common bariatric surgery performed in the United States is Roux-en-Y gastric bypass, which is a combined restrictive and malabsorptive procedure (**Figure 11**). Complications from these procedures can be divided into early (first 30 days after surgery) and late (after 30 days) complications (**Table 11**). Pulmonary embolism, which is an infrequent complication of bariatric surgery, is, however, one of the leading causes of death associated with the procedure, accounting for 50% of all deaths in these patients.

Bariatric surgery can be complicated by various nutritional deficiencies (**Table 12**). Iron deficiency occurs in nearly 50% of patients after Roux-en-Y gastric bypass as a result of alteration in gastric acid that affects iron reduction and from bypassing the proximal small bowel where iron absorption is maximal. Although a multivitamin containing iron is adequate iron replacement for many patients, supplemental iron may be required. The absorption of vitamin B_{12} is also significantly altered after Roux-en-Y gastric bypass, and multivitamin supplementation is not adequate to prevent vitamin B_{12} deficiency. Although folate deficiency can occur,

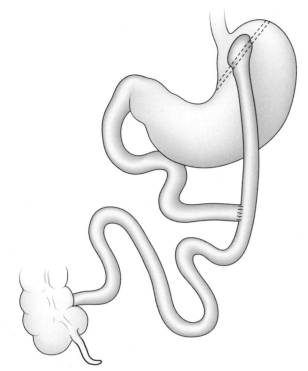

FIGURE 11.
Anatomy of Roux-en-Y gastric bypass surgery.
A small 50-mL pouch is made in the upper stomach, which is closed from the lower stomach with two staple lines. A Roux-en-Y loop is made with the jejunal end anastomosed to the small pouch. The gastric contents and the duodenal contents meet up when the two segments anastomose.

TABLE 11 Complications Related to Bariatric Surgery	
Complication	**Management**
Early	
Anastomotic leak	Antibiotics, re-explore
Bowel obstruction	Re-evaluate, re-explore
Hemorrhage	Resuscitate, re-explore
Venous thromboembolism	Anticoagulation
Wound infection	Antibiotics
Late	
Anastomotic stricture	Balloon dilation
Bacterial overgrowth	Antibiotics
Incisional hernia	Surgery with mesh
Marginal ulceration	PPI
Nutritional deficiencies	Appropriate replacement

PPI = proton pump inhibitor.

Gastric Resection Complications

There are various postgastrectomy syndromes. Dumping syndrome may occur in up to 20% of patients who undergo gastrectomy or vagotomy. Early dumping syndrome, which is caused by rapid emptying of hyperosmolar substances into the small bowel, occurs within 30 minutes after a meal and is characterized by diarrhea, bloating, nausea, and tachycardia. Late dumping syndrome occurs 1 to 3 hours after a meal and is characterized by neuroglycopenic symptoms. In early and late dumping syndromes, carbohydrate-rich foods and nutrient liquid drinks are poorly tolerated; patients should be encouraged to consume foods higher in fat and protein. Other post-ulcer surgery complications include afferent loop syndrome, which consists of chronic partial obstruction of the proximal loop of the duodenum and jejunum and results in duodenal distention, pain, and nausea after the patient eats; retained antrum syndrome, which is a rare condition in which an ulcer recurs associated with high levels of circulating gastrin; bile reflux gastropathy; and postvagotomy diarrhea. In addition, patients may present with features of maldigestion and malabsorption secondary to rapid transit, inadequate mixing of

it is usually transient because of the adaptive capability of the remaining small bowel for folate absorption. However, in women of childbearing age who have had bariatric surgery with intestinal bypass, folate supplementation should be provided given the risk of fetal neural tube defects if the patient becomes pregnant. Calcium and vitamin D supplementation may also be required. In some patients, weight loss may be more rapid and more severe than anticipated; in these cases, other causes for malabsorption need to be considered, such as bacterial overgrowth, unmasked celiac disease, and pancreatic insufficiency.

TABLE 12 Nutritional Deficiencies and Placement After Bariatric Surgery	
Nutrient Deficiency	**Replacement Therapy**
Iron	MVI with iron, or elemental iron 65 mg orally daily
Vitamin B_{12}	Vitamin B_{12} 500 µg orally daily, or 1000 µg IM monthly
Folic acid	MVI with folate, or folate 1 mg orally daily (women of childbearing age)
Calcium	Elemental calcium 1500 mg orally daily
Vitamin D	Vitamin D 400 IU orally daily
Thiamine (vitamin B_1)	Thiamine 50 mg orally daily (stop after 6 months)
Vitamin A	MVI daily; only use replacement therapy as needed

MVI = multivitamin; IM = intramuscularly.

digestive enzymes, loss of gastric acid, decreased absorptive surface area, and secondary bacterial overgrowth.

- Pulmonary embolism is an uncommon complication after bariatric surgery, but it accounts for 50% of all deaths in these patients.
- Nutritional deficiencies are common after bariatric surgery, and patients typically need supplementation with iron, vitamin B_{12}, calcium, and vitamin D.

Bibliography

Burt RW. Gastric fundic gland polyps. Gastroenterology. 2003; 125:1462-1469. [PMID: 14598262]

Camilleri M. Clinical practice: Diabetic gastroparesis [erratum in N Engl J Med. 2007;357:427]. N Engl J Med. 2007;356:820-9. [PMID: 17314341]

Chey WD, Wong BCY; Practice Parameters Committee of the American College of Gastroenterology. American College of Gastroenterology guideline on the management of Helicobacter pylori infection. Am J Gastroenterol. 2007;102:1808-25. [PMID: 17608775]

Correa P, Houghton J. Carcinogenesis of Helicobacter pylori. Gastroenterology. 2007;133:659-72. [PMID: 17681184]

Decker GA, Swain JM, Crowell MD, Scolapio JS. Gastrointestinal and nutritional complications after bariatric surgery. Am J Gastroenterol. 2007;102:2571-80. [PMID: 17640325]

Hwang JH, Rulyak SD, Kimmey MB; American Gastroenterological Association Institute. American Gastroenterological Association Institute technical review on the management of gastric subepithelial masses. Gastroenterology. 2006;130:2217-28. [PMID: 16762644]

Moayyedi P, Talley NJ, Fennerty MB, Vakil N. Can the clinical history distinguish between organic and functional dyspepsia? JAMA. 2006;295:1566-76. [PMID: 16595759]

Parkman HP, Hasler WL, Fisher RS; American Gastroenterological Association. American Gastroenterological Association technical review on the diagnosis and treatment of gastroparesis. Gastroenterology. 2004;127:1592-622. [PMID: 15521026]

Pusztaszeri MP, Genta RM, Cryer BL. Drug-induced injury in the gastrointestinal tract: clinical and pathologic considerations. Nat Clin Pract Gastroenterol Hepatol. 2007;4:442-53. [PMID: 17667993]

Talley NJ, Vakil NB, Moayyedi P. American gastroenterological association technical review on the evaluation of dyspepsia. Gastroenterology. 2005;129:1756-80. [PMID: 16285971]

Disorders of the Pancreas

Acute Pancreatitis

Acute pancreatitis is an acute or relapsing inflammatory process that may also involve peripancreatic tissues and other organs. The prevalence of acute pancreatitis appears to be rising in Western populations, with a range of 11 to 40 cases per 100,000. The mortality rate has remained constant at 7% to 8%.

The severity of acute pancreatitis is strongly correlated with the degree of pancreatic necrosis. Although most cases are self-limited, approximately 15% of patients develop significant pancreatic necrosis and organ compromise. Patients with multiorgan involvement and failure almost always have necrosis in 30% to 50% of the gland and a high mortality rate.

About 80% of all cases of acute pancreatitis are due to gallstones and alcohol abuse. About 10% of cases are classified as idiopathic; the remaining 10% of cases are caused by obstruction, drugs, and metabolic, genetic, infectious, and vascular disorders (**Table 13**).

Clinical Presentation and Diagnosis

Patients with acute pancreatitis usually have the sudden onset of epigastric pain, often radiating to the back. These symptoms are often accompanied by nausea, vomiting, fever, and tachycardia. The physical examination shows epigastric tenderness, abdominal distention, hypoactive bowel sounds, and occasional guarding.

The diagnosis is confirmed by laboratory results showing serum concentrations of amylase and lipase that are at least three times the upper limit of normal. The degree of elevation of pancreatic enzyme levels, however, does not correlate with severity of disease. Furthermore, serum tests are not sensitive because although approximately one third of patients with pancreatitis have elevated enzyme levels, they are often not three times above the upper limit of normal. Hyperamylasemia may also be caused by disorders of other organs that produce amylase such as the salivary glands or fallopian tubes and by a perforated ulcer, intestinal ischemia, or chronic renal insufficiency. Detection of an elevated serum lipase is more specific for acute pancreatitis but may be an incidental finding in asymptomatic patients (**Table 14**).

Although not required to make the diagnosis of acute pancreatitis, imaging can help grade the severity of the pancreatitis and sometimes provide a cause. Contrast-enhanced CT scan is the most specific test and in some cases can differentiate between edematous, interstitial pancreatitis and severe necrotizing pancreatitis. Common findings on CT scan in

TABLE 13 Causes of Acute Pancreatitis	
Obstructive	Gallstones (45%) Pancreas divisum Malignancy Choledochocele Parasites (*Ascaris lumbricoides*)
Toxins/Drugs	Alcohol (35%) Azathioprine Sulfa drugs Aminosalicylates Metronidazole Pentamidine Didanosine
Metabolic	Hyperlipidemia Hypercalcemia
Infectious	Viral (Cytomegalovirus, Epstein-Barr virus) Parasites (Toxoplasma, Cryptosporidium)
Vascular	Ischemia Vasculitis

TABLE 14 Nonpancreatic Causes of Elevated Serum Amylase and Lipase Levels

Amylase Elevation	Lipase Elevation
Intestinal ischemia, obstruction, radiation disease	Intestinal ischemia, obstruction
Parotitis	Duodenal ulcer
Ectopic pregnancy, salpingitis	Ketoacidosis
Renal failure	Celiac disease
Anorexia nervosa	Macrolipasemia
Alcoholism	Head trauma or intracranial mass
Ketoacidosis	Renal failure

acute pancreatitis include enlargement or irregular contour of the gland, peripancreatic inflammation, and fluid collections (**Figure 12**). MRI scanning may be helpful in patients with hypersensitivity to contrast media. Abdominal ultrasonography can be used to detect cholelithiasis in patients with suspected gallstone pancreatitis.

Prognostic Criteria for Acute Pancreatitis

Most episodes of acute pancreatitis are of the mild interstitial form. Almost all associated morbidity and mortality occurs in patients with necrotizing pancreatitis and particularly infected pancreatic necrosis, which has a mortality rate of 10% to 30%.

Various scoring systems are used to identify at-risk patients and to determine prognosis; these include the Ranson criteria, the Glasgow Scoring System, and the Acute Physiology and Chronic Health Evaluation (APACHE) II. Ranson criteria remains the most used scoring system while APACHE is

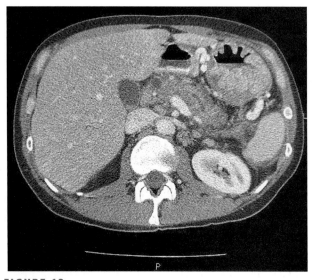

FIGURE 12.
Acute pancreatitis.
CT scan of a patient with acute interstitial pancreatitis with an inflamed, edematous pancreas.

the more complex. Neither test should substitute for close clinical judgment of the individual patient. The serum concentration of C-reactive protein increases with the severity of acute pancreatitis, but it is not a sensitive early marker of severity. Obesity (BMI >30) is also associated with severe disease.

Management

Mild acute interstitial pancreatitis usually resolves in a few days and does not result in organ dysfunction. Management consists of supportive measures, including bowel rest (nothing by mouth), intravenous fluid replacement, and narcotics for pain control.

In patients with severe acute pancreatitis whose condition is not improving or who continue to have fever after 3 to 5 days, contrast-enhanced CT scan should be performed to evaluate for necrosis. Prophylactic antibiotic therapy is useful only in patients with necrotizing pancreatitis; imipenem, cephalosporins, and fluoroquinolones have been shown to reduce mortality and morbidity. Patients with pancreatic necrosis should undergo percutaneous fine-needle aspiration for culture and Gram stain to evaluate for the presence of infected pancreatic necrosis. Infected pancreatic necrosis should be managed with surgical débridement.

Patients with severe pancreatitis often have prolonged hospitalizations with the inability to take food or liquids by mouth. Recent evidence suggests that the use of early nasoenteral (particularly nasojejunal) feeding may lower morbidity, particularly infectious complications, when compared with intravenous feeding.

Endoscopic retrograde cholangiopancreatography (ERCP) is recommended in patients with evidence of gallstone pancreatitis and suspected biliary obstruction. Biliary obstruction is suspected if cholelithiasis or choledocholithiasis is present, there is bile duct dilation, and there is elevation of liver enzymes. Aminotransferase concentrations rise initially in gallstone pancreatitis with subsequent rise of alkaline phosphatase and bilirubin if obstruction persists. ERCP with sphincterotomy has been shown to lower morbidity and mortality in these patients, significantly reducing rates of cholangitis and biliary sepsis.

Complications

Pancreatic pseudocysts (cysts of pancreatic juice that have a fibrous, nonepithelial lining that occurs around the gland) are the most common complication of acute pancreatitis. The cysts generally take at least 4 weeks to form, often resolve spontaneously, and are asymptomatic; they may, however, cause pain or obstruction by pressing against other organs (**Figure 13**). Symptomatic pseudocysts are treated with percutaneous drainage or endoscopic or surgical drainage via the stomach or duodenum.

A patient with an infected pseudocyst (pancreatic abscess) presents with worsening abdominal pain, fever, and an

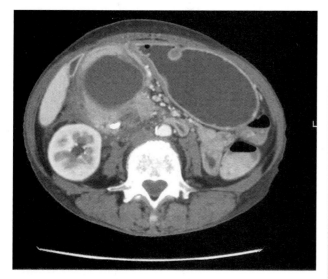

FIGURE 13.
Pancreatic pseudocyst.
CT scan showing pancreatic pseudocyst causing subsequent gastric outlet obstruction.

increasing leukocyte count. Treatment is usually percutaneous or surgical drainage and antibiotics.

Less common complications of acute pancreatitis are pancreatic tract leaks or fistulas that may present with pancreatic ascites. Treatment is bowel rest, endoscopic stenting, or surgery. Pancreatitis may also lead to splenic vein thrombosis with subsequent gastric varices and bleeding. Some patients with severe pancreatitis and significant necrosis may develop diabetes mellitus.

KEY POINTS

- Alcohol abuse and gallstones account for approximately 80% of cases of acute pancreatitis in the United States.
- Diagnosis of acute pancreatitis is made primarily through clinical evaluation and detection of elevated serum concentrations of amylase and lipase.
- The most important determinant of patient outcome in acute pancreatitis is the presence of pancreatic necrosis.
- Prophylactic antibiotic therapy in patients with acute pancreatitis should be limited to those patients with necrotizing pancreatitis.
- Nasojejunal feeding is the preferred route of nutrition in patients with acute pancreatitis.

Chronic Pancreatitis

Chronic pancreatitis is an irreversible chronic inflammatory condition of the pancreas characterized by fibrosis that progressively destroys exocrine and endocrine tissue. The prevalence of chronic pancreatitis is estimated at 3 to 10 cases per 100,000. There is a significant male predominance and strong association with alcohol consumption.

The most common cause of chronic pancreatitis in Western countries is alcohol abuse. The amount of alcohol consumed and the duration of consumption correlate with risk for chronic pancreatitis, but in patients who abuse alcohol, the risk may be increased also by nutritional and genetic factors. Approximately 20% of cases of chronic pancreatitis had previously been classified as idiopathic, but as more genetic causes have been identified and as diagnostic imaging has improved, more cases are now shown to have specific causes (**Table 15**).

Patients with chronic pancreatitis may present with one or more of the following: pain, malabsorption, and new-onset diabetes mellitus. The pain of chronic pancreatitis affects at least 85% of patients, is usually chronic and constant, is localized to the midepigastrium, radiates to the back, and is often exacerbated by food. Acute exacerbations may occur in addition to the constant pain. The pain results from chronic inflammation, increased intraductal pressure in the pancreatic ducts, and chronic stimulation of the nerves to the pancreas. When approximately 80% of the exocrine pancreas is damaged, malabsorption results, accompanied by steatorrhea, weight loss, and deficiencies of fat-soluble vitamins. Endocrine insufficiency in the form of diabetes mellitus occurs late in the disease when most of the gland has been damaged. In addition to the destruction of the insulin-producing β cells, chronic pancreatitis also leads to destruction of the glucagon-producing α cells; glucagon is the counterregulatory hormone that promotes gluconeogenesis, and the diabetes associated with chronic pancreatitis is therefore difficult to treat, with frequent episodes of hypoglycemia after insulin administration.

Diagnosis

Diagnostic tests for chronic pancreatitis consist of biochemical tests to evaluate pancreatic function and imaging tests to evaluate pancreatic structure. The most sensitive test for pancreatic function is the secretin stimulation test in which bicarbonate is collected and measured in the duodenum via an

TABLE 15 Causes of Chronic Pancreatitis
Alcohol Abuse
Obstruction
Tumor
Trauma
Pancreas divisum
Metabolic Disorders
Hyperlipidemia
Hypercalcemia
Genetic Disorders
Cystic fibrosis
Hereditary pancreatitis
Pancreatic secretory trypsin inhibitor mutations

oroduodenal tube after administration of intravenous secretin. The test has sensitivity of 75% to 95% but is very cumbersome for the patient and is rarely used. A 72-hour stool collection can be performed to test for fat malabsorption; ≥7 g of fat in the stool is considered abnormal. Chymotrypsin and elastase are stable products of pancreatic secretion that can be measured in feces; low values reflect insufficient pancreatic secretion of these enzymes. These tests all have low sensitivity, only being abnormal in patients with advanced chronic pancreatitis.

Imaging tests are used to evaluate for the structural changes of chronic pancreatitis. A plain radiograph showing pancreatic calcifications can confirm the diagnosis of chronic pancreatitis but is insensitive (approximately 30%). In the evaluation for duct dilation, duct irregularity, calcifications, or changes in the pancreatic parenchyma, abdominal ultrasonography (sensitivity 70%) and CT scan (sensitivity 90%) have been used. ERCP, the gold standard for diagnosing chronic pancreatitis, has a sensitivity of 95% when characterizing and examining the main duct and side branches (**Figure 14**). Endoscopic ultrasonography has recently been found to be almost equivalent to ERCP in establishing the diagnosis of chronic pancreatitis with less risk to the patient. Both ERCP and endoscopic ultrasonography, however, have a good deal of interobserver variability and may result in false-positive diagnoses of chronic pancreatitis. Magnetic resonance cholangiopancreatography (MRCP) has also been found to have sensitivities close to ERCP and endoscopic ultrasonography for the diagnosis of chronic pancreatitis, especially when MRCP imaging is combined with secretin stimulation.

Treatment

Treatment of chronic pancreatitis is directed at controlling pain and alleviating the manifestations of diabetes mellitus, malabsorption, and steatorrhea. Glucose control is managed as in patients with type 1 diabetes mellitus, but careful administration of insulin and careful glycemic control are essential because of the risk for hypoglycemia in these patients with impaired glucagon production. Malabsorption is treated with a low-fat diet and pancreatic enzyme supplementation. Generally, a minimum of 30,000 IU of pancreatic lipase before each meal is satisfactory to treat malabsorption secondary to chronic pancreatitis. Patients should abstain from alcohol.

Analgesia with narcotics is often required in patients with severe pain; such treatment can be challenging, particularly in patients with addiction problems such as those with alcoholism. Pancreatic enzyme replacement therapy may bring pain relief in selected patients by inhibiting the cholecystokinin feedback loop and thus decreasing pancreatic stimulation with meals.

Pain can be decreased by endoscopically removing obstructions to reduce intraductal pressure; this can be accomplished by dilating and stenting pancreatic strictures and removing stones. Percutaneous or endoscopically guided celiac plexus block can provide temporary relief. Surgical therapy is reserved for patients who fail to respond to medical therapy and continue to have severe pain. Drainage procedures can be performed, particularly a lateral pancreaticojejunostomy, when patients have a large dilated main duct. If the disease is localized to a portion of the pancreas, resection procedures such as a pancreaticoduodenectomy or distal pancreatectomy can be performed. Total pancreatectomy with autologous islet cell transplantation has been tried with success.

KEY POINTS

- Manifestations of chronic pancreatitis include abdominal pain, malabsorption, and diabetes mellitus.

- Diagnosis of chronic pancreatitis is made by imaging that shows pancreatic calcifications and ductal and parenchymal changes of the pancreas or biochemical tests that show impaired pancreatic function.

- Treatment of chronic pancreatitis includes pain control by medical, endoscopic, or surgical methods; pancreatic enzyme supplementation for malabsorption; and careful glucose control for diabetes mellitus.

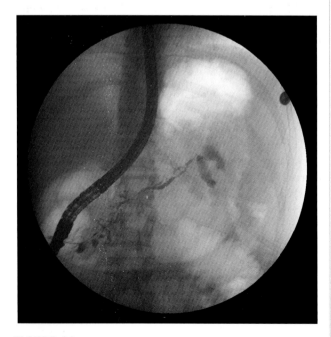

FIGURE 14.
Chronic pancreatitis.
Endoscopic retrograde pancreatography showing severe chronic pancreatitis with irregular duct, alternating strictures, and dilation, and filling of pseudocyst near the tail of the pancreas.

Pancreatic Adenocarcinoma

Pancreatic adenocarcinoma is an uncommon but deadly malignancy. Each year in the United States approximately

30,000 new cases are diagnosed and an equal number of affected patients die of the disease.

Age is the greatest risk factor associated with pancreatic cancer; the incidence rises with each decade after age 50 years. Tobacco smoking is the one clear risk factor. Chronic pancreatitis, which causes continued inflammation of the gland, increases the risk for pancreatic cancer tenfold. Hereditary pancreatitis, which affects the cationic trypsinogen gene, can increase the risk of pancreatic cancer by as much as 70- to 100-fold, with cancer presenting at an earlier age.

Clinical Presentation

The most common symptom of pancreatic cancer is constant epigastric pain that radiates to the back; the pain is secondary to ductal obstruction and perineural invasion. Patients with tumors of the body and tail of the gland usually present with pain because these tumors tend to be large when detected. The most common location of pancreatic cancers is in the head of the gland; these tumors are often accompanied by painless jaundice caused by obstruction of the common bile duct. Cachexia and weight loss of at least 10% of body weight are present in more than half of patients at diagnosis. New-onset diabetes mellitus may predate the diagnosis of pancreatic cancer by a few months, and acute pancreatitis due to pancreatic duct obstruction may be the first sign of pancreatic carcinoma.

Physical examination often shows weight loss, jaundice, abdominal tenderness, occasionally a nontender palpable gallbladder (Courvoisier sign) in a jaundiced patient, and, rarely, Trousseau syndrome of migrating thrombophlebitis.

Diagnosis

Laboratory findings in pancreatic cancer include elevation of liver enzymes in a cholestatic pattern if the tumor obstructs the bile duct and mild elevations of serum amylase and lipase concentrations. Serum concentration of cancer-associated antigen 19-9 (CA 19-9) increases with pancreatic cancer, particularly in unresectable tumors, but the test has a low sensitivity and specificity and cannot be used as a screening or diagnostic tool.

A pancreatic protocol contrast-enhanced spiral CT scan is the most important diagnostic and staging tool for pancreatic cancer, with a sensitivity of greater than 90% (**Figure 15**). Endoscopic ultrasonography is as accurate as CT scan for detecting tumors and may be more sensitive for tumors smaller than 2 cm in diameter. In addition, endoscopic ultrasonography when combined with CT scanning may aid in nodal and vascular staging to determine whether a tumor is surgically resectable. Endoscopic ultrasonography with fine-needle aspiration biopsy can provide specimens for histologic evaluation. ERCP is also very sensitive for detecting pancreatic cancer but because of its invasiveness is rarely used for diagnosis; the procedure is used primarily for therapeutic

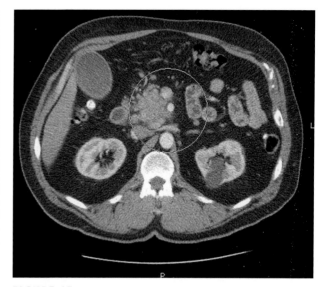

FIGURE 15.
CT scan of adenocarcinoma of the pancreas.
Large pancreatic head adenocarcinoma seen on CT scan.

purposes such as placing a stent in the bile duct for the treatment of obstructive jaundice.

Treatment

Surgery for pancreatic adenocarcinoma can be curative or palliative. Evidence of distant metastases or invasion of the tumor into the large local vessels makes the disease unresectable; approximately 80% to 85% of patients have unresectable disease at diagnosis. Cancer stage (**Table 16**) is determined with a combination of spiral CT, endoscopic ultrasonography, and sometimes laparoscopy.

If the disease is determined to be potentially resectable and if the patient is a candidate for surgery, surgery is the recommended approach. For cancer of the pancreatic head, pancreaticoduodenectomy (Whipple procedure) (**Figure 16**) is the indicated surgical procedure; for cancer of the body or tail of the pancreas, distal pancreatectomy is done. The operative mortality rate is 2% to 5% and operative morbidity is approximately 20%. Centers with the highest surgical volume have the lowest rate of perioperative complications and the highest survival rate. Even with surgical resection, the 5-year survival rate is only 10% to 25%. Adjuvant chemoradiotherapy has been shown to improve patient survival after resection.

Patients with unresectable, locally advanced disease usually survive for 10 months or less; patients with metastatic disease for 6 months or less. Chemotherapy is generally administered but with only a slight survival benefit. Pain relief with narcotic analgesia or celiac plexus block is essential. Biliary obstruction is usually treated with permanent metal stents placed via ERCP; duodenal obstruction is a serious complication that can be treated with surgical bypass or endoscopic stenting.

TABLE 16 Staging of Pancreatic Cancer, Treatment, and Prognosis

Stage	Findings	Treatment	Survival
Localized/resectable disease	No encasement of the celiac axis or SMA; patent SMPV confluence; no extrapancreatic disease	Surgical resection, with adjunctive radiation and chemotherapy	10%–25% 5-year survival
Locally advanced disease	Tumor extension to involve the celiac axis or SMA, or venous occlusion (SMV or SMPV confluence); no extrapancreatic disease	Radiation and chemotherapy	10 months
Metastatic disease	Metastatic disease (typically to liver and peritoneum and occasionally to lung)	Chemotherapy	6 months

SMA = superior mesenteric artery; SMPV = superior mesenteric-portal vein; SMV = superior mesenteric vein.

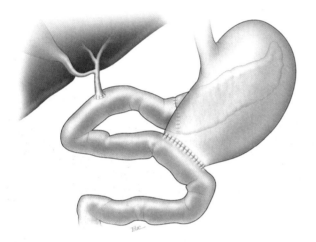

FIGURE 16.
Pancreatoduodenectomy for pancreatic cancer.
Drawing of anatomy after a pancreaticoduodenectomy or Whipple procedure for the treatment of pancreatic head adenocarcinoma. The pancreatic head, distal bile duct, duodenum, and distal stomach have been removed.

KEY POINTS

- Pancreatic adenocarcinoma is one of the deadliest cancers, with a 5-year survival rate less than 5% overall and only 10% to 25% in patients who undergo surgery with curative intent.

- Preoperative diagnosis and staging of pancreatic adenocarcinoma are performed with CT scanning and endoscopic ultrasonography; tumors that have not metastasized or invaded large local vessels are considered to be resectable.

- Surgery is the only curative option for pancreatic cancer: pancreatoduodenectomy is the procedure for cancer of the pancreatic head, and distal pancreatectomy for cancer of the body and tail; only 15% to 20% of patients are surgical candidates.

Cystic Neoplasms of the Pancreas

Cystic neoplasms of the pancreas are rare tumors comprising only 10% of pancreatic cysts and 1% of pancreatic cancers. However, with the increased use of CT and MRI imaging, incidental pancreatic cysts have been detected in up to 20% of the population.

If an inflammatory benign pseudocyst can be ruled out, the differential diagnosis of pancreatic cystic neoplasms includes the benign serous cystadenomas; the premalignant mucinous cystadenomas and frankly malignant mucinous cystadenocarcinoma; and main branch and side branch intraductal papillary mucinous neoplasms (**Figure 17**).

These neoplasms are often asymptomatic and detected incidentally. Symptoms, when present, are usually subtle and vague. The benign cystic lesions are differentiated from the potentially malignant lesions by imaging techniques including CT and MRI scanning and endoscopic ultrasonography. Cytologic examination of cyst fluid obtained by fine-needle

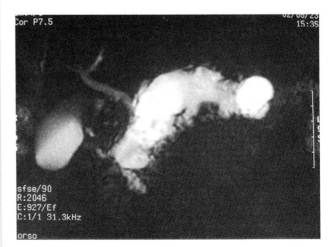

FIGURE 17.
Magnetic resonance cholangiopancreatography showing an intraductal papillary mucinous neoplasm.
MRCP image of a main branch intraductal papillary mucinous neoplasm demonstrating a massively dilated main pancreatic duct filled with mucin.

TABLE 17 Cyst Fluid Analysis of Pancreatic Cystic Lesions

Cyst Lesion	Amylase	Carcinoembryonic Antigen
Pseudocyst	High	Low
Serous cystadenoma	Variable	Low
Mucinous cystadenoma	Variable	High

aspiration as well as analysis for amylase and tumor markers, such as carcinoembryonic antigen, can aid in detecting malignant lesions (**Table 17**). Treatment of benign lesions consists of observation and follow-up; suspected premalignant and malignant lesions are surgically resected.

KEY POINT

- Management of pancreatic cystic lesions is determined by the presence of symptoms and malignant potential as determined by CT and MRI scanning, endoscopic ultrasonography, and cyst fluid analysis.

Pancreatic Neuroendocrine Tumors

Pancreatic neuroendocrine tumors are rare neoplasms that can arise in the pancreas and in other parts of the gastrointestinal system. The hallmark of pancreatic neuroendocrine tumors is an excessive, unregulated hormone secretion that leads to clinical symptoms; however, 15% do not secrete hormone and are termed "nonfunctioning" (**Table 18**).

The most common example of a functioning pancreatic neuroendocrine tumor is the gastrinoma. Gastrinomas are tumors that secrete an excess and unregulated amount of gastrin that in turn stimulates the parietal cells that lead to excess acid production. The acid leads to peptic ulcer formation and watery diarrhea with the clinical syndrome termed the Zollinger-Ellison syndrome. The diagnosis is made by identification of an elevated gastrin level with serum gastrin of greater than 1000 pg/mL (1000 ng/L) being essentially diagnostic of a gastrinoma. If the diagnosis is equivocal based on serum gastrin levels, the secretin stimulation test and gastric acid secretion test can be used.

After diagnosis and control of the hormonal effects of neuroendocrine tumors, the tumor must be accurately localized in the pancreas and the patient evaluated for metastatic disease. Pancreatic neuroendocrine tumors can be difficult to detect with CT and MRI imaging. Many pancreatic neuroendocrine tumors have receptors for somatostatin, and somatostatin receptor scintigraphy is the preferred first test in identifying both the primary pancreatic tumor and metastases in neuroendocrine tumors with the exception of insulinomas, which are rarely malignant. Endoscopic ultrasonography is highly sensitive for localizing the tumor in the pancreas and may be used as a complementary test to somatostatin receptor scintigraphy (**Figure 18**).

With the exception of insulinomas, tumors limited to the pancreas with no evidence of metastases should be surgically resected because of the high rate of malignancy. The primary determinant of survival is liver metastases; the 10-year survival rate in patients with no liver metastases is >90%; survival rate is 16% to 78% in patients with liver metastases. Metastatic disease is treated with chemotherapy, hepatic artery embolization, or radiolabeled somatostatin analogues (octreotide and lanreotide) with only limited to moderate success.

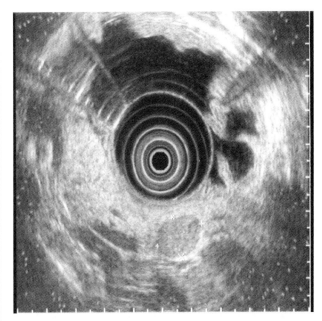

FIGURE 18.
Endoscopic ultrasonography localization of a pancreatic neuroendocrine tumor.
The image shows a round isoechoic to hypoechoic pancreatic tail neuroendocrine tumor.

TABLE 18 Features of Common Pancreatic Neuroendocrine Tumors

Tumor Type	Hormone	Symptoms	Malignancy Rate
Gastrinoma	Gastrin	Ulcers, diarrhea, gastroesophageal reflux disease	60%-90%
Insulinoma	Insulin	Hypoglycemia	<10%
VIPoma	Vasoactive intestinal	Diarrhea, dehydration, peptide hypokalemia	40%-70%
Glucagonoma	Glucagon	Dermatitis, diabetes	50%-80%

- Pancreatic neuroendocrine tumors lead to symptoms either through tumor mass effect or excessive secretion of hormones.

Bibliography

Bahra M, Jacob D, Pascher A, et al. Surgical strategies and predictors of outcome for malignant neuroendocrine tumors of the pancreas. J Gastroenterol Hepatol. 2007;22:930-5. [PMID: 17489964]

Brugge WR. Approach to cystic pancreatic lesions. Gastrointest Endosc Clin N Am. 2005;15:485-96. [PMID: 15990053]

Cahen DL, Gouma DJ, Nio Y, et al. Endoscopic versus surgical drainage of the pancreatic duct in chronic pancreatitis. N Engl J Med. 2007;356:676-84. [PMID: 17301298]

Forsmark CE, Baillie J; AGA Institute Clinical Practice and Economics Committee; AGA Institute Governing Board. AGA Institute technical review on acute pancreatitis. Gastroenterology. 2007;132:2022-44. [PMID: 17484894]

Schneider G, Siveke JT, Eckel F, Schmid RM. Pancreatic cancer: basic and clinical aspects. Gastroenterology. 2005;128:1606-25. [PMID: 15887154]

van Esch AA, Wilder-Smith OH, Jansen JB, van Goor H, Drenth JP. Pharmacological management of pain in chronic pancreatitis. Dig Liver Dis. 2006;38:518-26. [PMID: 16627019]

Villatoro E, Bassi C, Larvin M. Antibiotic therapy for prophylaxis against infection of pancreatic necrosis in acute pancreatitis. Cochrane Database Syst Rev. 2006;(4):CD002941. [PMID: 17054156]

Whitcomb DC. Clinical practice: Acute pancreatitis. N Engl J Med. 2006;354:2142-50. [PMID: 16707751]

Witt H, Apte MV, Keim V, Wilson JS. Chronic pancreatitis: challenges and advances in pathogenesis, genetics, diagnosis, and therapy. Gastroenterology. 2007;132:1557-73. [PMID: 17466744]

Yip D, Karapetis C, Strickland A, Steer CB, Goldstein D. Chemotherapy and radiotherapy for inoperable advanced pancreatic cancer. Cochrane Database Syst Rev. 2006;3:CD002093. [PMID: 16855985]

Disorders of the Intestines

Diarrhea

Diarrhea may be defined in terms of the frequency of defecation or the consistency, volume, or weight of the stool. Traditionally, a stool weight greater than 200 g/d is regarded as diarrhea; however, most patients associate an increase of the frequency of defecation to more than three times a day with a loose or liquid consistency to be the defining characteristic of diarrhea.

There are four types of diarrhea defined by mechanism: osmotic diarrhea is caused by the presence of large amounts of poorly absorbed solutes within the lumen of the gut; secretory diarrhea is caused by abnormal ion transport and subsequent water secretion; exudative or inflammatory diarrhea is caused by a disruption in the mucosal barrier secondary to infection or idiopathic inflammation; and motility-related diarrhea.

Duration, Severity, and Characteristics

Diarrhea can also be defined as acute and chronic. Acute diarrhea lasts no longer than 2 weeks and is usually secondary to infection (see MKSAP 15 Infectious Disease). Chronic diarrhea lasts longer than 4 weeks and usually has a noninfectious cause (**Table 19**); infectious causes of chronic diarrhea include *Clostridium difficile* and *Giardia* infection. Various medications may also cause chronic diarrhea (**Table 20**).

Small-bowel diarrhea is usually associated with large-volume stool and three to four bowel movements per day; large-bowel diarrhea is usually small-volume but consists of eight to ten bowel movements per day and may be associated with tenesmus if the rectosigmoid area is inflamed. In patients with chronic diarrhea, severe and unremitting abdominal pain is often indicative of an inflammatory destruction of the mucosa. If the pain is located in the right lower quadrant, terminal ileal Crohn disease should be considered. Inflammatory bowel disease may also be associated with extraintestinal manifestations, such as arthralgias or uveitis. Other disorders that cause chronic diarrhea have associated dermatologic manifestations; for example, inflammatory bowel disease is associated with erythema nodosum (**Figure 19**) or pyoderma gangrenosum (**Figure 20**), and celiac disease is associated with dermatitis herpetiformis (**Figure 21**). Weight loss is an important indicator of chronicity and severity but may be secondary to malabsorption, dehydration, or inadequate caloric intake.

Enteroinvasive processes (such as infection with *Escherichia coli* serotype O157:H7) are associated with a loss of an intact mucosa and commonly present with hematochezia. Malabsorptive processes are associated with steatorrhea (oily residue or globs of mucus) or passage of undigested food.

Management

Most episodes of diarrhea are self-limited, and the patient requires no therapy or diagnostic evaluation. However, if the patient is dehydrated from the diarrhea, intravenous fluids or oral rehydration solutions are required. In the setting of gastroenteritis, many patients become relatively lactose-intolerant. Empiric antibiotic therapy is often appropriate for acute traveler's diarrhea. Antidiarrheal agents such as loperamide or diphenoxylate/atropine may be used for symptomatic relief in this acute setting. If the diarrhea persists after such interventions, further evaluation is required.

Various diagnostic studies are used to determine the cause of noninfectious diarrheal disease (**Table 21**). Qualitative and quantitative fecal fat studies are sensitive noninvasive tests for fat malabsorption. However, it is important for the patient to be consuming a significant amount of fat (>100 g/d) at the time of the test for the result to be reliable.

Testing for fecal leukocytes rarely adds to the diagnosis of the cause of diarrhea. Measurement of the biomarkers fecal lactoferrin and calprotectin (proteins in the granules of

TABLE 19 Causes of Noninfectious Diarrhea

Disorder	Diagnosis	Clues or Risk Factors
Ischemia	Colon or small-bowel imaging and biopsies	Vascular disease, history of hematochezia, pain
Inflammatory Bowel Disease		
Ulcerative Colitis	Colon imaging and biopsies	Bloody diarrhea, tenesmus
Crohn Disease	Small-bowel imaging, ileocolonoscopy	Weight loss, anemia, hypoalbuminemia
Microscopic Colitis	Biopsies of colonic mucosa	Secretory diarrhea pattern; includes collagenous colitis, lymphocytic colitis
Irritable Bowel Syndrome (diarrhea-predominant)	History (bloating, abdominal discomfort relieved by a bowel movement)	Increased mucus in stool in ~50% of patients; no weight loss or alarm features
Celiac Sprue	Serologic studies (anti-tissue transglutaminase antibodies), small bowel biopsy	Dermatitis herpetiformis, iron deficiency anemia
Whipple Disease	Polymerase chain reaction, small-bowel biopsy	Arthralgias, neurologic or ophthalmologic symptoms
Carbohydrate Intolerance	Dietary exclusion, breath hydrogen test	Excess lactose—use of artificial sweeteners (sorbitol, mannitol), or fructose
Pancreatic Insufficiency	Tests for excess fecal fat and pancreatic calcifications, pancreatic function tests (secretin stimulation test)	Chronic pancreatitis, hyperglycemia, history of pancreatic resection
Small-Bowel Bacterial Overgrowth	Response to empiric antibiotics, duodenal aspirate	Diabetes mellitus, intestinal dysmotility (e.g., systemic sclerosis, jejunal diverticula)
Eosinophilic Enteritis	Small-bowel biopsy (often full-thickness biopsy)	Eosinophilia, hypoalbuminemia
Common Variable Immunodeficiency	Tests for hypogammaglobulinemia (multiple subclasses)	Pulmonary diseases, recurrent *Giardia* infection
Iatrogenic Disorders		
• Medications	History	See Table 20
• Enteral Feedings	History	Classic osmotic diarrhea
Bile Acid Malabsorption	Diagnosis of exclusion, empiric response to cholestyramine	History of resection of <100 cm of distal small bowel
Bile Acid Deficiency	Diagnosis of exclusion, tests for excess fecal fat	Cholestasis, history of resection of >100 cm of small bowel
Radiation Exposure	History, small-bowel and/or colon imaging	May begin years after exposure, strictures or hypervascular mucosa with characteristic biopsy findings

TABLE 20 Medications Commonly Associated with Diarrhea

Acarbose
Antibiotics (especially penicillins, macrolides)
Antineoplastic agents
Colchicine
Digoxin
Herbal and alternative medicines
Laxatives
Magnesium-based antacids, cathartics
Metformin
Misoprostol
NSAIDs
Proton pump inhibitors
Quinidine

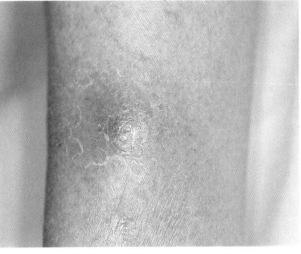

FIGURE 19.
Erythema nodosum.

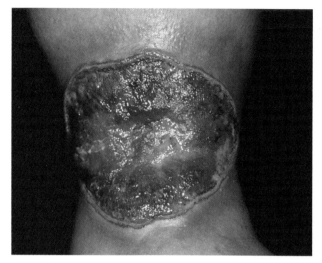

FIGURE 20.
Pyoderma gangrenosum.

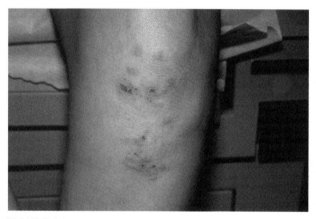

FIGURE 21.
Dermatitis herpetiformis.

neutrophils) is more sensitive than the fecal leukocyte test for detecting an inflammatory process or malignancy; however, these tests are not widely available. Flexible sigmoidoscopy and colonoscopy can help evaluate for infection; biopsies can detect pseudomembranes (present in *Clostridium difficile* infection) or viral inclusions (in cytomegalovirus infection).

Stool electrolytes (sodium and potassium) can be measured in liquid stool to calculate the fecal osmotic gap, which helps to differentiate osmotic from secretory diarrhea: the gap is calculated as $290 - 2 \times [Na + K]$; an osmotic gap <50 mosm/kg (50 mmol/kg) is consistent with secretory diarrhea; a gap greater than 125 mosm/kg (125 mmol/kg) suggests an osmotic diarrhea. Stool osmolarity less than 250 mosm/kg (250 mmol/kg) suggests factitious diarrhea associated with chronic laxative abuse. More commonly, however, a restriction of oral intake with concomitant diminution of diarrhea suggests an osmotic or malabsorptive cause. Persistent diarrhea despite no oral intake may imply a secretory cause.

Various neuropeptide are associated with secretory diarrhea secondary to a neuroendocrine disorder (for example, multiple endocrine neoplasia types 1 and 2). Assays for these neuropeptides should be considered in patients with an undiagnosed persistent secretory diarrhea and associated clinical findings.

KEY POINTS

- Acute diarrhea lasts less than 2 weeks; chronic diarrhea lasts longer than 4 weeks.
- Hydration is critical in a patient with severe diarrhea.
- Diagnostic evaluation is appropriate in diarrhea that is not self-limited and does not respond to empiric therapy.

Fat Malabsorption

Patients with chronic diarrhea and an oily residue in their stool should be evaluated for the various causes of fat malabsorption (**Table 22**), which is caused by disruption of any of the various stages of fat assimilation. Qualitative and quantitative fecal fat studies are useful in diagnosing fat malabsorption and steatorrhea. Some of the most common diseases that cause fat malabsorption are celiac disease, small-intestine bacterial overgrowth, short-bowel syndrome, and pancreatic insufficiency.

Celiac Disease

Celiac disease (also called celiac sprue, nontropical sprue, and gluten-sensitive enteropathy) was formerly considered to be a rare childhood disease but now is considered to be somewhat prevalent, with estimates of 1 in 133 to 1 in 250 persons. The disorder occurs in genetically predisposed persons with haplotype HLA-DQ2 or HLA-DQ8 and is triggered by ingestion of gluten, a composite of the proteins gliadin and glutenin that is present in wheat, rye, and barley. These haplotypes are present in 30% of the general population but in virtually all patients with celiac disease.

The clinical presentation of patients with celiac disease includes severe diarrhea, malabsorption, and malnutrition. Laboratory evaluation often shows asymptomatic liver chemistry abnormalities. Celiac disease is associated with various other disorders. Iron deficiency anemia, osteoporosis, and coagulopathy are direct results of disease-related malabsorption. As many as 10% of patients with type 1 diabetes mellitus and autoimmune thyroiditis have celiac disease. There is a 33-fold increase in rare lymphomas of the gut (enteropathy-associated T-cell lymphoma) as well as an increased risk for non-Hodgkin lymphoma at any site. Other associated conditions include ataxia, peripheral neuropathy, and epilepsy.

The inflammatory injury to the small intestine in celiac disease results from a T-cell–mediated immune response. The gold standard for diagnosis is biopsy from the duodenum, with the biopsy specimen showing intraepithelial lymphocytes, crypt hyperplasia, and partial to total villous atrophy (**Figure 22**).

TABLE 21 Diagnostic Studies for Noninfectious Diarrhea

Diagnostic Test	Indications	Interpretation/Usefulness
Stool Studies		
Qualitative fecal fat (Sudan stain)	Fat malabsorption	When properly performed, detects >90% of significant steatorrhea; low dietary fat consumption leads to false-negative results, and dietary Olestra® causes false-positive results.
Quantitative fecal fat (48- or 72-hour)	Fat malabsorption	Gold standard; patient must be on high-fat diet (>100 g/d); normal fecal fat value is <6 g/24 h, although most high-volume diarrheas result in mild elevations regardless of cause; values >10–24 g/24 h indicate fat malabsorption.
Fecal leukocytes or lactoferrin, calprotectin	Inflammation	Limited usefulness because of variable sensitivity and specificity.
Stool osmolarity	Verification of diarrhea	Normal is 280–300 mosm/kg (280-300 mmol/kg); a value of <250 mosm/kg (250 mmol/kg) is suggestive of factitious diarrhea (e.g., addition of water or hypotonic urine to stool sample).
Stool electrolytes (sodium, potassium)	Differentiation of secretory from osmotic diarrhea	Osmotic gap >125 mosm/kg (125 mmol/kg) suggests osmotic diarrhea; osmotic gap <50 mosm/kg (50 mmol/kg) suggests secretory diarrhea.
Stool magnesium	Factitious or iatrogenic diarrhea	>15 mmol/d (30 µg/d) or spot sample >45 µmol/L (90 meq/L) is abnormal; use of antacids is a common source.
Stool pH	Osmotic diarrhea	pH <6.0 suggests carbohydrate malabsorption.
Other Tests		
Serum antitissue transglutaminase (anti-tTG) antibody assay	Celiac sprue	Most reliable screening test for celiac sprue; diagnosis must be confirmed by small-bowel biopsies.
Antiendomysial antibody assay	Celiac sprue	More labor intensive, more expensive than anti-tTG antibody assay; positive result requires small-bowel biopsy for confirmation.
Antigliadin antibody assay	Celiac sprue	Useful in following dietary response to gluten withdrawal; less useful in diagnosis except for serum IgG in IgA deficiency.
Breath hydrogen test	Carbohydrate malabsorption	Increased hydrogen excretion after carbohydrate challenge; often replaced by an empiric trial of dietary exclusion.
D-Xylose test	Carbohydrate malabsorption	Decreased excretion of this orally administered agent indicates malabsorption; limited usefulness; mostly replaced by more specific testing.
Schilling test	Malabsorption	Limited usefulness; mostly replaced by more specific testing.
Small-bowel biopsy	Malabsorption, inflammation	Loss of villi (e.g., celiac disease) - inflammatory infiltrates (diastase resistance indicates Whipple disease, mast cells indicate mastocytosis).
Duodenal aspirates	Small-bowel bacterial overgrowth	Quantitative bacterial culture >10^5 is positive; mixed flora typically found; often replaced by empiric treatment.
Secretin stimulation test	Pancreatic insufficiency	Gold standard for pancreatic exocrine failure; limited availability; often replaced by empiric trial of pancreatic enzyme replacement therapy.
Neuropeptide assays[a]	Neuroendocrine tumors	Useful if persistent diarrhea >1 L/24 hr is present despite fasting and other indications of possible tumor (hypokalemia, mass, skin findings, etc.) are present.
Radiographic small-bowel follow-through	Inflammation, overgrowth	Presence of strictures, ulcers, fistulas suggests Crohn disease; diverticulosis predisposes to small-bowel bacterial overgrowth.
Colonoscopy with biopsies	Inflammation, secretory diarrhea	Diagnostic for ulcerative colitis, microscopic colitis, strictures, radiation enteropathy.

[a]Gastrin, vasoactive intestinal peptide, glucagon, somatostatin, pancreatic peptide, neurotensin, substance P, calcitonin, motilin, urine 5-hydroxyindoleacetic acid.

Celiac disease is associated with circulating antibodies to various substances, and serologic testing is used to screen for the disorder (**Figure 23**). The serologic tests for antitissue transglutaminase IgA antibodies and antiendomysial IgA antibodies both have a sensitivity greater than 90% and a specificity greater than 95%. The IgG antibody assays have a specificity greater than 95%, but their sensitivity of <40% makes them less useful as screening tests. Measurement of antigliadin IgA and IgG antibodies has a sensitivity and speci-ficity of approximately 80%. Therefore, the recommended serologic test is measurement of IgA antibodies to antitissue transglutaminase. However, 2% to 3% of patients with celiac disease have IgA deficiency, and, therefore, this test may give a false-negative result in such patients. In patients with a low serum IgA, the IgG antitissue transglutaminase antibody should be measured. False-negative results may also occur in patients with mild disease or in patients adhering to a gluten-free diet before diagnosis.

TABLE 22 Causes of Fat Malabsorption	
Type	**Cause**
Exocrine Pancreatic Insufficiency	Chronic pancreatitis
	Pancreatic resection
	Cystic fibrosis
Bile Salt Deficiency	Malabsorption
	Impaired synthesis-cholestatic liver disease
	Bacterial deconjugation
Mucosal Small-Intestine Disease	Celiac sprue
	Whipple disease
	Crohn disease
	Eosinophilic enteritis
	Mastocytosis
Surgical	Short bowel syndrome
	Gastric bypass surgery
Small Intestinal Parasites	*Giardia*
	Isospora
	Cryptosporidium
	Cyclospora
	Strongyloides
Impaired Lymphatic Drainage	Lymphangiectasia
	Lymphoma

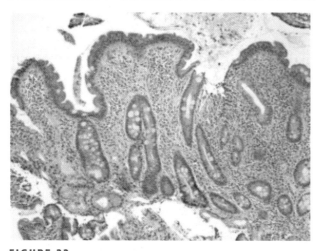

FIGURE 22.
Mucosal lesion in celiac sprue.
Biopsy specimen showing loss of the villous architecture and crypt hyperplasia and increased inflammatory infiltration of the lamina propria.

The only treatment for celiac disease is lifelong adherence to a gluten-free diet. Common grain substitutes for gluten include rice flour, cornstarch, quinoa, tapioca flour, and potato starch. Monitoring disease remission with both symptomatic relief and serial antibody testing is recommended; a disease in remission is characterized by symptomatic improvement, resolution of histologic changes, and normalization of serologic abnormalities. Recently, video capsule endoscopy has proved to be useful in evaluating patients with disease refractory to a gluten-free diet to determine whether there is evidence of distal abnormal mucosa. Rarely, immunosuppressive agents such as corticosteroids or tacrolimus have been used to treat refractory celiac disease. However, sources of unintentional gluten exposure should be identified because noncompliance is the most frequent cause of refractory disease.

Small-Intestine Bacterial Overgrowth

Small-intestine bacterial overgrowth is characterized by malabsorption of nutrients due to an excessive number of colonic bacteria in the small intestine. Symptoms include flatulence, bloating, and constipation. The disorder can be especially problematic in the elderly, who may have hypochlorhydria or impaired intestinal motility leading to failed bacterial clearance. Risk factors for bacterial overgrowth are shown in **Table 23**. A common sign is a low serum vitamin B_{12} concentration associated with vitamin malabsorption with an elevated folate concentration secondary to bacterial production in a patient with megaloblastic anemia.

Because excessive bacterial growth in the upper intestine leads to premature metabolism of food, there is an excess of sugar fermentation and a reduction of calories reaching the distal intestines. Therefore, testing with a lactose or lactulose challenge can identify patients with overactive bacterial flora. An empiric trial of antibiotics may be necessary to corroborate the diagnosis and begin therapy. Common treatments include tetracycline, amoxicillin-clavulanic acid, or rifaximin for 10 to 14 days.

Diarrhea, bloating, or flatulence may recur after antibiotic therapy, and some patients may require a prolonged course, a rotating series of antibiotics, or a scheduled period of intermittent therapy. Such patients should adhere to a low-carbohydrate, high-fat diet to minimize substrate for the bacteria.

Short-Bowel Syndrome

The short-bowel syndrome is a malabsorptive state that usually occurs secondary to small-bowel resection; it is defined in adults as residual small intestine less than 200 cm. It may also result from such congenital conditions as jejunal or ileal atresia. The degree of nutrient, electrolyte, and fluid absorption is related to the amount of residual intestine after resection. Patients at the highest risk for dehydration, chronic liver disease, and protein calorie malabsorption are those with a jejunocolic or ileocolic anastomosis and less than 60 cm of residual small intestine or end jejunostomy with less than 115 cm of residual small intestine. The remaining intestine adapts to facilitate more efficient absorption that allows for an enteral feeding regimen. The most important aspect of providing nutritional support is to prevent energy malnutrition and specific vitamin and nutrient deficiencies. Initial or intermittent

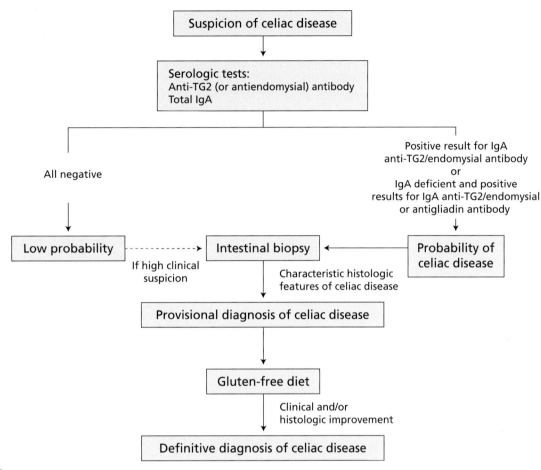

FIGURE 23.
Diagnostic approach to celiac sprue.

TG2 = antitissue transglutaminase.

Reproduced with permission from Alaedini A, Green PHR. Narrative review: celiac disease: understanding a complex autoimmune disorder. Ann Intern Med. 2005;142:289-298. [PMID: 15710962] Copyright 2005, American College of Physicians.

TABLE 23 Risk Factors for Bacterial Overgrowth
Hypochlorhydria
Postoperative
Gastric atrophy
Medication-induced (H$_2$-receptor antagonists, proton pump inhibitors)
Intestinal dysmotility syndromes
Diabetes mellitus
Systemic sclerosis
Persistent small intestinal dilatation
Secondary to strictures
Small intestinal diverticulosis
Surgically created blind loops of intestine
Afferent loop dysfunction post-gastrojejunostomy
Surgically absent ileocecal valve

parenteral nutrition is often required, and patients with a shorter intestine require ongoing parenteral nutrition.

Certain dietary restrictions are required in patients with the syndrome. Oxalate in the diet normally binds to calcium and is excreted in the stool; in patients with significant fat malabsorption, dietary calcium binds to free fatty acids and the oxalate passes into the colon where it is absorbed and renally filtered before being bound to calcium. The resultant hyperoxaluria can lead to nephrolithiasis; therefore, a low-oxalate diet is recommended.

Intestinal transplantation is an option for patients requiring lifelong parenteral nutrition and those with serious complications of their disease.

Pancreatic Insufficiency

The pancreas normally secretes 600 to 1200 mL daily, consisting primarily of pancreatic enzymes, bicarbonate, and water. Fluid and bicarbonate are stimulated by secretin; however the pancreatic acinar cells are likely regulated by gastrin-releasing peptide and the cholinergic nervous system. Pancreatic function of 10% to 20% is required to produce requisite proteolytic enzymes for normal digestion (for example, trypsin, chymotrypsin, and elastase). Patients with impaired pancreatic function typically present with diarrhea and other symptoms of fat malabsorption and have steatorrhea, with a fecal fat concentration of greater than 8 to 10 g/24 hours (8-10 g/d). Resolution of the diarrhea after an empiric trial of enzyme supplementation is often the confirmatory test for pancreatic insufficiency. A secretin stimulation test or endoscopic ultrasonography may rarely be needed to assess pancreatic exocrine function.

Acute pancreatitis can sometimes lead to exocrine dysfunction. However, patients with chronic pancreatitis, as evidenced by calcification on radiologic imaging or endoscopic ultrasonography, more commonly have pancreatic insufficiency. Cystic fibrosis is also associated with exocrine dysfunction, and testing for the *CFTR* gene mutation is recommended in patients with idiopathic pancreatic insufficiency; however, not all mutations are screened for in the commercially available assays.

Reducing fat intake to less than 20 g/d may be adequate for some of these patients. However, they often require pancreatic lipase supplementation, 30,000 to 50,000 units per meal, with titration for an individual patient. Supplementation can also be given with snacks, with an accordingly reduced dose.

KEY POINTS

- Patients with chronic diarrhea with an oily residue in their stool should be evaluated for fat malabsorption.

- Celiac disease is associated with other autoimmune diseases such as type 1 diabetes mellitus.

- A response to an empiric course of antibiotics is often the best test for small-intestine bacterial overgrowth.

- Patients with less than 200 cm of functioning small intestine should be carefully monitored for short-bowel syndrome.

- The diarrhea associated with pancreatic insufficiency often responds to supplementation with pancreatic lipase enzymes.

Inflammatory Bowel Disease

Inflammatory bowel disease is an idiopathic chronic inflammatory disease of the gastrointestinal tract that consists of two distinct clinical entities: ulcerative colitis and Crohn disease (also known as regional enteritis). The pathogenesis of the disease is not fully understood but likely involves a genetic predisposition and a dysregulated immunologic response to the local microenvironment of luminal bacteria.

Ulcerative colitis and Crohn disease are usually differentiated on the basis of differences in the distribution of pathology in the bowel and histopathologic appearance of the lesion. However, these diseases are more likely an immunoinflammatory spectrum of chronic and recurring diseases of the intestines. As many as 10% of patients cannot be shown to have either Crohn disease or ulcerative colitis and are considered to have indeterminate colitis.

Risk Factors for Inflammatory Bowel Disease

The peak incidence of these diseases is in the second, third, and fourth decades of life, with a second peak in the seventh and eighth decades. There are no sex differences, but patients of Ashkenazi Jewish descent have a higher risk. There is a 5% to 10% risk for first-degree relatives of affected patients. Many candidate genes have been proposed. There has been an established link between Crohn disease and variants of the *CARD15* (also known as *NOD2*) gene, but this gene plays a role in only some patients with Crohn disease and does not affect the risk for colitis. Recently, the interleukin-23 (IL-23) receptor gene has been shown to have a much larger effect on the risk for both Crohn disease and colitis. IL-23 holds particular promise, as studies of the monoclonal antibody against the p40 subunit have demonstrated benefit in the treatment of Crohn disease.

Clinical Manifestations of Inflammatory Bowel Disease

Patients with ulcerative colitis generally present with bloody diarrhea with rectal urgency, discomfort, and cramps. They have profound tenesmus (feelings of urgency and incomplete evacuation), which is secondary to proctitis. This inflammation of the rectum can cause constipation to be a more common manifestation than diarrhea; in such patients, determining the activity of the disease and treating it can be challenging. Ulcerative colitis extends proximally from the anal verge and can progress to pancolitis involving the cecum. Fever is infrequent, but weight loss secondary to the inflammatory disease itself or to the chronic diarrhea is common. Physical examination findings can range from mild lower abdominal tenderness to abdominal distention with rebound tenderness and hypoactive bowel sounds, suggestive of toxic megacolon.

Crohn disease is more protean in its manifestations than ulcerative colitis, as the disease can affect any portion of the gastrointestinal tract and frequently has so-called "skip lesions" with areas of normal mucosa juxtaposed with severe inflammation. The transmural nature of the disease results in three distinct manifestations: inflammatory, fistulizing, and fibrostenotic.

In Crohn disease, large-volume diarrhea can occur; diarrhea is associated with both small- and large-bowel Crohn disease, whereas hematochezia is almost always a sign of colonic disease. The inflamed tissue causes a secretory diarrhea and a protein-losing enteropathy, steatorrhea from fat malabsorption (with patients who have ileal or ileocolic disease frequently being vitamin B_{12}– and vitamin D–deficient), and other types of malabsorption. Patients who have had their terminal ileum resected are also at risk for a choleretic diarrhea secondary to bile salt wasting.

Fistulae are abnormal connections between the bowel and adjacent organs. Abscesses may form, and the fistula acts as a natural drainage mechanism, causing pus to emerge from the fistulae. The fistulae become symptomatic with drainage of fecal material around the anus (perianal fistulae), seepage of bowel contents through the skin (enterocutaneous fistulae), passage of feces through the vagina (rectovaginal fistulae), and pneumaturia or recurrent urinary tract infections (enterovesical fistulae). The intestinal inflammation may extend to adjacent musculature and result in neuromuscular sequelae; for example, a patient with Crohn disease and a new limp likely has a psoas muscle abscess.

Patients with intestinal strictures present with signs of obstruction: fever, abdominal distention, pain, nausea, and vomiting. Strictures may be secondary to severe inflammation or to fibrosis of the bowel and can be relieved only by surgical resection. The most common site of strictures is in the terminal ileum where they result in partial or complete small-bowel obstruction. However, patients with duodenal Crohn disease may develop gastric outlet obstruction.

In patients with ileal disease, the abdominal examination commonly shows right lower quadrant tenderness; a phlegmonous mass may be present. A detailed anorectal examination is important in patients with suspected Crohn disease: the presence of skin tags suggests the diagnosis, and the examination may also show fistulae.

Extraintestinal Manifestations

Extraintestinal manifestations occur in approximately 10% to 20% of patients with inflammatory bowel disease at some time in the course of their disease. Arthritis, the most common such manifestation, can either be related to the intestinal inflammation itself or be part of an overlap syndrome with rheumatoid arthritis. This unexpected relationship is made more interesting in that the anti–tumor necrosis factor α protocols for treatment of Crohn disease were initially developed for the treatment of rheumatoid arthritis. Sacroiliitis and ankylosing spondylitis, in association with HLA B27, occur in 5% to 10% of patients with inflammatory bowel disease. Uveitis and episcleritis may also occur. Erythema nodosum, which manifests as small exquisitely tender nodules on the anterior tibial surface, occurs more commonly in Crohn disease, whereas pyoderma gangrenosum is more common in ulcerative colitis and can range from small lesions to large ulcers. Even small amounts of trauma to the skin can activate this inflammatory process.

Primary sclerosing cholangitis occurs in approximately 5% of patients with ulcerative colitis and may occur in Crohn disease as well. The relationship between chronic inflammatory disease of the bile ducts and the disease of the intestines is unclear, but up to 80% of patients with primary sclerosing cholangitis have underlying inflammatory bowel disease.

Affected patients may present with only an isolated elevation in serum alkaline phosphatase concentration or with jaundice, biliary obstruction, and evidence of portal hypertension. These patients may have recurrent episodes of cholangitis as well as a malignant transformation to cholangiocarcinoma. In addition, there is a much higher than normal incidence of colorectal cancer in patients with inflammatory bowel disease and concurrent primary sclerosing cholangitis. Therapy with ursodeoxycholic acid has been shown to be chemoprotective against colon cancer in this setting.

There is also an increased risk for colon cancer in patients with inflammatory bowel disease; the risk is associated with the age of onset of inflammatory bowel disease; duration, extent, and severity of disease; and whether the patient has a family history of colorectal cancer. The most reliable estimates suggest an annual colorectal cancer rate in extensive colitis of at least 0.5% per year after the first decade of colitis. Screening recommendations include colonoscopy every 1 to 2 years beginning 8 years after diagnosis. Unlike sporadic colorectal cancer that develops primarily from colon polyps, inflammatory bowel disease–associated colon cancer can arise from flat dysplastic mucosa which is not readily detectable from underlying inflammatory tissue.

Nearly half of patients with inflammatory bowel disease have osteopenia, with a substantially increased risk of osteoporosis and fracture. The risk is present in patients with ulcerative colitis and Crohn disease, in both sexes, and in patients who are taking corticosteroids and those who have never taken them.

Diagnosis

Inflammatory bowel disease should be considered in any young patient with chronic diarrhea or hematochezia. Infection should be excluded by stool culture for ova and parasites, *Giardia*, and *Clostridium difficile*. Laboratory findings suggestive of inflammatory bowel disease include anemia, hypoalbuminemia, leukocytosis, and vitamin deficiencies (more likely in small-intestinal Crohn disease than ulcerative colitis). Approximately two thirds of patients with ulcerative colitis, but only 15% to 20% of patients with Crohn disease and less than 5% of persons without inflammatory bowel disease have p-ANCA, a serum antibody directed against a particular histone H1 antigen and detectable by immunofluorescence or specific enzyme immunoassay. By contrast, approximately half of patients with Crohn disease have anti-*Saccharomyces cerevisiae* antibodies (ASCA), as opposed to less than 5% of patients with ulcerative colitis and control subjects. Therefore, measuring both serum p-ANCA and ASCA is reasonably reliable for the diagnosis of Crohn disease or ulcerative colitis. Newer antibody tests, such as those directed against the outer membrane porin of *Escherichia coli* (Omp-C) and against the flagellum of pathogenic polyflagellated organisms (Cbir1), are also predictive of Crohn disease. However, these tests are most accurate in classic cases of each condition, and the problem of differentiating atypical presentations or diagnosing indeterminate colitis remains.

At presentation, almost half of patients with ulcerative colitis have proctosigmoiditis only; an additional 15% to 20% have left-sided disease. Approximately one third of patients present with pancolitis. Patients with proctitis generally have a benign course, but 11% develop more extensive disease by 5 years and 19% by 10 years. Endoscopic findings range from a decreased vascular pattern and minimal friability in patients with mild disease to spontaneous bleeding and deep ulcerations in severe disease. Histopathology typically consists of crypt abscesses with branching and architecture distortion, as well as acute and chronic inflammation.

Crohn disease has a different pattern of distribution than ulcerative colitis, with 30% of patients having isolated small-bowel disease, 25% colonic disease, and 40% ileocolonic disease. A few patients have upper gastrointestinal tract or isolated perianal disease in the absence of colonic inflammation. The mildest endoscopic lesions are aphthous ulcers, which can, however, coalesce to form deep ulcerations and a cobblestone appearance. Affected areas are commonly separated by normal mucosa, the so-called "skip lesions" that are the hallmark of Crohn disease. Granulomas are almost pathognomonic of Crohn disease but are rarely seen on endoscopic mucosal biopsies.

Radiographic studies establish the location, extent, and severity of inflammatory bowel disease. The plain abdominal radiograph can show a dilated colon and small-bowel obstruction. A barium-contrast small-bowel series or enteroclysis (a minimally invasive radiographic procedure of the small intestine that requires the introduction of a catheter into the small intestine followed by the injection of barium and methylcellulose) provides information about location and amount of inflammatory or stricturing small-bowel disease. Separation of

loops of bowel, thumbprinting, and spiculation (that is, formation of needle-like projections) are all indicators of jejunoileitis. CT enterography is the most comprehensive study and highlights the areas of bowel inflammation and stricture and can identify abscesses, fistulae, and mesenteritis. Video capsule endoscopy provides the most direct evidence of small bowel ulcerations and is approved by the FDA to aid in the diagnosis of Crohn disease. This procedure is highly sensitive, and therefore, the detection of small lesions can lead to a false-positive diagnosis because up to 15% of normal volunteers have been found to have ulcerations in the small bowel. In a patient with possible obstruction, a patency capsule, which is a capsule system designed to determine small-bowel patency before video capsule endoscopy, should be ingested by the patient.

Treatment
Treatment of inflammatory bowel disease involves drug therapy and in certain cases surgery (**Table 24**).

Crohn Disease

5-Aminosalicylates
The mechanism of action of 5-aminosalicylates (5-ASA) is not well-understood, but they have anti-inflammatory effects believed to be secondary to inhibition of arachidonic acid in the bowel mucosa by cyclooxygenase. The oldest 5-ASA sulfasalazine was originally used to treat rheumatoid arthritis; five other oral formulations have since been developed. Two mesalamines are released in the small bowel in a pH- and time-dependent manner and are used to treat both Crohn disease and ulcerative colitis. Mesalamine is available in suppository and enema formulations, which are effective alone in patients who have inflammation limited to the rectosigmoid and may also be used in combination with an oral 5-ASA.

TABLE 24 Medical Therapy for Inflammatory Bowel Disease

Medication	Indication	Side Effects/Adverse Events
5-ASA (sulfasalazine, olsalazine, balsalazide, mesalamine: oral, rectal)	UC: induction/maintenance CD (weak): induction/maintenance	Interstitial nephritis (rare) Diarrhea (olsalazine)
Antibiotics: Metronidazole, Ciprofloxacin	CD: perianal and colonic disease	Metronidazole: peripheral neuropathy, metallic taste, antabuse effect Ciprofloxacin: arthropathy, seizure
Corticosteroids (oral, intravenous, rectal)	UC/CD: induction, not maintenance	Acne, moon facies, truncal obesity, osteoporosis, osteonecrosis, diabetes, hypertension, cataracts, infection
Budesonide	CD (ileal/R colon): induction	Minimal corticosteroid effects
Methotrexate	CD: induction/maintenance	Bone marrow suppression, hepatotoxicity, pulmonitis
6-MP, Azathioprine	UC/CD: steroid withdrawal, maintenance	Pancreatitis, fever, infection, leukopenia, hepatotoxicity, lymphoma
Anti–TNF-α: Infliximab Adalimumab	UC/CD: induction/maintenance CD: induction/maintenance	Infusion reaction, tuberculosis reactivation, demyelination, infection, heart failure, lymphoma
Cyclosporine	UC: steroid refractory	Hypertension, nephro and neurotoxicity

ASA = aminosalicylate; UC = ulcerative colitis; CD = Crohn disease; MP = mercaptopurine; TNF = tumor necrosis factor.

Because Crohn disease is a transmural disease, the 5-ASA agents have not proved to be as efficacious as they are in ulcerative colitis but are often used in the treatment of mild disease. Whether these agents should be used at all in Crohn disease is controversial, but delayed-release mesalamine is commonly used for small-bowel disease. Other preparations of mesalamine are released in the distal ileum and therefore may have a role in treating ileal disease. The azo-bonded 5-ASAs, such as balsalazide, olsalazine, and sulfasalazine have a potential effect only in Crohn colitis.

Corticosteroids

Ileal-release preparations of budesonide are indicated for the treatment of patients with mild ileal and right-sided colonic Crohn disease. Budesonide is a topically active corticosteroid with a very high affinity for the glucocorticoid receptor (15 times that of prednisolone and 195 times that of hydrocortisone). Only 10% to 15% of the drug reaches the systemic circulation; the rest is converted in the liver to inactive metabolites. Conventional corticosteroids are effective in the short-term induction of remission in patients with Crohn disease but are generally used in patients with moderate disease at any location or in patients with ileal disease who have failed to respond to the 5-ASAs or budesonide. Because of the toxic effects of long-term corticosteroid therapy (for example, osteoporosis, avascular necrosis, and psychosis), it is important to devise a strategy for tapering the dosage and discontinuing corticosteroid therapy before the therapy is started.

Immunomodulators

Azathioprine and 6-mercaptopurine are immunomodulators that are believed to act through metabolites. Their onset of full activity is slow and may take up to 3 months. These drugs are effective for the maintenance of remission in patients with Crohn disease regardless of disease distribution. Adverse side effects of therapy with these agents include leukopenia and hepatotoxicity. Before being treated with these agents, patients should be tested for thiopurine methyltransferase, the enzyme involved in the conversion of 6-mercaptopurine to inactive metabolites; patients who have low enzyme activity (or who are homozygous deficient in thiopurine methyltransferase) should not be treated with these agents.

Methotrexate is an immunomodulator that has been shown to induce and maintain remission in Crohn disease but not in ulcerative colitis. There is a risk for hepatotoxicity, and patients with persistently elevated liver tests may need to undergo liver biopsy. Methotrexate is both a teratogen and abortifacient and is therefore contraindicated in pregnant patients and those who are breastfeeding.

Biologic Agents

Tumor necrosis factor α (TNF-α) is a potent proinflammatory cytokine involved in the pathogenesis of both Crohn disease and ulcerative colitis. Infliximab and adalimumab are monoclonal antibodies against TNF-α: infliximab is a chimeric antibody given intravenously; adalimumab and certolizumab are fully humanized antibodies given subcutaneously. These medications can reduce and close fistulae and induce remission in inflammatory Crohn disease within 4 to 8 weeks.

There is ongoing investigation into the earlier use of potent biologic therapies to induce remission quickly while sparing the effects of systemic corticosteroid therapy. All three anti-TNF-α agents are contraindicated in patients with active tuberculosis, and a tuberculin skin test and chest radiograph are required before the initiation of therapy. Patients with latent tuberculosis require isoniazid prophylaxis because the disease can reactivate. Treatment can lead to the reactivation of viral hepatitis and also results in other infections and possibly lymphoma. There have also been a few reported cases of a rare hepatosplenic T-cell lymphoma with the concomitant use of infliximab and 6-mercaptopurine.

Surgery

In fibrostenotic stricturing disease leading to bowel obstruction, there is generally no viable medical therapy. Limited small-bowel or ileocolic resection or bowel-sparing small-bowel stricturoplasties are the only therapy in this setting. Recurrence of disease at the sites of previous surgery is common, and therefore surgery is not a preferred strategy for inflammatory disease. Studies have shown that 3 months of metronidazole therapy reduced severe recurrences 12 months after surgery. Furthermore, 6-mercaptopurine (and likely azathioprine) is modestly effective for decreasing both endoscopic and clinical postoperative recurrences in patients with Crohn disease.

Ulcerative Colitis

The choice of medications for ulcerative colitis depends on both severity and extent of disease. The 5-ASAs, which are not widely effective in Crohn disease, have well-documented efficacy and remain the mainstay of both induction and maintenance therapy in mild to moderate ulcerative colitis. The 5-ASAs are the only medications shown to be effective as chemoprophylaxis for colorectal cancer in patients with ulcerative colitis. In patients not responsive to the 5-ASAs or in those with more severe disease, corticosteroids may induce remission. In hospitalized patients intravenous therapy is usually administered, whereas in the outpatient setting oral and rectal corticosteroids are used. No dose effect above the equivalent of prednisone 60 mg/d has been found. Corticosteroid therapy does not maintain remission and is appropriate only as short-term therapy. Although some patients may transition successfully back to 5-ASA as maintenance therapy after corticosteroid induction therapy, often an immunomodulator such as 6-mercaptopurine or its prodrug azathioprine is warranted; these agents are corticosteroid-sparing and maintain remission.

If corticosteroid therapy does not induce remission, patients may be treated with either infliximab or cyclosporine; in hospitalized patients, these medications are considered after a 7- to 10-day trial of corticosteroids. Cyclosporine requires close monitoring for hypertension and neurologic and renal toxicity, and therefore physicians may favor inflix-imab despite its increased risk for opportunistic infection and possibly malignancy. Medically refractory ulcerative colitis is treated surgically with curative total proctocolectomy with either end-ileostomy or ileal pouch–anal anastomosis, in which a neorectum is constructed from a segment of ileum and connected to the anus to retain continence. Total proc-tocolectomy may also be warranted in patients with neopla-sia, toxic megacolon, perforation, and refractory bleeding.

Microscopic Colitis

Microscopic colitis is another type of inflammatory bowel dis-ease and may be classified as lymphocytic colitis or collage-nous colitis. The incidence of microscopic colitis parallels that of ulcerative colitis and is more common in northern indus-trialized countries. The disorder occurs disproportionately in middle-aged women, with a peak incidence at age 65 years. Symptoms include a chronic relapsing-remitting pattern of watery diarrhea that varies in severity and may be accompa-nied by weight loss, abdominal pain, fatigue, and nausea. Comorbid autoimmune diseases are common, including thy-roid disorders, celiac disease, diabetes mellitus, and rheuma-toid arthritis. The cause of microscopic colitis is probably multifactorial and likely represents an abnormal mucosal response to various luminal exposures including infection and drugs such as NSAIDs. The mucosa usually appears normal macroscopically, and the diagnosis is made solely on charac-teristic histologic findings. Collagenous colitis is characterized by a thickened subepithelial collagen layer, whereas an increased number of intraepithelial lymphocytes is found in lymphocytic colitis. Supportive treatment with antidiarrheal agents, such as loperamide, bismuth subsalicylate, and diphe-noxylate, may be effective for mild cases. Otherwise, budes-onide has the best-documented efficacy; prednisolone, 5-ASA, antibiotics, and probiotics have been studied but the data is less robust.

KEY POINTS

- 5-Aminosalicylates (5-ASAs) are the mainstay of ther-apy for mild to moderate ulcerative colitis; when 5-ASAs are not effective, corticosteroids may need to be used as short-term induction therapy.

- Microscopic colitis typically manifests with loose, watery diarrhea and is most commonly seen in mid-dle-aged or elderly women.

- Treatment for mild microscopic colitis is supportive, but budesonide is the most effective treatment in more severe cases.

Dysmotility Syndromes

Constipation

Chronic constipation is a common condition, with prevalence in the United States estimated at approximately 15% and is much more common in women than in men. Although con-stipation may occur secondary to metabolic or neurologic disease (**Table 25**), obstruction, or various medications (**Table 26**), there is often no identifiable primary cause.

TABLE 25 Secondary Causes of Functional Constipation (Partial List)

Metabolic and Endocrine Disorders
Diabetes mellitus
Hypothyroidism
Hypercalcemia, hypokalemia
Pregnancy
Porphyria
Panhypopituitarism
Anorexia

Neurogenic Disorders
Hirschsprung disease
Chagas disease
Neurofibromatosis
Ganglioneuromatosis
Autonomic neuropathy
Intestinal pseudo-obstruction (myopathy, neuropathy)
Multiple sclerosis
Spinal cord lesions
Parkinson disease

Collagen Vascular and Muscle Disorders
Systemic sclerosis
Amyloidosis
Dermatomyositis
Myotonic dystrophy

Reproduced from Wald A. Chronic constipation: advances in management. *Neurogastroenterol Motil.* 2007;19(1):4-10. [PMID: 17187583]. Copyright 2007, John Wiley & Sons. Reproduced with permission of Blackwell Publishing Ltd.

TABLE 26 Some Drugs Associated with Constipation

Anticholinergics
Antispasmodics
Antidepressants
Antipsychotics

Cation-Containing Agents
Iron supplements
Aluminum (antacids, sucralfate)

Neurally Active Agents
Opiates
Antihypertensives
Ganglionic blockers
Vinca alkaloids
Calcium channel blockers
$5HT_3$ antagonists

Reproduced from Wald A. Chronic constipation: advances in management. *Neurogastroenterol Motil.* 2007;19(1):4-10. [PMID: 17187583]. Copyright 2007, John Wiley & Sons. Reproduced with permission of Blackwell Publishing Ltd.

Constipation is typically thought of as a decrease in frequency of bowel movements, but affected patients often complain of constipation even with daily stools because of a qualitative change in their bowel habits. The Rome III criteria for functional constipation account for these additional features (**Table 27**).

There are two mechanisms of chronic constipation: slow transit and outlet delay. In the former, also known as colonic inertia, patients have prolonged transit of radiopaque markers through the proximal colon; although resting colonic motility is generally normal, there is colonic hypomotility in response to meals or a stimulant laxative. Colonic inertia is likely the result of an abnormality in the enteric nerve plexus, including decreased numbers of the interstitial cells of Cajal, also known as the "pacemaker" cells of the gut. Patients with outlet delay have normal transit time through the colon but impaired rectal expulsion. In patients without another primary cause such as Hirschsprung disease (a congenital absence of intramural neural plexus or aganglionosis, rarely with adult-onset presentation), dyssynergic defecation may be the underlying pathogenesis of outlet delay. Dyssynergic defecation consists of the loss of the coordinated relaxation (or paradoxic contraction) of the puborectalis muscle and external anal sphincter, which thus narrows the anorectal angle and increases the anal canal pressure, making defecation more difficult and less effective. Dyssynergic defecation is likely learned and does not have an organic basis. Slow transit and outlet delay can coexist in a patient.

Diagnosis

The medical history in a patient with constipation should focus on the patient's specific complaints with regard to bowel habits; a 2-week stool diary may be helpful in this regard. A patient's perceptions of what constitutes normal defecation may be inaccurate. A detailed history of medication use (including over-the-counter drugs) and comorbid illnesses should be obtained. Physical examination may be helpful in identifying perianal abnormalities such as hemorrhoids or fissures, and a rectal examination can assess resting sphincter tone as well as a patient's ability to relax the puborectalis and external anal sphincter when asked to mimic a bowel movement. Alarm features include rectal bleeding or occult blood–positive stool, weight loss, a family history of colon cancer or inflammatory bowel disease, anemia, and acute onset in an older person; in the absence of such findings, further laboratory tests, imaging, and endoscopy are not indicated. In patients older than 50 years, however, colonoscopy should be recommended if not previously performed. In patients with alarm signs or symptoms, evaluation may include plain radiographs of the abdomen to assess for significant stool retention and megacolon, and radiopaque marker studies to assess for slow transit and outlet delay. Defecography and anorectal manometry studies are highly specialized tests that may be useful in the evaluation of dyssynergic defecation.

Treatment

Treatment of constipation includes correction of underlying metabolic abnormalities, such as hypothyroidism, and discontinuation of any potentially putative medications. Increased fiber intake to the recommended 25 to 30 g/d augments stool bulk and facilitates stool transit time. Osmotic laxatives are often the next step in the treatment of constipation, including lactulose, magnesium-based compounds, and polyethylene glycol solutions. Fiber and osmotic laxatives may cause bloating and discomfort and should be introduced gradually, although polyethylene glycol is usually well tolerated. Although stimulant laxatives are often avoided by physicians because of fears regarding dependency and abuse, these fears are largely unsubstantiated and these medications are frequently helpful in patients with slow transit. Common stimulant laxatives include anthraquinones (such as senna) and diphenylmethanes (such as bisacodyl). Tegaserod, a partial 5-hydroxytryptamine-4 (5-HT$_4$) receptor agonist, was previously approved for the treatment of both constipation-predominant irritable bowel syndrome in women as well as chronic constipation in men and women younger than 65 years; however, it was voluntarily withdrawn from the market in early 2007 after an association between this medication and cardiovascular events was discovered. Lubiprostone, an intestinal chloride channel agonist that increases intestinal fluid secretion, was recently approved for the treatment of chronic functional constipation. In patients with dyssynergia, biofeedback training may be effective. Very rarely, in the case of severe refractory and disabling constipation in which other gastrointestinal motility is normal and in patients without dyssynergia, a subtotal colectomy with ileorectal anastomosis may offer relief.

TABLE 27 Diagnosis of Functional Constipation: The Rome III Criteria

1. Must include *two* or *more* of the following:

   Straining during at least 25% of defecations

   Lumpy or hard stools in at least 25% of defecations

   Sensation of incomplete evacuation for at least 25% of defecations

   Sensation of anorectal obstruction/blockage for at least 25% of defecations

   Manual maneuvers to facilitate at least 25% of defecations (e.g. digital evacuation, support of the pelvic floor)

   Fewer than three defecations per week

2. Loose stools are rarely present without the use of laxatives

3. There are insufficient criteria for irritable bowel syndrome

Reproduced from Longstreth GF, Thompson WG, Chey WD, Houghton LA, Mearin F, Spiller RC. Functional bowel disorders. Gastroenterology. 2006;130:1480-91. [PMID: 16678561]. Copyright 2006, reproduced with permission from Elsevier.

Ileus and Pseudo-Obstruction

Ileus, the functional inhibition of normal bowel motility, most commonly occurs after abdominal surgery but can also be associated with metabolic disturbances such as electrolyte abnormalities; medications including narcotics and anticholinergic agents; and neurologic disorders, inflammatory conditions, and sepsis (**Table 28**).

Postoperatively, the pathogenesis of ileus is likely multifactorial: impaired electrical activity of the stomach, small intestine, and colon; increased inhibitory sympathetic nervous system output; increased activity of inhibitory neurotransmitters, local factors, hormones, and inflammatory mediators; and the dysmotility effect of anesthesia. Manifestations of ileus include an inability to tolerate oral intake, bloating, abdominal pain, and lack of flatus and stool. Physical examination often reveals abdominal distention, normal or decreased bowel sounds, and diffuse mild tenderness. Plain radiographs of the abdomen reveal air throughout the intestine, although often ileus can share radiographic features of a mechanical small-bowel obstruction, including air-fluid levels and a paucity of gas in the colon (**Figure 24**). The distinction is important because small-bowel obstruction can lead to ischemia, necrosis, and perforation.

CT scan and barium studies may aid in differentiating ileus from obstruction. Treatment of ileus is generally supportive, with removal of any offending medications and correction of electrolyte abnormalities. Nasogastric intubation does not seem to shorten the duration of ileus but may provide symptomatic relief from vomiting. Early postoperative feeding, gum chewing, laxatives, and NSAIDs are potential therapeutic options; the role of promotility agents remains

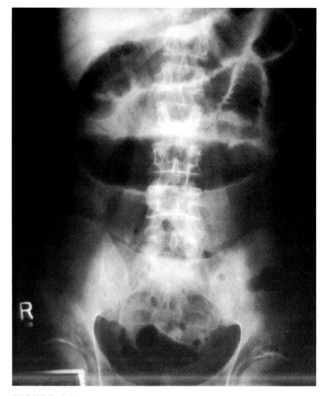

FIGURE 24.
Small-bowel obstruction.
A flat plate radiograph of the abdomen reveals small intestine and colonic dilation in a patient with diffuse cutaneous systemic sclerosis with pseudo-obstruction.

unclear. Laparoscopic procedures and local epidural anesthesia may reduce length of postoperative ileus.

Intestinal pseudo-obstruction, which is a motility disorder that mimics mechanical bowel obstruction in the absence of an obstructive lesion, may affect the small and/or large bowel and can be either acute or chronic. In the affected segment, motility is slowed or absent, and the bowel is dilated on radiographic studies. Chronic intestinal pseudo-obstruction may be idiopathic and some familial forms have been identified, but it is more often secondary to an underlying paraneoplastic syndrome or a neurologic, smooth muscle, or metabolic disorder. Clinically, patients most commonly present with abdominal pain and distention, but constipation, early satiety/fullness, nausea, and vomiting are also features. Weight loss and diarrhea may occur when malabsorption and bacterial overgrowth are present. Symptoms may wax and wane and indeed even completely resolve between episodes, although in the most severe cases, chronic intestinal pseudo-obstruction is unremitting.

Physical examination may reveal distention, tympany, and a succussion splash; signs of systemic diseases should also be sought. Plain radiographs of the abdomen and an upper gastrointestinal/small-bowel series should be performed on

TABLE 28 Disorders Associated with Chronic Intestinal Pseudo-obstruction
Neurologic Disorders
Brainstem tumor
Dysautonomia
Familial visceral neuropathy
Neurofibromatosis
Parkinson disease
Smooth Muscle Disorders
Amyloidosis
Familial visceral myopathy
Mitochondrial myopathy
Muscular dystrophy
Systemic lupus erythematosus
Systemic sclerosis (scleroderma)
Systemic Disorders
Diabetes mellitus (rare)
Hypothyroidism

all patients, both to support the diagnosis and rule out other diseases (for example, Crohn disease); dilated loops of bowel and air-fluid levels may be demonstrated, and it may be difficult to distinguish between pseudo-obstruction and mechanical obstruction. Endoscopy may be helpful in both ruling out an obstructive lesion and obtaining biopsies. Colonoscopy may yield helpful diagnostic information and rarely may function to decompress the bowel. Laboratory tests may be useful in testing for systemic disorders as well as monitoring electrolytes and nutritional status, including vitamin levels and essential elements in patients with signs of malabsorption. Manometry and histopathologic findings may be supportive but not diagnostic of chronic intestinal pseudo-obstruction. Treatment includes therapy for any underlying disorders, nutritional support, which may involve enteral or parenteral feeding, and antibiotic treatment when bacterial overgrowth is present. Acute exacerbations may be treated with prokinetic agents including erythromycin, metoclopramide, and neostigmine; octreotide may be useful in cases of underlying scleroderma, and cisapride, although not available in the United States because of an association with fatal cardiac arrhythmias, can be obtained directly through the manufacturer when need is documented and risk is shown to be minimal. Surgery may be useful to bypass, remove, or decompress affected segments of bowel.

Dysmotility Disorders in Patients with Diabetes Mellitus

In patients with type 1 or type 2 diabetes mellitus, autonomic dysfunction manifesting in altered motility is common, especially after prolonged disease and in association with other diabetic complications. Upper gastrointestinal disorders including esophageal dysmotility and gastroparesis are common in such patients. There are likely multiple mechanisms in the setting of autonomic neuropathy: abnormal small-intestinal and colonic motility can result in constipation and diarrhea, bacterial overgrowth, anorectal dysfunction, increased intestinal secretion and possibly bile salt malabsorption, and exocrine pancreatic insufficiency. Additionally, celiac disease is more common in patients with diabetes than in the general population, and medications such as metformin are associated with diarrhea as are dietetic foods that contain artificial sweeteners such as sorbitol. Treatment is both supportive and directed at the underlying mechanism: antidiarrheal agents such as loperamide may decrease motility, and clonidine has been used to decrease secretory diarrhea. Antibiotics should be used to treat bacterial overgrowth. Octreotide has also been used in patients with diarrhea, but its long-term efficacy is questionable. Fecal incontinence may also be treated with biofeedback.

KEY POINTS

- Chronic constipation is more prevalent in women than in men; most cases are idiopathic, but causes include medications and metabolic, neurologic, and collagen-vascular disorders.

- Alarm features in patients with functional constipation include rectal bleeding or occult blood–positive stool, weight loss, a family history of colon cancer or inflammatory bowel disease, anemia, and acute onset in an older person; patients without alarm features do not need extensive evaluation.

- Treatment of chronic constipation includes fiber supplementation and osmotic and stimulant laxatives; biofeedback training may be used for patients with dyssynergia.

- Ileus most commonly occurs after abdominal surgery but can also be associated with metabolic disturbances, medications, inflammatory conditions, sepsis, and neurologic injury.

- Chronic idiopathic pseudo-obstruction, a motility disorder that mimics intestinal obstruction, may be secondary to paraneoplastic syndrome or neurologic, smooth muscle, or metabolic disorders.

- Altered motility secondary to autonomic dysfunction in diabetes mellitus is common, especially after prolonged disease and in association with other diabetic complications.

Irritable Bowel Syndrome

Irritable bowel syndrome (IBS) is a common disorder, with a 7% prevalence estimate in the United States based on population studies. Women are 1.5 times more likely to be affected than men, most commonly between ages 20 and 40 years. Onset after the age of 50 years is uncommon. The pathophysiology of the disorder is not well understood and may vary depending on the subtype. Abnormal gastrointestinal motility, visceral afferent hypersensitivity, and autonomic innervation abnormalities have been implicated as possible mechanisms. Altered activation of the mucosal immune system may occur, particularly in patients with diarrhea and who develop symptoms after having had acute gastroenteritis, a syndrome known as postinfectious irritable bowel syndrome. Depression, anxiety, a history of sexual abuse, phobias, and somatization are commonly associated with the syndrome, but psychosocial factors do not appear to be causal. Health-related quality of life (HRQOL) scores are lower in patients with IBS than in unaffected persons, but it is unclear whether IBS leads to lower HRQOL or vice versa. Compared with affected patients who do not seek medical care, patients who seek evaluation and treatment are more likely to have comorbid psychiatric illness, and psychological stress is likely to exacerbate symptoms. IBS is costly, with direct and indirect (including decreased work productivity) costs estimated at $20 billion, with IBS patients consuming greater than 50% more in health care resources than matched controls. Increased health care utilization in IBS patients is directly related to somatization levels.

Diagnosis is based solely on clinical grounds. As no biochemical, radiographic, endoscopic or histologic marker exists, several clinical indices have been published to aid in the diagnosis of IBS, with the Rome criteria being the most widely known. While the third version of the Rome criteria (**Table 29**) was recently released, only Rome I criteria have been evaluated for accuracy, with a sensitivity of 71% and a specificity of 85%. The American College of Gastroenterology (ACG) task force on IBS has recommended a simpler definition: abdominal pain associated with altered bowel habits (change in stool form or frequency) over a period of at least 3 months. Rome III criteria describes four subtypes of IBS: constipation-predominant, diarrhea-predominant, mixed, and unsubtyped (**Table 30**). Supportive symptoms may include abnormal stool frequency (>3/d, <3/week), abnormal stool form (lumpy/hard or loose/watery), straining or urgency or a sensation of incomplete evacuation, mucus, and bloating.

In addition to meeting the diagnostic criteria for IBS, the absence of alarm symptoms (see Table 29) and signs has also been touted as reassuring that the patient does not have organic disease such as inflammatory bowel disease, colorectal cancer or celiac disease. Recent review of the literature has suggested that nocturnal symptoms as well as rectal bleeding in particular are not helpful in separating IBS from patients

---

TABLE 30 Subtyping Irritable Bowel Syndrome (IBS) by the Predominant Stool Pattern (Rome III Criteria)

1. IBS with constipation (IBS-C) - hard or lumpy stools[a] ≥25% and loose (mushy) or watery stools[b] <25% of bowel movements[c]

2. IBS with diarrhea (IBS-D) - loose (mushy) or watery stools[b] ≥25% and hard or lumpy stool[a] <25% of bowel movements[c]

3. Mixed IBS (IBS-M) - hard or lumpy stools[a] ≥ 25% and loose (mushy) or watery stools[b] ≥25% of bowel movements[c]

4. Unsubtyped IBS (IBS-U) - insufficient abnormality of stool consistency to meet criteria IBS-C, D or M[c]

[a]Bristol Stool Form Scale 1-2 [separate hard lumps like nuts (difficult to pass) or sausage shaped but lumpy].

[b]Bristol Stool Form Scale 6-7 (fluffy pieces with ragged edges, a mushy stool or watery, no solid pieces, entirely liquid).

[c]In the absence of use of antidiarrheals or laxatives.

Reproduced from Ersryd A, Posserud I, Abrahamsson H, Simren M. Subtyping the Irritable Bowel Syndrome by Predominant Bowel Habit: Rome II versus Rome III. Alimentary Pharmacology & Therapeutics. 2007;26:953-61. [PMID: 17767480]. Copyright 2007, John Wiley and Sons. Reproduced with permission from Blackwell Publishing Ltd.

---

with organic disease. While other alarm criteria such as anemia and weight loss lack sensitivity for the diagnosis of organic disease, they are specific. Affected patients may describe nongastrointestinal somatic symptoms such as headache, urinary symptoms, backache, and fatigue.

Evaluation

Patients with potential IBS should not undergo a potentially expensive or harmful evaluation that may undermine their confidence in the diagnosis and in the physician.

However, anemia is an alarm sign; a complete blood count should be performed after the onset of symptoms. Furthermore, patients with IBS with diarrhea and mixed IBS should have serologic tests for celiac disease, which occurs more commonly in patients with these IBS subtypes than in the general population. Although many recent studies have focused on the possible link between IBS and small intestine bacterial overgrowth, the ACG task force finds insufficient evidence to recommend routine testing. Testing for lactose intolerance, which is more common among IBS patients, should be conducted only if this diagnosis is unclear on clinical grounds. Colonoscopy is indicated only if patients are older than 50 years. In any patient with alarm features, however, further evaluation is mandated and should be tailored to symptoms; for example, patients with constipation need imaging to rule out a mechanical obstruction. In patients with IBS with diarrhea who undergo colonoscopy, random biopsies of the colon should be done to evaluate for microscopic colitis, particularly if there is suggestion of a secretory diarrhea.

Treatment

Treatment of IBS depends greatly on a patient's predominant symptoms. Although patients often link diet to symptoms, no

---

TABLE 29 Rome III Diagnostic Criteria for Irritable Bowel Syndrome

Recurrent abdominal pain or discomfort (abnormal sensation not described as pain) at least 3 days a month in past 3 months (with onset > 6 months prior) associated with two or more of the following:

    Improvement with defecation

    Onset associated with change in frequency of stool

    Onset associated with change in form (appearance) of stool

Alarm indicators that suggest other diseases:

    Age >50 years

    Male

    Short history of symptoms

    Documented weight loss

    Nocturnal symptoms

    Family history of colon cancer

    Rectal bleeding

    Recent antibiotic use

Reproduced from Spiller R. Clinical update: irritable bowel syndrome. The Lancet. 2007;369:1586-88. [PMID: 17499587]. Copyright 2007, with permission from Elsevier.

clear data support elimination diets or food allergy testing, but if individual patients identify clear food triggers, these can be eliminated or reduced. Bulking agents, in particular fiber in the form of psyllium hydrophilic mucilloid (ispaghula husk) and possibly calcium polycarbophil, may improve global IBS symptoms but can be associated with bloating and flatulence. Laxatives appear to be effective in chronic constipation, but they have not been studied sufficiently in IBS; although laxatives appear to improve frequency of bowel movements in those with constipation, it remains unclear whether they have any effect on pain. (Osmotic laxatives such as milk of magnesia as well as nonabsorbable polyethylene glycol, sorbitol, and lactulose are generally believed to be safer than stimulant laxatives, but they may be associated with bloating and flatulence; therefore, senna and bisacodyl may be appropriate for intermittent use for constipated patients.) Tegaserod, a 5-HT_4 (serotonin) agonist had been previously approved to treat IBS with constipation in women and improved bowel movements, abdominal pain, and global IBS symptoms; as noted above the drug was withdrawn from the market in March 2007. Lubiprostone is a chloride channel antagonist approved to treat chronic constipation in adults, but it does not alleviate abdominal pain.

In IBS with diarrhea, loperamide is the only antidiarrheal agent that has been studied in randomized controlled trials. Although this medication improved both bowel movement frequency and consistency, it had no effect on other IBS symptoms. Alosetron, a 5-HT_3 antagonist, alleviates abdominal pain, global IBS symptoms, and diarrhea and urgency in women and men with IBS with diarrhea; potential serious but uncommon side effects include both severe constipation and ischemic colitis. Because of these adverse events, this drug is available only through an FDA restricted program administered by its manufacturer. It should be reserved for patients who have failed to respond to conventional therapies.

Antispasmodic agents, including dicyclomine, hyoscyamine, and possibly peppermint oil, function as gastrointestinal smooth muscle relaxants. Although these agents may reduce abdominal pain in the short term, their efficacy is not well substantiated, and because their action is not specific to the gut, they may be associated with side effects that preclude their use; furthermore, they may cause constipation. Tricyclic antidepressants and possibly selective serotonin reuptake inhibitors have analgesic properties; tricyclics also have an anticholinergic effect and thus may induce constipation. Smaller doses than are used in the treatment of depression are generally recommended. Comorbid depression may best be treated with a selective serotonin reuptake inhibitor. Psychosocial stressors should also be addressed.

While the link between small intestinal bacterial overgrowth and IBS remains unclear, the short-term (10 to 14 days) use of the nonabsorbed antibiotic rifaximin at doses between 1000 and 1200 mg/day has demonstrated improvement in global IBS symptoms, bloating and diarrhea in

several well-designed randomized controlled trials conducted predominantly in patients with IBS and diarrhea. The efficacy and safety of longer term or intermittent use of rifaximin are unknown. Other antibiotics such as neomycin may be effective as well but have not been as well studied. The efficacy of probiotics is yet to be determined adequately.

Finally, antibiotic and probiotic therapy has been used because bacterial overgrowth has been implicated in the pathogenesis of the syndrome, possibly through abnormal motility or as a sequela of postinfectious IBS. Rifaximin has been effective in relieving symptoms in patients with bacterial overgrowth. *Bifidobacterium infantis* is the only probiotic that has proven efficacy in the treatment of IBS.

KEY POINTS

- Irritable bowel syndrome is a functional bowel disorder that most commonly affects women aged 20 to 40 years.
- Possible mechanisms of irritable bowel syndrome include abnormal gastrointestinal motility, visceral afferent hypersensitivity, and altered activation of the mucosal immune system.
- Irritable bowel syndrome is a clinical diagnosis based on the Rome III criteria; in the absence of alarm features, extensive diagnostic evaluation is unnecessary.
- There are four subtypes of irritable bowel syndrome: constipation-predominant, diarrhea-predominant, mixed, and unsubtyped.
- Treatment of irritable bowel syndrome is targeted at the predominant symptoms and includes fiber, laxatives, antidiarrheal and antispasmodic agents, and antidepressants.

Colonic Diverticular Diseases

Diverticulosis

Diverticulosis consists of the presence of diverticula in the colon. An acquired colonic diverticulum is actually a "false" or "pseudo" diverticulum because only the mucosa and submucosa are contained within this sac-like outpouching that herniates through the muscularis propria at points of weakness where the vasa recta blood vessels penetrate the colon. Diverticulosis is so common in aging Western populations that some do not consider it pathologic: in the United States, diverticulosis is found in up to 50% of persons in their eighth and ninth decade of life compared with less than 10% of those younger than 40 years. In contrast, rural Africa and Asia have a prevalence of less than 1%. Diverticular disease encompasses both diverticular hemorrhage and diverticulitis. Additionally some patients have nonspecific symptoms, including bloating, cramping, irregular bowel movements, and excessive flatulence, symptoms that may, however, be related to irritable bowel syndrome rather than directly related to diverticula.

The pathogenesis of diverticulosis likely relates to the interplay between dietary fiber, colonic wall structure, and intestinal motility. Fiber augments stool bulk and volume, which increases colonic diameter and thus decreases segmentation and intraluminal pressures. The sigmoid colon has the smallest width and thus is the most commonly affected part of the colon in Western countries, although in Asia, right-sided diverticula are more common. Traditional Western diets are deficient in fiber, generally not meeting the recommended 25 to 30 g/d; diverticulosis is less common in populations from regions with high fiber diets and in vegetarians. Abnormalities in the regulation of the colonic extracellular matrix as well as decreased intestinal transit and excessive contractility are also implicated in the pathogenesis of diverticulosis. Asymptomatic diverticulosis does not warrant further evaluation, although it is reasonable to suggest a high-fiber diet.

Diverticulitis

Diverticulitis results from obstruction at the diverticulum neck by fecal matter, leading to mucus and bacterial overgrowth. Approximately 15% to 25% of patients with diverticula develop diverticulitis. Because 85% of diverticulitis occurs in the sigmoid or left colon, left lower quadrant pain is the most common clinical manifestation, often accompanied by fever. Other symptoms that may occur include a change in bowel habits, and rarely bleeding, nausea, vomiting, and anorexia; 10% to 15% of affected patients have urinary symptoms induced by diverticulitis in close proximity to the bladder. Bowel sounds are usually decreased but may be hyperactive in patients with obstruction. More than half of patients with diverticulitis have leukocytosis.

Diagnosis

The diagnosis of diverticulitis is made on the basis of history and physical examination, but imaging is often helpful when the diagnosis is unclear or when complications are suspected. Plain radiographs of the chest and abdomen can detect free air in patients with peritoneal signs, and up to 50% of patients with acute diverticulitis will be found to have ileus, obstruction, or a soft-tissue mass. CT scan of the abdomen and pelvis with oral and intravenous contrast has become the imaging modality of choice to diagnose acute diverticulitis, with a sensitivity and specificity up to 97% and 100%, respectively. CT findings consistent with diverticulitis include the presence of diverticula with pericolic fatty infiltration, bowel wall thickening, phlegmon, and pericolic fluid. CT scan can also show complications including fistula, obstruction, and abscess. Single-contrast enema studies and ultrasonography are second-line imaging modalities and are not now commonly used. Colonoscopy should be avoided in the acute setting because air insufflation may increase the risk for perforation.

After resolution, however, patients who have not had a recent colonoscopy should undergo the procedures to rule out malignancy.

Treatment

Treatment of diverticulitis consists of antibiotics. Patients with mild symptoms, no signs of peritonitis, and no significant comorbidities and who can tolerate oral intake may be treated at home with oral antibiotics, whereas others should be hospitalized for intravenous antibiotics, hydration, and bowel rest. Antibiotic choice should cover gram-negative bacilli and anaerobes: commonly used regimens include a fluoroquinolone combined with metronidazole. Symptomatic improvement is expected within 2 to 4 days, and patients should complete a 7- to 10-day course. Because only 25% develop recurrent diverticulitis, surgery is not recommended after one uncomplicated episode but should be considered in patients with repeated episodes.

The treatment of complicated diverticulitis varies. Small abscesses may be managed successfully with antibiotics and bowel rest, whereas nonresolving or larger abscesses may require CT-guided percutaneous drainage with subsequent elective one-stage surgery. Patients who have multiloculated or inaccessible abscesses as well as those with peritoneal signs may need surgery as an initial treatment, which sometimes requires two stages. In these cases, resection with diverting colostomy and Hartmann pouch is performed; after sufficient healing, colostomy take-down and reanastomosis are done in a second surgery. Fistulae result when colonic inflammation and/or abscess extends to an adjacent organ. Colovesical fistulae are the most common, particularly in men, while colovaginal fistulae are the next most frequent type; enteric, uterine, and rectal fistulae may also occur. Fistulae are generally managed surgically. Obstruction secondary to diverticulitis often resolves with conservative management, but persistent strictures should be evaluated for neoplasia and may necessitate endoscopic or surgical management.

KEY POINTS

- Diverticulosis is a common finding in elderly persons in the West; a lack of dietary fiber may be a factor in the pathogenesis.

- Diverticulitis and diverticular bleeding are the major complications of diverticulosis and are seen in less than a quarter of patients.

- Diverticulitis presents most commonly with left lower quadrant pain, fever, and an elevated leukocyte count; diagnosis is generally made on clinical and CT findings; colonoscopy should be avoided in the acute setting.

- Diverticulitis is treated with antibiotics; complications include abscess, fistula, and obstruction, which may require surgical intervention.

Intestinal Ischemic Disease

Intestinal ischemia consists of a decreased blood supply to the bowel, resulting in diminished delivery of oxygen and nutrients.

Acute Mesenteric Ischemia

Acute mesenteric ischemia is a life-threatening condition that must be recognized and treated emergently. Although the disorder is rare, its incidence is rising, which may be the result of improved awareness but also likely stems from a growing aging population who are at increased risk. Acute mesenteric ischemia should not be confused with acute colonic ischemia, which is a very different entity and will be discussed in detail later in this section (**Table 31**).

Acute mesenteric ischemia is categorized into superior mesenteric artery embolus, nonocclusive mesenteric ischemia, superior mesenteric artery thrombosis, focal segmental ischemia, and acute mesenteric venous thrombosis. Superior mesenteric artery embolus, which is the most common type, accounting for approximately 50% of cases, usually develops from ventricular or left atrial thrombi in the context of atrial fibrillation. Superior mesenteric artery thrombosis occurs in patients with severe atherosclerotic disease and most often occurs at the origin of the superior mesenteric artery; 20% to 50% of patients have postprandial abdominal pain and weight loss consistent with chronic mesenteric ischemia. Nonocclusive mesenteric ischemia accounts for 25% of acute mesenteric ischemia and begins as physiologic protective vasoconstriction in response to a cardiovascular event or hypovolemia; other risk factors are cirrhosis, end-stage renal failure requiring hemodialysis, and use of splanchnic vasoconstrictors such as digitalis. Acute mesenteric venous thrombosis generally occurs in younger patients with hypercoagulable conditions, portal hypertension, intra-abdominal inflammation, sepsis, trauma and after surgery. Unlike the other subtypes, focal segmental ischemia involves only small segments of bowel and therefore does not carry the same high mortality rate; causes include atheromatous emboli, strangulated hernias, vasculitis, radiation therapy, and use of oral contraceptive pills.

Most patients with acute mesenteric ischemia are older than 50 years. Abdominal pain is almost invariably present; elderly patients may have more vague symptoms including mental status change and tachypnea. Forceful bowel evacuation may occur in superior mesenteric artery embolus, and although occult blood–positive stool is common, overt bleeding is rare. Late signs and symptoms include nausea, vomiting, fever, hematemesis, obstruction, back pain, and shock. Physical examination early in the presentation may be unremarkable, thus illustrating the classic teaching of "pain out of proportion to examination." As the initial insult progresses to bowel infarction, distention with peritoneal signs develop.

Diagnosis

The key to the diagnosis of acute mesenteric ischemia is a high index of suspicion. Traditional angiography has been the diagnostic gold standard as well as being used for administration of therapeutic vasodilators and stenting. CT angiography is becoming increasingly recognized as a highly sensitive and specific modality to diagnose acute mesenteric ischemia. The procedure is more readily available than traditional angiography and also permits the evaluation of the abdomen in addition to the vasculature. Magnetic resonance angiography is also an excellent diagnostic modality in this setting, especially in patients with hypersensitivity to contrast dye or with renal insufficiency. Both imaging modalities are limited in the diagnosis of nonocclusive mesenteric ischemia, however. Standard CT scanning is useful only in mesenteric venous thrombosis. Plain radiographs of the abdomen are generally normal early in the course of acute mesenteric ischemia but later may show thumbprinting, an ileus, bowel thickening, and pneumatosis. Doppler ultrasonography may be helpful in evaluation of the proximal mesenteric vessels, but it has multiple limitations and is not recommended. Laboratory tests are neither adequately sensitive nor specific, especially early in the course. Later, the leukocyte count may be elevated above 15,000/μL (15×10^9/L) in more than three quarters of patients, along with a metabolic acidosis and elevated lactate, creatine kinase, lactate dehydrogenase, aspartate aminotransferase, and alkaline phosphatase. Plasma D-dimer, glutathione S-transferase α, and

TABLE 31 Distinguishing Features of Acute Colonic and Small-Bowel Ischemia	
Acute Colonic Ischemia	**Acute Mesenteric Ischemia Involving Small Bowel**
90% of patients over age 60	Age varies with etiology of ischemia
Acute precipitating cause is rare	Acute precipitating cause is typical
Patients do not appear ill	Patients appear very ill
Mild abdominal pain, tenderness present	Pain is usually severe, tenderness is not prominent early
Rectal bleeding, bloody diarrhea typical	Bleeding uncommon until very late
Colonoscopy is procedure of choice	Angiography indicated

Adapted from Reinus JF, Brandt LJ, Boley SJ. Ischemic diseases of the bowel. Gastroenterology Clinics of North America. 1990;19:319-43. [PMID: 2194948]. Copyright 1990, with permission from Elsevier.

intestinal fatty acid binding protein show promise as serologic markers of intestinal ischemia but are not used routinely.

Treatment

The overall mortality rate of acute mesenteric ischemia remains high; survival rates are greatly improved when diagnosis is made promptly and treatment is initiated immediately. A patient suspected of having acute mesenteric ischemia should be given prompt supportive treatment with volume resuscitation and broad-spectrum antibiotics that cover anaerobic and gram-negative organisms. Suspected underlying mechanisms such as arrhythmias and heart failure should be corrected. Specific treatment depends on the subtype and whether peritoneal signs are present. Patients with superior mesenteric artery embolus or thrombosis who have peritoneal signs should undergo exploratory laparotomy. Surgical interventions include peritoneal lavage, resection of necrotic and perforated bowel, thrombolectomy, patch angioplasty, endarterectomy, and bypass procedures. In patients with questionable bowel viability, second-look surgeries are advocated. Papaverine, a nonspecific vasodilator, is frequently used pre- and postoperatively to minimize splanchnic vasoconstriction and reperfusion injury. In patients without peritoneal signs, thrombolytic agents such as streptokinase and tissue plasminogen activator have been used successfully in case series and reports. In nonocclusive mesenteric ischemia, intra-arterial papaverine should be initiated as soon as angiographic diagnosis is confirmed, with repeat angiography in 24 hours to assess for improved or persistent vasospasm; papaverine may be continued for up to 5 days, but if not effective or peritoneal signs develop, then surgical exploration is warranted. Treatment of mesenteric venous thrombosis usually entails surgical resection and/or thrombolectomy; lifelong anticoagulation is necessary when an underlying hypercoagulable state is identified. Focal segmental ischemia is treated with bowel resection.

Chronic Mesenteric Ischemia

Chronic mesenteric ischemia, also called intestinal angina or claudication, is characterized by postprandial abdominal pain that usually begins 30 minutes after eating and may last up to 3 hours; sitophobia or fear of eating typifies the disorder and invariably leads to weight loss. Most cases arise in the setting of severe mesenteric atherosclerotic disease, such that in 90% of cases at least two of the three major splanchnic arteries are occluded and in half the cases all three are occluded. Although MR or CT angiography is useful in detecting mesenteric vessel occlusions, chronic mesenteric ischemia should not be diagnosed without the proper clinical history and without excluding other causes such as malignancy, pancreatitis, peptic ulcer disease, and biliary colic. Surgical bypass is the definitive treatment. Percutaneous angioplasty and stenting procedures may have equivalent initial success rates as surgery, but long-term efficacy has not been established.

Colonic Ischemia

Colonic ischemia, also called ischemic colitis, is much more common than acute or chronic mesenteric ischemia. The disorder is characterized by a wide spectrum of ischemic injury to the colon including reversible colonopathy, transient colitis, chronic colitis, stricture, gangrene, and fulminant universal colitis; it is rarely fatal. Although an underlying cause is often not identified, colonic ischemia can occur in association with colonic hypoperfusion in the setting of aortic or cardiac bypass surgery, prolonged physical exertion (for example, long-distance running), and any cardiovascular event accompanied by hypotension. Medications such as oral contraceptives, drugs such as cocaine, vasculitides, and hypercoagulable states have also been identified as risk factors (**Table 32**).

The most commonly affected sites of colonic ischemia are the descending, sigmoid, and splenic flexure. When the right colon is affected, concomitant mesenteric ischemia can occur because the superior mesenteric artery supplies the proximal colon. Most patients with colonic ischemia are older than 60 years and usually present with left-lower quadrant pain, urgent defecation, and red or maroon rectal bleeding that does not require transfusion. Patients may have mild tenderness over the involved segment of colon; hypovolemia and peritonitis are rare and generally herald the existence of gangrenous bowel, perforation, or transmural necrosis. In the past, diagnosis was made by the findings of thumbprinting representing submucosal hemorrhages on barium enema studies, but colonoscopy is now the primary diagnostic procedure. Colonoscopic findings are generally segmental and include hemorrhagic nodules, linear and circumferential ulceration, and gangrene. Macro- and microscopic abnormalities may

TABLE 32 Causes of Ischemic Colitis
Arterial
Hypoperfusion: Decreased cardiac output, cardiac arrhythmias, sepsis with shock
Thrombotic: Thrombosis of the inferior mesenteric artery
Embolic: Arterial emboli, cholesterol emboli
Drug-Induced
Cocaine
Digoxin
Estrogens
Pseudoephedrine
Postoperative
Coronary artery bypass graft surgery
Abdominal aortic surgery
Vasculitis
Systemic lupus erythematosus
Hypercoagulable State
Protein C and S and antithrombin III deficiency; factor V Leiden mutation
Miscellaneous

overlap with those of infectious and inflammatory colitides. Therapy includes intravenous fluids and antibiotics to cover anaerobes and gram-negative bacteria, although data to support this latter practice are weak. Underlying causes and offending medications should be identified and rectified. If peritoneal signs of hypovolemic shock or sepsis develop, immediate exploratory laparotomy is necessary.

KEY POINTS

- Acute mesenteric ischemia is a life-threatening condition that typically occurs in older patients with cardiovascular and peripheral vascular disease.

- A high suspicion is the key to early diagnosis of acute mesenteric ischemia, which is essential to reduce morbidity and mortality. The diagnosis is usually made by radiographic and traditional angiography.

- Treatment for acute mesenteric ischemia includes surgery, vasodilator therapy, and in patients with mesenteric venous thrombosis and a hypercoagulable state, anticoagulation.

- Chronic mesenteric ischemia occurs in the setting of significant atherosclerotic disease in which usually two or three splanchnic vessels are occluded; a history of postprandial abdominal pain and weight loss are essential features of the diagnosis.

- Colonic ischemia usually occurs in older patients with cardiovascular disease and in younger patients who are long-distance runners; diagnosis is made by colonoscopy and histology; treatment is supportive.

Bibliography

American College of Gastroenterology. An Evidence-Based Systematic Review on the Management of Irritable Bowel Syndrome . American College of Gastroenterology Task Force on IBS. Am J Gastroenterol. 2009;104: Suppl 1

Antonucci A, Fronzoni L, Cogliando L, et al. Chronic intestinal pseudo-obstruction. World J Gastroenterol. 2008;14:2953-61. [PMID: 18494042]

Baumgart DC, Sandborn WJ. Inflammatory bowel disease: clinical aspects and established and evolving therapies. Lancet. 2007; 369:1641-57. [PMID: 17499606]

Green PH, Cellier C. Celiac Disease. N Engl J Med. 2007;357:1731-43 [PMID: 17960014]

Kornbluth A and Sachar D; Practice Parameters Committee of the American College of Gastroenterology. Ulcerative colitis practice guidelines in adults (update): American College of Gastroenterology, Practice Parameters Committee. Am J Gastroenterol. 2004;99:1371-85. [PMID: 15233681]

Longstreth GF, Thompson WG, Chey WD, Houghton LA, Mearin F, Spiller RC. Functional bowel disorders [erratum in Gastroenterology. 2006;131:688]. Gastroenterology. 2006;130:1480-91. [PMID: 16678561]

Mayer, EA. Irritable Bowel Syndrome. N Engl J Med. 2008;358:1692-9. [PMID: 18420501]

Nyhlin N, Bohr J, Eriksson S, Tysk C. Systematic review: microscopic colitis. Aliment Pharmacol Ther. 2006;23:1525-34. [PMID: 16696800]

Petruzziello L, Iacopini F, Bulajic M, Shah S, Costamagna G. Review article: uncomplicated diverticular disease of the colon. Aliment Pharmacol Ther. 2006;23:1379-91. [PMID: 16669953]

Spiller R. Chronic diarrhoea. Gut. 2007;56:1756-7. [PMID: 17998327]

Colorectal Neoplasia

Pathophysiology of Colorectal Neoplasia

The transformation of a normal colonocyte into cancer is the result of a series of molecular changes that induce unregulated cellular proliferation and culminate in malignancy. The biologic roles of the genes involved in sporadic and familial colorectal cancer have been elucidated, thereby leading to an understanding of the pathways of colon carcinogenesis. In addition, various environmental and dietary factors have been shown to affect the risk for colon cancer. Although the mechanisms by which these factors interact in colon carcinogenesis are not well understood, recognizing their contribution offers potential for prevention of colonic neoplasia and intervention in disease.

Knudsen's two-hit hypothesis of carcinogenesis, which proposes that two mutations (or "hits") are required for carcinogenesis, is most evident in colorectal cancer in the familial colon cancer syndromes. In hereditary cancer syndromes, the first hit is an inherited mutation that is present in the zygote and therefore exists in every cell (a germline mutation); the second hit is a somatic mutation, and cancer develops in a high proportion of such patients and at an early age. In sporadic cancers both hits are somatic mutations in a single cell, a much less likely event than the single somatic mutation in hereditary cancers, although one that occurs in nearly 5% of the population.

Genetics

Adenoma-to-Carcinoma Sequence

The multistep model of colon carcinogenesis proposes a series of genetic abnormalities resulting in progression from normal mucosa to dysplastic adenoma to carcinoma (**Figure 25**). Early in the process a hyperproliferative epithelium develops, whereas later multiple mutations accumulate, contributing to increasing degrees of chromosomal instability and dysplasia. Cellular expansion becomes clonal and eventually cancer develops. The progression from normal mucosa to adenoma to cancer takes approximately 15 years.

Tumor Suppressor Genes

In most sporadic cancers and some familial syndromes, mutations occur in the *APC* gene. The normal *APC* gene regulates the growth of the colonocyte. When both copies (alleles) of the *APC* gene within a cell are mutated, cell growth

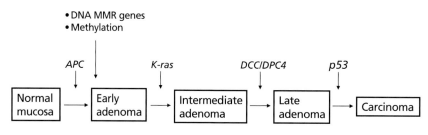

FIGURE 25.
Genetic mutations in the pathophysiology of colorectal cancer.

APC = adenomatous polyposis gene; *DCC* = deleted in colorectal cancer gene; *DPC4* = deleted in pancreatic cancer 4 gene; *K-ras* = K-ras oncogene; *MMR* = mismatches repair genes; *p53* = *p53* tumor suppressor gene.

becomes dysregulated. This type of gene is called a tumor suppressor gene because its normal function suppresses oncogenesis. Mutations in the *APC* gene, which tend to occur early in the process of colon carcinogenesis, are the cause of most cases of the familial adenomatous polyposis syndrome.

Mutations in the tumor suppressor gene *p53* occur in 70% of colon cancers. The *p53* gene facilitates cell repair and initiates apoptosis (a form of programmed cell death that eliminates old, unnecessary, and unhealthy cells). When the *p53* gene is inactivated by a mutation, apoptosis is not initiated and the cell may become "immortalized" and harbor abnormal DNA. Mutations in the *p53* gene often occur late in the transformation from dysplasia to carcinoma.

Oncogenes

Oncogenes promote cell growth and replication, and their normal suppression in the healthy cell prevents cancer; mutations of oncogenes are oncogenic. Mutations of the *ras* oncogene occur in half of the cases of sporadic colon cancer but do not appear to be a dominant molecular feature of hereditary cancers. Other oncogenes are involved in the development of colon cancer (**Table 33**).

Mismatch Repair Genes and Base Excision Repair Genes

Mismatch repair genes assist in the repair of errors in DNA that occur during replication. When these genes are defective, small abnormal sequences of DNA called microsatellites are inserted into the genetic code, resulting in microsatellite instability, which predisposes the cell to malignant transformation. Mutations of mismatch repair genes are implicated as the primary aberration in hereditary nonpolyposis colorectal cancer but are also present in 15% of sporadic colon cancers. The adenoma-to-carcinoma sequence is markedly accelerated in cancers that result from mutations to mismatch repair genes. Base excision repair genes function to remove DNA damaged from the byproducts of cellular metabolism, such as oxidative damage from reactive oxygen species. Mutations of base excision repair genes play a role in familial adenomatous polyposis that is inherited in an autosomal recessive pattern.

TABLE 33 Genetics of Colon Cancer		
Gene Function	**Affected Gene**	**Clinical Manifestation**
Tumor suppressor genes	*APC* *p53* *DCC*	FAP, AFAP Sporadic colon cancer Non-syndromic familial colon cancer[a]
Oncogenes	*myc* *ras* *src* *erbB2*	Sporadic colon cancer
Mismatch repair genes	*MLH1* *MLH3* *MSH2* *MSH6* *PMS1* *PMS2*	HNPCC Sporadic colon cancer
Base excision repair genes	*MYH*	FAP, AFAP—autosomal recessive inheritance

APC = Adenomatous polyposis coli; *DCC* = Deleted in colon cancer; FAP = Familial adenomatous polyposis; AFAP = Attenuated FAP; HNPCC = Hereditary nonpolyposis colon cancer.

[a]A mutation of the *APC* gene that does not result in altered structure of the gene product but predisposes to other sporadic mutations occurs in Ashkenazi Jews.

Epidemiology and Risk Factors of Colonic Neoplasia

One in twenty persons in the United States will develop colorectal cancer in their lifetime. In 2007 more than 140,000 new cases of colorectal cancer were diagnosed in the United States, making it the third most common cancer diagnosis in both men (behind prostate and lung) and women (behind breast and lung). Colon cancer is also the third most common cause of cancer death in both sexes despite the decline in colon cancer–related mortality over the past decade. Almost 40% of patients diagnosed with colorectal cancer die of the disease. Colon cancer affects men and women equally and occurs in all ethnic groups, although the incidence is greater in black Americans than in other populations. Moreover, black Americans have more advanced clinical stage at diagnosis and a worse overall prognosis than other ethnic groups.

Environmental Factors

Various dietary and environmental factors have been shown to affect the development of colorectal cancer. Diets rich in fruits, vegetables, and dietary fiber have been associated with fewer colon cancers, as have diets that are low in fat and red meat. High intake of calcium, folate, and selenium has also been associated with a decreased overall risk. The biologic rationale for these findings is postulated as decreased exposure of the colonic epithelium to carcinogenic factors and mitigation of the carcinogenic potential of luminal carcinogens.

TABLE 34 Extracolonic Manifestations of Familial Adenomatous Polyposis

Benign
  Mandibular osteomas
  Supernumerary teeth
  Congenital hypertrophy of the retinal pigment epithelium
  Desmoid tumors
  Epidermoid and sebaceous cysts
  Gastric polyps
Premalignant/Malignant
  Small-bowel adenomas and cancer
  Thyroid cancer
  Gastric cancer
  Central nervous system tumors
  Biliary cancer

Despite the convincing epidemiologic data, trials designed to reduce colon cancer risk through dietary modification have yielded disappointing results.

Obesity and a sedentary lifestyle have been associated with the development of adenomas and an increased risk for colorectal cancer. Obesity also reduces survival in patients diagnosed with colon cancer. Smoking and alcohol use have both been consistently found to be associated with the development of colon adenomas and cancer and to adversely affect survival.

Hereditary Colon Cancer Syndromes

Familial Adenomatous Polyposis

Less than 1% of all cases of colon cancer are due to familial adenomatous polyposis, which is a condition transmitted in an autosomal dominant fashion and characterized by the presence of hundreds to thousands of adenomatous polyps and the inevitable development of colon cancer. The colonic manifestation of florid polyposis is most often due to a germline mutation in the *APC* gene. Less commonly, polyposis results from biallelic mutations of the *MYH* gene with a recessive pattern of transmission. Mutations are detectable in 70% of patients; polyps typically develop during the teenage years, and cancer develops between age 30 and 50 years. In addition to the polyposis, various benign and malignant extracolonic manifestations occur in affected kindreds (**Table 34**). The next most common site of cancer in these patients is the periampullary region of the duodenum, and screening protocols include evaluation of the upper and lower gastrointestinal tract.

Attenuated Familial Adenomatous Polyposis

In attenuated familial adenomatous polyposis, 10 to 100 adenomas develop, and the polyps and cancer develop about 10 years later than in the classic form of familial adenomatous polyposis. The attenuated form most commonly is the result of mutations in the 3′ or 5′ end of the *APC* gene, although biallelic *MYH* mutations also result in this phenotype. The extracolonic manifestations of the classic form also occur in patients with the attenuated form, and are present in those with both *APC* and *MYH* mutations.

Hereditary Nonpolyposis Colorectal Cancer

Hereditary nonpolyposis colorectal cancer (HNPCC, also known as Lynch syndrome) is an autosomal dominant syndrome that carries an 80% lifetime risk for colon cancer. HNPCC is the most common of the hereditary colon cancer syndromes, accounting for 2% to 3% of all colorectal adenocarcinomas. Mutations in *MLH1* and *MSH2* mismatch repair genes are the most commonly detected genetic abnormality. HNPCC-associated cancer generally becomes clinically apparent in patients with fewer than 10 adenomas, and although cancer may occur at an early age, it generally develops after age 50 years. The cancers tend to occur in the right side of the colon and have a mucinous histopathology with infiltrating lymphocytes. The pathophysiology through the mismatch repair gene pathway is an accelerated adenoma-to-carcinoma sequence, with cancer often occurring within a few years of a colonoscopy during which all polyps were removed. HNPCC-associated extracolonic cancers include uterine cancer (40% to 60% lifetime risk) and ovarian cancer (10% to 12% lifetime risk). Cancers of the small bowel, stomach, pancreas, renal pelvis, and ureter also occur in association with HNPCC and may occur in affected kindreds even in the absence of colon cancer.

Peutz-Jeghers Syndrome and Juvenile Polyposis Syndrome

The Peutz-Jeghers syndrome is a rare autosomal dominant hereditary condition that consists of polyposis of the colon and small bowel. The polyps are predominantly hamartomas, although they may undergo malignant transformation, and affected persons have an 80-fold increased risk for colon cancer over the general population. The genetic abnormality occurs as a germline mutation in the *STK11* gene. Patients may be readily identified by the classic perioral pigmentation, although the typical presentation consists of bleeding and abdominal pain from large polyps. Extracolonic tumors of the breast, pancreas, ovaries, and lung occur at an increased rate.

Juvenile polyposis syndrome is an autosomal dominant condition with hamartomatous polyps occurring most often in the distal colon, accompanied by congenital malformations of the gastrointestinal tract, genitourinary system, and heart. Germline mutations of the *SMAD4* gene are implicated in this syndrome. The lifetime colon cancer risk in juvenile polyposis syndrome is approximately 70%.

Diagnosis and Management of Patients at Increased Risk for Colon Cancer

Genetic Testing

Patients who may have a hereditary cancer syndrome include those with more than the expected number of cancers in their family, those with cancer at an earlier age than anticipated, and those with endoscopically detected multiple polyps. Evaluation of such patients should be performed under the guidance of a genetic counselor who can evaluate the many implications of both positive and negative results (especially a negative result in an at-risk person) and address the personal, social, and financial aspects of genetic testing. If a family carries a defined genetic mutation and an at-risk family member tests negative for the mutation, it is likely that the tested person does not carry the mutation and will not develop the disease. However, a negative test is not helpful if the genetic mutation in the family is unknown. In this case the test is not informative and the patient must be treated as if he or she remains at risk for the syndrome.

Adenomatous Polyposis

Familial adenomatous polyposis and attenuated familial adenomatous polyposis are most commonly diagnosed after polyposis is detected on endoscopy. The endoscopy may be performed due to a suggestive family history or because of bleeding or abdominal pain. Commercial testing for mutations in the *APC* gene is available. If an *APC* mutation is not detected, then testing for *MYH* should be performed. In 30% of cases, a genetic mutation will not be detected in patients with polyposis.

Management for patients with familial adenomatous polyposis and for at-risk persons includes annual flexible sigmoidoscopy beginning as early as age 10 to 12 years. Colectomy should be considered when polyposis is detected, although because the mean age of the onset of cancer in these patients is 40 years, decisions may be individualized. In patients with attenuated familial adenomatous polyposis, annual complete colonoscopy is required because polyps may only be present in the proximal colon. Many patients can be managed with endoscopic polypectomy rather than with surgery, but surgery is recommended if the polyp burden cannot be managed at colonoscopy. Upper endoscopy is performed initially between ages 25 and 30 years and at 1- to 3-year intervals thereafter.

Hereditary Nonpolyposis Colorectal Cancer

Most patients with HNPCC are identified from their medical history. The diagnosis should be suspected in persons who have multiple family members with cancers of the colon, endometrium and ovaries, small bowel, ureter, renal pelvis, and pancreaticobiliary system. The Amsterdam II clinical criteria for HNPCC use the 3-2-1 rule: three relatives with an HNPCC-associated cancer, two generations affected, one person diagnosed before age 50 years. The Amsterdam criteria are not sensitive enough to detect many affected families, and, therefore, they were expanded in the form of the Bethesda criteria (**Table 35**). A decision procedure for testing persons in whom HNPCC is suspected is shown in **Figure 26**.

Management of patients with HNPCC or those who are considered at risk for the disease consists of colonoscopy every 1 to 2 years beginning at age 20 to 25 years or 10 years before the age at diagnosis of the youngest family member diagnosed with colon cancer. Annual colonoscopy is recommended after age 40 years. The risk for gynecologic malignancies is greatly reduced in affected women who undergo prophylactic hysterectomy and salpingo-oophorectomy, and many physicians advocate surgery for women who no longer wish to bear children. Women who do not choose prophylactic surgery should have a pelvic examination with endometrial sampling, transvaginal ultrasonography, and measurement of serum CA-125 every 1 to 2 years from age 30 years. Screening for urinary tract cancers with urine cytology and renal ultrasonography

TABLE 35 Clinical Criteria for Hereditary Nonpolyposis Colon Cancer

Amsterdam II Criteria

At least three relatives affected with an HNPCC-associated cancer[a]

One affected member is the first-degree relative of the other two

Two or more successive generations are affected

One or more affected relatives is diagnosed with colon cancer at age <50 years

Familial adenomatous polyposis is excluded

Tumors are verified by pathologic examination

Modified Bethesda Guidelines[b]

Individuals with cancer in families that meet the Amsterdam Criteria

Individuals with two HNPCC-related cancers regardless of age[c]

Individuals with CRC or endometrial cancer diagnosed at age <50 years

Individuals with CRC and a first-degree relative with CRC or HNPCC-related extracolonic cancer or adenoma; one of the cancers diagnosed at age <50 years or adenoma diagnosed at age <40 years

Individuals with histology consistent with microsatellite instability at age <60 years

Individuals with adenomas diagnosed at age <40 years

HNPCC = hereditary nonpolyposis colorectal cancer; CRC = colorectal cancer.

[a]HNPCC-associated cancers include cancers of the colorectum, endometrium, small bowel, renal pelvis, and ureter.

[b]Bethesda Guidelines are for identifying persons who should undergo testing for microsatellite instability.

[c]Bethesda Guidelines include hepatobiliary cancers and cancer of the ovaries, brain, and stomach in addition to those in the Amsterdam criteria. Synchronous or metachronous colorectal cancer are considered a second HNPCC-associated cancer.

should also be performed every 1 to 2 years beginning at age 30 years.

Inflammatory Bowel Disease

Patients with ulcerative colitis and Crohn disease have an increased risk for colon cancer, a risk that increases with increased duration of disease, the extent of colonic involvement, and the coexistence of sclerosing cholangitis. The annual cancer risk is estimated to be 1% to 2% per year after 8 years of disease, and, therefore, colonoscopic surveillance should be started in patients who have had inflammatory bowel disease for 8 years or longer. For patients with inflammation limited to the left colon, recommendations vary, with some authorities initiating surveillance after 15 years' duration of disease. If dysplasia is detected on biopsy in a patient with colitis, the risk for colon cancer is markedly increased even at sites distant from the site of biopsy; colectomy should, therefore, be considered even in the absence of a preoperative cancer diagnosis.

Other Predisposing Conditions

Other conditions that increase the risk for colorectal cancer include a history of radiation injury to the colon, acromegaly,

and urinary diversion with implantation of the ureters into the colon. Patients with these conditions should have an accelerated surveillance program, although there are no uniform surveillance guidelines for such patients.

KEY POINTS

- Evaluation of patients with a suspected familial colon cancer syndrome should be performed under the guidance of a genetic counselor.
- Patients with hereditary colon cancer syndromes such as familial adenomatous polyposis and hereditary nonpolyposis colorectal cancer have a very high risk of developing colon cancer and extracolonic malignancy; these patients require aggressive screening and surveillance strategies.
- In addition to being at high risk for colon cancer, patients with familial adenomatous polyposis are at risk for cancers of the small bowel, thyroid gland, stomach, central nervous system, and biliary system.
- Hereditary nonpolyposis colorectal cancer should be suspected clinically in persons who have multiple family members with cancers of the colon, endometrium and ovaries, small bowel, ureter, renal pelvis, and pancreaticobiliary system.
- Clinical diagnostic criteria for hereditary nonpolyposis colorectal cancer include the 3-2-1 rule: 3 relatives with an associated cancer; 2 generations affected; and 1 person diagnosed before age 50 years.
- Medical conditions that increase the risk for colorectal cancer include inflammatory bowel disease, acromegaly, a history of radiation injury to the colon, and urinary diversion with implantation of ureters into the colon.

Screening and Surveillance for Colonic Neoplasia

Assessing a person's risk for colon cancer is central to formulating an appropriate screening and surveillance protocol. There has been a decrease in the incidence of colorectal cancer over the past 10 years, a fact that may be a result of screening and surveillance. Guidelines for screening have been issued by various professional organizations independently or as part of the United States Preventive Services Task Force. The guidelines include various screening modalities, and the choice of test for an individual patient should be based on a discussion between physician and patient on the risks and benefits to the patient. The likelihood of patient compliance with follow-up of a positive screening test as well as surveillance testing must be factored into the decision.

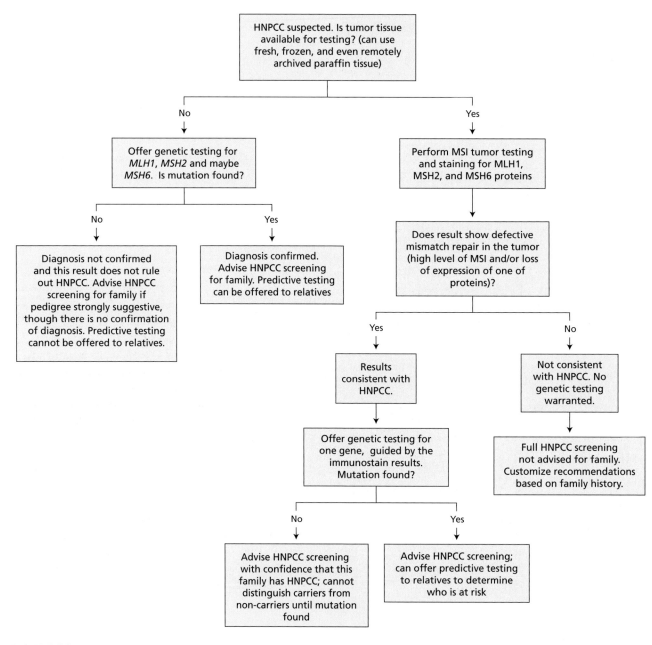

FIGURE 26.
Testing for hereditary nonpolyposis colorectal cancer.

HNPCC = hereditary nonpolyposis colorectal cancer; MLH1 = MLH1 gene; MSH2 = MSH2 gene; MSH6 = MSH6 gene; MSI = microsatellite instability.

Adapted from Lindor NM. Recognition of genetic syndromes in families with suspected hereditary colon cancer syndromes. Clin Gastroenterol Hepatol. 2004;2:366-375. [PMID: 15118973] Copyright 2004, with permission from Elsevier.

Average-Risk Patients

Persons at average risk for colorectal cancer include those with no personal or family history of colon adenoma or cancer who do not have a condition that predisposes them to cancer. Screening in this population should be started at age 50 years, with surveillance intervals depending upon the screening modality.

Nonsyndromic Family History

A family history of colon cancer or adenomatous polyps significantly increases a person's risk for colon cancer; up to 30% of those screened have such a history. The magnitude of risk depends on whether the affected family member is a first-degree relative (parent, sibling, child) or second-degree relative (grandparent, aunt, uncle), the number of affected family members, and their age at onset of disease. The presence of colon cancer in a first-degree relative carries a two- to threefold increased lifetime risk over the general population; that risk is doubled again if the affected relative was diagnosed before age 45 years. If two first-degree relatives have colon cancer, the colon cancer risk approaches 20%. Therefore, physicians should ask their patients about the presence of a first-degree relative with colon cancer and age of onset of the cancer. For persons with a family history of colorectal cancer in a first-degree relative, screening is initiated either at age 40 years or beginning 10 years earlier than the diagnosis of the youngest affected family member (**Table 36**).

Screening Tests

Screening for colorectal cancer is cost effective and well tolerated; it also saves lives. Screening is feasible because the 10 to 15 years needed for a polyp to develop into cancer are sufficient time to detect and remove an adenoma. Most screening strategies result in cost-effectiveness ratios of $10,000 to $25,000 per year of life saved, although a dominant cost-effectiveness strategy has not emerged across studies.

Fecal Occult Blood Test

When performed correctly, fecal occult blood testing (FOBT) is an effective screen for colorectal cancer; proper performance requires a dedicated physician and a motivated patient. The test is inexpensive, noninvasive, generally acceptable to patients, and can detect bleeding anywhere in the colon. Occult blood is detected by either a guaiac-based test (gFOBT) or fecal immunochemical test (FIT). gFOBT testing detects hemoglobin by a peroxidase reaction; the procedure requires annual testing, that two samples be collected from each of three spontaneously passed stools, and that diets be modified during the testing period to avoid aspirin, red meat, and certain fruits and vegetables. Performed correctly, gFOBT has been shown to reduce colorectal cancer–related mortality by

33%. FIT detects human globin and is more specific than gFOBT. FIT requires fewer precollection restrictions and in some cases the need for fewer samples, thereby improving patient compliance. The amount of reduction in colorectal cancer–related mortality with FIT is not known. The U.S. Multi-Society Task Force on Colorectal Cancer recommends annual stool testing with either gFOBT or FIT for colorectal cancer screening.

At present one third of primary care physicians report the use of a digital rectal examination as the principal means of obtaining the stool sample, a practice that reduces the efficacy of FOBT five-fold. Moreover, only 52% of physicians recommend colonoscopy in patients in whom blood is detected on FOBT.

Flexible Sigmoidoscopy

Endoscopic screening of the distal colon decreases colon cancer diagnoses in the screened colonic segment and decreases colorectal cancer–related mortality by 45%. Advanced adenomas (≥1 cm in diameter, villous histology, high-grade dysplasia or cancer) are detected three times more often by sigmoidoscopy than by fecal occult blood testing. Combined occult blood testing and sigmoidoscopy modestly increases the detection rate from 70% to 76%. Small polyps detected during sigmoidoscopy can be biopsied or removed safely with a snare without cautery. Cautery should be avoided in the uncleansed colon because of the possibility of colonic rupture. Removing large polyps requires a colonic preparation and snare polypectomy. If a polyp removed during sigmoidoscopy is found to be an adenoma, complete colonoscopy is required. Factors at sigmoidoscopy that are associated with finding advanced adenomas on follow-up colonoscopy include multiple adenomas, adenomas ≥1 cm, patient age >65 years, and villous adenomas.

Guidelines from professional societies recommend that sigmoidoscopy be performed at 5-year intervals if no adenomas are detected. Sigmoidoscopy is well tolerated and does

TABLE 36 Screening Recommendations for Patients with a Family History of Colorectal Cancer or Adenomatous Polyps		
Patient Category	**Screening**	**Surveillance**
First-degree relative(s) with colorectal cancer diagnosed at age <60 years	Colonoscopy at age 40 or 10 years younger than affected relative (whichever is younger)	If normal, repeat every 3-5 years
First-degree relative(s) with colorectal cancer diagnosed at ≥60 years	Colonoscopy at age 40 years	If normal, repeat every 10 years
First-degree relative(s) with adenomatous polyp <60 years	Colonoscopy at age 40 years or 10 years younger than affected relative	If normal, repeat every 5 years
First-degree relative with adenomatous polyp >60 years	Colonoscopy beginning at age 40 years	Individualized; if normal, same as average risk
Second- or third degree relative with cancer or polyps	Colonoscopy as average-risk persons	If normal, same as average risk

Reprinted from Davila RE, Rajan E, Baron TH, et al. ASGE guideline: the role of endoscopy in the surveillance of premalignant conditions of the upper GI tract. Gastrointestinal Endoscopy. 2006;63:546-57. [PMID: 16564854] Copyright 2006, with permission from Elsevier.

not require sedation. There are fewer complications from sigmoidoscopy than from colonoscopy, although bleeding and perforation can occur.

Colonoscopy

Colonoscopy is both a diagnostic and therapeutic procedure that evaluates the entire colon and allows biopsy and/or polypectomy. The National Polyp Study found that colonoscopy reduced the incidence of colorectal cancer by 76% to 90% when compared to control populations. European studies show a similar effect, with a 66% to 80% reduction in colorectal cancer incidence. There have been no randomized controlled trials of colonoscopy in the reduction of colorectal cancer–related mortality; however, extrapolation of sigmoidoscopy and fecal occult blood testing data would support endoscopic polypectomy throughout the colon as an effective means of reducing colorectal cancer–related deaths. Half of patients with advanced adenomas of the proximal colon that are detectable on colonoscopy do not have polyps within the reach of a sigmoidoscope. If an adenoma is detected on colonoscopy, the patient is most likely to benefit from an accelerated surveillance program. If a high-quality colonoscopy yields normal results, there is no need for another colonoscopic surveillance for 10 years.

Colonoscopy is generally well tolerated, the primary source of discomfort being the colon preparation. Colonoscopy is not acceptable to all persons, thereby decreasing adherence rates and disproportionately so in women and ethnic minorities. Complications include bleeding (0.20%) and perforation (0.02%) and are not inconsequential. The miss rate for polyps >1 cm is 6% to 11%. Nevertheless, colonoscopy is the preferred screening modality by most U.S. physicians and medical societies.

Double-Contrast Barium Enema

The most recent recommendations from the U.S. Multi-Society Task Force and the National Comprehensive Cancer Network include double-contrast barium enema among the options for colorectal cancer screening. However, the U.S. Preventive Services Task Force no longer lists barium enema amongst the screening options. Double-contrast barium enema has not been shown to reduce the incidence of colorectal cancer or cancer-related mortality. The rate of detection of both small and large polyps is half that of colonoscopy, and the cancer detection rate is 83% compared with 95% for colonoscopy. The current role of double-contrast barium enema is limited to the patient in whom a complete examination of the colon is desired but cannot be performed by other methods.

CT Colonography

CT colonography (virtual colonoscopy) is an emerging modality for colorectal cancer screening and has been endorsed by the U.S. Multi-Society Task Force as an acceptable mode of screening. The optimal procedure requires a bowel preparation similar to that for colonoscopy, insertion of a rectal tube and insufflation to establish pneumocolon. Scanning is then performed supine, and the procedure repeated in the prone position. Sensitivity for polyp detection by CT colonography is extremely variable. The sensitivity of CT colonography for polyps <5 mm varies from 30% to 60% whereas the range for lesions ≥1 cm is 60% to 95%. These data reflect variation in technique, scanner technology, and operators and readers.

Concerns unique to CT colonography include radiation exposure, the relevance of small lesions, surveillance intervals, and how to address incidental findings. The radiation exposure of a single examination is low; however, such exposure would result in a radiation-induced tumor in 1 in 714 persons, and the exposure increases with subsequent examinations. A consensus group of radiologists states that polyps <5 mm need not be reported; however, the ethical and medical implications of this proposal must be considered as multiplicity of polyps irrespective of size is a strong predictor of advanced neoplasia.

The recent recommendations for CT colonography include a 5-year surveillance interval. However, reimbursement for the test is low, and there are many concerns regarding standardization of the tests and results reporting. The choice of CT colonography as a primary screening modality must be individualized and consider patient preferences and burdens and local expertise. CT colonography is most useful when colonoscopy is either not feasible or contraindicated and structural colonic imaging is required.

Fecal DNA Testing

Exfoliation of DNA is a constant event within the colon. This DNA can be recovered from the stool and analyzed for a panel of molecular aberrations linked with colorectal neoplasia. Stool DNA testing requires submission of a single stool sample in its entirety. The sensitivity of fecal DNA for detecting advanced adenomas ranges widely. In a study of more than 2500 persons comparing fecal DNA to FOBT, fecal DNA testing was superior in detecting advanced adenoma (18% vs. 11%) and cancer (52% vs. 13%). Sensitivity of fecal DNA testing has been reported to be as high as 91%. There are no studies demonstrating a reduction in colorectal cancer–related mortality. The panel of molecular abnormalities continues to be refined, and studies are ongoing to optimize yield and clinical efficacy. Fecal DNA testing has recently been endorsed as an option for screening for colorectal neoplasia; however, the surveillance interval after initial screening remains unknown.

- Colorectal cancer screening is well tolerated, cost-effective, and saves lives.

- Screening for colorectal cancer is feasible because of the 10 to 15 years that are needed for a polyp to develop into cancer, an ample time to detect and remove an adenoma.

- Fecal occult blood testing, flexible sigmoidoscopy, and colonoscopy are appropriate options for screening for colorectal cancer in average-risk patients.

Surveillance of Patients with Colon Polyps or Cancer

Colon Polyps

The surveillance interval after colonoscopic polypectomy depends on the location, size, number, and histology of the removed polyps, along with the personal risk assessment of the patient. Surveillance should be done with colonoscopy. Surveillance reduces the incidence and disease-related mortality of colorectal cancer, and the positive predictive value of other strategies is unacceptably low. Factors associated with advanced adenomas and cancers on subsequent colonoscopy include adenomas >1 cm, three or more polyps detected in a single colonoscopy, villous histology, and advanced dysplasia. Although hyperplastic polyps are not a risk factor for colorectal cancer, serrated adenomas (which have a unique histologic architecture) are associated with dysplasia and colorectal cancer and affected patients are at risk for cancer

(Table 37). Hyperplastic polyposis syndrome is defined by the World Health Organization as: (1) at least five histologically diagnosed hyperplastic polyps proximal to the sigmoid colon, of which two are greater than 1 cm in diameter; or (2) any number of hyperplastic polyps occurring proximal to the sigmoid colon in an individual who has a first-degree relative with hyperplastic polyposis; or (3) greater than 30 hyperplastic polyps of any size distributed throughout the colon.

When cancers occur after colonoscopy, they tend to be smaller and to occur at sites of previous polypectomy as well as in the proximal colon. Therefore, follow-up surveillance must be performed carefully because these cancers tend to be smaller than cancers detected at a single colonoscopy.

Colon Cancer

After colon cancer is diagnosed, a perioperative complete colonic evaluation, either before resection or 3 to 6 months thereafter, is required. CT colonography is useful in the case of obstructing cancers to evaluate the rest of the colon before surgery. Surveillance of the colon is recommended at 1, 3, and 5 years after the perioperative colonoscopy if no new lesions are detected. If adenomas or cancers are detected during postresection surveillance, shorter intervals between evaluations may be needed, and the patient may have to be evaluated for a familial colon cancer syndrome. In the case of a low-anterior resection for rectal cancer, proctosigmoidoscopy is recommended every 3 to 6 months for up to 3 years in addition to colonoscopy.

Surveillance for patients with colon cancer must include strategies for detecting local recurrence as well as distant metastases, particularly for patients with advanced disease.

TABLE 37 Post-Polypectomy Surveillance Recommendations of the US Multi-Society Task Force on Colorectal Cancer and the American Cancer Society

1. **Patients with small rectal hyperplastic polyps** should be considered to have normal colonoscopies, and therefore the interval before the subsequent colonoscopy should be 10 years. An exception is patients with a hyperplastic polyposis syndrome.

2. **Patients with only one or two small (<1 cm) tubular adenomas with only low-grade dysplasia** should have their next follow-up colonoscopy in 5 to 10 years.

3. **Patients with 3 to 10 adenomas, or any adenoma ≥1 cm, or any adenoma with villous features, or high-grade dysplasia** should have their next follow-up colonoscopy in 3 years providing that piecemeal removal has not been done and the adenoma(s) are completely removed. If the follow-up colonoscopy is normal or shows only one or two small tubular adenomas with low-grade dysplasia, then the interval for the subsequent examination should be 5 years.

4. **Patients who have more than 10 adenomas at one examination** should be examined at a shorter (<3 years) interval established by clinical judgment, and the clinician should consider the possibility of an underlying familial syndrome.

5. **Patients with sessile adenomas that are removed piecemeal** should be considered for follow up at short intervals (2 to 6 months) to verify complete removal. Once complete removal has been established, subsequent surveillance needs to be individualized based on the judgment of the endoscopist. Completeness of removal should be based on both endoscopic and pathologic assessments.

6. **More intensive surveillance is indicated when the family history may indicate hereditary nonpolyposis colorectal cancer.**

Adapted from Winawer SJ, Zauber AG, Fletcher RH, et al. Guidelines for colonoscopy surveillance after polypectomy: a consensus update by the US Multi-Society Task Force on Colorectal Cancer and the American Cancer Society. CA: A Cancer Journal for Clinicians. 2006;56:143-59. [PMID: 16737947]. Copyright 2006, American Cancer Society. Reproduced with permission from John Wiley & Sons.

Intensive surveillance strategies require a combination of a patient history and physical examination, blood tests including measurement of serum carcinoembryonic antigen, and periodic CT scans. Intensive surveillance improves disease-free survival and may detect recurrent or metastatic disease when therapeutic and even curative interventions are possible.

Clinical Presentation of Colonic Neoplasia

Colon adenomas are usually discovered incidentally. The strongest predictor of finding an adenoma on index colonoscopy is the presence of blood in the stool. Adenomas are less commonly found when the indication for colonoscopy is abdominal pain, changes in bowel function, or weight loss. Abdominal pain, bleeding, and altered bowel habits are the most common presenting symptoms of colon cancer; less common are anemia and weight loss. Colon cancer may present with local invasion and fistula formation or unexplained intra-abdominal abscess, resulting in a clinical picture similar to that of complicated diverticulitis. Patients with diverticulitis should undergo colonoscopy after the acute inflammation resolves. Bacteremia from *Streptococcus bovis* and *Clostridium septicum* has been associated with colon cancer and should prompt colonoscopy. Adenocarcinoma of unknown primary site originates from the colon in approximately 6% of cases.

Staging of Colon Cancer

After the diagnosis of colon cancer, comprehensive staging work-up is performed; the work-up consists of a thorough medical history and physical examination, complete evaluation of the colon, and CT scan of the abdomen and pelvis. MRI is more sensitive for detecting liver metastases than CT, although long scanning times and availability limit the use of MRI. Scanning with 2-[^{18}F] fluoro-2-deoxy-D-glucose (FDG) and positron emission tomography (PET) scan (the FDG-PET scan) is sensitive for detecting extrahepatic metastases but is not superior to CT scan for detecting spread to the liver. Many centers perform combined PET-CT, which offers the benefits of both tests. The most accurate procedure for locoregional staging for rectal cancer is endoscopic ultrasonography (**Figure 27**), which provides high-resolution imaging and the ability to sample suspicious nodal disease. A preoperative measurement of serum carcinoembryonic antigen provides prognostic information and serves as a marker for recurrent disease. Staging most commonly follows the TNM staging of the American Joint Committee on Cancer (**Table 38**).

The strongest determinant of recurrence of colorectal cancer and survival is the pathologic staging, which correlates with prognosis and thereby determines the need for adjuvant therapy. Molecular targets that can diagnose micrometastases not detected by histologic assessment will likely have a role in staging evaluation in the near future. At present, the 5-year survival rate for patients diagnosed with stage I disease exceeds 90%; however, for patients with stage IV disease, the survival rate is only 8%. The overall colon cancer–related mortality rate approaches 40%.

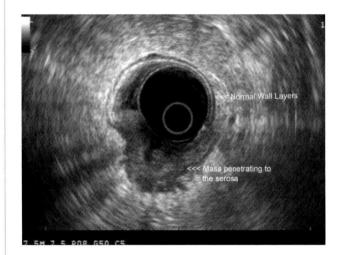

FIGURE 27.
Endoscopic ultrasonography of rectal cancer.
Endoscopic ultrasound image of a rectal cancer extending through the colonic wall to the serosa.

TABLE 38 Stage Groupings for Colorectal Cancer				
AJCC Stage Groupings	**Tumor**	**Node**	**Metastasis**	**Dukes Stage (Astler-Coller modification)**
Stage 0	Tis	N0	M0	–
Stage I	T1	N0	M0	A
	T2	N0	M0	B1
Stage IIA	T3	N0	M0	B2
Stage IIB	T4	N0	M0	B3
Stage IIIA	T1-T2	N1	M0	C1
Stage IIIB	T3-T4	N1	M0	C2/C3

Bibliography

Cappell MS. The pathophysiology, clinical presentation, and diagnosis of colon cancer and adenomatous polyps. Med Clin North Am. 2005;89:1-42, vii. [PMID: 15527807]

Davila RE, Rajan E, Baron TH, et al; Standards of Practice Committee, American Society for Gastrointestinal Endoscopy. ASGE guideline: colorectal cancer screening and surveillance [erratum in Gastrointest Endosc. 2006;63:892]. Gastrointest Endosc. 2006;63:546-57. [PMID: 16564851]

Farrar WD, Sawhney MS, Nelson DB, Lederle FA, Bond JH. Colorectal cancers found after a complete colonoscopy. Clin Gastroenterol Hepatol. 2006;4:1259-64. [PMID: 16996804]

Hawk ET, Umar A, Richmond E, Viner JL. Prevention and therapy of colorectal cancer. Med Clin North Am. 2005;89:85-110, viii. [PMID: 15527810]

Imperiale TF, Ransohoff DF, Itzkowitz SH, Turnbull BA, Ross ME; Colorectal Cancer Study Group. Fecal DNA versus fecal occult blood for colorectal-cancer screening in an average-risk population. N Engl J Med. 2004;351:2704-14. [PMID: 15616205]

Levin B, Lieberman DA, McFarland B, et al; American Cancer Society Colorectal Cancer Advisory Group; US Multi-Society Task Force; American College of Radiology Colon Cancer Committee. Screening and surveillance for the early detection of colorectal cancer and adenomatous polyps, 2008: a joint guideline from the American Cancer Society, the US Multi-Society Task Force on Colorectal Cancer, and the American College of Radiology. Gastroenterology. 2008;134:1570-95. [PMID: 18384785]

Rex DK, Kahi CJ, Levin B, et al; American Cancer Society; US Multi-Society Task Force on Colorectal Cancer. Guidelines for colonoscopy surveillance after cancer resection: a consensus update by the American Cancer Society and the US Multi-Society Task Force on Colorectal Cancer. Gastroenterology. 2006;130:1865-71. [PMID: 16697749]

Segnan N, Senore C, Andreoni B, et al; SCORE2 Working Group-Italy. Randomized trial of different screening strategies for colorectal cancer: patient response and detection rates. J Natl Cancer Inst. 2005;97:347-57. [PMID: 15741571]

Syngal S, Bandipalliam P, Boland CR. Surveillance of patients at high risk for colorectal cancer. Med Clin North Am. 2005;89:61-84, vii-viii. [PMID: 15527809]

Umar A, Boland CR, Terdiman JP, et al. Revised Bethesda Guidelines for hereditary nonpolyposis colorectal cancer (Lynch syndrome) and microsatellite instability. J Natl Cancer Inst. 2004;96:261-8. [PMID: 14970275]

Winawer SJ, Zauber AG, Fletcher RH, et al. Guidelines for colonoscopy surveillance after polypectomy: a consensus update by the US Multi-Society Task Force on Colorectal Cancer and the American Cancer Society. CA Cancer J Clin. 2006;56:143-59; quiz 184-5. [PMID: 16737947]

Disorders of the Liver, Gallbladder, and Bile Ducts

Approach to the Patient with Abnormal Liver Chemistry Studies

Up to 4% of asymptomatic persons have abnormal results on liver biochemical tests performed as part of general medical evaluations or screening programs. Tests that reflect liver injury include alanine aminotransferase (ALT), aspartate aminotransferase (AST), alkaline phosphatase, and bilirubin. Tests that reflect liver function include albumin and prothrombin time.

Liver Injury Test Patterns

Hepatocellular injury most often results in an elevation of serum ALT and AST, which are released from injured hepatocytes. AST is also released, however, from other tissues, such as the heart and skeletal muscle. Therefore, elevations of ALT, which is minimally produced in nonhepatic tissues, are more sensitive for diagnosing liver disease.

Cholestatic injury, which consists of lack of or abnormality in the flow of bile, is indicated by an elevation of serum alkaline phosphatase. Cholestasis may occur without jaundice, however, because of the capacity of the liver to secrete bile sufficiently, until the injury to the bile ducts is significant. Profound disruption of the bile secretory mechanisms is likely to result in elevation of the serum bilirubin and therefore jaundice. Bilirubin is measured as conjugated (direct) and unconjugated (indirect) fractions. In patients with cholestatic diseases leading to jaundice, approximately half of the bilirubin is measured as the conjugated fraction. Predominance of the unconjugated fraction indicates either the overproduction of bilirubin (as occurs in hemolysis) or impairment of bilirubin conjugation. The latter situations are not uncommon, given the 5% prevalence of Gilbert syndrome in the general population. This benign syndrome, also known as constitutional hepatic dysfunction and familial nonhemolytic jaundice, is characterized by total bilirubin concentrations up to 3.0 mg/dL (51.3 mmol/L) resulting from a reduced expression of the enzyme that conjugates bilirubin.

Liver Function Tests

Measurement of the serum albumin and prothrombin time (or INR) reflects the liver's synthetic capacity. Reduction in the albumin concentration may indicate significant hepatic dysfunction. Similarly, elevation in the prothrombin time may indicate impaired hepatic production of clotting factors; however, these parameters may also be elevated in the setting of vitamin K deficiency, such as in malnutrition or malabsorption.

Clinical Approach to Abnormal Liver Studies

In the patient without known liver disease, elevated liver test results must be interpreted in the context of the clinical presentation and the pattern, degree, and duration of the biochemical abnormalities. A diagnosis of hepatitis requires further characterization to determine whether the injury is hepatocellular or cholestatic and its severity. Next, it is important to determine whether the patient has symptoms of liver disease, which may be constitutional, such as malaise, listlessness, weight loss, and nausea or, more specific, such as jaundice or right upper quadrant pain. The duration of liver test abnormalities can be determined through the patient's history and laboratory records: disorders present for less than 6 months are considered acute forms of hepatitis (**Table 39**); the disease is considered a form of chronic hepatitis when it has been present for greater than 6 months (**Table 40**). Cholestatic liver diseases are shown in **Table 41**.

Viral Hepatitis

Hepatitis A Virus

Hepatitis A virus (HAV) causes approximately half of the cases of acute hepatitis in the United States. Most patients who contract hepatitis A develop a clinical syndrome consisting of malaise, jaundice, and such nonspecific gastrointestinal symptoms as nausea and poor appetite. The typical incubation period is 2 to 3 weeks. The major routes of infection include ingestion of contaminated food or water and close contact with an infected person. Persons at high risk for acquisition of hepatitis A include men who have sex with men and those who travel to areas of the world where hepatitis A infection is endemic.

The diagnosis of acute hepatitis A depends on detecting an IgM antibody to hepatitis A virus (IgM anti-HAV), which is the earliest marker of infection, arising at the onset of symptomatic illness and becoming undetectable by 6 months; thereafter, IgG anti-HAV becomes detectable. The IgG antibody indicates prior infection and immunity; there is no chronic state of hepatitis A infection.

Prevention of hepatitis A infection consists of judicious use of hepatitis A immune globulin and the hepatitis A vaccine. Immune globulin and the vaccine should be given to all nonimmune contacts within 2 weeks of exposure to an infected person. In addition, persons at high risk and those with chronic liver disease should be vaccinated. The vaccine schedule is two doses separated by 6 to 12 months. There is also a combined hepatitis A/hepatitis B vaccine available.

Hepatitis B Virus

An estimated 350 million persons worldwide are infected with hepatitis B virus (HBV); approximately 1.25 million persons in the United States are chronically infected. Hepatitis B virus causes approximately one third of cases of acute viral hepatitis in the United States and approximately 15% of cases of chronic viral hepatitis.

Hepatitis B is transmitted parenterally by percutaneous exposure, for example, by sharing needles or syringes in injection drug use and intimate person-to-person contact with an infected person, including sexual contact (especially in men who have sex with men). In addition, perinatal acquisition can occur and is most common in newly developing countries and Eastern Europe and Russia.

TABLE 39 Characteristics of Acute Hepatitis				
	Liver Enzyme Pattern			
Disease	**ALT**	**AST**	**Historical Features**	**Diagnostic Evaluation**
Viral hepatitis A	↑↑↑	↑↑	Fecal oral exposure	IgM antibodies to hepatitis A (IgM anti-HAV)
Viral hepatitis B	↑↑↑	↑↑	Blood/body fluid exposure	IgM antibodies to hepatitis B core antigen (IgM anti-HBc) and to hepatitis B surface antigen (HBsAg)
Viral hepatitis C	↑↑	↑	Recent intravenous drug use	Hepatitis C RNA (HCV RNA); variable presence of antibody to hepatitis C (anti-HCV) within the first 3 months after exposure
Alcoholic hepatitis	↑	↑↑	Heavy alcohol use, either binge or chronic	Absence of other diagnostic markers of liver disease; improvement with cessation of alcohol use; ratio of AST:ALT >2, AST usually <500
Drug-induced hepatitis	↑↑↑↑	↑↑	History of drug/medication use within 3 months, often of a drug previously associated with liver injury	Absence of other diagnostic markers of liver disease
Fatty liver, nonalcohol	↑↑↑	↑↑↑	Late pregnancy, amiodarone	History of medication use, absence of other diagnostic markers of liver disease
Ischemic hepatitis	↑↑↑↑	↑↑↑↑	Severe hypotension	Absence of other diagnostic markers of liver disease; rapid improvement with resolution of hypotension
Acute liver failure	↑↑↑	↑	Ingestion of an associated agent; rapid progression from jaundice to encephalopathy (within 12-24 weeks)	Signs of impaired hepatic synthetic function

ALT = alanine aminotransferase; AST = aspartate aminotransferase.

TABLE 40 Characteristics of Chronic Hepatitis

Disease	Liver Enzyme Pattern		Historical Features	Diagnostic Findings
	ALT	**AST**		
Viral hepatitis B	↑↑	↑	Fecal oral exposure, born in an endemic area	HBsAg; may have hepatitis B DNA (HBV DNA)
Viral hepatitis C	↑↑	↑	Intravenous drug use, blood transfusion prior to 1992, born to an infected mother, other parenteral exposures	Anti-HCV, HCV RNA
Fatty liver, nonalcohol	↑↑	↑	Presence of metabolic syndrome (obesity, insulin resistance, hypertriglyceridemia)	Absence of other diagnostic markers of liver disease; hepatic imaging shows fat
Alcoholic liver disease	↑	↑↑	Remote history of heavy alcohol use	Absence of other diagnostic markers of liver disease
Autoimmune hepatitis	↑↑	↑	More common in women	Positive autoantibodies, including antinuclear and anti–smooth-muscle antibodies
Hemochromatosis	↑	↑	Arthritis, diabetes, family history	Elevated ferritin (>1000) and iron saturation (>55%), presence of *HFE* gene mutations
Wilson disease	↑↑	↑↑	Young, movement disorders, psychiatric disease, Kayser-Fleischer rings	Hemolysis, low alkaline phosphatase, low ceruloplasmin
α_1-Antitrypsin deficiency	↑	↑	Lung disease	Low serum A1AT, liver biopsy

ALT = alanine aminotransferase; AST = aspartate aminotransferase; HBsAg = hepatitis B surface antigen; Anti-HCV = antibody to hepatitis C virus; A1AT = α1-antitrypsin.

TABLE 41 Characteristics of Cholestatic Liver Diseases

Disease	Liver Biochemistry Pattern		Historical Features	Diagnostic Evaluation
	AP	**TBili**		
Primary biliary cirrhosis	↑↑	↑	More common in women, fatigue, pruritus	Antimitochondrial antibodies present in 95%, liver biopsy
Primary sclerosing cholangitis	↑↑	↑	More common in men, history of inflammatory bowel disease	Cholangiography
Large bile duct obstruction	↑↑	↑	Pain and fever	Cholangiography
Drug-induced cholestasis	↑↑	↑	History of drug/medication use within 3 months, often of a drug previously associated with liver injury	Improvement with cessation
Infiltrative liver disease	↑↑			CT, MRI, liver biopsy

AP = alkaline phosphatase; TBili = total bilirubin.

Diagnosis

The diagnosis of hepatitis B depends on accurately interpreting serologic tests (**Table 42**). The HBV DNA assays are commonly used. Most assays are based on polymerase chain reaction technology with lower limits of detection of 50 to 200 IU/mL (corresponding to 25 to 1000 copies/mL). Newer assays have increased sensitivity, with a lower limit of detection of 5 to 10 IU/mL. High levels of HBV DNA are associated with more severe disease, and treatment is monitored for effectiveness by dropping HBV DNA levels.

Various subgroups of infected patients reflect the natural history of infection: these subgroups include the immune-tolerant patient, the patient in a phase of immune clearance, and the inactive carrier. The immune-tolerant patient acquired HBV perinatally, is HBeAg positive, and has high levels of HBV DNA. As such patients age, the risk for active hepatitis increases. The patient with detectable HBeAg, high HBV DNA, elevated serum ALT levels, and inflammation on liver biopsy is in a phase of immune clearance (that is, the phase when the immune system is attempting to eliminate the virus). In this phase, elevations in liver enzymes may indicate the onset of HBeAg seroconversion. The inactive carrier is a patient in whom spontaneous seroconversion to HBeAg negativity occurs. In these patients, there is low or undetectable HBV DNA with little or no inflammation on liver biopsy. In this group, periodic reversions back to HBeAg

TABLE 42 Interpretation of Hepatitis B Diagnostic Serologies

Interpretation	HBsAg	Anti-HBs	IgM anti-HBc	IgG anti-HBc	HBeAg	Anti-HBe	HBV DNA
Acute infection	Positive	Negative	Positive	Negative	Positive	Negative	Positive
Chronic infection, nonreplicative	Positive	Negative	Negative	Positive	Negative	Positive	Negative
Chronic infection, replicative	Positive	Negative	Negative	Positive	Positive	Negative	Positive
Chronic infection, replicative, eAg negative	Positive	Negative	Negative	Positive	Negative	Positive	Positive
Immune, prior infection	Negative	Positive	Negative	Positive	Negative	Negative	Negative

HBsAg = hepatitis B surface antigen; Anti-HBs = antibody to hepatitis B surface antigen; IgM anti-HBc = IgG antibody to hepatitis B core antigen; IgG anti-HBc = IgG antibody to hepatitis B core antigen; HBeAg = hepatitis B e antigen; anti-HBe = antibody to hepatitis B e antigen; HBV DNA = hepatitis B virus DNA.

positivity may occur and be associated with elevation of liver tests and an increase in HBV DNA levels.

Patients with serologic findings characterized by the presence of HBsAg but absence of HBeAg may harbor HBV variants in the precore or promoter regions. Such patients tend to be older and have lower HBV DNA levels and more advanced disease.

Most adults who acquire hepatitis B develop symptoms during an incubation period of between 1 and 4 months after exposure. These symptoms are similar to those of hepatitis A and may include jaundice as well as other nonspecific constitutional complaints. In most patients the acute infection resolves within 6 months, that is, they become HBsAg-negative and develop anti-HBsAb. Patients with persistent HBsAg positivity beyond 6 months have chronic infection. Even in patients with chronic infection, HBsAg clears at a rate of approximately 0.5% per year. Various risk factors have been associated with the development of HBV-associated liver disease in patients with chronic infection (**Table 43**).

Management

Management of acute hepatitis B consists of history and physical examination and laboratory tests, including hepatitis B serologic tests and measurement of liver enzymes and prothrombin time. The clinical examination should be alert to the development of asterixis or any subtle neurologic changes, such as somnolence, or changes in mental status. Such clinical findings signal the onset of encephalopathy, which defines the patient as having fulminant hepatic failure. A patient suspected of being at high risk for development of fulminant hepatic failure should be transferred to a liver transplantation center for an expedited liver transplant evaluation. Transfer to a transplantation facility should ideally be arranged when a patient shows signs of worsening liver function marked by a rising prothrombin time and worsening liver function tests but before the development of mental status changes. After mental status changes develop, the patient needs to be closely monitored for the development of cerebral edema, which in

TABLE 43 Factors Associated with Progression of HBV-Associated Liver Disease

HBV-Associated Liver Disease	
Cirrhosis	**Hepatocellular Carcinoma**
Older age	Older age
Longer duration of infection	Male sex
High HBV DNA	High HBV DNA
Long-term alcohol use	Family history of hepatocellular carcinoma
HIV or HCV coinfection	Presence of cirrhosis
Smoking	History of reversion to HBeAg positivity from negative
	HBV genotype C
	Core promoter mutation
	HCV coinfection

HBV = hepatitis B virus; HBV DNA = hepatitis B virus DNA; HCV = hepatitis C virus; HBeAg = hepatitis B e antigen.

extreme cases can lead to cerebral herniation and death before liver transplantation can be performed. The physical examination should involve a thorough and frequent neurologic and ophthalmologic examination ensuring that the pupils remain equal and reactive to light. Dilation or fixation of the pupils is often a sign of worsening cerebral edema and may signify cerebral herniation.

If there are no clinical or laboratory findings consistent with liver failure, management consists of observation and follow-up testing. It is prudent to reassess the hepatitis B serologic profile every 1 to 3 months until the acute infection resolves (signified by loss of HBsAg and appearance of anti-HBsAb). Acute hepatitis B may rarely cause severe illness with impaired liver function. In such cases, antiviral therapy (usually consisting of lamivudine or entecavir in combination with adefovir) is indicated. This therapy offers the immediate potency of lamivudine/entecavir, with the reduced risk of resistance resulting from the combination with adefovir.

Management of patients with chronic hepatitis B virus infection with active viral replication and some degree of liver disease includes hepatitis B serologies to include an HBeAg and, if positive, HBV DNA. **Figure 28** shows a suggested management approach guided by the results of these tests.

The goals of therapy in chronic hepatitis B are suppression of viral replication, conversion of a positive HBeAg to negative, and mitigation of hepatic inflammation as evidenced by a reduction in the serum concentration of liver enzymes. An additional goal of therapy is sustained suppression of viral replication, indicated by lack of recurrent HBV DNA after antiviral therapy is discontinued. There are six approved therapies for chronic, replicative hepatitis B: interferon (standard and pegylated), lamivudine, adefovir, entecavir, and telbivudine (**Table 44**). The advantages of interferon are its limited duration of therapy, the lack of resistance, and the high response rate. However, patients with advanced liver disease or decompensated cirrhosis should not be given interferon therapy because they may be at risk for decompensation of liver disease and infection. In such patients, the oral agents are used; however, these agents are limited in their ability to achieve a sustained suppression of viral replication, cost, and propensity for drug resistance.

Screening and Prevention

Prevention of hepatitis B is predicated on providing prophylaxis and immunization to patients recently exposed or at risk for exposure. It is now universal practice to provide the hepatitis B vaccine to all newborns. However, those persons who were born before the onset of universal vaccination should be offered vaccination especially if they are at risk of being exposed. Such persons include all children and adolescents who did not get the vaccine when they were younger. Other people who should be vaccinated include sex partners of people infected with HBV, men who have sex with men, people who inject street drugs, people with more than one sex partner, people with chronic liver or kidney disease, people with jobs that expose them to human blood, household contacts of people infected with HBV, residents and staff in institutions for the developmentally disabled, kidney dialysis patients, people who travel to countries where HBV is common, and people with HIV infection. If someone is suspected of having been exposed to HBV and has not been previously vaccinated, that patient should receive passive immunization with hepatitis B immune globulin followed by the vaccination series as soon as possible.

Patients with established chronic infection must be monitored for the development of cirrhosis and hepatocellular carcinoma. Hepatic ultrasonography and measurement of serum α-fetoprotein every 6 to 12 months are adequate to screen for hepatocellular carcinoma. In general, patients with chronic infection should be counseled to avoid alcohol and be immunized against hepatitis A; close contacts should also be immunized. Infected pregnant women should be given hepatitis B immune globulin immediately after delivery, and the infant should be vaccinated, which can result in a 95% reduction in prenatal transmission.

Hepatitis C

Hepatitis C virus (HCV) infection is the most prevalent bloodborne infection in the United States, affecting an estimated 4 million persons. Most patients acutely infected with HCV are asymptomatic and do not clear the infection spontaneously; approximately 85% develop chronic infection. Of patients with chronic infection, 20% to 25% develop cirrhosis over 20 years. Of patients who develop cirrhosis, the risk for

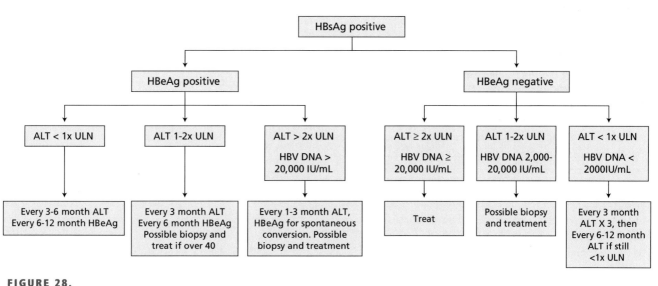

FIGURE 28.
Management of chronic hepatitis B virus infection.

ALT = alanine aminotransferase; AST = aspartate aminotransferase; HBeAg = hepatitis B e antigen; HBV = hepatitis B virus.

TABLE 44 Therapies for Chronic Hepatitis B

Therapy	Duration of Therapy		Potency	HBeAg + to − conversion	HBsAg + to − conversion	Resistance	Cost/Year
	HBeAg+	HBeAg−					
Subcutaneous Pegylated Interferon	1 year	1 year		27%	5-10%	None	$$$$
Lamivudine	Until 6 months after seroconversion to HBeAg−	Until loss of HBsAg	++	20%	Rare	Very high	$
Adefovir	Until 6 months after seroconversion to HBeAg−	Until loss of HBsAg	+	15%	Rare	Moderate	$$
Entecavir	Until 6 months after seroconversion to HBeAg−	Until loss of HBsAg	+++	21%	Rare	Low	$$$
Telbivudine	Until 6 months after seroconversion to HBeAg−	Until loss of HBsAg	++	22%	Rare	Low	$$

hepatocellular carcinoma is approximately 5% per year. The incidence of acute infections has been declining owing to better hygiene practices among injection drug users.

Patients at risk for hepatitis C include persons who have ever injected illegal drugs, have received hemodialysis, or were born to an infected mother and health care workers who have sustained needlestick accidents. The anti-HCV antibody test is the screening test for at-risk persons; a positive test in a person with one of the risk factors confirms exposure to the virus. The HCV RNA test is required to determine active infection rather than just exposure to the virus. In patients with none of the risk factors who have a positive anti-HCV antibody test and a negative HCV RNA test, the recombinant immunoblot assay (RIBA), which detects antibodies to any of several viral antigens, should be done. A positive RIBA, in the absence of detectable HCV RNA confirms that the patient has been infected with hepatitis C but has spontaneously cleared the infection.

Liver biopsy is not required for the diagnosis of hepatitis C infection; however, biopsy is useful in some patients to determine the extent of fibrosis and degree of inflammation. In infected patients with persistently normal liver tests, biopsy may also identify those who have minimal inflammation and the absence of fibrosis and may, therefore, forgo therapy and opt for observation. Enzyme levels might be normal in the presence of significant fibrosis rather than inflammation; patients with normal enzymes who undergo liver biopsy, therefore, may at that point opt for treatment based on advanced histology rather than false reassurance of normal aminotransferases.

Therapy for hepatitis C infection consists of the combination of pegylated interferon and ribavirin. The ideal candidate for therapy is the patient with detectable virus, some

indication of hepatic inflammation (elevated liver tests or inflammation on the biopsy), and no contraindication to therapy. The goal of therapy is to achieve a sustained virologic response, which is defined as undetectable HCV beyond 6 months after the end of treatment. Eleven distinct genotypes of the virus have been identified; the genotypes differ in their pathogenicity and in their response to therapy. The most important variable affecting the response rate is the genotype of the virus. Patients infected with genotype 1 have an approximately 45% sustained response rate if treated for 48 weeks. Patients who achieve at least a two-log reduction in the HCV RNA by the twelfth week have a higher likelihood (approximately 66%) of achieving a sustained response. Failure to achieve this degree of viral suppression by the twelfth week of therapy is associated with a sustained response of approximately 1%, and treatment can be stopped at that time. Patients with genotypes 2 and 3 have a sustained virologic response rate in excess of 80% and require only 24 weeks of therapy; the dosage of ribavirin can also be reduced in these patients.

Most patients treated with pegylated interferon and ribavirin experience side effects, which include a flulike illness, bone marrow suppression, depression, and thyroid inflammation. Contraindications to therapy include severe preexisting bone marrow suppression, severe depression, and advanced liver disease.

Hepatitis D

Hepatitis D virus (HDV or delta agent) depends upon the presence of HBsAg for its replication and, therefore, cannot survive on its own. In an HBV-infected patient, HDV infection may present as an acute hepatitis (in which case it is a coinfection) or an exacerbation of preexisting chronic hepatitis (in which case it is a superinfection). Patients with a history of injection drug use are at greatest risk for acquiring HDV infection.

Hepatitis E

Hepatitis E virus (HEV) can produce an acute hepatitis and is most likely to occur in residents of or recent travelers to underdeveloped nations. It results from fecal-oral transmission. Pregnant woman with acute HEV infection are at greatest risk for developing severe hepatitis or liver failure.

KEY POINTS

- Hepatitis A can rarely cause fulminant hepatic failure and almost always is self-limited.
- Chronic hepatitis B is defined by persistent viral replication 6 months after exposure.
- Treatment of chronic hepatitis B is recommended in patients with elevated viral load in combination with abnormal liver test results, and/or evidence of histologic inflammation or fibrosis.
- All patients with chronic liver disease should be vaccinated against hepatitis A and B.
- The ideal candidate for therapy is the patient with detectable virus, some indication of hepatic inflammation (elevated liver tests or inflammation on the biopsy), and no contraindication to therapy.
- Treatment regimen and length of treatment for hepatitis C depend on the genotype of the hepatitis C virus.

Alcohol- and Drug-Induced Liver Disease

Alcohol-Induced Liver Disease

Alcohol-induced liver injury begins with fatty infiltration and then progresses to inflammation, fibrosis, and cirrhosis. Men who consume more than 60 grams of ethanol a day (six or more alcoholic drinks) and women who consume more than 30 grams a day (approximately three alcoholic drinks) for more than 10 years are at risk for alcohol-related cirrhosis. Other factors, including genetic predisposition and underlying liver disease, may influence alcohol's effects on the liver.

Acute alcoholic hepatitis is diagnosed by finding hepatic inflammation in a patient with recent alcohol consumption. Inflammation is indicated by modest elevation of liver tests, with the serum AST concentration usually being less than 400 U/L and approximately twice the concentration of the serum ALT. Affected patients may present with leukocytosis, jaundice, hepatomegaly, and right upper quadrant pain, findings that may suggest infection. Liver biopsy specimen shows fat with acute inflammation and sinusoidal fibrosis. However, biopsy is not required in these patients,

and the risk is often greater than the benefit. Assessment of the severity of acute alcoholic hepatitis is important because, in addition to abstinence from alcohol and nutritional therapy, pharmacologic therapy may be beneficial. The discriminant function (DF) calculation, which helps to identify patients whose short-term survival is improved by corticosteroid therapy, is calculated as follows:

$$DF = 4.6 \text{ (prothrombin time [s] – control prothrombin time [s]) + serum bilirubin (mg/dL)}$$

Patients with a DF greater than 32 have a more than 50% short-term (30-day) mortality risk. Such patients are candidates for therapy with prednisone, 40 mg/d, for 30 days. Corticosteroid therapy is also beneficial in patients with acute alcoholic hepatitis and encephalopathy. Patients with renal failure were excluded from the initial corticosteroid trials, and some patients with infection may not be candidates for this therapy. An alternative therapy shown to have benefit on renal function and survival is pentoxifylline.

Drug- and Toxin-Induced Liver Injury

Any drug, including complementary and alternative medications, can cause liver injury through such mechanisms as the formation of protein adducts that disrupt cell membranes, an immunologic response, and the generation of injurious free radicals. Drug-induced liver injury may be either dose-dependent and predictable or idiosyncratic. The classic example of a dose-dependent hepatotoxin is acetaminophen; a massive single ingestion of more than 12 grams can lead to fatal hepatic necrosis. Acetaminophen toxicity is the most common cause of acute liver failure in the United States. Patients who consume alcohol or who are malnourished may experience acetaminophen injury, even in the absence of massive ingestion.

There are many idiosyncratic hepatotoxins, but a few have become known for their patterns of injury, sometimes termed "signature hepatotoxicity" (**Table 45**). However, other causes of liver injury must be excluded before a diagnosis of drug-induced hepatotoxicity is made, and it must be established that the patient took the drug before the onset of injury. **Figure 29** shows a differential diagnostic approach to a suspected case of drug-associated liver injury.

Treatment of drug-induced liver injury is primarily supportive and involves withdrawal of the suspected offending agent. However, there are a few specific antidotes, including *N*-acetylcysteine for acetaminophen intoxication and silymarin or penicillin for *Amanita phalloides* (mushroom) poisoning. If a drug is implicated as a cause of idiosyncratic liver injury, therapy with the agent must not be restarted because the hepatic response may be more vigorous and injurious than the initial event.

TABLE 45 Signature Pattern of Drug-induced Hepatotoxicity

Signature Pattern	Specific Agents
Acute liver injury	Acetaminophen, isoniazid
Chronic liver injury	Nitrofurantoin, minocycline, methyldopa
Fibrosis and Cirrhosis	Methotrexate, vitamin A
Jaundice	Erythromycin, amoxicillin/clavulanic acid, chlorpromazine, estrogens
Hypersensitivity	Phenytoin
Fatty liver	Amiodarone, tamoxifen, valproic acid, didanosine

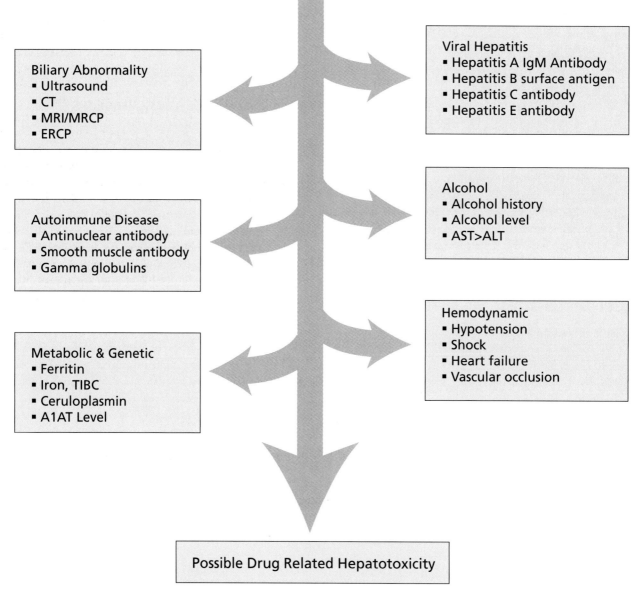

Liver Injury

Biliary Abnormality
- Ultrasound
- CT
- MRI/MRCP
- ERCP

Viral Hepatitis
- Hepatitis A IgM Antibody
- Hepatitis B surface antigen
- Hepatitis C antibody
- Hepatitis E antibody

Autoimmune Disease
- Antinuclear antibody
- Smooth muscle antibody
- Gamma globulins

Alcohol
- Alcohol history
- Alcohol level
- AST>ALT

Metabolic & Genetic
- Ferritin
- Iron, TIBC
- Ceruloplasmin
- A1AT Level

Hemodynamic
- Hypotension
- Shock
- Heart failure
- Vascular occlusion

Possible Drug Related Hepatotoxicity

FIGURE 29.
Diagnosing drug-related hepatotoxicity.

A1AT = α_1-antitrypsin; ALT = alanine aminotransferase; AST = aspartate aminotransferase; MRCP = magnetic resonance cholangiopancreatography; MRI = magnetic resonance imaging; TIBC = total iron binding capacity.

- Severe alcoholic hepatitis should be treated with corticosteroids if the calculated discriminant function (DF) is greater than 32 and there are no contraindications.
- Acetaminophen is the most common cause of drug-induced acute hepatic failure in the United States.
- Acetaminophen toxicity can occur at a lower dose in patients with concomitant malnutrition or alcohol use.

Autoimmune Hepatitis

Autoimmune hepatitis is a chronic condition characterized by fluctuating degrees of clinical, biochemical, and histologic manifestations. The diagnosis of autoimmune hepatitis depends on the presence of certain serologic and histologic findings and the exclusion of other causes of liver disease (**Table 46**).

Autoimmune hepatitis is more common in women and usually presents in adulthood. Approximately 50% of patients are asymptomatic and are diagnosed as a result of screening tests; some patients have nonspecific symptoms such as malaise, rash, and arthralgias. Findings on physical examination are also nonspecific. Some patients have only hepatomegaly, whereas others have jaundice or signs of hepatic decompensation, such as ascites or encephalopathy. The presence of other autoimmune disorders may also be a clue to the diagnosis. Patients who present with a very severe form of autoimmune hepatitis, either with or without cirrhosis, are at risk for hepatic necrosis and fulminant hepatic failure.

No single biochemical test can confirm or exclude the diagnosis. In most cases, serum aminotransferases are elevated, ranging from mild increases in serum concentrations to values greater than 1000 U/L. Hyperbilirubinemia may occur with a normal or near-normal serum alkaline phosphatase level. Certain autoantibodies may be elevated, including anti–smooth-muscle antibody, antinuclear antibody, and rarely anti–liver-kidney-microsomal antibody type 1 (anti-LKM1). In addition, serum IgG and IgM are also elevated. In some patients, the diagnosis has to be confirmed by histologic evaluation, which typically reveals a predominant lymphocytic and plasmacytic periportal infiltrate. However, in severe cases, the lobule can also be involved and hepatocyte necrosis occurs, with or without cirrhosis.

Early recognition of autoimmune hepatitis, especially in patients who present with a subfulminant course, can favorably affect the outcome. Prednisone is the first-line treatment of active disease and may induce remission. Generally, patients who present with greater than a fivefold increase in serum aminotransferase concentrations and who have active inflammation on liver biopsy specimen should be considered for treatment. Patients who present with very high aminotransferase levels can have up to a 40% 6-month mortality rate, and patients with hepatic necrosis on biopsy even without cirrhosis have a 45% 5-year mortality rate. The decision to initiate treatment is unambiguous in these patients. However, the decision to treat is less clear in patients with milder biochemical and/or histologic findings. Progression to cirrhosis is much less likely in these patients. The decision to start treatment in these patients with medications that have significant side effects must be individualized. Treatment is generally not recommended for patients with inactive cirrhosis, that is, advanced fibrosis in the absence of significant hepatitis.

TABLE 46 Features Supporting or Militating Against a Diagnosis of Autoimmune Hepatitis

Positive Features	Negative Features
Female sex	High serum alkaline phosphatase
Elevates serum aminotransferases	AMA seropositive
Low serum alkaline phosphatase	Positive hepatotropic virus serology
Hypergammaglobulinemia with elevated serum IgG	Positive drug/alcohol history
ANA, SMA, anti-LKM1, pANNA, or anti-SLA/LP positive	Morphologic changes in liver biopsy specimen suggestive of other cause
AMA seronegative	
Negative drug and alcohol history	
Interface hepatitis on liver biopsy	
Concurrent immunologic disorders in patient or family	
Compatible HLA markers	
Response to corticosteroid therapy	

AMA = antimitochondrial antibodies; ANA = antinuclear antibodies; SMA = anti–smooth muscle antibodies; anti-LKM1 = type 1 liver–kidney microsomal antibodies; pANNA = peripheral anti-neutrophil nuclear antibodies; anti-SLA/LP = anti-soluble liver antigen/liver-pancreas antigen antibodies; HLA = human leukocyte antigen.

Reproduced from McFarlane IG. Definition and classification of autoimmune hepatitis. Seminars in Liver Disease. 2002;22(4):317-24. [PMID: 12447704]. Copyright 2002, reprinted with permission from Thieme.

Treatment for autoimmune hepatitis consists of prednisone alone or more commonly in combination with azathioprine, with the goal of reducing the dosage of prednisone to the lowest level possible and continuing azathioprine. Treatment can be discontinued once remission is achieved; however, histologic remission often lags behind biochemical remission by at least 6 months. Relapse occurs in 20% to 100% of cases; however, reinitiation of treatment usually induces remission in patients who relapse. Indefinite low-dose treatment should be considered after relapse.

KEY POINTS

- Autoimmune hepatitis is more common in women and can lead to subfulminant liver failure.

- In most patients with autoimmune hepatitis, serum aminotransferase levels are elevated, ranging from mild increases in serum concentrations to values greater than 1000 U/L, along with hyperbilirubinemia with a normal or near-normal serum alkaline phosphatase level.

- Therapy for patients with autoimmune hepatitis consists of prednisone along with azathioprine, with the goal of reducing the prednisone dosage to the lowest effective dose.

Metabolic Liver Disease

Nonalcoholic Fatty Liver Disease

Nonalcoholic fatty liver disease consists of variable degrees of fat accumulation, inflammation, and fibrosis in the absence of significant alcohol intake. It is increasingly recognized as possibly the most common form of liver disease in the United States and accounts for a large portion of previously termed cryptogenic liver disease. Fatty liver disease in the absence of inflammation is more common in women than in men and occurs in 60% of obese patients. Steatohepatitis, the presence of inflammation in patients with fatty liver disease, occurs in about 20% of obese patients, and 2% to 3% have cirrhosis. This spectrum of fatty liver disease is most commonly seen in patients with underlying consequences of obesity, including insulin resistance, hypertension, and/or hyperlipidemia, the classic metabolic syndrome. It is estimated that up to 75% of patients with insulin resistance have some degree of fatty liver disease.

The pathophysiology of fatty liver disease is generally believed to be the result of a "two-hit" phenomenon, involving first the abnormal accumulation of fat in the liver from underlying risk factors. The second "hit" involves beta oxidation as well as lipid peroxidation of fatty acids, leading to the accumulation of reactive oxidative species and to mitochondrial and cell injury, which can progress to cirrhosis.

The diagnosis is usually made when patients with characteristic clinical risk factors are found to have mildly to moderately elevated serum aminotransferase concentrations.

Imaging with ultrasonography, CT, or MRI can confirm the presence of steatosis, although all these imaging modalities are considered insensitive for mild degrees of steatosis.

There is no definitive treatment for nonalcoholic fatty liver disease. The reduction of underlying risk factors is essential. Weight loss, exercise, and aggressive control of plasma glucose, lipids, and blood pressure are the mainstay of treatment. Antioxidant drugs, including S-adenosyl-L-methionine (SAMe) and betaine are ineffective. Silymarin is under study as a potential agent. Numerous studies have evaluated oral hypoglycemic drugs in this disorder. The thiazolidinediones have shown promising results, as have previous studies with metformin. Patients with fatty liver disease are not necessarily at increased risk from statin therapy than nonaffected patients, and statins are treatment options in these patients.

Wilson Disease

Wilson disease is a rare autosomal recessive disorder that affects 1 in 30,000 to 1 in 100,000 people. It is characterized by the reduced excretion of copper into the bile secondary to a transport abnormality, leading to the pathologic accumulation of copper in the liver and other tissues, particularly the brain. The gene responsible for Wilson disease is *ATP7B* located on chromosome 13. Affected patients can present with neurologic, psychiatric, ophthalmologic (**Figure 30**), hematologic, or hepatologic abnormalities.

Patients may present with fulminant disease, although underlying liver injury may already be established even in patients who present in this manner from previously undiagnosed and therefore untreated disease. Patients with fulminant hepatic failure from Wilson disease have elevated serum aminotransferase concentrations in the setting of hemolytic anemia. Such patients also usually have normal or even reduced serum alkaline phosphatase levels. These patients are at risk of progressive hepatic necrosis and may require urgent evaluation for liver transplantation. Less fulminant presentations can

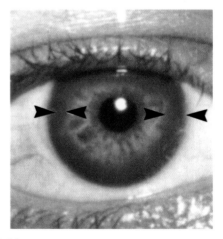

FIGURE 30.
Kayser-Fleischer ring characteristic of Wilson disease.
Note the circumferential discoloration that occurs at the sclera-iris border due to copper deposition in Descemet membrane.

be difficult to diagnose, and Wilson disease should be suspected in a young patient with liver disease and associated neuropsychiatric symptoms.

The diagnosis of Wilson disease can be confirmed by liver biopsy; nonspecific early histologic changes include the presence of steatosis or steatohepatitis. An elevated hepatic copper content in the absence of long-standing cholestasis, which can also elevate the intrahepatic copper content, is often diagnostic of the disease. Other helpful biochemical findings include a low serum ceruloplasmin and an increased serum copper concentration and urinary copper excretion.

Treatment of Wilson disease is directed at reducing the copper overload with the use of various copper chelators, such as penicillamine and trientine, or the use of agents that reduce copper absorption, such as zinc. Ammonium tetrathiomolybdate, which both chelates copper and reduces its absorption, is also effective, although it is not available in the United States. Use of penicillamine can be associated with hypersensitivity reactions, neurologic deterioration, and proteinuria, as well as blood dyscrasias. Therefore, trientine may be a better first-line agent.

First-degree relatives of patients with Wilson disease should be screened for the disorder by measurement of serum copper and ceruloplasmin and urinary copper excretion, along with liver tests.

Hereditary Hemochromatosis

Hereditary hemochromatosis is a common genetic disorder in white persons, characterized by excessive iron deposition in tissues, especially the liver, heart, pancreas, and pituitary gland. The iron overload in these tissues can lead to cirrhosis, heart disease, and diabetes mellitus. The gene mutations leading to phenotypic hereditary hemochromatosis are the C282Y mutation and H63D mutation of the *HFE* gene. Patients with abnormal liver studies should be screened for hemochromatosis. Patients who are suspected of having iron overload or patients older than 20 years who have a first-degree relative with hereditary hemochromatosis should also be screened (**Figure 31**).

Initial evaluation involves measuring the transferrin saturation and the serum ferritin. If the fasting transferrin saturation is greater than 50% in women and greater than 60% in men, the diagnosis should be strongly suspected. Other disease states that elevate the iron saturation include alcohol use, hepatitis C virus infection, fatty liver disease, and neoplasms. Patients with none of these other causes of elevated iron saturation should undergo genetic screening. Liver biopsy is indicated to determine the degree of fibrosis and in cases where the diagnosis remains uncertain. Iron will stain blue with Prussian blue stain. The hepatic iron index, which consists of the hepatic iron concentration in micromoles per gram divided by the patient's age in years, is used to evaluate for the degree of iron overload. A hepatic iron index greater than 1.9 μmol/g/y is diagnostic. Treatment of hereditary

hemochromatosis involves therapeutic phlebotomy to extract excess iron or to prevent accumulation of iron before symptomatic overload occurs (**Table 47**).

α_1-Antitrypsin Deficiency

α1-Antitrypsin deficiency affects the liver, lungs, and skin. Disease in the liver is the result of the abnormal accumulation of the variant protein, which accumulates in hepatocytes and can be identified as inclusions that stain with the PAS stain. Intrahepatic disease occurs only in patients with either the homozygous ZZ alleles or the heterozygous MZ alleles. The disease can manifest in early childhood or in adulthood and is associated with an increased risk of cirrhosis and hepatocellular carcinoma, which can occur even in the absence of cirrhosis. Although there is no treatment for hepatic disease, liver transplantation is an option for patients who develop hepatic decompensation. First-degree relatives of affected patients should be screened.

KEY POINTS

- Risk factors for nonalcoholic fatty liver disease include obesity, insulin resistance, and hyperlipidemia.
- Treatment of nonalcoholic fatty liver disease includes weight loss, exercise, statins and oral hypoglycemic agents.
- Patients with abnormal liver tests should be screened for hereditary hemochromatosis with iron studies.
- First-degree relatives of patients with hereditary hemochromatosis should be screened with iron studies.
- Wilson disease should be excluded in any young patient who presents with abnormal liver tests or acute liver failure especially with associated neuropsychiatric manifestations.
- α_1-Antitrypsin deficiency can manifest in early childhood or in adulthood and is associated with an increased risk for cirrhosis and hepatocellular carcinoma.

Cholestatic Liver Disease

Primary Biliary Cirrhosis

Primary biliary cirrhosis is a slowly progressive autoimmune disease that mainly affects women older than 25 years. In the United States, the reported prevalence is between 160 and 402 per million. There is a familial predisposition to the disorder, and female first-degree relatives of affected patients are at increased risk. Other risk factors include the presence of other autoimmune disorders, a history of tobacco smoking, a history of urinary tract infection, and possibly exposure to environmental causes, such as bacteria, viruses, and toxins.

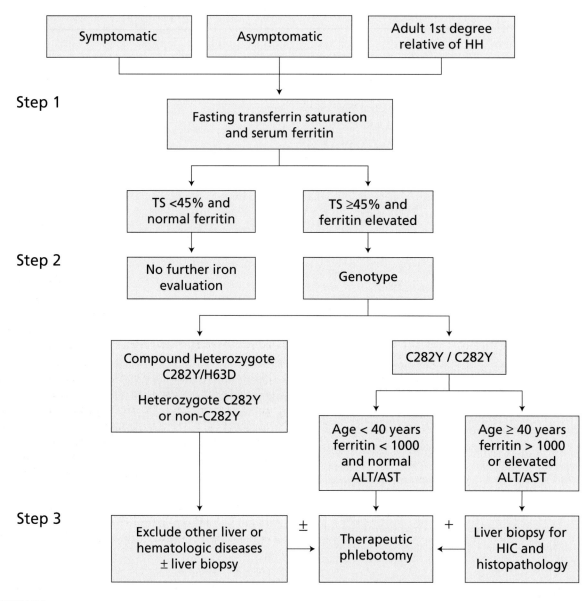

FIGURE 31.
Screening for hereditary hemochromatosis.

ALT = alanine aminotransferase; AST = aspartate aminotransferase; HH = hereditary hemochromatosis; HIC = hepatic iron concentration; TS = transferrin saturation.

Reproduced with permission from Tavill AS; American Association for the Study of Liver Diseases; American College of Gastroenterology; American Gastroenterological Association. Diagnosis and management of hemochromatosis. Hepatology. 2001 May;33(5):1321-1328. [PMID: 11343262] Copyright 2001, John Wiley & Sons.

Because of an increased awareness of the disease, more patients are being diagnosed while asymptomatic. In symptomatic patients, fatigue and pruritus are the most common presenting symptoms. Pruritus usually predates the development of jaundice, which can occur months to years thereafter. Other clinical findings largely depend on the stage of the disease. However, immune disorders such as hypothyroidism, Sjögren disease, sicca syndrome, and systemic sclerosis (scleroderma) may coexist with primary biliary cirrhosis. As the disease progresses, patients may manifest the effects of chronic malabsorption of the fat-soluble vitamins A, D, E, and K. They are thus likely to have hyperlipidemia and osteoporosis.

Other than excoriations from pruritus or xanthelasmas from hyperlipidemia, most patients do not have any characteristic findings until advanced liver disease develops.

Serologic and biochemical findings are useful in making the diagnosis of primary biliary cirrhosis. Most patients have antimitochondrial antibodies and elevated serum IgM and alkaline phosphatase levels, sometimes with elevations in aminotransferase levels. The serum bilirubin level is usually increased in progressive disease. Liver biopsy is not necessary to make the diagnosis of primary biliary cirrhosis, but it can help determine the stage of disease.

TABLE 47 Treatment of Iron Overload
Hereditary Hemochromatosis
One phlebotomy (removal of 500 mL of blood) weekly or biweekly
Check hematocrit before each phlebotomy; allow hematocrit to fall by no more than 20% of previous level
Check serum ferritin level every 10 to 12 phlebotomies
Stop frequent phlebotomy when serum ferritin level falls below 50 ng/mL (50 mg/L)
Continue phlebotomy at intervals to keep serum ferritin level between 25 and 50 ng/mL (25-50 mg/L)
Avoid vitamin C supplements
Secondary Iron Overload Due to Dyserythropoiesis
Deferoxamine, 20 to 40 mg/kg body weight per day
Consider follow-up liver biopsy to ascertain adequacy of iron removal
Avoid vitamin C supplements

Reproduced with permission from Tavill AS; American Association for the Study of Liver Diseases; American College of Gastroenterology; American Gastroenterological Association. Diagnosis and management of hemochromatosis. Hepatology. 2001;33:1321-8. [PMID:11343262]. Copyright 2001, John Wiley & Sons Inc.

The progression of primary biliary cirrhosis is affected by when the diagnosis is made and ursodeoxycholic acid therapy is initiated. A recent study found that initiation of treatment in patients diagnosed with stage I or II disease resulted in a long-term survival similar to that of healthy matched controls. However, in patients diagnosed with later stages, the disease is progressive, and despite treatment many of these patients die of the disease or require liver transplantation. More recently, a systematic review and meta-analysis of randomized controlled trials of treatment with ursodeoxycholic acid in patients with primary biliary cirrhosis calls into question the impact of this agent on the mortality and morbidity outcomes of these patients despite the stage of disease. Ursodeoxycholic acid acts as a choleretic agent, which if used early in the disease can delay progression. A large part of the treatment of advanced primary biliary cirrhosis involves symptom management. Pruritus that does not respond to topical lotions can be managed with bile acid resins such as cholestyramine. For refractory pruritus, hydroxyzine, rifampin, and opioid antagonists can be considered. Ursodeoxycholic acid also may have antipruritic effects. Patients should be screened for deficiencies of vitamins A, D, E, and K, and appropriate supplementation should be instituted. Although patients with primary biliary cirrhosis often have hypercholesterolemia, they have not been shown to have increased cardiovascular risk as a result of the hypercholesterolemia.

Primary Sclerosing Cholangitis

Primary sclerosing cholangitis is a chronic condition that usually presents in the fourth or fifth decade of life; it is more common in men than in women and is characterized by progressive bile duct inflammation and destruction and ultimately fibrosis of both the intrahepatic and extrahepatic bile ducts, leading to cirrhosis. The cause of the disorder is unknown, but there is a strong association with ulcerative colitis, which is present in 80% of patients with primary sclerosing cholangitis. However, the severity of ulcerative colitis does not correlate with the severity of primary sclerosing cholangitis, and treatment of ulcerative colitis does not significantly affect the prognosis of cholangitis.

The most common symptoms of primary sclerosing cholangitis are pruritus and fatigue; as the disease progresses, most patients develop jaundice. Cholangiocarcinoma occurs in approximately 10% of affected patients, is not always related to severity of disease, and is associated with a poor prognosis. Primary sclerosing cholangitis is also commonly complicated by cholangitis and is frequently a consequence of endoscopic intervention. The disorder variably affects the bile ducts: 75% of patients have involvement of both large and small ducts; 15% have involvement of the small ducts only; and 10% have involvement of the large duct only.

The diagnosis of primary sclerosing cholangitis depends on detecting multifocal strictures with beading of the bile ducts on cholangiographic imaging usually with ERCP (**Figure 32**).

This classic finding often occurs in association with cholestatic biochemical abnormalities, including elevated alkaline phosphatase with mild elevations of aminotransferase levels. Liver biopsy is not required to make the diagnosis, and in patients with small duct involvement, the liver biopsy specimen may appear normal. In disease affecting larger ducts, biopsy specimen shows the classic "onion-skin" lesion, which is caused by concentric fibrosis of the bile ducts. As the disease progresses, the smaller involved ducts become obliterated, and the portal tracts become infiltrated with inflammatory cells, which leads to periportal fibrosis, bridging fibrosis, and ultimately cirrhosis.

No medical therapy affects the natural history of primary sclerosing cholangitis or the prognosis of affected patients. Ursodeoxycholic acid therapy may alleviate the biochemical abnormalities associated with the disease, but it does not affect the clinical or histologic course.

Patients with primary sclerosing cholangitis, like those with advanced primary biliary cirrhosis, develop steatorrhea with complications from deficiencies of fat-soluble vitamins.

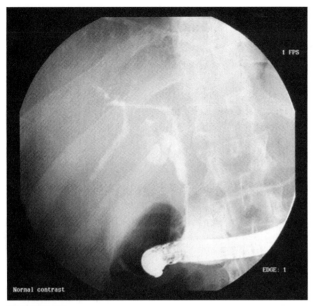

FIGURE 32.
Endoscopic retrograde cholangiopancreatography showing primary sclerosing cholangitis.
Note the beading of the bile ducts.

Complications related to progressive duct destruction include recurrent cholangitis, bile duct stones, large strictures, and cholangiocarcinoma. Dominant strictures can sometimes be managed by placement of endoscopic stents across the stricture. However, liver transplantation is the only treatment that reverses the complications of end-stage liver disease in primary sclerosing cholangitis, and patients who undergo transplantation have a favorable survival outcome.

KEY POINTS

- Primary biliary cirrhosis more commonly affects women than men and is associated with an elevated antimitochondrial antibody titer.
- Ursodeoxycholic acid therapy may affect long-term outcome in patients with primary biliary cirrhosis.
- Primary sclerosing cholangitis can be identified radiographically by the classic beads-on-a-string appearance of the bile ducts.
- Primary sclerosing cholangitis is commonly associated with inflammatory bowel disease, especially ulcerative colitis.
- There is no specific medical treatment for primary sclerosing cholangitis.

Complications of Liver Disease

Portal Hypertension and Gastroesophageal Varices

Cirrhosis is the predominant cause of portal hypertension, which results from a combination of increased splanchnic blood flow secondary to splanchnic vasodilation and increased resistance to blood flow secondary to intrahepatic fibrosis and endothelial dysfunction. Portal hypertension is calculated by measuring the pressure gradient in the liver, that is, the difference in pressure between the portal vein and the hepatic veins. A gradient greater than 6 mm Hg defines portal hypertension. Thrombocytopenia in the setting of cirrhosis should raise suspicion for the presence of portal hypertension and congestive splenomegaly.

One of the most significant complications of portal hypertension is gastroesophageal variceal bleeding. Although varices can occur anywhere along the gastrointestinal tract, including the small intestine and the rectum, the most dangerous site relative to bleeding is the area nearest the gastroesophageal junction. The risk for variceal bleeding is increased when the pressure gradient exceeds 12 mm Hg. The lifetime risk for a first-time variceal bleed in the setting of cirrhosis is 30% and carries a mortality risk of 30% to 50%. Therefore, primary prophylaxis is crucial. All patients with a diagnosis of cirrhosis should undergo endoscopic screening for varices. Primary prophylaxis with a nonselective β-blocker, such as nadolol or propranolol, should be initiated if large varices are detected, especially if they have stigmata of bleeding such as red wale signs (longitudinal red streaks on the variceal surface). Primary prophylaxis decreases the risk of a first variceal bleed by 30% to 40%.

An acute variceal bleed should be treated in the intensive care unit. Appropriate resuscitation should be performed with correction of hypovolemia and coagulopathy. Medical treatment includes initiation of prophylactic antibiotics because these patients are at increased risk of bacterial infection. Splanchnic vasoconstrictors such as octreotide should also be used to reduce portal blood flow. However, the mainstay of treatment of an acute variceal bleed is endoscopic band ligation and/or endoscopic sclerotherapy. Esophageal band ligation is the first line of endoscopic therapy because of the complications associated with sclerotherapy. If band ligation does not control primary bleeding, or if bleeding recurs or is due to gastric varices, balloon tamponade followed by portal decompression by placement of a transjugular intrahepatic portosystemic shunt (TIPS) can be performed. The incidence of rebleeding is reported to be as high as 70%, and the use of nonselective β-blockers to prevent rebleeding is recommended; the goal of this therapy is a reduction in the heart rate of 25% or attaining a systolic blood pressure of 90 mm Hg or less.

Ascites

Ascites is the most common complication of portal hypertension secondary to cirrhosis. Any patient who develops new-onset ascites should undergo diagnostic paracentesis. Coagulopathy in the absence of disseminated intravascular coagulation is not a contraindication to paracentesis. Initial evaluation of ascitic fluid should include measurement of albumin along with cell count with differential, Gram stain, and culture (**Table 48**). The serum-to-ascites albumin

TABLE 48 Test Used in Evaluation of Ascites
Initial Evaluation
Protein
Albumin
Cytology
Cell count with differential
Gram stain
Blood culture
Special Tests
Tuberculosis culture
Repeat cytology
Bilirubin
Amylase
Triglycerides

gradient is calculated by subtracting the ascitic fluid albumin level from the serum albumin level. A gradient >1.1 indicates that the patient has portal hypertension (**Table 49**).

Management of ascites secondary to portal hypertension involves dietary restriction of sodium to less than 2 g/d and implementation of diuretics. A combination of spironolactone and furosemide as a one-time morning dose is the initial therapy. The dose-limiting factor of diuretic therapy is the development of significant hyponatremia and/or renal insufficiency or failure to achieve a response at very high doses. The occurrence of such complications defines diuretic-resistant ascites or refractory ascites. In this setting large volume paracentesis can be performed with the use of albumin supplementation when greater than 5 liters of fluid are removed at one time to prevent hemodynamic instability. A TIPS can also be placed; however, this can result in worsening synthetic function and difficult-to-manage encephalopathy and therefore should be considered with caution in advanced cirrhosis.

Spontaneous Bacterial Peritonitis

Spontaneous bacterial peritonitis, which occurs most commonly in patients with cirrhosis and ascites, is associated with significant morbidity and mortality. Suggestive symptoms include fever, abdominal tenderness or pain, altered mental status, diarrhea, and paralytic ileus. The criteria for the diagnosis are an ascitic fluid absolute neutrophil count >250/µL

TABLE 49 Disease Associations with Serum to Ascites Albumin Gradient (SAAG)	
SAAG >1.1	**SAAG <1.1**
Cirrhosis	Nephrotic syndrome
Heart failure	Peritoneal carcinomatosis
Noncirrhotic portal hypertension	Pancreatitis
Budd-Chiari Syndrome	Tuberculosis
Infiltrative hepatic disease	Serositis

or a positive ascitic fluid culture. Treatment consists of a third-generation cephalosporin for at least 5 days. Diagnostic paracentesis should be repeated to document successful therapy if the patient does not show clinical improvement. Any patient who has had spontaneous bacterial peritonitis should receive antibiotic prophylaxis indefinitely. Any patient who is hospitalized and has a total ascitic fluid protein concentration <1 g/dL should also receive antibiotic prophylaxis, even in the absence of documented spontaneous bacterial peritonitis. Patients with low-protein ascites should receive either daily low-dose or weekly high-dose fluoroquinolones as prophylaxis during hospitalization. Patients with a history of spontaneous bacterial peritonitis should be maintained on this antibiotic long term.

Hepatorenal Syndrome

The hepatorenal syndrome is a form of functional renal failure in patients with cirrhosis and portends a poor prognosis in the absence of liver transplantation. It is largely a result of splanchnic vasodilation and the consequential activation of the renin–angiotensin system, leading to renal vasoconstriction. The syndrome is a diagnosis of exclusion characterized by a urine sodium concentration <10 meq/L (10 mmol/L) and the absence of intrinsic renal injury. Common precipitating events include the use of NSAIDs or the development of spontaneous bacterial peritonitis, especially in the absence of concomitantly administered albumin. The syndrome is reversible in its early stages with successful liver transplantation. There are two types of hepatorenal syndrome: type 1 is an acute progressive form associated with a 2-week mortality rate of 80%; type 2, which is more indolent, often occurs in the setting of diuretic-resistant ascites and has a better prognosis. Combined treatment with the systemic vasoconstrictor midodrine, the splanchnic vasoconstrictor octreotide, and albumin has been shown to reverse renal failure due to the hepatorenal syndrome; however, liver transplantation remains the most successful long-term treatment.

Hepatopulmonary Syndrome

The hepatopulmonary syndrome, which is characterized by hypoxemia resulting from intrapulmonary vasodilation, occurs in up to 25% of patients with advanced cirrhosis. The syndrome should be suspected in patients with cirrhosis who have a Pao_2 less than 70 mm Hg or a alveolar-arterial oxygen gradient greater than 20 mm Hg. Most patients present with signs of liver disease, but dyspnea is the presenting symptom in some patients. Other forms of intrinsic lung disease should be excluded before this diagnosis is made. Like the hepatorenal syndrome, the hepatopulmonary syndrome, if not significantly advanced, can resolve with liver transplantation. The diagnosis is confirmed by documenting the presence of intrapulmonary shunting by either a bubble echocardiographic study or a ^{99}Tc macro-aggregated albumin lung perfusion scan. In the bubble study, the observation of bubbles of agitated saline in the left side of the heart within 3 to 6 beats is diagnostic. Similarly, detecting albumin in the brain upon injection into the systemic circulation suggests the presence of a significant intrapulmonary shunt. After the diagnosis is confirmed, the patient should be evaluated for liver transplantation. However, severe disease, defined by a Pao_2 less than 50 mm Hg or shunt greater than 20% on lung perfusion scan, is associated with a high mortality rate.

Hepatic Encephalopathy

Hepatic encephalopathy is a potentially reversible complication of cirrhosis that can manifest variously as mild personality changes, reduced memory, or sleep perturbations or as frank coma. The pathophysiology of hepatic encephalopathy is complex and incompletely understood but is believed to consist predominantly of the accumulation of glutamine in the brain secondary to increased ammonia levels. The increased concentration of glutamine causes brain edema, which leads to encephalopathy. Hepatic encephalopathy can be precipitated by gastrointestinal bleeding, dehydration, and electrolyte abnormalities, often as a result of over-aggressive diuresis, spontaneous bacterial peritonitis, or renal failure, or iatrogenically as a result of a TIPS placement.

There are various treatment modalities for encephalopathy. Nonabsorbable disaccharides such as lactulose are used to decrease the gut ammonia. Antibiotics, such as neomycin, metronidazole, and rifaximin, have also been used. Certain antibiotics, however, especially neomycin, should be used with caution because they can precipitate renal failure. Other agents used for treatment of hepatic encephalopathy include L-ornithine L-aspartate, and benzoate and benzodiazepine receptor antagonists (such as flumazenil), but large clinical trials documenting their reliable efficacy are lacking.

Hepatocellular Carcinoma

Hepatocellular carcinoma is the most common primary intrahepatic tumor and the fastest growing cause of cancer-related death in men in the United States. The cancer usually develops in patients with advanced chronic liver disease; however, patients with hepatitis B may develop hepatocellular carcinoma in the absence of advanced liver disease. Hepatocellular carcinoma in patients with hepatitis C usually occurs in the setting of cirrhosis at a rate of 3% to 5% per year. In the United States, the rate of hepatocellular carcinoma in Asians is two times greater than the rate in black Americans whose rate is two times greater than that of whites. Hepatocellular carcinoma is more common in men than in women. Hepatocellular cancers derive their blood supply through neovascularization, whereby the cancer develops a new blood supply fed through small branches of the hepatic artery. It is this characteristic vascular supply that helps identify potential cancers on contrast-enhanced imaging, such as triple-phase CT and gadolinium MRI. Although these modalities tend to be better at identifying hepatocellular carcinoma than ultrasonography, the current screening guidelines for hepatocellular carcinoma recommend ultrasonography and measurement of serum

α-fetoprotein every 6 months. Detecting a suspicious lesion on ultrasonography or a very elevated serum α-fetoprotein level should prompt confirmatory imaging with MRI or CT (**Figure 33**).

Biopsy is rarely needed to confirm the diagnosis, and there is the small but real chance of tumor seeding on biopsy, which needs to be considered especially if the patient meets the criteria for liver transplantation. A patient should be referred for transplantation if the tumor meets the Milan criteria, that is, one tumor no larger than 5 cm in diameter or no more than three tumors, none of which is larger than 3 cm. The post-transplant survival rate in such patients is similar to that of patients transplanted without malignancy: 85% at 1 year, 75% at 3 years, and 67% at 5 years. Surgical resection of an isolated tumor is less likely to be tolerated in patients with cirrhosis and is more often considered in patients without advanced chronic liver disease. Patients who undergo surgical resection have a 50% 5-year survival rate.

Local ablative treatments include radiofrequency ablation, percutaneous ethanol ablation, or transarterial chemoembolization. The two former options are reserved for patients who have no more than two tumors, both less than 3 cm. In chemoembolization, a chemotherapeutic agent along with lipiodol is injected into the hepatic artery and the artery is occluded. The effect on survival of these local modalities needs further study.

KEY POINTS

- Primary prophylaxis with nonselective β-blockers should be given to all patients with large varices on endoscopy and continued indefinitely after a variceal bleed.

- Esophageal band ligation is the treatment of choice for an esophageal variceal bleed; transjugular intrahepatic portosystemic shunt (TIPS) should be reserved for patients who fail to respond to endoscopic therapy.

- New-onset ascites should be evaluated by measuring ascitic fluid albumin along with cell count with differential, Gram stain, and culture.

- Patients with spontaneous bacterial peritonitis should receive long-term antibiotic therapy.

- Development of the hepatorenal syndrome is an indication of progressive liver disease and is associated with a high mortality rate in the absence of liver transplantation.

- The hepatopulmonary syndrome should be suspected in patients with cirrhosis who have a Pao_2 less than 70 mm Hg or an alveolar-arterial oxygen gradient greater than 20 mm Hg.

- Any patient with cirrhosis is at risk for hepatocellular carcinoma and should be screened with ultrasonography and measurement of serum α-fetoprotein every 6 months.

- Patients with hepatitis B virus infection can develop hepatocellular carcinoma in the absence of cirrhosis.

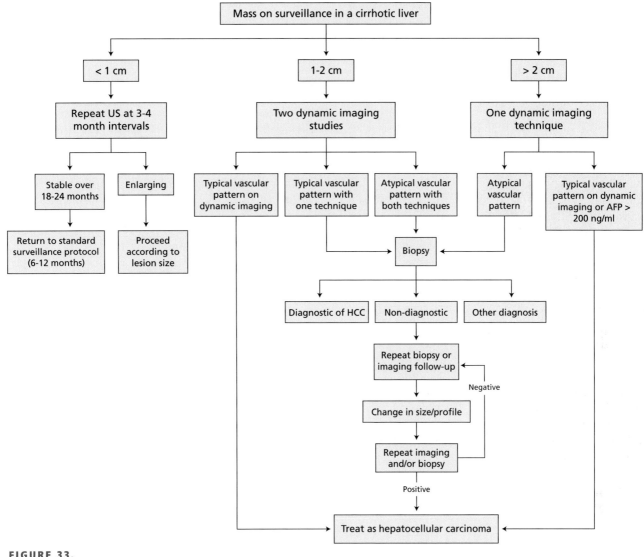

FIGURE 33.
Evaluation of hepatocellular carcinoma.

AFP = α-fetoprotein; HCC = hepatocellular carcinoma; US = ultrasonography.

Reprinted from Varela M, Sanchez W, Bruix J, Gores GJ. Hepatocellular carcinoma in the setting of live transplantation. Liver Transpl. 2006;12:1028-1036. [PMID: 16799950] Copyright 2006, John Wiley & Sons. Reproduced with permission of Blackwell Publishing Ltd.

Fulminant Hepatic Failure

Fulminant hepatic failure consists of the rapid development of acute or subacute liver injury accompanied by mental status changes. The time between the onset of liver disease and the development of encephalopathy is usually weeks, but encephalopathy can develop over a period of 3 to 6 months. One classification of fulminant hepatic failure defines the development of jaundice to encephalopathy within 1 week as hyperacute, within 4 weeks as acute, and within 1 to 12 weeks as subacute. Patients with hyperacute liver failure have the best survival rate. Fulminant hepatic failure is rare in the United States and accounts for 6% of liver disease–related deaths and 6% of liver transplants. The most common cause of fulminant hepatic failure in the United States is acetaminophen toxicity,

which can occur even in patients taking therapeutic doses of acetaminophen if they have underlying liver disease (especially alcoholic liver disease) (**Table 50**). Therapy with *N*-acetylcysteine is effective for the fulminant hepatic failure caused by acetaminophen toxicity. The only other effective medical treatments are penicillamine or silymarin (milk thistle) for *Amanita* mushroom poisoning and acyclovir for herpesvirus-induced liver failure. In other cases, liver transplantation is the only effective therapy; the survival rate with transplantation for fulminant hepatic failure is 65% to 80%. Therefore, recognition is important so that affected patients can be transferred to a liver transplantation center.

The development of cerebral edema is the most common cause of death in patients with fulminant hepatic failure.

TABLE 50 Causes of Fulminant Hepatic Failure

Viral Hepatitis
  Hepatitis A, B, C, D, and E virus
  Herpes simplex virus
  Cytomegalovirus
  Epstein-Barr virus
  Herpes zoster virus

Drugs
  Acetaminophen
  Isoniazid
  Tetracycline
  3,4-methylenedioxy-N-methylamphetamine (MDMA, the street drug Ecstasy)

Toxins
  Amanita phalloides
  Bacillus cereus

Budd-Chiari Syndrome

Veno-occlusive Disease

Acute Fatty Liver of Pregnancy

HELLP Syndrome (hemolysis, elevated liver enzymes, low platelets)

Wilson Disease

Management of cerebral edema includes reducing stimulation, elevating the patient's head, preventing fluid overload, and inducing hypothermia. Pharmacotherapy for cerebral edema includes use of mannitol. Other features of fulminant hepatic failure include worsening coagulopathy; metabolic abnormalities, including hypoglycemia and electrolyte abnormalities; and multiorgan involvement, including renal failure, high cardiac output, and lactic acidosis.

Liver Transplantation

Patients with advanced cirrhosis should be evaluated for liver transplantation. The two types of liver transplantation are deceased-donor transplant, in which the entire liver from a donor is placed into the recipient and live-donor transplant, in which part of the liver from a compatible donor is used. The 1-year patient survival rate for liver transplantation is 84% and higher in some centers. Donor livers are allocated by the United Network for Organ Sharing (UNOS) through a point system referred to as the Model for End-stage Liver Disease (MELD). The MELD score is a calculation based on the INR (or prothrombin time) and the serum total bilirubin and creatinine levels (a calculator is available at www.unos.org/resources/meldPeldCalculator.asp).

Additional points are given to patients with hepatocellular carcinoma within the Milan criteria (one nodule less than or equal to 5 cm, up to three separate nodules none larger than 3 cm).

The evaluation for liver transplantation involves a multidisciplinary approach and includes hepatologists, surgeons, radiologists, and social workers. There are various contraindications to liver transplantation (**Table 51**), but patients who are acceptable candidates require ongoing evaluation and medical management to ensure they remain acceptable candidates.

KEY POINTS

- Any patient suspected of fulminant hepatic failure should be transferred to a liver transplant center.
- Liver transplantation should be considered for any patient with advanced cirrhosis and evidence of clinical or biochemical decompensation.
- Liver transplantation for disorders other than fulminant hepatic failure is based on the Model for End-stage Liver Disease (MELD) score.

Hepatic Tumors, Cysts, and Abscesses

Common benign liver lesions include cysts, adenomas, focal nodular hyperplasia, and abscesses. Hepatic cysts are by far the most common of these lesions and are usually detected incidentally on imaging obtained for other reasons. The cysts are usually asymptomatic unless they become very large and cause symptoms from mass effect on other organs. If a cyst becomes symptomatic or if there is evidence that it may not be a simple cyst, resection should be considered. However, cystadenomas may undergo malignant transformation and therefore, if suspected, should be resected. Cystadenomas can be differentiated from simple cysts by their radiographic appearance; cystadenomas have thicker irregular walls than simple cysts or internal thickened irregular septations.

Focal nodular hyperplasia, a nonmalignant tumor more common in women than in men, is usually detected on imaging by the identification of a central scar. On pathologic examination, it appears as a large central artery running through this central scar that radiates outward as smaller vessels which run through fibrous tissue throughout the lesion, mimicking cirrhosis. The lesion is not hormone-responsive and, therefore, affected women do not have to discontinue birth control. The lesion should be resected only in the rare cases in which it causes mass effect on other organs.

TABLE 51 Contraindications to Liver Transplantation

Severe cardiac/pulmonary disease

Extrahepatic malignancy (excluding some skin cancers)

Advanced hepatocellular cancer

Cholangiocarcinoma

Systemic infections

Morbid obesity

Ongoing substance abuse

Hepatic adenomas, which are also more common in women than in men, are hormone-responsive and have a small but real malignant potential. Histologically, adenomas are characterized by sheets of benign-appearing hepatocytes and an absence of any biliary structures. Adenomas may rupture, leading to intraperitoneal bleeding; the risk of rupture is increased during pregnancy, and adenomas should be resected in women considering pregnancy. An alternative approach in women not seeking pregnancy who have adenomas that are less than 5 cm in diameter and are taking hormones is to stop hormone treatment and repeat imaging after some time to determine whether the lesion has become smaller.

Hepatic abscesses usually arise either from direct seeding of infected peritoneum or from hematogenous spread. The most common abdominal infections found to be associated with the development of hepatic abscesses are appendicitis and cholangitis; however, a cause is not found in up to 40% of patients. Pyogenic abscess should be considered in any patient who presents with fever, previous infection, and right upper quadrant discomfort. The most common organisms implicated in pyogenic liver abscesses include *Escherichia coli* and anaerobes; however, there have been increasing reports of pyogenic liver abscesses caused by *Klebsiella pneumoniae* in Japan, and therefore this should be taken into consideration when choosing antibiotic regimens. Most pyogenic abscesses are also managed with percutaneous drainage. Pus should be cultured for aerobes and anaerobes to guide antibiotic therapy.

Amebic liver abscesses are caused by *Entamoeba histolytica*, and usually occur in patients who are from countries where amebiasis is endemic (such as Mexico and the countries of South America) or who have recently traveled to these countries. This infection also seems to be more common in patients who are HIV positive. Treatment of amebic liver abscess is important to prevent growth and rupture of the abscess, which can be life-threatening. In patients who have been in an endemic area and who have fever and right upper quadrant pain, serologic tests for *E. histolytica* are appropriate.

If the test is positive, treatment with metronidazole should be instituted.

KEY POINTS

- Hepatic adenomas carry a risk for bleeding and malignant transformation, and therefore should be considered for resection.
- Women with hepatic adenomas who are taking oral contraceptives should discontinue hormone treatment.
- Focal nodular hyperplasia does not undergo malignant transformation and is not hormone-responsive.
- Nonobstructing simple hepatic cysts do not require intervention.
- Hepatic abscess is often the result of hematogenous or local spread of extrahepatic infection such as appendicitis or cholangitis; most hepatic abscesses require drainage.

Pregnancy-Related Liver Disease

There are various liver diseases associated with pregnancy (**Table 52**). Cholestasis of pregnancy is the most common and most benign pregnancy-related liver disease. The disorder, which has a genetic predisposition, is usually seen in the late second or third trimester of pregnancy. Affected women usually present with pruritus and cholestasis with total bilirubin levels not exceeding 10 mg/dL (171 mmol/L). In some patients, serum aminotransferases are mildly elevated. Although most cases are benign, there is an increase in fetal mortality and an association with preterm delivery. Treatment consists of symptomatic relief to the mother, with ursodeoxycholic acid being the first drug of choice.

The HELLP syndrome, which consists of microangiopathic hemolytic anemia, elevated liver tests, and a low platelet count, is a significantly more serious pregnancy-related liver

TABLE 52 Characteristics of Pregnancy-Related Liver Diseases			
	Cholestasis of Pregnancy	**HELLP**	**Acute Fatty Liver of Pregnancy**
Trimester	Third	Second and third and after delivery	Third
Bilirubin	< 6 mg/dL (103 µmol/L), increased bile acids	2-3 mg/dL (34-51 µmol/L)	Elevated
Aminotransferases	<500 U/L	<500 U/L	500-1000 U/L
Other Abnormal Laboratory Studies		Low platelet count Microangiopathic hemolytic anemia	Increased leukocyte count Increased uric acid Decreased glucose
Treatment	Ursodeoxycholic acid	Delivery	Delivery
Prognosis	Good Can recur	High fetal mortality Recurs Can lead to fulminant hepatic failure	High fetal mortality Recurs; may lead to fulminant hepatic failure

HELLP = hemolysis, elevated liver enzymes, low platelets syndrome.

disease. The disorder also occurs mainly in the second and third trimester of pregnancy and often in the presence of preeclampsia and eclampsia. It should be suspected in any patient who presents with clinical signs of preeclampsia and develops signs of acute liver disease. The syndrome is associated with a significant degree of fetal morbidity and a high risk of fetal and maternal mortality. The only treatment is immediate delivery of the fetus. In extreme cases, despite delivery the mother develops fulminant hepatic failure and requires liver transplantation.

Acute fatty liver of pregnancy is rare, occurring in fewer than 1 in 16,000 deliveries. It usually occurs in the third trimester, and, like the HELLP syndrome, it can be associated with preeclampsia. It usually occurs in first pregnancies or in women pregnant with more than one fetus. The cause is believed to be associated with a defect in the beta oxidation of fatty acids in the fetus leading to acute accumulation of hepatic fat and the formation of microsteatosis in the mother. Presenting symptoms are usually vague; however, biochemical markers can be significantly abnormal including serum aminotransferase levels up to 1000 U/L as well as a significant elevation in the bilirubin. The development of encephalopathy or coagulopathy requires emergent delivery. Despite delivery, emergent liver transplantation for the mother may be rarely required.

KEY POINTS

- Cholestasis of pregnancy is the most common and benign pregnancy-related liver disease presenting as pruritus and cholestasis in the late second or third trimester of pregnancy.

- The HELLP syndrome consists of microangiopathic hemolytic anemia, elevated liver tests, and a low platelet count.

- Delivery is the treatment of choice for the HELLP syndrome and acute fatty liver of pregnancy.

Gallstones and Acute Cholecystitis

The prevalence of gallstones in the United States ranges from 5% for black men to 27% for Mexican-American women. Native Americans have the highest prevalence: 30% in men and 64% in women. However, most gallstones are asymptomatic, the risk of developing symptoms being approximately 1% to 2% per year. Most patients with asymptomatic stones are managed conservatively. Bile binding agents are unlikely to be extremely effective in dissolving stones but may help prevent development of additional ones.

There are three main types of gallbladder stones: cholesterol stones, brown pigment stones, and black pigment stones. Cholesterol stones, which are the most common type, classically occur in older obese women with a family history of gallstones. Brown pigment stones usually occur in the setting of biliary infections. Black pigment stones form as a consequence of increase in bilirubin load as occurs in hemolytic anemia. Microlithiasis, or sludge, can result in similar symptoms and complications as those in gallstones.

Complications of Gallstones

Complications of gallstones include cholecystitis, choledocholithiasis, Mirizzi syndrome, cholecystenteric fistula, and acute pancreatitis.

Acute Cholecystitis

Acute cholecystitis is the most common complication of gallstones and one of the most common causes of surgical emergencies. It is usually caused by the impaction of a gallstone in the neck of the gallbladder, thus inhibiting biliary drainage and leading to distention and edema of the gallbladder wall. Clinical symptoms usually include right upper quadrant abdominal pain associated with nausea, vomiting, and fever. On physical examination, deep palpation during inspiration can elicit pain in the right upper quadrant and cause inspiratory arrest, a finding known as a Murphy sign, which has a specificity of 79% to 96% for acute cholecystitis. The leukocyte count is elevated in acute cholecystitis, but there are no blood tests specific to the diagnosis. On ultrasonography, characteristic findings include an enlarged gallbladder often with a thickened wall. There is often evidence of stones or debris in the gallbladder and a reproducible sonographic Murphy sign. If the diagnosis is uncertain after ultrasonography, cholescintigraphy (HIDA scan) can also be performed to confirm the diagnosis. If the gallbladder cannot be visualized on HIDA scan because of outlet obstruction by stone or sludge, the test is considered positive. However, this study is not helpful in patients with intrinsic liver disease and elevated serum bilirubin levels.

The treatment of acute cholecystitis depends on the severity of the symptoms and the health of the patient. When the diagnosis is suspected, the patient should not take anything by mouth and be supported with intravenous fluids, antibiotics such as metronidazole and ciprofloxacin or ampicillin-sulbactam, and intravenous analgesia if needed. Patients who present with mild symptoms can proceed directly to laparoscopic cholecystectomy. If the patient presents with significant inflammation or multiorgan system involvement, it may be necessary to proceed with percutaneous drainage followed by cholecystectomy when surgically appropriate.

Acalculous Cholecystitis

Acalculous cholecystitis accounts for approximately 10% of all cases of cholecystitis. It often occurs in patients who have other serious comorbidities, such as trauma, burns, or prolonged fasting states, as well as a result of certain infections, especially in immunosuppressed patients. The disorder usually results from chronic stasis of bile in the gallbladder secondary to underlying disease, resulting in inflammation and distention of the gallbladder wall and ultimately infection and even per-foration in severe cases.

Management of acalculous cholecystitis is similar to that of acute calculous cholecystitis, but very ill patients may need to be initially managed with percutaneous drainage if they are too unstable to tolerate immediate surgical cholecystectomy. The mortality rate of acalculous cholecystitis is linked to the stability of the patient and ranges from 10% to as high as 90% in very ill patients.

Common Bile Duct Stones

Common bile duct stones (choledocholithiasis) are the most common cause of acute cholangitis in the United States. Acute cholangitis results from either complete or intermittent obstruction of the bile duct with stone or sludge complicated by bacterial infection originating from the intestinal flora. Patients typically present with Charcot triad consisting of right upper quadrant pain, fever, and jaundice. In severely affected patients, mental status changes and hypotension may also be present. Most patients present with leukocytosis and elevated serum bilirubin and alkaline phosphatase levels; aminotransferases may also be significantly elevated. The dis-order can be distinguished from other causes of elevated aminotransferases by the sharp rise in the levels followed by an acute large decrease indicative of intermittent obstruction. Ultrasonography is often diagnostic if biliary ductal dilatation is noted in the presence of associated clinical symptoms. Magnetic resonance cholangiopancreatography (MRCP) is a more sensitive study than ultrasonography; it has a sensi-tivity of greater than 90% and offers the advantage of avoid-ing invasive ERCP. ERCP carries the risk of pancreatitis or bile duct or duodenal perforation of up to 3% with a mor-tality rate of 0.2%.

Medical management of the patient requires prompt ini-tiation of broad-spectrum antibiotics with coverage of enteric gram-negative bacteria such as *Escherichia coli* and *Klebsiella* species. Fluoroquinolones are often an adequate initial choice. Severely ill patients with hypotension or sepsis, how-ever, also require emergent decompression of the biliary tract with ERCP, percutaneous drainage, or surgery. ERCP is asso-ciated with less morbidity and mortality and is therefore the first-choice management if available. Cholecystectomy should be considered after the patient is stable and adequately treated with antibiotics to reduce the recurrence of choledo-cholithiasis.

Mirizzi Syndrome

Mirizzi syndrome is an uncommon disorder that occurs in approximately 0.1% of all patients presenting with gallstones. It is defined by the external compression of the common hepatic duct that most often results from a large stone that becomes lodged in the cystic duct or distal portion of the gall-bladder. The resulting compression of the common hepatic duct leads to cholestasis, pain, and jaundice. In advanced

stages, cholecystocholedochal fistula formation can occur. Diagnosis is usually made with ultrasonography and can be confirmed by either a CT scan or MRCP. Common reported findings include dilatation of the common hepatic duct at the level of the cystic duct. Sometimes, an impacted stone in the cystic duct or neck of the gallbladder is seen, especially with CT or MRCP. An additional finding is the lack of dilatation below the level of the obstruction in the common bile duct. If confirmed, decompression and sometimes stenting before surgery are often required.

KEY POINTS

- Any patient with complications of gallstones should be evaluated for cholecystectomy.
- Patients with choledocholithiasis may need ERCP before cholecystectomy to decompress the bile duct and prevent cholangitis.

Biliary Tract Neoplasms

Gallbladder Carcinoma

Gallbladder cancer, the most common malignancy of the bil-iary tract, is usually diagnosed at an advanced stage and there-fore has a very poor prognosis; most studies report a 5-year survival rate of 0 to 10%. Up to 2% of patients who undergo elective cholecystectomy for gallstones are incidentally found to have carcinoma of the gallbladder. In the United States, whites are more commonly affected than blacks.

The pathogenesis of gallbladder carcinoma is not entirely known, but gallstones are a significant risk factor; 65% to 90% of patients with gallbladder cancer also have gallstones, although only 1% to 3% of patients with known gallstones develop cancer. Other risk factors for gallbladder cancer include a calcified gallbladder (porcelain gallbladder), gall-bladder polyps, anomalous pancreaticobiliary duct anatomy, obesity, and estrogens. It is recommended that polyps larger than 1 cm in diameter be treated with cholecystectomy.

Early gallbladder cancer is asymptomatic. Presenting symptoms include jaundice, weight loss, and anorexia and occur when the cancer is usually advanced and likely unre-sectable. Approximately 80% of patients have invasion of either adjacent organs or distant metastases at diagnosis. The best case is the incidental diagnosis made during surgery for acute cholecystitis, which occurs in 1% of cholecystectomy specimens.

The diagnosis can be made with ultrasonography, which may show an irregular fixed polypoid lesion without acoustic shadowing. Endoscopic ultrasonography can help in both diagnosing and staging the disease. CT scan and/or MRI can confirm the extent of spread and involvement of vessels and lymph nodes.

Optimal treatment is surgical resection, which often requires resection of not only the gallbladder but also parts of the regional anatomy. Simple cholecystectomy is felt to be curative only for disease limited to the mucosa. Adjuvant radiation therapy or chemotherapy has been shown in some studies to offer benefit, but results have been conflicting and the studies small. Palliative surgery is the only option for some patients with advanced disease.

Cholangiocarcinoma

Cholangiocarcinomas are tumors that arise from the biliary tract. They have an overall low incidence reported to be approximately 8 in one million in the United States; however, the incidence is rising. Risk factors include primary sclerosing cholangitis, ulcerative colitis, intrahepatic bile duct stones, and, less commonly in the United States, liver fluke infections. The tumors are classified by their anatomic location as hilar (Klatskin tumor), intrahepatic, and distal extrahepatic bile duct cancer. Symptoms are more common with tumors that obstruct the hilum or extrahepatic bile duct. Symptomatic patients usually present with painless jaundice and pruritus with associated weight loss. The tumor marker CA19-9 may be elevated in cholangiocarcinoma, but it can also be elevated in other disease states even in the absence of malignancy.

Ultrasonography may be sufficient for diagnosis if there is ductal dilatation as a result of the tumor. However, MRI with magnetic resonance cholangiopancreatography (MRCP) is the radiologic modality of choice as it can also assist in staging. CT angiography can delineate vasculature involvement. With ERCP, biopsy samples can be taken and therapeutic stents can be placed, but the procedure cannot stage the disease. Endoscopic ultrasonography with fine-needle aspiration can also be used to obtain tissue samples. Although a tissue diagnosis is confirmatory, a negative result does not rule out malignancy. Cholangioscopy is a newer technology that allows for intraductal visualization to assess for malignancy and may become a more commonly used diagnostic modality in the future.

Surgical resection is the only curative treatment for cholangiocarcinoma; however, even with successful resection the 5-year survival rate is 20% to 35%. The survival rate in patients who do not achieve clear margins during surgery is dismal. Although good outcomes with liver transplantation have been reported in a few centers, liver transplantation is not an option for most patients with cholangiocarcinoma because of the very high recurrence risk. The outcome in patients treated with either radiation therapy or chemotherapy is poor.

Adenocarcinoma of the Ampulla of Vater

The ampulla of Vater comprises the muscle fibers that surround the duodenal portion of the common bile duct and pancreatic duct and open into the duodenal lumen through the papilla of Vater. Tumors can arise from any structure in this area, including the bile duct, pancreatic duct, or duodenum.

Patients at increased risk for this tumor include those with familial adenomatous polyposis or hereditary nonpolyposis colorectal cancer syndromes. These patients should, therefore, be screened for ampullary cancer. Tumor markers are not very specific for ampullary cancers, but serum CA 19-9 and carcinoembryonic antigen (CEA) may be elevated. Most tumors become evident when the patient presents with painless jaundice or with signs of gastric outlet obstruction from duodenal obstruction. Initial imaging is usually ultrasonography; however, CT or MRI with MRCP is more definitive and can assist in staging disease. ERCP and endoscopic ultrasonography allow for tissue sampling, and ERCP has the added benefit of allowing the decompression of ductal obstruction by the placement of a stent. The treatment for adenocarcinoma of the ampulla of Vater is pancreaticoduodenectomy if there is no evidence of advanced disease.

KEY POINTS

- Gallbladder cancer has a very poor prognosis and is rarely resectable at the time of diagnosis.
- Porcelain gallbladder and gallbladder polyps greater than 1 cm in diameter are risk factors for gallbladder cancer, and should be treated with cholecystectomy.
- Cholangiocarcinoma carries a poor prognosis and should be suspected in patients with primary sclerosing cholangitis or long-term biliary abnormalities who develop new-onset jaundice.

Bibliography

Benjaminov FS, Heathcote J. Liver disease in pregnancy. Am J Gastroenterol. 2004;99:2479-88. [PMID: 15571598]

Blei AT. Portal hypertension and its complications. Curr Opin Gastroenterol. 2007;23:275-82. [PMID: 17414843]

Cullen SN, Chapman RW. The medical management of primary sclerosing cholangitis. Semin Liver Dis. 2006;26:52-61. [PMID: 16496233]

Hoofnagle JH, Doo E, Liang TJ, Fleischer R, Lok AS. Management of hepatitis B: summary of a clinical research workshop. Hepatology. 2007;45:1056-75. [PMID: 17393513]

Hoofnagle JH, Seeff LB. Peginterferon and ribavirin for chronic hepatitis C. N Engl J Med. 2006;355:2444-51. [PMID: 17151366]

Kaplan MM, Gershwin ME. Primary biliary cirrhosis [erratum in N Engl J Med. 2006;354:313]. N Engl J Med. 2005;353:1261-73. [PMID: 16177252]

Krawitt EL. Autoimmune hepatitis. N Engl J Med. 2006;354:54-66. [PMID: 16394302]

LaRusso NF, Shneider BL, Black D, et al. Primary sclerosing cholangitis: summary of a workshop. Hepatology. 2006;44:746-64. [PMID: 16941705]

Parikh S, Hyman D. Hepatocellular cancer: a guide for the internist. Am J Med. 2007;120:194-202. [PMID: 17349437]

Qaseem A, Aronson M, Fitterman N, et al; Clinical Efficacy Assessment Subcommittee of the American College of Physicians. Screening for Hereditary Hemochromatosis: A Clinical Practice Guideline from the American College of Physicians [erratum in Ann Intern Med. 2006;144:380]. Ann Intern Med. 2005;143:517-21. [PMID: 16204164]

Sanders G, Kingsnorth AN. Gallstones. BMJ. 2007;335:295-9. [PMID: 17690370]

Sass DA, Shakil AO. Fulminant hepatic failure. Liver Transpl. 2005; 11:594-605. [PMID: 15915484]

Gastrointestinal Bleeding

Introduction

Blood loss from the gastrointestinal tract is a major source of morbidity and accounts for greater than 300,000 hospitalizations per year. Upper gastrointestinal tract bleeding requiring hospitalization is five times more common than lower bleeding and has a mortality rate of up to 10%. Nonvariceal hypertensive bleeding is generally the result of an underlying disorder such as cancer, ulceration, vascular malformation, or inflammation. Additionally, the widespread use of NSAIDs and the increasing use of anticoagulants and antiplatelet agents have complicated the management of patients with bleeding. The approach to the patient must therefore consider the acuity of the bleeding, anatomic site of blood loss, and underlying pathophysiology. The introduction of endoscopic clips, wireless capsule endoscopy, and double-balloon enteroscopy have broadened the options for diagnosis and treatment. Treatment often involves a multidisciplinary approach, including a gastroenterologist, radiologist, and surgeon.

Upper Gastrointestinal Bleeding

Upper gastrointestinal bleeding may have variceal and nonvariceal causes. Variceal bleeding, which is associated with portal hypertension and often chronic liver disease, is discussed under the complications of liver disease.

The most common cause of nonvariceal bleeding is peptic ulcer disease, including both gastric and duodenal ulcers and accounting for 35% to 50% of all cases of upper gastrointestinal bleeding. Most peptic ulcers occur secondary to *Helicobacter pylori* infection or use of NSAIDs. Esophagitis and gastritis, which account for up to 25% of upper gastrointestinal bleeding, and a Mallory-Weiss tear of the gastroesophageal junction secondary to retching, which accounts for up to 15%, are other common causes. Malignancy of the upper gastrointestinal tract is a rare cause. Gastric antral vascular ectasia (GAVE syndrome, also called watermelon stomach) and arteriovenous malformations can cause both chronic and acute gastrointestinal bleeding. Rarer causes include Dieulafoy lesion (an exposed arteriole), hemobilia (bleeding from the biliary tree), and hemosuccus pancreaticus (blood loss from the pancreatic duct). A rare cause but one with high morbidity in a patient with recent vascular surgery is an aortoenteric fistula.

Evaluation of the Patient with Upper Gastrointestinal Bleeding

In a patient with suspected upper gastrointestinal bleeding, medical history should focus on previous gastrointestinal bleeding, chronic liver disease, peptic ulcer disease, and use of anticoagulants and NSAIDs. The presenting symptoms can suggest the degree and volume of blood loss. The presence of melena (black, tarry stools) suggests an upper gastrointestinal tract source but can be associated with loss of as little as 150 to 200 mL of blood. Hematemesis of bright red blood is associated with ongoing upper bleeding, whereas hematochezia secondary to an upper source is suggestive of brisk ongoing bleeding of at least 1000 mL of blood. Presyncope and syncope may occur with hypovolemia secondary to bleeding.

The physical examination should concentrate on stigmata of chronic liver disease (which would suggest a variceal source of bleeding), any scars from recent surgery, and abdominal tenderness consistent with peptic ulcer disease. Resting tachycardia (heart rate >100/min) suggests a 15% to 30% loss of blood volume, while a blood pressure that is below normal is consistent with a loss of more than 30% of blood volume. Signs of orthostatic hypotension with a decrease in blood pressure and/or an increase in pulse rate of more than 30/minute may indicate large volume loss when resting heart rate and blood pressure are normal but may be insensitive for smaller amounts of blood loss. With severe blood loss the respiration rate can increase, with confusion and mental status changes.

Management of Upper Gastrointestinal Bleeding

The first step in the management of acute upper gastrointestinal bleeding is fluid resuscitation. Volume loss is estimated by pulse rate, blood pressure, and presence of orthostatic hypotension. Endoscopic or surgical treatment should generally not be performed until the patient has been resuscitated with intravenous fluids and/or blood products. Two large-bore intravenous sites or central access should be obtained for volume infusion. In the first 24 hours hemoglobin and hematocrit are often inaccurate determinants of blood loss due to hemoconcentration.

Patients with significant volume loss, liver disease, or comorbid conditions should be admitted to a monitored care or intensive care unit setting. Therapy with an intravenous proton pump inhibitor has been shown to reduce the risk of recurrent bleeding. If it is unclear whether the bleeding is variceal, the vasodilating drug octreotide should be given.

Upper endoscopy should be performed within the first 24 hours of admission and emergently for patients with rapid bleeding or with suspected end-stage liver disease. Endoscopy can determine the cause of bleeding and distinguish high-risk lesions for both continued bleeding and rebleeding, such as a bleeding ulcer, from low-risk lesions, such as a Mallory-Weiss tear.

Acutely bleeding nonvariceal sources can be treated endoscopically with injection of normal saline which tamponades the small mucosal and submucosal vessels or more commonly diluted 1:10,000 epinephrine. Coagulation of the bleeding source can be performed with contact thermal probes passed through the endoscope or noncontact techniques such as argon plasma coagulation. Combination therapy with injection therapy followed by thermal therapy is often performed. Endoclips, which are metallic mechanical devices that function like a suture, can be used in endoscopy to provide sufficient hemostasis for most upper gastrointestinal bleeding sources.

With endoscopic therapy, outcomes are poorer and rebleeding rates are higher in the elderly and patients with comorbid disease, particularly cardiac disorders, malignancy, and cirrhosis. Patients who present with hypotension/shock, hematochezia from an upper source, a frankly bloody nasogastric aspirate, or a large transfusion requirement are more likely to fail to respond to initial endoscopic treatment or to rebleed in the first few days after endoscopic treatment whether or not they have comorbidities.

Patients with bleeding from sources secondary to portal hypertension, such as esophageal or gastric varices, are at high risk for rebleeding despite advancements in endoscopic and nonendoscopic treatment. Patients with arterial spurting during endoscopy can have a rebleeding rate as high as 90%. Patients with a visible vessel or adherent clot on an ulcer may have rebleeding rates of 50% and up to 30%, respectively. Patients who have a pigmented flat spot associated with an ulcer or a clean-based ulcer are at low risk for rebleeding, and if they are stable with few other comorbid illnesses can usually be discharged after only a short time in the hospital.

When endoscopic therapy is ineffective, interventional radiology or surgery should be considered, especially in patients who continue to bleed despite endoscopic therapy or who have multiple rebleeding episodes, large ulcers along the lesser curvature of the stomach or posterior wall of the duodenum, or aortoenteric fistulae. Interventional radiology may achieve hemostasis with angiography and embolization. Surgical management, particularly of bleeding ulcers, is the most definitive therapy but is associated with significant morbidity and even death in patients with active bleeding.

KEY POINTS

- The most common cause of nonvariceal upper gastrointestinal bleeding is peptic ulcer disease secondary to *Helicobacter pylori* infection or use of NSAIDs.

- The most important part of treating upper gastrointestinal bleeding is establishment of intravenous access and correction of volume loss with fluid resuscitation and transfusion of blood products when needed.

- Upper endoscopy provides diagnosis of the cause of bleeding, treatment of the bleeding source, and prognosis for the risk of rebleeding.

- Surgery or interventional radiology for upper gastrointestinal bleeding should be reserved for patients who fail to respond to medical and endoscopic therapy.

Lower Gastrointestinal Bleeding

Lower gastrointestinal bleeding is defined as bleeding into the lumen of the gastrointestinal tract that emanates from a source distal to the ligament of Treitz. Acute lower gastrointestinal bleeding is defined as bleeding for less than 3 days, whereas chronic bleeding consists of an intermittent and slow loss of blood over several days or longer. The most common causes of chronic bleeding include neoplasms, angiectasias, and inflammatory bowel disease. The annual incidence of lower gastrointestinal bleeding requiring hospitalization is approximately 21 per 100,000 adults in the United States. The risk increases with age, with a mean age ranging from 63 to 77 years. Lower bleeding accounts for approximately 20% of all episodes of gastrointestinal bleeding requiring hospitalization, and the most common source is the colon.

Causes

Diverticular Bleeding

Up to 15% of patients with diverticulosis develop bleeding, a complication that occurs more frequently in the elderly. Diverticular bleeding accounts for 24% to 50% of cases of lower gastrointestinal bleeding. While diverticulosis occurs more commonly in the sigmoid or left colon, diverticular bleeding more commonly occurs in the right colon. Bleeding is arterial, resulting from medial thinning of the vasa recta as they drape over the dome of the diverticulum. Generally patients do not have other symptoms; diverticulitis and bleeding almost never coexist. Physical examination is generally unremarkable unless large blood loss results in tachycardia, hypotension, and orthostasis. Volume resuscitation via two large-bore intravenous catheters is mandated first before any diagnostic or therapeutic procedures. Blood products are transfused as needed. Colonoscopy, generally after a purge with polyethylene glycol, may identify the bleeding diverticulum and permit endoscopic treatment with epinephrine and/or electrocautery; colonoscopy may also help identify other causes of bleeding such as vascular ectasias. If a specific bleeding source cannot be identified, a bleeding scan may be performed to localize the source. Angiography is 100% specific in identifying the affected artery, but bleeding must be active at the time of the test; vasopressin administration and embolization may also be performed in this manner. Surgery is reserved for refractory bleeding, and ideally when the site is known a segmental resection can be done rather than a subtotal colectomy. In 70% to 90% of cases, the bleeding spontaneously remits; rebleeding occurs in 22% to 38% of patients.

Ischemic Colitis

Ischemic colitis, which accounts for between 1% and 19% of episodes of lower gastrointestinal bleeding, results from a sudden temporary reduction in mesenteric blood flow. This hypoperfusion typically affects the "watershed" areas of the colon, that is, the splenic flexure and rectosigmoid junction. Patients may report dizziness but may not recall any such episodes. They present with sudden onset of mild crampy abdominal pain and subsequent passage of bloody stool or bloody diarrhea. Endoscopically, there is a well-defined segment of cyanotic or ulcerated mucosa. CT scan, which is increasingly used to make the diagnosis, shows a segmental colitis. Most episodes resolve spontaneously with supportive care, such as intravenous fluids and pain control.

Ischemic colitis is fundamentally different from acute mesenteric ischemia, which presents with pain out of proportion to physical examination and is usually secondary to a thrombotic event.

Vascular Ectasias

Angioectasias, also known as vascular ectasias or angiodysplasias (or errantly arteriovenous malformations), account for up to 11% of episodes of lower gastrointestinal bleeding. They are painless dilated submucosal vessels that radiate from a central feeding vessel. Affected patients may present with iron deficiency anemia and occult gastrointestinal bleeding or with hematochezia that is indistinguishable from diverticular hemorrhage.

Hemorrhoids

Typically patients with hemorrhoidal bleeding report streaks of bright red blood on the toilet paper or on the outside of a firm stool. There is usually pain associated with defecation. However, the hemorrhoids themselves are not painful because there is no enervation to the colonic mucosa proximal to the dentate line. Hemorrhoids are unlikely to cause serious bleeding.

Other Causes

Significant lower gastrointestinal bleeding may also be caused by inflammatory bowel disease, neoplasms, infectious colitis, radiation colitis, Meckel diverticulum, NSAIDs and ulcers, post-polypectomy ulcer, and rarely colonic varices and Dieulafoy lesions.

Evaluation

Patients with acute lower gastrointestinal bleeding present with hematochezia, clots per rectum, or melena. Associated symptoms and signs include chest pain, shortness of breath, orthostasis, and syncope. These findings may indicate a rapid upper gastrointestinal bleed, and upper endoscopy should be considered.

In patients with suspected lower gastrointestinal bleeding, previous episodes of gastrointestinal bleeding should be noted, as should use of antiplatelet or anticoagulation therapy and aspirin and NSAIDs. A history of pelvic radiation therapy for prostate, rectal, or cervical cancer should be elicited as well. The results of previous endoscopic examinations should

be obtained, especially if there was a colonoscopy with polypectomy in the preceding 2 weeks. Independent risk factors for lower gastrointestinal bleeding are a hematocrit less than 35%, tachycardia, hypotension, and gross blood on rectal examination.

Management

If the patient is hemodynamically unstable, the patient should be resuscitated as in the case of a nonvariceal upper gastrointestinal bleed. Although most episodes of lower gastrointestinal bleeding resolve spontaneously, it is important to establish the cause of bleeding. Approximately 10% to 15% of patients with hematochezia have an upper source. Nasogastric lavage is not recommended to exclude an upper gastrointestinal bleed, because a duodenal ulcer may yield a false-negative result.

Colonoscopy is recommended within the first 48 hours of admission for a suspected lower gastrointestinal bleed; early colonoscopy has been correlated with decreased length of hospital stay and improved outcome. The procedure should be performed after first purging the colon with polyethylene glycol, which improves endoscopic visualization and diagnostic yield. The yield of colonoscopy in this setting ranges from 48% to 90%.

Endoscopic treatments to control intestinal bleeding of either the upper or lower tract include coaptive bipolar cautery, injection of epinephrine, endoclips, and argon plasma coagulation. The therapy depends on the type of lesion. Treatment of bleeding and nonbleeding visible vessels and adherent clots decreases recurrence rates.

If colonoscopy does not identify a discrete lesion or endoscopic therapy does not control the bleeding, radiologic evaluation or surgery may be indicated. The two primary types of radiologic evaluation are technetium-99m (^{99m}Tc) pertechnetate red blood cell scanning and angiography. Red blood cell scanning is positive in 45% of patients with an active bleed and has an overall accuracy for localizing the bleeding of 78%. It can detect ongoing bleeding occurring at a rate of 0.1 to 0.5 mL/min. This scan is more sensitive than angiography and is often the first radiologic test performed. A technetium-99m (^{99m}Tc) pertechnetate scan should also be considered in younger patients with undiagnosed overt lower gastrointestinal bleeding. Angiography cannot detect the bleeding site if the bleeding rate is less than 1 mL/min; however, the advantage of angiography as a primary modality is its ability to provide selective embolization. Initial control of hemorrhage with angiotherapy ranges from 60% to 100%.

If technetium-99m (^{99m}Tc) pertechnetate red blood cell scanning and angiography are negative and the bleeding continues, a small bowel evaluation via video capsule endoscopy or push enteroscopy should be attempted. The yield of detecting the source of occult gastrointestinal bleeding by capsule endoscopy is highest in a patient with active bleeding. If the source of bleeding cannot be identified and bleeding persists, surgery should be considered. Preoperative localization of the region of bleeding is imperative to avoid an extensive subtotal colectomy. This can be the case with diverticular disease where the exact source is not visualized on angiography.

The mortality rate from lower gastrointestinal bleeding is generally less than 5%, but is highest in patients who are hospitalized for other reasons when the bleeding occurs. Elderly patients with comorbid conditions who are undergoing aggressive transfusions and fluid resuscitation should be treated in the intensive care unit.

KEY POINTS

- Up to 20% of episodes of acute gastrointestinal bleeding result from a lower gastrointestinal source.
- Colonoscopy is effective in the early diagnosis and treatment of lower gastrointestinal bleeding.
- The most common causes of acute lower gastrointestinal bleeding are diverticulosis, vascular ectasias, and ischemic colitis.
- Most episodes of lower gastrointestinal bleeding resolve spontaneously and simply require supportive care.

Obscure Gastrointestinal Bleeding

Obscure gastrointestinal bleeding is defined as recurrent blood loss without an identified source of bleeding, despite investigation with standard upper endoscopy and colonoscopy. Patients with obscure bleeding present with either overt bleeding in which there is clinically evident hemorrhage in the form of melena or hematochezia or with occult bleeding in which blood loss is not clinically evident but may be detected with fecal occult blood testing. Obscure recurrent bleeding accounts for 5% of hospitalizations for gastrointestinal hemorrhage.

Differential Diagnosis

The sources of gastrointestinal bleeding may not be readily identified for various reasons. Lesions may bleed intermittently, such as in the Dieulafoy lesion, a submucosal artery that protrudes through the mucosa and causes acute recurrent brisk hemorrhage. Volume contraction or a low hemoglobin concentration may alter the appearance of a bleeding source. For example, an esophageal varix may decompress with an episode of bleeding, or a site of angiodysplasia may not be evident in the setting of profound anemia. The source of bleeding may not originate in the intestinal lumen as is the case in hemosuccus pancreaticus and hemobilia. Subtle or rare causes of bleeding may not be recognized at endoscopy if careful inspection is not performed or if the endoscopist is not familiar with uncommon findings. Finally, the cause of bleeding may be located within the small bowel and therefore not within the reach of the endoscope or colonoscope.

The history and physical examination for obscure gastrointestinal bleeding are similar to those for upper and lower bleeding. Patient age is important to the differential diagnosis because causes of bleeding in young patients may be different from those in older patients (**Table 53**). For example, Meckel diverticulum is more likely in a young patient, whereas angiodysplasia is more common in the elderly. The physical examination findings of perioral pigmentation that occurs in Peutz-Jeghers syndrome should raise suspicion of a small-bowel polyp, and mucosal telangiectasias are a clue to hereditary hemorrhagic telangiectasia (Osler-Weber-Rendu syndrome).

Diagnostic Evaluation

In a patient with recurrent bleeding, endoscopy and/or colonoscopy should be repeated. Studies of push enteroscopy have found that the source of blood loss is located within the reach of the diagnostic endoscope in 37% of cases. If a repeat study is nondiagnostic, the next step depends upon the severity and suspected location of blood loss.

Angiography

In a patient with brisk overt bleeding, urgent angiography may be both diagnostic and therapeutic. Angiographically evident bleeding typically requires blood loss at a rate of 1 mL/min. Therefore, for patients who are not aggressively bleeding, the sensitivity is poor, and even in the setting of active bleeding, the sensitivity only reaches 40%. The diagnostic yield for angiography is maximized if an immediate preprocedure nuclear medicine scan identifies bleeding. In the case of a positive test, angiographic embolization can halt bleeding in 70% to 90% of cases. Complications from angiography include renal failure, vascular dissection, aneurysm formation, and ischemia of the embolized segment. Complications occur in 11% of patients who undergo therapeutic embolization.

Technetium Labeled Nuclear Scan

Nuclear medicine scans can identify bleeding at much lower rates of hemorrhage than angiography. A technetium-99m (^{99m}Tc) radiolabeled red blood cell scan can visualize bleeding rates as low as 0.10 mL/min, whereas a technetium-labeled sulfur colloid scan requires only 0.05 mL/min. In the case of the sulfur colloid scan, however, rapid uptake and the liver and spleen limits the ability to assess sources of blood loss in the upper abdomen. The findings on nuclear medicine bleeding scans are nonspecific; bleeding may be observed and localized to a general region, but distinguishing between colonic and small-bowel sources of bleeding is difficult. The primary role of nuclear medicine bleeding scans is in stratifying patients likely to benefit from angiography or surgery.

TABLE 53 Age-dependent Differential Diagnosis of Obscure Bleeding

Age (Years)	Differential Diagnosis	Type of Bleeding	Diagnostic Clues
<20	Peutz-Jeghers syndrome	Occult	Perioral pigmentation; obstructive symptoms
	Meckel diverticulum	Overt	Possible abdominal pain
	Hemangioma	Overt	Possible cutaneous hemangiomas
	Congenital arteriovenous malformation	Overt	Bruit
	Dieulafoy lesion	Overt	Recurrent massive bleeding with normal endoscopic studies
20-60	Crohn disease	Occult or overt	Extraintestinal manifestations; family history; abdominal pain
	Chronic radiation therapy or NSAID-induced ulcers	Occult	History; medication review
	Large hiatal hernia – Cameron erosion	Occult	Previous upper gastrointestinal radiographs; chest radiograph
	Meckel diverticulum[a]	Overt	Possible abdominal pain
	Gastric antral vascular ectasia (watermelon stomach)	Occult or overt	
	Post-radiation angiectasia	Occult or overt	History
	Dieulafoy lesion	Overt	Recurrent massive bleeding with normal endoscopic studies
	Tumors	Occult or overt	Weight loss; lymphadenopathy
	von Willebrand disease	Occult	Epistaxis; other bleeding sites
>60[b]	Amyloidosis	Occult or overt	Organomegaly, purpura, renal involvement
	Angiectasia	Occult or overt	
	Hereditary hemorrhagic telangiectasia	Occult or overt	Telangiectasias on mouth, face, fingers
	Malignancy	Occult or overt	Weight loss; pain

[a]Up to age 35–40 years.

[b]Includes all diagnoses in the 20–60 age group.

Wireless Capsule Endoscopy

In wireless capsule endoscopy, a patient swallows a video capsule that by intestinal motility passes through the stomach and into the small intestine. The video capsule transmits images to a recording device worn by the patient. The images are downloaded onto a computer where they can be reviewed. With capsule endoscopy the small bowel can be visualized in its entirety, and the procedure, which has been shown to detect sources of bleeding in 70% of patients, is considered the test of choice to follow standard endoscopy in patients with obscure bleeding. The most common abnormalities detected on capsule endoscopy are vascular ectasias, with small-bowel ulceration and tumors of the small intestine being the next most frequent findings. The miss rate for capsule endoscopy based upon a pooled analysis of studies is 11%. The primary complication is retention of the capsule because of an obstructing mass or stricture. Retained capsules deep within the small bowel can often be removed by double-balloon endoscopy, although surgery may be required.

Push Enteroscopy

Push enteroscopy consists of direct insertion of an endoscope longer than the standard upper endoscope and has the advantage of being both diagnostic and therapeutic. The working channel of the endoscope allows for biopsy of lesions and treatment of bleeding sites. The push enteroscope can be advanced up to 150 cm beyond the pylorus; however, the depth of insertion varies greatly and depends on the operator as well as on the patient's anatomy. The yield for enteroscopy varies from 13% to 78%. Push enteroscopy is complementary to capsule endoscopy and is most often performed for the evaluation of lesions detected on capsule endoscopy that are within the reach of the enteroscope or if capsule endoscopy is unavailable. Complications of push enteroscopy include mucosal ulceration and avulsion, bleeding, and perforation.

Double-Balloon Endoscopy

The double-balloon endoscope is a system that uses two latex balloons, one mounted on the endoscope and a second balloon on the overtube, which are successively inflated and deflated to pleat the bowel over the endoscope and achieve deep intubation of the small intestine. Double-balloon endoscopy may be performed via the oral or transanal route and has replaced intraoperative enteroscopy in many cases. The role for double-balloon endoscopy is to evaluate or treat findings seen on capsule endoscopy, for evaluation of ongoing bleeding when bleeding is brisk enough that the need for endoscopic hemostasis is expected, and as a complementary test when a small-bowel source of bleeding remains a concern despite a nondiagnostic capsule endoscopy. The chief complication of double-balloon endoscopy is perforation. Contraindications include severe ulceration, recent surgical anastomosis, radiation enteritis, or any other cause of a weakened bowel wall.

Small-Bowel Radiography

Evaluation of the small bowel with barium radiography and single-contrast small-bowel follow-through or enteroclysis (small-bowel barium enema) has little role in the evaluation of patients with obscure bleeding. The diagnostic yield (5% to 20%) is inadequate to support its use, and angiodysplasia, which accounts for most cases of obscure bleeding, is routinely missed on small-bowel barium studies. Small-bowel radiography may detect tumors, Crohn disease, Meckel diverticulum, and jejunal diverticulosis, which may be causes of obscure bleeding.

Intraoperative Endoscopy

Intraoperative endoscopy is not usually required for diagnosis because wireless capsule endoscopy and double-balloon endoscopy have improved the ability to diagnose and treat small-bowel sources of bleeding. Nevertheless, intraoperative endoscopy may be required for ongoing life-threatening bleeding without an identified source. Rebleeding rates up to 24% have occurred after surgical treatment. This finding is more representative of the multifocal and dynamic nature of the cause of obscure bleeding rather than suboptimal surgical technique.

Treatment

Treatment of obscure gastrointestinal bleeding depends on the cause of blood loss. Angiodysplasia can generally be treated endoscopically with electrothermal cautery or argon plasma coagulation, although rebleeding is common in such cases. Angiography is often central to treatment, particularly in the setting of brisk bleeding. If angiography is ineffective, intraoperative endoscopy may be required.

Cessation of offending medications may be all that is needed to treat the cause of bleeding. In NSAID-induced small-bowel ulceration, stopping the offending agent will allow mucosal healing. Similarly, avoiding antiplatelet agents or anticoagulants may be considered on a case-by-case basis. There is some evidence suggesting that estrogen-progesterone and octreotide may be beneficial for recurrent bleeding from enteric angiodysplasia. Bleeding from malignancy generally requires surgical resection, although if surgery is not feasible, angiography and endoscopy have had limited short-term success.

KEY POINTS

- Repeating upper endoscopy or colonoscopy detects the cause of obscure gastrointestinal bleeding in a significant number of patients.
- Capsule endoscopy and double-balloon endoscopy play central roles in identifying and treating small-bowel sources of bleeding.

Bibliography

DiMaio CJ, Stevens PD. Nonvariceal upper gastrointestinal bleeding. Gastrointest Endosc Clin N Am. 2007;17:253-72. [PMID: 17556147]

Dorward S, Sreedharan A, Leontiadis GI, Howden CW, Moayyedi P, Forman D. Proton pump inhibitor treatment initiated prior to endoscopic diagnosis in upper gastrointestinal bleeding. Cochrane Database Syst Rev. 2006;(4):CD005415. [PMID: 17054257]

Hartmann D, Schmidt H, Bolz G, Schilling D, Kinzel F, Eickhoff A, et al. A prospective two-center study comparing wireless capsule endoscopy with intraoperative enteroscopy in patients with obscure GI bleeding. Gastrointest Endosc 2005;61:826-32. [PMID: 15933683]

Lau JY, Leung WK, Wu JC, et al. Omeprazole before endoscopy in patients with gastrointestinal bleeding. N Engl J Med. 2007;356: 1631-40. [PMID: 17442905]

Lin S, Rockey DC. Obscure gastrointestinal bleeding. Gastroenterol Clin North Am. 2005;34:679-98. [PMID: 16303577]

Lewis BS. Obscure GI bleeding in the world of capsule endoscopy, push, and double balloon enteroscopies. Gastrointest Endosc. 2007;66: S66-8. [PMID: 17709036]

Targownik LE, Nabalamba A. Trends in management and outcomes of acute nonvariceal upper gastrointestinal bleeding: 1993-2003 [erratum in Clin Gastroenterol Hepatol. 2007;5:403]. Clin Gastroenterol Hepatol. 2006;4:1459-1466. [PMID: 17101296]

Self-Assessment Test

This self-assessment test contains one-best-answer multiple-choice questions. Please read these directions carefully before answering the questions. Answers, critiques, and bibliographies immediately follow these multiple-choice questions. The American College of Physicians is accredited by the Accreditation Council for Continuing Medical Education (ACCME) to provide continuing medical education for physicians.

The American College of Physicians designates MKSAP 15 Gastroenterology and Hepatology for a maximum of 16 *AMA PRA Category 1 Credits*™. Physicians should only claim credit commensurate with the extent of their participation in the activity. Separate answer sheets are provided for each book of the MKSAP program. Please use one of these answer sheets to complete the Gastroenterology and Hepatology self-assessment test. Indicate in Section H on the answer sheet the actual number of credits you earned, up to the maximum of 16, in ¼-credit increments. (One credit equals one hour of time spent on this educational activity.)

Use the self-addressed envelope provided with your program to mail your completed answer sheet(s) to the MKSAP Processing Center for scoring. Remember to provide your MKSAP 15 order and ACP ID numbers in the appropriate spaces on the answer sheet. The order and ACP ID numbers are printed on your mailing label. If you have *not* received these numbers with your MKSAP 15 purchase, you will need to acquire them to earn CME credits. E-mail ACP's customer service center at custserv@acponline.org. In the subject line, write "MKSAP 15 order/ACP ID numbers." In the body of the e-mail, make sure you include your e-mail address as well as your full name, address, city, state, ZIP code, country, and telephone number. Also identify where you have made your MKSAP 15 purchase. You will receive your MKSAP 15 order and ACP ID numbers by e-mail within 72 business hours.

CME credit is available from the publication date of July 31, 2009, until July 31, 2012. You may submit your answer sheets at any time during this period.

Self-Scoring Instructions:

Gastroenterology and Hepatology

Compute your percent correct score as follows:

Step 1: Give yourself 1 point for each correct response to a question.

Step 2: Divide your total points by the total number of questions: 110.

The result, expressed as a percentage, is your percent correct score.

	Example	Your Calculations
Step 1	93	
Step 2	93 ÷ 110	÷ 110
% Correct	85%	%

*Each of the numbered items is followed by lettered answers. Select the **ONE** lettered answer that is **BEST** in each case.*

Item 1

A 38-year-old man is evaluated for persistent dyspepsia 2 months after a duodenal ulcer was detected and treated. He originally presented with new-onset epigastric pain, and esophagogastroduodenoscopy showed a duodenal ulcer; biopsy specimens showed the presence of *Helicobacter pylori*. The patient, who does not use NSAIDs and is penicillin-allergic, completed a 10-day course of therapy with omeprazole, metronidazole, and clarithromycin.

At this time, urea breath testing for *H. pylori* shows persistent infection.

In addition to a proton pump inhibitor, which of the following regimens is indicated for this patient?

(A) Amoxicillin and levofloxacin
(B) Bismuth subsalicylate, metronidazole, and tetracycline
(C) Clarithromycin and amoxicillin
(D) Clarithromycin and metronidazole
(E) Trimethoprim–sulfamethoxazole and erythromycin

Item 2

A 19-year-old woman is evaluated for a 2-week history of nausea and new-onset jaundice. Six weeks ago she had an uncomplicated cystitis, which resolved after a 3-day course of therapy with trimethoprim-sulfamethoxazole.

On physical examination, the temperature is 37.3 °C (99.2 °F), the blood pressure is 120/85 mm Hg, the pulse rate is 88/min, and the respiration rate is 14/min; the BMI is 31. There is conjunctival icterus, jaundice, and right upper quadrant tenderness on deep palpation. Murphy sign is not elicited, and there is no asterixis or stigmata of chronic liver disease. Stool is negative for occult blood.

Laboratory studies:

Leukocyte count	7800/µL (7.8×10^9/L) with normal differential
Bilirubin (total)	12.0 mg/dL (205.2 µmol/L)
Bilirubin (direct)	5.6 mg/dL (95.6 µmol/L)
Aspartate aminotransferase	23 U/L
Alanine aminotransferase	35 U/L
Alkaline phosphatase	464 U/L
Antinuclear antibody titer	Negative
Anti–smooth muscle antibody	Negative
Antimitochondrial antibody	Negative

Ultrasonography of the right upper quadrant shows normal caliber of the hepatic ducts, a normal gallbladder without wall thickening, and no cholelithiasis.

Which of the following is the most appropriate management for this patient?

(A) Cholecystectomy
(B) Endoscopic retrograde cholangiopancreatography
(C) Liver biopsy
(D) Observation

Item 3

A 35-year-old woman is evaluated for symptomatic ulcerative colitis. One year ago, she was diagnosed with pan-ulcerative colitis and responded well to initial and maintenance therapy with balsalazide. However, 2 months ago she developed urgent bloody diarrhea several times a day and lower abdominal cramping; prednisone, 40 mg/d, alleviated her acute symptoms, but her symptoms have returned with prednisone tapering. The patient is otherwise healthy, and her medications are balsalazide, 750 mg three times a day, prednisone, 15 mg/d, and calcium with vitamin D.

On physical examination, vital signs and other findings are normal. Laboratory studies reveal hemoglobin 11.4 g/dL (114 g/L) and plasma glucose 140 mg/dL (7.77 mmol/L). Stool analysis for *Clostridium difficile* toxin A and B is negative.

Which of the following is the most appropriate next step in the treatment of this patient?

(A) Add olsalazine
(B) Add budesonide
(C) Add metronidazole
(D) Increase prednisone dosage to 40 mg/d and add 6-mercaptopurine

Item 4

A 27-year-old woman with an 8-year history of ulcerative colitis is evaluated during a follow-up examination. The initial colonoscopy after diagnosis showed pancolitis. She has been treated with mesalamine since diagnosis and has had episodes of bloody diarrhea two or three times a year but has otherwise done well. Her most recent colonoscopy 1 year ago when she had increased diarrhea and bleeding showed no progression of disease. Since then she has been clinically stable. The patient's medical history includes nephrolithiasis, and her only medications are mesalamine, 2.4 g/d, and a multivitamin. There is no family history of inflammatory bowel disease or colorectal cancer.

On physical examination, vital signs are normal; BMI is 20.5. There is mild abdominal tenderness in the right lower quadrant without rebound or guarding. The rest of the physical examination is normal. Laboratory studies reveal a normal complete blood count, including leukocyte differential, and a serum C-reactive protein level of 0.8 mg/dL (8 mg/L).

Which of the following is the most appropriate management of this patient's risk for colorectal cancer?

(A) Annual capsule endoscopy
(B) Annual flexible sigmoidoscopy
(C) Colonoscopy now and annually thereafter
(D) Increasing the dose of mesalamine to 3.6 g/d

Item 5

A 71-year-old man is evaluated for chronic epigastric discomfort, heartburn, and diarrhea of 4 years' duration. His weight has been stable during this time period. The patient has no significant medical history and takes no medications.

On physical examination, there is mild epigastric tenderness but no rebound or guarding. Rectal examination reveals brown stool that is positive for occult blood. Laboratory studies reveal hemoglobin of 12.3 g/dL (123 g/L) with a mean corpuscular volume of 75 fL. Test for serum *Helicobacter pylori* antibody is negative. Esophagogastroduodenoscopy shows prominent gastric folds, mild linear erosions, and multiple ulcers in the stomach and the duodenum.

Which of the following is the most appropriate next step in the evaluation of this patient?

(A) CT scan of the abdomen and pelvis
(B) Endoscopic ultrasonography
(C) Measurement of serum gastrin
(D) Somatostatin receptor scintigraphy

Item 6

A 44-year-old woman is evaluated for a 6-month history of dyspepsia, regurgitation of sour fluid, and eructation. There is no associated fever, chills, weight loss, or vomiting. The condition failed to respond to a 6-week trial of omeprazole therapy. The patient's medical history includes hypertension, type 2 diabetes mellitus, and obesity (BMI 36); her medications are lisinopril, metformin, and insulin glargine.

On examination, vital signs are normal; there is mild epigastric tenderness without rebound, and stool is negative for occult blood.

Which of the following is the most appropriate next diagnostic step in the evaluation of this patient?

(A) Ambulatory esophageal pH monitoring
(B) Barium esophagography
(C) CT scan of the chest
(D) Esophageal manometry

Item 7

A 71-year-old woman is evaluated for a 2-day history of progressive dyspnea on exertion. She has also had two episodes of black, tarry stool in the past week. She has not had fever, chills, cough, or abdominal pain or bright red rectal bleeding. The patient has a history of osteoarthritis for which she takes ibuprofen, 600 mg twice daily.

On physical examination, the temperature is 37.0 °C (98.6 °F), the blood pressure is 136/84 mm Hg, the pulse rate is 78/min, and the respiration rate is 12/min; the BMI is 24. Cardiac examination shows a grade 2/6 early systolic murmur at the base and regular rhythm with normal heart sounds. The lungs are clear, and there is no peripheral edema. Rectal examination reveals brown stool that is positive for occult blood. Laboratory studies reveal hemoglobin of 9.8 g/dL (98 g/L) with a mean corpuscular volume of 80 fL; serum biochemistry tests, including liver chemistry tests, and prothrombin time, activated partial thromboplastin time, and INR are normal. Chest

radiography and echocardiography are normal; esophagogastroduodenoscopy, colonoscopy, and push enteroscopy are normal. Small-bowel capsule endoscopy shows a nonbleeding white ulcer in the mid-ileum.

Which of the following is the most appropriate next step in the management of this patient?

(A) Discontinue ibuprofen therapy
(B) Double-balloon enteroscopy
(C) Estrogen/progesterone therapy
(D) Mesenteric angiography
(E) Octreotide therapy

Item 8

A 41-year-old woman is evaluated for a 4-month history of intermittent mid-upper-abdomen pain, which does not radiate and is not affected by eating. She had gastroesophageal reflux when she was pregnant, but she says that the current symptoms are not like those of reflux or heartburn. She occasionally feels nauseated and mildly bloated, but she has not vomited, felt early satiety, or lost weight. She does not have difficulty swallowing or painful swallowing. Her bowel movements are normal. She has been pregnant twice and had two healthy children, both delivered by cesarean section. Her medical history also includes a cholecystectomy 5 years ago. Her only current medication is a multivitamin.

On physical examination, she is afebrile; the pulse rate is 65/min and the blood pressure is 110/65 mm Hg. There is no jaundice or scleral icterus; mild epigastric tenderness is present. Bowel sounds are normal; there are no abdominal bruits, palpable masses, or lymphadenopathy. Complete blood count and liver chemistry tests are normal.

Which of the following is the most appropriate next diagnostic test in the evaluation of this patient?

(A) Abdominal ultrasonography
(B) Esophagogastroduodenoscopy
(C) Gastric scintigraphy
(D) *Helicobacter pylori* stool antigen
(E) Small-bowel radiograph

Item 9

A 38-year-old woman is evaluated for elevated results of liver chemistry tests detected in an evaluation for new-onset fatigue, joint pains, and jaundice. The patient recently started a job in a hospital and received a hepatitis B vaccination. She has a history of hypothyroidism, and her only medications are levothyroxine and a multivitamin. She has never used illicit drugs and does not drink alcohol. Her mother has rheumatoid arthritis.

On physical examination, the patient is afebrile; the blood pressure is 130/75 mm Hg, the pulse rate is 80/min, and the respiration rate is 14/min. The BMI is 26. There is scleral icterus; the rest of the examination is normal.

Laboratory studies:

Leukocyte count	3400/μL (3.4 × 10⁹/L) with a normal differential
Bilirubin (total)	6.0 mg/dL (102.6 μmol/L)
Bilirubin (direct)	3.6 mg/dL (61.6 μmol/L)
Aspartate aminotransferase	890 U/L
Alanine aminotransferase	765 U/L
Alkaline phosphatase	120 U/L
Antinuclear antibody	Titer 1:40
Anti–smooth muscle antibody	Titer 1:640
Antimitochondrial antibody	Negative

Viral serologic tests are negative.

Which of the following is the most likely diagnosis?

(A) Acute cholecystitis
(B) Autoimmune hepatitis
(C) Drug-induced liver injury
(D) Primary biliary cirrhosis
(E) Primary sclerosing cholangitis

Item 10

A 32-year-old man is evaluated in the emergency department for a 5-day history of worsening crampy abdominal pain and eight to ten loose bowel movements a day. The patient has a 5-year history of ulcerative colitis treated with azathioprine and topical mesalamine; before this episode, he had one or two bowel movements of well-formed stool a day. The patient had sinusitis recently, which resolved with antibiotic therapy. He has otherwise been healthy and has not traveled recently, had contact with sick persons, or been noncompliant with medication.

On physical examination, the temperature is 38.3 °C (101 °F), the blood pressure is 130/76 mm Hg sitting and 105/60 mm Hg standing, the pulse rate is 90/min sitting and 120/min standing, and the respiration rate is 18/min. The abdomen is diffusely tender without rebound or guarding. Laboratory studies reveal hemoglobin 12.3 g/dL (123 g/L), leukocyte count of 28,000/μL (28 × 10⁹/L) with 15% band forms, and platelet count of 234,000/μL (234 × 10⁹/L). Intravenous fluids are started and stool studies are obtained.

Which of the following is the most appropriate next step in the management of this patient?

(A) Increase dosage of azathioprine
(B) Start oral vancomycin
(C) Start oral mesalamine
(D) Small-bowel radiographic series

Item 11

A 34-year-old woman is evaluated for continued severe mid-epigastric pain that radiates to the back, nausea, and vomiting 5 days after being hospitalized for acute alcohol-related pancreatitis. She has not been able eat or drink and has not had a bowel movement since being admitted.

On physical examination, the temperature is 38.2 °C (100.8 °F), the blood pressure is 132/84 mm Hg, the pulse rate is 101/min, and the respiration rate is 20/min. There is no scleral icterus or jaundice. The abdomen is distended and diffusely tender with hypoactive bowel sounds.

Laboratory studies:

Leukocyte count	15,400/μL (15.4 × 10⁹/L)
Aspartate aminotransferase	189 U/L
Alanine aminotransferase	151 U/L
Bilirubin (total)	1.1 mg/dL (18.8 μmol/L)
Amylase	388 U/L
Lipase	924 U/L

CT scan of the abdomen shows a diffusely edematous pancreas with multiple peripancreatic fluid collections, and no evidence of pancreatic necrosis.

Which of the following is the most appropriate next step in the management of this patient?

(A) Enteral nutrition by nasojejunal feeding tube
(B) Intravenous imipenem
(C) Pancreatic débridement
(D) Parenteral nutrition

Item 12

A 42-year-old woman is evaluated for a 20-year history of constipation. She has approximately one or two bowel movements a week consisting of lumpy or hard stool. She strains at defecation and has a sense of incomplete evacuation after a bowel movement. She does not have bloody stool, abdominal pain or discomfort, weight loss, or diarrhea. She is otherwise healthy, and her only medication is an occasional over-the-counter laxative or stool softener.

On physical examination, vital signs are normal. The anorectal tone is normal, and on rectal examination, the patient is able to expel the examiner's finger when asked to mimic a bowel movement. Laboratory studies are normal. Radiopaque marker study shows delayed transit time through the right colon.

Which of the following is the most likely diagnosis?

(A) Chronic intestinal pseudo-obstruction
(B) Constipation-predominant irritable bowel syndrome
(C) Pelvic floor dysfunction (dyssynergic constipation)
(D) Colonic inertia (slow-transit constipation)

Item 13

A 60-year-old man hospitalized for advanced cirrhosis complicated by ascites and encephalopathy is evaluated for massive hematemesis and hypotension. The patient's medications are spironolactone, furosemide, and lactulose.

On physical examination, the temperature is 35.6 °C (96 °F), the blood pressure is 80/50 mm Hg, the pulse rate is 146/min, and the respiration rate is 20/min. The patient has just vomited red blood and has large-volume ascites; the stool is brown and positive for occult blood. Laboratory studies show hemoglobin of 9 g/dL (90 g/L), platelet count of 60,000/μL (60 × 10^9/L), and INR of 3.

In addition to rapid volume resuscitation, which of the following is the most appropriate management of this patient?

(A) Arteriography
(B) Esophagogastroduodenoscopy
(C) Intravenous nadolol
(D) Mesocaval shunt
(E) Transjugular intrahepatic portosystemic shunt

Item 14

A 48-year-old man is evaluated 3 weeks after presenting with epigastric pain and early satiety with no weight loss. He underwent an esophagogastroduodenoscopy that showed thickened and nodular gastric folds in the body of the stomach with patchy erosions in the antrum. Biopsy specimens of the nodularity showed low-grade B-cell lymphoma; specimens of the antrum showed chronic active gastritis and no *Helicobacter pylori*. Endoscopic ultrasonography showed no invasion through the wall of the stomach; CT scan of the abdomen showed only gastric wall thickening. The patient's medical history includes intermittent heartburn and occasional headache; his medications include as-needed antacids and an NSAID.

On physical examination, vital signs are normal. Examination of the abdomen reveals mild epigastric tenderness but no hepatosplenomegaly or lymphadenopathy. Complete blood count and serum chemistry tests are normal.

Which of the following is the most appropriate next step in the management of this patient?

(A) Evaluation for HIV infection
(B) Initiation of systemic chemotherapy
(C) *Helicobacter pylori* stool antigen test
(D) Measurement of serum tissue transglutaminase antibody
(E) Surgical resection of the tumor

Item 15

A 56-year-old woman is evaluated for a 3-year history of progressive dysphagia for solids and liquids; she has had a 6.8-kg (15-lb) weight loss during this time. The dysphagia was initially intermittent, but recently swallowing almost all food or drink causes a feeling of chest tightness and discomfort with increasingly frequent regurgitation of undigested food. The dysphagia is sometimes alleviated by standing upright. Her medical history is significant only for hypertension, and her medications include lisinopril and a multivitamin.

On physical examination, the patient appears uncomfortable and restless; she is thin but does not have thenar wasting. She is afebrile; the blood pressure is 142/92 mm Hg, the pulse rate is 96/min, and the respiration rate is 22/min. The BMI is 23.

Barium esophagography shows a dilated esophagus with an air/fluid level and tapered narrowing of the distal esophagus. Esophagogastroduodenoscopy shows a dilated esophagus with retained food and a tight lower esophageal sphincter, which allowed passage of the endoscope.

Which of the following is the most likely diagnosis?

(A) Achalasia
(B) Diffuse esophageal spasm
(C) Peptic stricture
(D) Scleroderma esophagus

Item 16

A 45-year-old woman is evaluated for a 2-week history of right leg and flank pain and a slight limp. The patient was diagnosed with Crohn disease at age 20 years when she was evaluated for abdominal pain, nausea, and vomiting, and small-bowel radiographic series revealed a stenotic area in her terminal ileum with proximal dilatation and an enteroenteric fistula. She had an elective ileocolic resection with a primary anastomosis when her disease proved to be refractory to corticosteroid therapy. She has since been pain-free but has required intermittent courses of antibiotics and mesalamine for diarrheal flares of disease. She has had routine colonoscopic examinations with colonic biopsies showing scattered aphthous ulcerations and biopsy specimens revealing non-necrotizing granulomas in the colon and neo-terminal ileum. Her most recent colonoscopy was 5 years ago. She is otherwise healthy and takes no medication.

On physical examination, the temperature is 38.0 °C (101.0 °F), the blood pressure is 120/80 mm Hg, and the pulse rate 90/min; there is right-sided abdominal tenderness and restricted painful extension of the right hip; otherwise, the range of motion of the hip is normal and without pain. She has an abnormal gait, favoring her right leg.

Which of the following is the most likely diagnosis?

(A) Avascular necrosis of the hip
(B) Crohn disease-related arthritis
(C) Osteoporosis-related fracture of the femoral neck
(D) Psoas muscle abscess

Item 17

A 57-year-old woman is evaluated for a 1-month history of increased abdominal girth. The patient has a 15-year history of alcohol abuse, drinking a bottle of wine a day. She also has type 2 diabetes mellitus, hypertension, and hyperlipidemia, and her medications are metformin, hydrochlorothiazide, propranolol, simvastatin, and aspirin.

On physical examination, the temperature is 37.1 °C (98.8 °F), the blood pressure is 90/50 mm Hg, the pulse rate is 99/min, and the respiration rate is 13/min; the BMI is 21. Examination reveals scleral icterus; bulging flanks; a small umbilical hernia; caput medusae; spider angiomata of the face, arms, and chest; and mild asterixis. There is no abdominal tenderness.

Laboratory studies:

Leukocyte count	5200/µL (5.2 × 10⁹/L) with a normal differential
Platelet count	65,000/µL (65 × 10⁹/L)
INR	2.2
Bilirubin (total)	3.4 mg/dL (58.1 µmol/L)
Bilirubin (direct)	1.8 mg/dL (30.8 µmol/L)
Aspartate aminotransferase	120 U/L
Alanine aminotransferase	65 U/L
Alkaline phosphatase	196 U/L
Albumin	2.7 g/dL (27 g/L)
Creatinine	2.7 mg/dL (206.0 µmol/L)
Urinalysis	Normal

Blood cultures are negative. Ultrasonography of the abdomen shows massive ascites, patent vessels, no ductal dilatation, and a shrunken liver with no masses.

Which of the following is the most appropriate management for this patient?

(A) Diagnostic paracentesis

(B) Cefotaxime and albumin

(C) Furosemide and spironolactone

(D) Transjugular intrahepatic portosystemic shunt

Item 18

A 25-year-old man is evaluated for a 6-month history of eight loose, nonbloody stools a day; he also has abdominal pain and small-joint arthritis. The patient has a 5-year history of Crohn disease, initially treated with corticosteroids but then maintained on azathioprine therapy. Small-bowel radiographic series shows no stricturing disease but some active jejuno-ileitis. Azathioprine metabolites were recently measured and were found to be at therapeutic concentration.

Which of the following is the most appropriate additional therapy for this patient?

(A) 5-Aminosalicylate

(B) Anti–tumor necrosis factor α-inhibitor

(C) Calcineurin inhibitor

(D) Corticosteroids

Item 19

A 53-year-old man is evaluated after a recent episode of substernal chest pain. He was evaluated in the emergency department for chest pain, and serial electrocardiograms and measurement of cardiac enzymes showed no evidence of myocardial ischemia. An outpatient stress test also showed no evidence of myocardial disease. The patient has a history of medically controlled hypertension, and his only medication is amlodipine.

On physical examination, the patient appears healthy and vital signs are normal. Barium esophagography shows a segmented or "corkscrew" esophagus. Esophageal manometry shows simultaneous contractions in the distal esophagus with 50% of swallows.

Which of the following is the most appropriate therapy for this patient?

(A) Esophageal bougienage

(B) Laparoscopic myotomy

(C) Oral anticholinergic therapy

(D) Oral proton pump inhibitor therapy

(E) Pneumatic dilatation

Item 20

A 38-year-old man is evaluated for a 3-month history of bloating and increased frequency of defecation. He has four to six bowel movements a day, including nocturnal bowel movements several times a week. The stool tends to be loose but there is no blood or melena. He has significant bloating but no abdominal pain. The patient underwent a Roux-en-Y gastric bypass procedure 2 years ago for morbid obesity; he lost 45.5 kg (100 lb) after the procedure. His weight stabilized 1 year ago, but he has lost 2.2 to 4.5 kg (5 to 10 lb) in the past few months. His medical history also includes hypertension, which resolved after the bariatric surgery, and his medications include a daily multivitamin with iron and daily oral calcium, vitamin D, and vitamin B₁₂ supplements. The patient's sister has Crohn disease, and he has twin 15-month-old daughters who attend a daycare center.

On physical examination, the blood pressure is 110/62 mm Hg, and the BMI is 29. He has redundant abdominal skin and healed abdominal incisions. The abdomen is not distended or tender; bowel sounds are normal. There is normal rectal tone and no palpable rectal abnormalities or perianal disease.

Laboratory studies:

Hemoglobin	11.7 g/dL (117 g/L)
Mean corpuscular volume	103 fL
Vitamin B₁₂	185 pg/mL (136.5 pmol/L)
Folate	30 ng/mL (67.9 nmol/L)
C-reactive protein	0.6 mg/dL (6.0 mg/L)
Tissue transglutaminase antibodies (IgA and IgG)	Negative

Stool culture and examination for fecal leukocytes and ova and parasites on three stool specimens are negative. Colonoscopy with terminal ileal examination is grossly normal. Esophagogastroduodenoscopy shows altered anatomy consistent with the bypass procedure; small-bowel biopsy specimens are negative. CT enterography is normal.

Which of the following is the most likely diagnosis?

(A) Celiac disease

(B) Crohn disease

(C) Giardiasis

(D) Irritable bowel syndrome

(E) Small intestinal bacterial overgrowth

Item 21

A 55-year-old man is evaluated for a 4-month history of frequent and urgent defecation with loose and bloody stool, mild abdominal cramping, and fatigue. He has up to eight bowel movements a day and often wakes at night with symptoms; before this episode he had one bowel movement a day with well-formed stool. He does not have fever, nausea, or vomiting, but he has lost 3 kg (7 lb). He has mild joint pain in his knees and ankles that also began 4 months ago, which is worse in the morning and resolves somewhat during the day. The patient is a former cigarette smoker but quit smoking 2 years ago. His medical history includes hypertension, and his only medication is hydrochlorothiazide.

On physical examination, vital signs are normal. There is mild lower abdominal tenderness without rebound or guarding; there are no palpable abdominal masses. Examination of the rectum shows gross blood. Laboratory studies reveal hemoglobin 12.3 g/dL (123 g/L) with a mean corpuscular volume of 76 fL. Fecal leukocytes are present, but stool analysis is negative for infection. Colonoscopy shows continuous erythema, friability, and loss of vascular pattern from the rectum to the splenic flexure; the rest of the colon and terminal ileum is normal. Histology shows cryptitis, crypt abscesses, and crypt architecture distortion.

Which of the following is the most likely diagnosis?

(A) Crohn colitis
(B) Infectious colitis
(C) Ischemic colitis
(D) Microscopic colitis
(E) Ulcerative colitis

Item 22

A 44-year-old man with a long history of alcohol abuse is evaluated on the sixth day of hospitalization for acute pancreatitis. On admission to the hospital, he was afebrile, the blood pressure was 150/88 mm Hg, the pulse rate was 90/min, and the respiration rate was 16/min. Abnormal findings were limited to the abdomen, which was flat and tender to palpation without peritoneal signs. Bowel sounds were normal. Plain abdominal and chest radiographs were normal. Abdominal ultrasonography revealed a diffusely enlarged, hypoechoic pancreas without evidence of gallstones or dilated common bile duct. He was treated with aggressive intravenous hydration and opioid analgesia. For the past 2 days, the patient has had repeated febrile episodes, persistent severe abdominal pain, and increasing shortness of breath.

On physical examination, the temperature is 38.6 °C (101.5 °F), the blood pressure is 98/60 mm Hg, the pulse rate is 112/min, and the respiration rate is 22/min; oxygen saturation is 92% with the patient breathing oxygen 3 L/min. Breath sounds are decreased at the base of both lungs. The abdomen is distended and diffusely tender with hypoactive bowel sounds. Laboratory studies reveal leukocyte count of 19,800/µL (19.8 × 10⁹/L), creatinine 1.4 mg/dL (106.8 µmol/L), amylase 388 U/L, and lipase 842 U/L.

Which of the following is the most appropriate next step in the evaluation of this patient?

(A) CT scan of the abdomen with intravenous contrast
(B) Endoscopic retrograde cholangiopancreatography
(C) Endoscopic ultrasonography
(D) Stool chymotrypsin

Item 23

A 55-year-old man is hospitalized for a 2-week history of jaundice and altered mental status. The patient has a 10-year history of alcohol dependence and has failed several attempts to stop drinking. His family reports that he had been drinking heavily every day until about 3 weeks ago.

On physical examination, the patient is confused and lethargic; the temperature is 38.0 °C (100.0 °F), the blood pressure is 90/60 mm Hg, the pulse rate is 120/min, and the respiration rate is 30/min. The BMI is 24. Examination reveals scleral icterus. There is no guarding on palpation of the abdomen. The liver edge is tender and easily palpable 3 cm below the right costal margin. There is no ascites, edema, or evidence of bleeding.

Laboratory studies:

Leukocyte count	17,000/µL (17 × 10⁹/L)
Platelet count	103,000/µL (103 × 10⁹/L)
Prothrombin time	26.2 s
INR	4.0
Bilirubin (total)	37.0 mg/dL (632.7 µmol/L)
Bilirubin (direct)	17.0 mg/dL (290.7 µmol/L)
Aspartate aminotransferase	98 U/L
Alanine aminotransferase	50 U/L
Alkaline phosphatase	230 U/L
Albumin	2.0 g/dL (20 g/L)
Ammonia	110 µg/dL

Chest radiograph is normal. Ultrasonography shows an enlarged, fatty liver, with no nodules, ascites, pericholecystic fluid, or bile duct dilatation. Blood and urine cultures are negative.

In addition to enteral nutrition, which of the following is the most appropriate management for this patient?

(A) Ceftriaxone
(B) Methylprednisolone
(C) Fresh frozen plasma
(D) Liver transplantation

Item 24

A 64-year-old woman is evaluated in the emergency department for her second episode of painless bloody stool. Four weeks ago, she was evaluated in the hospital for maroon stool; the hemoglobin at that time was 2 g/dL (20 g/L) lower than previous complete blood counts; esophagogastroduodenoscopy was normal; colonoscopy showed some old blood but no active bleeding. The patient was observed for 2 days and discharged with instructions for outpatient follow-up. Her current episode consisted of two maroon stools, one this morning and one 2 hours ago. Nasogastric lavage yields coffee grounds that clear with 1 L of saline.

The patient had a colonoscopy 2 years ago at which time a single adenomatous polyp was detected and removed. She has no personal or family history of bleeding or gastrointestinal malignancy and is otherwise healthy; she has no upper gastrointestinal symptoms, does not use alcohol, and her only medication is a multivitamin.

On physical examination, the temperature is 37.1 °C (98.7 °F), the blood pressure is 98/62 mm Hg, the pulse rate is 94/min, and the respiration rate is 14/min; the BMI is 23.5. There is no scleral icterus; examinations of the heart and lungs are normal. The abdomen is soft with increased bowel sounds but no hepatosplenomegaly. Rectal examination reveals the presence of maroon and red blood but no palpable masses or hemorrhoids. Laboratory studies reveal hemoglobin of 9.4 g/dL (94 g/L) with a mean corpuscular volume of 86 fL; leukocyte count with differential and platelet count are normal. Prothrombin time, activated partial thromboplastin time, and INR are normal, as are liver chemistry tests. Serum blood urea nitrogen is 34 mg/dL (12.1 mmol/L), and creatinine is normal.

Which of the following is the most appropriate next step in the evaluation of this patient?

(A) Colonoscopy
(B) Double-balloon enteroscopy
(C) Esophagogastroduodenoscopy
(D) Technetium red blood cell scan
(E) Wireless capsule endoscopy

Item 25

A 68-year-old man with a history of alcoholism is evaluated in the emergency department for a 7-month history of diarrhea during which he has noted an increased volume of stool and decreased consistency. He has had intermittent abdominal pain but not severe enough to prevent him from eating or drinking. He is not taking any medications.

On physical examination, he is afebrile; the blood pressure is 108/72 mm Hg, the pulse rate is 80/min, and the respiration rate is 16/min. The abdomen is soft with mild periumbilical tenderness but no distention.

Laboratory studies:

Aspartate aminotransferase	155 U/L
Alanine aminotransferase	88 U/L
Alkaline phosphatase	96 U/L
Bilirubin (total)	1.1 mg/dL (18.8 µmol/L)
Amylase	65 U/L
Lipase	70 U/L

CT scan of the abdomen shows calcifications but no mass. There is fat in the stool.

Which of the following is the most appropriate management for this patient?

(A) Fiber
(B) Cholestyramine
(C) Loperamide
(D) Pancreatic enzymes

Item 26

A 74-year-old woman is evaluated for 3 years of progressive dysphagia, first for solid foods and now for both solid foods and liquids; she has had frequent episodes of regurgitation of undigested food and has lost 6.8 kg (15 lb) during the past 6 months. Her medical history includes stenting of the left anterior descending coronary artery 1 year ago after which she has had symptomatic residual distal stenosis. She had a cerebrovascular accident 2 years ago and still has mild residual right hemiparesis. Her medications include metoprolol, clopidogrel, enalapril, aspirin, and hydrochlorothiazide.

On physical examination, the patient is thin (BMI 20) and appears ill, although not in distress. Vital signs are normal. Chest radiograph shows a dilated esophagus with an air/fluid level and changes of chronic aspiration in the right lung base. Barium esophagography shows "bird beak" narrowing of the distal esophagus and mega-esophagus with retained fluid in the esophageal body. Esophageal manometry shows aperistalsis of the esophageal body and incomplete lower esophageal sphincter relaxation with swallowing. On esophagogastroduodenoscopy, the endoscope passes through the lower esophageal sphincter without resistance; there are no masses in the esophagus or the gastric cardia.

Which of the following is the most appropriate therapy for this patient?

(A) Anticholinergic therapy
(B) Botulinum toxin injection
(C) Laparoscopic myotomy
(D) Pneumatic dilatation

Item 27

A 56-year-old woman is evaluated for iron-deficiency anemia detected during her annual examination. An esophagogastroduodenoscopy showed diffuse linear antral erosions and small clean-based ulcers; gastric biopsy specimens were negative for *Helicobacter pylori*, and small-bowel biopsy specimens were normal. A subsequent colonoscopy was normal. The patient's medical history includes longstanding rheumatoid arthritis and diarrhea-predominant irritable bowel syndrome, and her medications include methotrexate, hydroxychloroquine, nabumetone (an NSAID); daily calcium, vitamin D, and iron supplements; and loperamide. The patient has taken NSAIDs for many years; she once tried to switch to celecoxib, but it did not provide sufficient pain relief.

On physical examination, vital signs are normal; she has slight joint swelling of the metacarpophalangeal and proximal interphalangeal joints consistent with rheumatoid arthritis. Abdominal examination is normal. Laboratory studies reveal hemoglobin of 10.6 g/dL (106 g/L).

Which of the following is the most appropriate management for this patient?

(A) Add an H$_2$-receptor antagonist
(B) Add misoprostol
(C) Add a proton pump inhibitor
(D) Add sucralfate

Item 28

A 65-year-old man is evaluated in the emergency department for fever and abdominal pain. The patient has a history of diverticulitis, and his latest flare 2 months ago was treated as an outpatient with antibiotics. While improved, he still has residual pain in the left lower quadrant. He has no other significant medical history and has not traveled recently.

On physical examination, the temperature is 38.8 °C (101.8 °F), the blood pressure is 120/85 mm Hg, the pulse rate is 100/min, and the respiration rate is 18/min; the BMI is 25. There is right upper quadrant abdominal pain with normal bowel sounds and no peritoneal signs, scleral icterus, or ascites.

Laboratory studies:

Hemoglobin	14.2 g/dL (142 g/L)
Leukocyte count	17,000/µL (17 × 10⁹/L) with 15% band forms
Platelet count	320,000/µL (320 × 10⁹/L)
INR	1.0
Bilirubin (total)	1.6 mg/dL (27.4 µmol/L)
Bilirubin (direct)	0.6 mg/dL (10.3 µmol/L)
Aspartate aminotransferase	97 U/L
Alanine aminotransferase	86 U/L
Alkaline phosphatase	220 U/L

CT scan of the abdomen and pelvis shows a mass with a fluid level consistent with a hepatic abscess. Antibiotic therapy is begun.

Which of the following is the most appropriate next step in the management of this patient?

(A) Endoscopic retrograde cholangiopancreatography
(B) Lobectomy
(C) MRI with gadolinium
(D) Percutaneous drainage of the hepatic lesion

Item 29

A 55-year-old woman is evaluated in the hospital for a 2-day history of epigastric abdominal pain, nausea and vomiting, and anorexia. The patient has no significant medical history and takes no medications.

On physical examination, the temperature is 38.0 °C (100.5 °F), the blood pressure is 124/76 mm Hg, the pulse rate is 99/min, and the respiration rate is 16/min. There is scleral icterus and a slight yellowing of the skin. There is mid-epigastric and right upper quadrant tenderness. There is no palmar erythema, spider angiomata, or other evidence of chronic liver disease.

Laboratory studies:

Leukocyte count	14,900/µL (14.9 × 10⁹/L)
Aspartate aminotransferase	656 U/L
Alanine aminotransferase	567 U/L
Bilirubin (total)	5.6 mg/dL (95.8 µmol/L)
Amylase	1284 U/L
Lipase	6742 U/L

Abdominal ultrasonography shows a biliary tree with a dilated common bile duct of 12 mm and cholelithiasis but no choledocholithiasis.

Which of the following is the most appropriate next step in the management of this patient?

(A) CT scan of the abdomen and pelvis with pancreatic protocol
(B) Endoscopic retrograde cholangiopancreatography
(C) Hepatobiliary iminodiacetic acid (HIDA) scan
(D) Magnetic resonance cholangiopancreatography

Item 30

A 74-year-old man is evaluated in the hospital for severe diffuse abdominal pain. He was hospitalized 5 days ago for chest pain and was found to be in rapid atrial fibrillation and a myocardial infarction was diagnosed. He underwent cardiac catheterization and double stent placement after which he has had intermittent hypotension and has remained in atrial fibrillation with a controlled ventricular rate. At the bedside the patient is sweating, nauseated, and holding his abdomen. He cannot respond to questions. His wife says that he has never had any gastrointestinal problems, but that he has not had a bowel movement since he entered the hospital. The patient has chronic atrial fibrillation but he discontinued his anticoagulation therapy 6 months ago; he also has hyperlipidemia. His medications are heparin, metoprolol, simvastatin, clopidogrel, and aspirin.

On physical examination, the temperature is 38.0 °C (99.5 °F), the blood pressure is 102/60 mm Hg, the pulse rate is 94/min, and the respiration rate is 25/min. There is mild, diffuse abdominal tenderness to palpation without rebound or guarding; there are no palpable abdominal masses. Laboratory studies reveal only a leukocyte count of 13,000/µL (13 × 10⁹/L). Radiograph of abdomen shows no evidence of perforation or obstruction.

Which of the following would be the most appropriate management for this patient?

(A) CT arteriography
(B) Colonoscopy
(C) Intravenous famotidine
(D) Lactulose

Item 31

A 35-year-old woman with a history of chronic hepatitis C virus infection is evaluated 4 weeks after starting therapy with pegylated interferon and ribavirin. The patient also has a history of hypothyroidism, and her medications include interferon, ribavirin, and levothyroxine. The patient's mother has rheumatoid arthritis and hypothyroidism.

On physical examination, the patient is afebrile; the blood pressure is 100/78 mm Hg, the pulse rate is 65/min, and the respiration rate is 12/min. The BMI is 26. There is scleral icterus; there is no edema, ascites, or spider angioma.

Laboratory studies:

	1 Month Ago	Current
Bilirubin (total, mg/dL)	1.2 (20.5 µmol/L)	4.0 (68.4 µmol/L)
Bilirubin (direct, mg/dL)	0.3 (5.1 µmol/L)	2.3 (39.3 µmol/L)
Aspartate aminotransferase (U/L)	37	770
Alanine aminotransferase (U/L)	39	890
Alkaline phosphatase (U/L)	90	167
Albumin (g/dL)	4.0 (40 g/L)	3.6 (36 g/L)
Antinuclear antibody	Negative	Titer 1:80
Anti–smooth muscle antibody	Negative	Titer 1:640
Antimito-chondrial antibody	Negative	Negative
Hepatitis C virus RNA	580,000 copies/mL	540,000 copies/mL

Ultrasonography of the liver is normal.

Which of the following is the most appropriate next step in the management of this patient?

(A) Continue interferon and ribavirin at current dosages
(B) Continue interferon and hold ribavirin
(C) Discontinue interferon and ribavirin
(D) Discontinue interferon and ribavirin for 1 week

Item 32

A 30-year-old woman is evaluated for a 9-month history of cramping midepigastric discomfort that is relieved by defecation; the discomfort is sometimes accompanied by bloating. The stool is often watery. She has not had fever, chills, or weight loss. The patient is otherwise healthy and takes no medications; there is no family history of gastrointestinal disease.

On physical examination, the patient is afebrile; the blood pressure is 105/70 mm Hg, the pulse rate is 72/min, the respiration rate is 14/min, and the BMI is 23. The abdomen is soft and not tender or distended; the stool is brown and negative for occult blood. Complete blood count and serum biochemistry studies, including liver studies, vitamin B_{12}, vitamin D, and thyroid-stimulating hormone, are normal.

Which of the following is the most appropriate management for this patient?

(A) Colonoscopy
(B) CT enteroscopy
(C) Gluten-free diet
(D) Symptomatic management

Item 33

A 32-year-old man is evaluated in the emergency department for chest discomfort of 2 hours' duration and that occurred after he ate a large meal. He has difficulty swallowing and feels as though something is stuck in his chest; he is barely able to swallow his saliva and frequently spits into a cup. He has had two similar but less severe episodes in the past 6 months. The patient's only significant medical history is a 20-year history of seasonal allergic rhinitis treated with nasal corticosteroids and oral antihistamines.

On physical examination, he is well developed and well nourished but uncomfortable. Esophagogastroduodenoscopy shows multiple esophageal rings with raised white specks, longitudinal furrows, and friable esophageal mucosa. Histologic examination of the mucosa shows intense inflammation of the lamina propria with more than 15 eosinophils per high-power field. No strictures are detected.

Which of the following is the most appropriate management for this patient?

(A) Endoscopic esophageal dilatation
(B) Leukotriene receptor antagonist therapy
(C) Oral topical (swallowed) corticosteroid therapy
(D) Proton pump inhibitor therapy

Item 34

A 64-year-old man is evaluated for a 3-month history of abdominal bloating and mid-epigastric discomfort associated with a 6.8-kg (15-lb) weight loss. The patient has no significant medical history and takes no medications.

On physical examination, vital signs are normal, and the only significant finding is mild epigastric tenderness.

Laboratory studies:

Complete blood count	Normal
Aspartate aminotransferase	55 U/L
Alanine aminotransferase	67 U/L
Amylase	184 U/L
Lipase	382 U/L

Helical CT scan of the abdomen shows a 2.8-cm pancreatic body mass. There are no liver lesions and no invasion into surrounding major vessels. Endoscopic ultrasonography confirms the presence of an approximately 3-cm lesion without vascular invasion. Fine-needle aspiration specimen is positive for adenocarcinoma.

Which of the following is the most appropriate next step in the management of this patient?

(A) Combined radiation therapy and chemotherapy
(B) Distal pancreatectomy
(C) Palliative care consultation
(D) Pancreatic enzyme supplementation

Item 35

A 37-year-old woman is evaluated for diffuse musculoskeletal pain at her 1-year follow-up after a Roux-en-Y gastric bypass for medically complicated obesity. Before surgery she had type 2 diabetes mellitus for which she required insulin therapy; after surgery the diabetes was manageable with diet modification alone. She also had hyperlipidemia, for which she took a statin, but after surgery her hyperlipidemia resolved and she discontinued statin therapy 6 months ago. She has lost 36.4 kg (80 lb) since surgery but she thinks that her weight has stabilized over the past few months. She has two to three bowel movements of well-formed stool a day. She has some diffuse musculoskeletal pain but otherwise feels well. Her medical history includes the gastric bypass, a cholecystectomy, diet-controlled type 2 diabetes mellitus, and hypothyroidism. Her medications include levothyroxine, a multivitamin containing iron, vitamin B_{12} by injection, and over-the-counter calcium and vitamin D.

On physical examination, vital signs are normal; the BMI is 29. There is redundant skin over the arms and trunk and mild thyromegaly. There is no jaundice or scleral icterus. Abdominal examination reveals no tenderness or hepatomegaly; there is normal muscle strength with no focal muscle tenderness. Laboratory studies show a serum alkaline phosphatase of 314 U/L; all other tests, including complete blood count, aminotransferases, bilirubin, γ-glutamyltranspeptidase, serum thyroid-stimulating hormone, free thyroxine, and calcium, are normal.

Which of the following is the most appropriate next step in the evaluation of this patient?

(A) Anti–smooth muscle antibody test
(B) Measurement of 25-hydroxyvitamin D
(C) Measurement of serum creatine kinase
(D) Measurement of triiodothyronine
(E) Ultrasonography of the liver

Item 36

A 37-year-old man is evaluated to determine his risk for colon cancer because his 62-year-old mother was recently diagnosed with colon cancer. The patient is healthy and takes no medications. He has a bowel movement daily, has not noticed any change in bowel habits, and has never seen blood in his stool. He does not have any abdominal pain, weight loss, or jaundice.

His mother's cancer was in the ascending colon, and she is recovering from surgery. His maternal uncle was diagnosed with colon cancer at age 48 years, and he died of the disease a year later. His mother's other two siblings, aged 44 and 46 years, are healthy. His maternal grandfather was diagnosed with colon cancer in his 60s but died of complications of heart disease. His maternal grandmother survived endometrial cancer diagnosed in her 50s and died in her 70s of a stroke. There is no history of cancer on his father's side.

Which of the following is the most appropriate management for this patient?

(A) Blood test of the mother to evaluate for microsatellite instability
(B) Colonoscopy when he reaches age 50 years
(C) Flexible sigmoidoscopy now
(D) Referral for genetic counseling

Item 37

A 32-year-old woman is evaluated for a 5.2-cm mass in the right lobe of the liver detected during evaluation for possible appendicitis, which was ruled out. The patient has a history of migraine and a 6-year history of irregular menses, and her medications include sumatriptan as needed and an oral contraceptive pill.

On physical examination, the patient is afebrile; the blood pressure is 110/65 mm Hg, the pulse rate is 80/min, and the respiration rate is 14/min. The BMI is 21. There are no palpable abdominal masses; bowel sounds are normal, and Murphy sign is not present. Laboratory tests are all normal. CT scan of the abdomen shows a well-circumscribed lesion in the right lobe of the liver with an enhancing central scar; the rest of the liver appears to be normal, and there is no intra- or extrahepatic duct dilatation.

Which of the following is the most appropriate management for this patient?

(A) Discontinuation of oral contraceptive pills
(B) Evaluation for liver transplantation
(C) Observation
(D) Referral for surgical resection

Item 38

A 25-year-old woman is evaluated for a 2-year history of almost daily bloating and lower abdominal cramping; the symptoms are associated with constipation, relieved with bowel movements, and seem worse when she is under stress. She has one or two small bowel movements a week and often has a feeling of incomplete evacuation. She never has diarrhea and has not had blood in the stool, nocturnal awakening with pain or for bowel movements, or weight loss. She has taken a fiber supplement without relief. The patient is otherwise healthy, and her only medication is an oral contraceptive pill that she has been taking for 1 year. Her mother had a similar condition when she was younger, but both her parents are alive and well.

On physical examination, vital signs are normal; there is mild lower abdominal tenderness with no rebound, guarding, or palpable abdominal masses. Laboratory studies reveal hemoglobin 13.1 g/dL (131 g/L); serum biochemistry tests, including thyroid-stimulating hormone, are normal.

Which of the following is the most appropriate next step in the management of this patient?

(A) Colonoscopy
(B) CT scan of the abdomen and pelvis
(C) Discontinue the oral contraceptive
(D) Reassurance and polyethylene glycol

Item 39

A 26-year-old man is evaluated in the emergency department for shortness of breath and fatigue. He has had maroon stools for the past 2 weeks associated with occasional mild, crampy periumbilical pain but no severe pain. He has had no stools for the past 48 hours.

On physical examination, the temperature is 37.1 °C (98.8 °F), the blood pressure is 94/62 mm Hg supine, the pulse rate is 116/min, and the respiration rate is 14/min; the BMI is 19.5. He has pale conjunctivae and regular tachycardia. The chest is clear and the abdomen is normal with no organomegaly. Examination of the stool is positive for occult blood. Laboratory studies reveal hemoglobin 6.8 g/dL (68 g/L) with a mean corpuscular volume of 74 fL and a platelet count of 446,000/μL (446×10^9/L); serum biochemistry tests, prothrombin time, activated partial thromboplastin time, and INR are normal. Following volume resuscitation, esophagogastroduodenoscopy is normal and colonoscopy shows some old blood but no active bleeding. Wireless capsule endoscopy fails to identify a source of bleeding.

Which of the following is the most appropriate next step in the evaluation of this patient?

(A) Small-bowel barium contrast study
(B) CT scan of the chest and abdomen
(C) Mesenteric angiography
(D) Technetium-99m (^{99m}Tc) pertechnetate (Meckel) scan

Item 40

A 58-year-old man is evaluated for a 4-week history of progressive difficulty swallowing liquids. The symptom begins immediately with the initiation of a swallow and has recently been associated with coughing. The patient does not have fever or weight loss. His only significant medical history is atherosclerotic cardiovascular disease; his only medications are a β-blocker, a statin, and aspirin.

Vital signs are normal, and physical examination shows only crackles at the posterior base of the right lung field.

Which of the following is the most appropriate next diagnostic test in the evaluation of this patient?

(A) Ambulatory esophageal pH monitoring
(B) CT scan of the chest and abdomen
(C) Esophageal manometry
(D) Videofluoroscopy

Item 41

A 48-year-old man is evaluated 8 weeks after having been hospitalized for an episode of sudden nausea, hematemesis, and profound hypotension. He was treated in the emergency department with fluids and an erythrocyte transfusion. An esophagogastroduodenoscopy showed a 1.5-cm clean-based ulcer in the duodenal bulb; biopsy specimens of the body of the stomach and antrum showed chronic active gastritis and the presence of *Helicobacter pylori*. He was discharged from the hospital and prescribed a 10-day course of omeprazole, clarithromycin, and amoxicillin. He had taken omeprazole for the past 8 weeks and has just completed therapy before his visit. The patient's father had gastric cancer.

On examination, the patient is asymptomatic and afebrile; the blood pressure is 118/72 mm Hg and the pulse rate is 88/min. Physical examination and complete blood count are normal.

Which of the following is the most appropriate next step in the management of this patient?

(A) *Helicobacter pylori* serum antibody test
(B) *Helicobacter pylori* urea breath test in 8 weeks
(C) *Helicobacter pylori* urea breath test now
(D) Repeat esophagogastroduodenoscopy with biopsies
(E) No further testing

Item 42

A 51-year-old man is evaluated for an 8-month history of mid-epigastric pain that is worse after eating, six to eight bowel movements a day usually occurring after a meal, and loss of 6.8 kg (15 lb) over the past 6 months. The patient drinks six to eight cans of beer a day. He takes no medications.

On physical examination, the patient is thin (BMI 21) and has normal bowel sounds, mid-epigastric tenderness, but no evidence of hepatosplenomegaly or masses. Rectal examination reveals brown stool that is occult blood negative. The remainder of the examination is normal. Plain radiograph of the abdomen shows a normal bowel gas pattern and is otherwise normal.

Laboratory studies:

Leukocyte count	6800/μL (6.8×10^9/L)
Platelet count	69,000/μL (69×10^9/L)
Fasting plasma glucose	104 mg/dL (5.77 mmol/L)
Aspartate aminotransferase	191 U/L
Alanine aminotransferase	82 U/L
Amylase	122U/L
Lipase	289 U/L

Which of the following tests is most likely to establish the diagnosis in this patient?

(A) Colonoscopy
(B) CT scan of the abdomen
(C) Measurement of serum antiendomysial antibodies
(D) Stool for leukocytes, culture, ova, and parasites

Item 43

A 32-year-old man is evaluated for a 2-week history of nausea, malaise, low-grade fever, vomiting, and jaundice. He has no other significant medical history and takes only ibuprofen for headache and fever.

On physical examination, the temperature is 37.6 °C (99.7 °F), the blood pressure is 110/75 mm Hg, the pulse rate is 90/min, and the respiration rate is 22/min; the BMI is 25. Examination reveals scleral icterus, jaundice, 1+ pitting lower extremity edema, hepatomegaly, mild asterixis, and somnolence. There are no stigmata of chronic liver disease.

Laboratory studies:

Bilirubin (total)	17.5 mg/dL (393.3 µmol/L)
Bilirubin (direct)	7.2 mg/dL (123.1 µmol/L)
Aspartate aminotransferase	8790 U/L
Alanine aminotransferase	7650 U/L
Alkaline phosphatase	195 U/L
INR	2.3
Hepatitis B surface antigen	Positive
Hepatitis B core antigen (IgM)	Positive
Hepatitis C antibody	Negative
Hepatitis A total antibody	Positive
Blood alcohol	Negative
Acetaminophen	Undetectable

Ultrasonography shows hepatomegaly and increased echogenicity, a normal spleen, and perihepatic ascites. There is no ductal dilatation.

Which of the following is the most appropriate management for this patient?

(A) Begin interferon therapy
(B) Evaluation for liver transplantation
(C) Endoscopic retrograde cholangiopancreatography
(D) Corticosteroids

Item 44

A 55-year-old woman is evaluated for elevated liver chemistry tests detected on examination for life insurance. She has no symptoms of liver disease and no history of jaundice, ascites, lower extremity edema, or encephalopathy. She used recreational injection drugs between the ages of 20 and 25 years. She has no significant medical history and takes no medications. She drinks about six cans of beer a day.

On physical examination, vital signs are normal. There are spider angiomata on the upper body and the presence of a nodular liver edge and splenomegaly.

Laboratory studies:

Platelet count	88,000/µL (88 × 10⁹/L)
INR	1.4
Bilirubin (total)	1.1 mg/dL (18.8 µmol/L)
Aspartate aminotransferase	48 U/L
Alanine aminotransferase	96 U/L
Alkaline phosphatase	186 U/L
Albumin	3.6 g/dL (36 g/L)
Hepatitis B surface antigen	Negative
Hepatitis C virus antibody	Positive
HCV RNA in serum	500,000 copies/mL

Ultrasonography shows coarsened hepatic echotexture; CT scan shows changes in the liver consistent with cirrhosis and splenomegaly.

Which of the following is the most appropriate next step in the management for this patient?

(A) Esophagogastroduodenoscopy
(B) Evaluation for liver transplantation
(C) Lamivudine
(D) Pegylated interferon and ribavirin

Item 45

A 25-year-old man is evaluated after being turned down as a blood donor because of abnormal liver chemistry tests. The patient is healthy, takes no medications, does not smoke, and drinks alcohol socially. His parents and siblings are alive and healthy; his maternal grandfather developed type 2 diabetes mellitus at age 75 years. The review of systems is normal.

On physical examination, vital signs and BMI are normal.

Laboratory studies:

Hemoglobin	11.9 g/dL (119 g/L)
Mean corpuscular volume	76 fL
Cholesterol (total)	155 mg/dL (4.01 mmol/L)
LDL cholesterol	85 mg/dL (2.2 mmol/L)
HDL cholesterol	33 mg/dL (0.85 mmol/L)
Bilirubin (total)	0.5 mg/dL (8.55 µmol/L)
Aspartate aminotransferase	25 U/L
Alanine aminotransferase	58 U/L
Alkaline phosphatase	110 U/L

Serologic tests for hepatitis virus infection are normal.

Which of the following is the most appropriate diagnostic test for this patient?

(A) Anti-tissue transglutaminase antibody
(B) α_1-Antitrypsin concentration
(C) Blood alcohol level
(D) Liver biopsy

Item 46

A 78-year-old woman is evaluated in the hospital after being admitted 5 days ago for a 2-week history of abdominal pain and nausea, along with black, tarry stools for the past 36 hours. On day 1 esophagogastroduodenoscopy showed a clean-based bleeding gastric ulcer that was positive for *Helicobacter pylori* infection; the ulcer was treated with injection therapy and coagulation therapy with probe cautery, and proton pump inhibitor therapy was initiated. The bleeding did not stop, and esophagogastroduodenoscopy was repeated on day 3 with endoclip therapy. The bleeding continued, and the patient has received eight units of packed erythrocytes.

On physical examination on day 5, the temperature is 37.2 °C (99.0 °F), the blood pressure is 95/50 mm Hg, the pulse rate is 103/min, and the respiration rate is 16/min. Rectal examination reveals melanotic stool. Laboratory studies reveal hemoglobin of 10.8 g/dL (108 g/L); all other tests, including coagulation parameters, are normal.

Which of the following is the most appropriate next step in the management of this patient?

(A) Bleeding scan
(B) *Helicobacter pylori* eradication therapy
(C) Intravenous octreotide
(D) Surgery

Item 47

A 45-year-old man is brought to the emergency department by fire rescue after his wife found him in bed lethargic and disoriented. The previous 2 days, the patient had been agitated and irritable and his speech was slurred. The patient has a history of cirrhosis complicated by esophageal variceal bleeding, ascites, and lower extremity edema, and his medications are furosemide, spironolactone, propranolol, and lactulose. He has a long history of alcohol dependence but has been sober for 1 year.

On physical examination, the patient is somnolent but arousable although not responsive to commands; he is afebrile. The blood pressure is 100/78 mm Hg, the pulse rate is 65/min, and the respiration rate is 12/min; the BMI is 26. There are no focal neurologic deficits; the pupils are equal and reactive to light. There is shifting abdominal dullness and 2+ lower extremity edema. The stool is negative for occult blood.

Laboratory studies:

Leukocyte count	5600/µL with normal differential (5.6×10^9/L)
Glucose (random)	112 mg/dL (6.21 mmol/L)
Sodium	135 meq/L (135 mmol/L)
Potassium	3.5 meq/L (3.5 mmol/L)
Chloride	100 meq/L (100 mmol/L)
Bicarbonate	28 meq/L (28 mmol/L)
Bilirubin (total)	4.0 mg/dL (68.4 µmol/L)
Bilirubin (direct)	2.3 mg/dL (39.3 µmol/L)
Aspartate aminotransferase	78 U/L
Alanine aminotransferase	45 U/L
Alkaline phosphatase	167 U/L
Albumin	2.7 g/dL (27 g/L)
Ammonia	230 µg/dL (135 µmol/L)
Blood alcohol	Negative

Urinalysis is negative. Dipstick is positive for 3+ leukocyte esterase and nitrites. CT scan of the head is normal. A diagnostic peritoneal fluid tap excludes spontaneous bacterial peritonitis. Empiric antibiotic therapy is started.

Which of the following is the most appropriate management for this patient?

(A) Corticosteroids
(B) Increase lactulose therapy
(C) Intravenous albumin
(D) Transjugular intrahepatic portosystemic shunt (TIPS)

Item 48

A 73-year-old man is evaluated for a 3-month history of progressive, dull, epigastric pain. The pain is constant and does not radiate. The patient has had early satiety during this time and has lost 13.5 kg (30 lb); he has had mild nausea but no vomiting. The patient has a history of peptic ulcer disease and occasional heartburn; his only medication is an over-the-counter antacid as needed.

On physical examination, the patient appears cachectic; BMI is 19. There is tenderness and fullness in the epigastric region with hepatomegaly. Laboratory studies reveal hemoglobin 10.4 g/dL (104 g/L) with a mean corpuscular volume of 74 fL; bilirubin, aspartate aminotransferase, alanine aminotransferase, and alkaline phosphatase concentrations are normal. Esophagogastroduodenoscopy shows a large ulcerated mass in the gastric body with heaped-up edges; biopsy specimens show adenocarcinoma.

Which of the following is the most appropriate next step in the management for this patient?

(A) CT scan of the abdomen
(B) Endoscopic ultrasonography
(C) *Helicobacter pylori* stool antigen test
(D) Positron emission tomography

Item 49

A 73-year-old woman who has been hospitalized for 3 weeks for urosepsis requiring parenteral nutrition is evaluated for 2 days of pain in the right upper quadrant of the abdomen and new-onset fever. The patient required mechanical ventilation but was recently weaned from the ventilator. Her medications include intravenous imipenem, furosemide, and omeprazole.

On physical examination, the temperature is 38.7 °C (101.7 °F), the blood pressure is 140/80 mm Hg, the pulse rate is 98/min, and the respiration rate is 18/min; the BMI is 35. The abdomen is diffusely tender with increased discomfort in the right upper quadrant with guarding and rebound. Bowel sounds are hypoactive and there is no ascites.

Laboratory studies:

Leukocyte count	17,000/µL (17×10^9/L) with 15% band forms
INR	1.3
Bilirubin (total)	2.4 mg/dL (41.0 µmol/L)
Bilirubin (direct)	1.7 mg/dL (29.0 µmol/L)
Aspartate aminotransferase	44 U/L
Alanine aminotransferase	35 U/L
Alkaline phosphatase	150 U/L
Albumin	3.8 g/dL (38 g/L)
Urinalysis	Negative

Ultrasonography of the abdomen shows a distended gallbladder with an edematous wall and pericholecystic fluid, pancreatic edema unchanged from previous imaging, and increased liver echotexture consistent with fatty infiltration; there is no cholelithiasis or sludge or dilatation of biliary duct.

Which of the following is the most appropriate next step in the management of this patient?

(A) Addition of an antifungal agent
(B) Endoscopic retrograde cholangiopancreatography
(C) Observation on current therapy
(D) Percutaneous cholecystostomy

Item 50

A 37-year-old man is evaluated for several weeks of progressive dysphagia, primarily for solid foods but also for liquids, associated with regurgitation of undigested food, nausea and vomiting, chest pain, and a 6.8-kg (15-lb) weight loss. The patient's only significant medical history is Hodgkin disease diagnosed 15 years ago, which was treated with mantle radiation.

On physical examination, the patient appears anxious but not in distress. Vital signs and physical examination are normal. Barium esophagography shows a dilated atonic esophagus with a tapered narrowing at the gastroesophageal junction. Esophageal manometry shows incomplete relaxation of a hypertensive lower esophageal sphincter with aperistalsis of the esophageal body. CT scan of the chest and abdomen confirms the dilated esophagus but shows no masses or lymphadenopathy. Esophagogastroduodenoscopy shows a mildly dilated esophagus with retained secretions and a 3-cm mass at the gastroesophageal junction. Biopsy specimens of the mucosa are negative for cancer.

Which of the following is the most appropriate management for this patient?

(A) Botulinum toxin injection of the distal esophagus
(B) Endoscopic ultrasonography of the esophagus with needle biopsy
(C) Pneumatic dilatation of the esophagus
(D) Repeat mucosal biopsy
(E) Thoracoscopic exploration

Item 51

A 30-year-old woman is evaluated for her risk for colon cancer. Her father and her sister both have colon cancer; her father was diagnosed at age 51 years and her sister at age 26 years. Her paternal uncle was diagnosed with colon cancer at age 57 years and with transitional cell cancer of the ureter at age 61 years. The patient had a screening colonoscopy 3 years ago that was normal; she is healthy and takes no medications.

On physical examination, vital signs are normal; BMI is 21.5. Physical examination is normal. Blood testing for germline mutations of the *MLH1* and *MSH2* genes is negative.

Which of the following is the most appropriate next step in the management of this patient?

(A) Abdominal CT scan
(B) Colonoscopy
(C) Mammography
(D) Repeat genetic testing

Item 52

A 57-year-old woman is evaluated in the intensive care unit for rapidly progressive renal failure requiring dialysis. The patient had been hospitalized for advanced liver disease including mental status changes secondary to encephalopathy. She has ascites. The liver disease is the result of chronic hepatitis C virus infection. The patient has no history of renal insufficiency and has not received antibiotics, intravenous contrast agents, or other nephrotoxic agents. Her medications are lactulose, nadolol, midodrine, octreotide, and albumin. She does not drink alcohol.

On physical examination, the temperature is 36.6 °C (97.8 °F), the blood pressure is 110/70 mm Hg, the pulse rate is 97/min, and the respiration rate is 12/min; the BMI is 22.

Laboratory studies:

Creatinine	5.4 mg/dL (412.0 µmol/L)
Urea nitrogen	120 mg/dL (42.8 mmol/L)
Urine sodium	less than 5 meq/L (5 mmol/L)
Urinalysis	Negative

Ultrasonography shows normal-size kidneys and no obstruction.

Which of the following is the most appropriate management for this patient?

(A) Add lisinopril
(B) Kidney and liver transplantation
(C) Kidney transplantation
(D) Liver transplantation
(E) Peritoneovenous shunt

Item 53

A 72-year-old man is evaluated for a 2-month history of epigastric discomfort associated in the past 6 weeks with a 4.6-kg (10 lb) weight loss; he has had 2 weeks of dark urine and light stool. The patient has no significant medical history and takes no medications.

On physical examination, vital signs are normal. There is scleral icterus, visibly jaundiced skin, and mild epigastric tenderness. Laboratory studies are significant for total bilirubin of 8.2 mg/dL (140.2 µmol/L) and alkaline phosphatase of 648 U/L. CT scan of the abdomen shows fullness in the head of the pancreas and biliary dilation but no evident pancreatic mass.

Which of the following is the most appropriate next step in the management of this patient?

(A) Endoscopic ultrasonography
(B) Measurement of CA 19-9 concentration
(C) Surgical exploration
(D) Ultrasonography of the abdomen
(E) Visceral angiography

Item 54

A 63-year-old man is evaluated in the hospital 3 days after having undergone a left hemicolectomy for adenocarcinoma of the colon. The patient has bloating and mild diffuse abdominal discomfort. He has not defecated or passed gas since surgery. He is nauseated but has not vomited. His medical history also includes hypertension and type 2 diabetes mellitus, and his medications are oxycodone, lisinopril, and glyburide.

On physical examination, the abdomen is distended with mild diffuse tenderness, tympany, and hypoactive bowel sounds but without rebound or guarding; there are no abdominal masses or organomegaly. Laboratory studies reveal random glucose 290 mg/dL (16.1 mmol/L), potassium 3.1 meq/L (3.1 mmol/L), and magnesium 1.1 mg/dL (0.45 mmol/L); complete blood count, serum thyroid-stimulating hormone, liver chemistry tests, and amylase are normal. Plain radiograph of the abdomen shows diffusely dilated loops of small bowel; CT scan of the abdomen and pelvis also shows dilated loops of bowel without evidence of obstruction.

In addition to glucose control and correction of electrolytes, which of the following is the most appropriate next step in the management of this patient?

(A) Insertion of a nasogastric tube to gravity drainage
(B) Insertion of a rectal tube
(C) Intravenous metoclopramide
(D) Minimization of oxycodone

Item 55

A 58-year-old woman is evaluated in the emergency department for substernal chest pain of 18 hours' duration. She describes the pain as a tightening that is not associated with eating or exertion and that radiates to the neck. The pain is not accompanied by dyspnea, nausea, or diaphoresis. She had a similar episode 1 month ago, and an exercise stress test showed no areas of ischemia. The patient's medical history includes hypertension and type 2 diabetes mellitus; her medications include ramipril, metformin, and aspirin.

On physical examination, the patient appears uncomfortable but not acutely ill. The temperature is 37.2 °C (99.0 °F), the blood pressure is 130/74 mm Hg, the pulse rate is 88/min, and the respiration rate is 16/min; the BMI is 31.5. The lungs are clear; the heart rate is regular and there are no murmurs. Electrocardiography shows nonspecific ST and T wave abnormalities, which are unchanged from a previous examination.

Which of the following is the most appropriate management for this patient?

(A) Ambulatory esophageal pH monitoring
(B) Esophageal manometry
(C) Esophagogastroduodenoscopy
(D) Oral proton pump inhibitor therapy
(E) Repeat exercise stress test

Item 56

A 39-year-old woman is evaluated for a 6-week history of nausea and intermittent vomiting, which began after a 3-day episode of severe nausea, vomiting, and diarrhea. At the same time, her school-age children had a similar episode that resolved spontaneously. However, since that time, the patient has had daily nausea worsened by eating, early satiety, bloating, and vomiting of large volumes of nonbilious food. She does not have abdominal pain, but in the past 6 weeks, she has lost 4.5 kg (10 lb). The patient's medical history includes a transsphenoidal resection of a nonfunctioning pituitary adenoma 3 years ago and two deliveries by cesarean section. Her mother has depression, and her father has primary sclerosing cholangitis.

On physical examination, she is thin (BMI 19); vital signs are normal. She responds appropriately and makes normal eye contact; there is no jaundice or scleral icterus. There is mild abdominal distention and normal bowel sounds without succussion splash or tenderness. Laboratory studies, including liver enzymes, are normal. Esophagogastroduodenoscopy reveals retained gastric contents but no obstruction. Radiograph of the small bowel is normal.

Which of the following is the most appropriate next step in the evaluation of this patient?

(A) Biliary ultrasonography
(B) Gastric scintigraphy
(C) MRI of the head
(D) Referral for biofeedback training
(E) Viral culture of stool

Item 57

A 65-year-old woman is evaluated in routine follow-up. Three months ago she was evaluated for fatigue and pruritus and was found to have an elevated serum alkaline phosphatase concentration and antimitochondrial antibody positive at a titer of 1:640. Liver biopsy specimen was consistent with stage 1 primary biliary cirrhosis. The pruritus is controlled with cholestyramine therapy. The patient is taking calcium, 1500 mg/d, and vitamin D, 800 IU/d. She has no other medical problems or symptoms.

On physical examination, vital signs are normal; BMI is 26. The rest of the examination is normal.

Laboratory studies:
Bilirubin (total)	1.0 mg/dL (17.1 µmol/L)
Aspartate aminotransferase	65 U/L
Alanine aminotransferase	70 U/L
Alkaline phosphatase	200 U/L

Dual energy x-ray absorptiometry scan shows normal bone mineral density.

Which of the following is the most appropriate therapy for this patient?

(A) Alendronate
(B) Estrogen replacement
(C) Evaluation for liver transplantation
(D) Ursodeoxycholic acid

Item 58

A 42-year-old man is evaluated for a 1-month history of progressive jaundice, pruritus, and dark urine. The patient has a 15-year history of ulcerative colitis; he is poorly compliant with mesalamine therapy and occasionally requires corticosteroid therapy. He drinks two cans of beer a day and has never used injection drugs or received a blood transfusion. He takes no other medications.

On physical examination, vital signs are normal. There is mild jaundice and hepatomegaly but no splenomegaly, ascites, or abdominal tenderness. There is no asterixis.

Laboratory studies:

Platelet count	350,000/μL (350 × 10⁹/L)
INR	1.1
Aspartate aminotransferase	150 U/L
Alanine aminotransferase	180 U/L
Bilirubin (total)	4.2 mg/dL (71.8 μmol/L)
Alkaline phosphatase	450 U/L
Total protein	6.0 g/dL (60 g/L)
Albumin	3.8 g/dL (38 g/L)

Which of the following is the most likely diagnosis?

(A) Autoimmune hepatitis

(B) Hepatitis A

(C) Hepatitis C

(D) Primary sclerosing cholangitis

Item 59

A 57-year-old woman is evaluated as a new patient. She is asymptomatic and has no significant medical history. Her father died of a myocardial infarction at age 71 years, and her 81-year-old mother is alive and healthy. There is no family history of cancer, but the patient has a friend who was recently diagnosed with colon cancer and is concerned about her risk for the disease.

On physical examination, vital signs are normal; BMI is 25.5; the rest of the physical examination is normal. Laboratory results are all within normal limits.

Which of the following is an appropriate screening strategy for colon cancer in this patient?

(A) Annual digital rectal examination every year

(B) Colonoscopy every 10 years

(C) Double-contrast barium enema every 3 years

(D) Flexible sigmoidoscopy every 10 years

Item 60

A 74-year-old man is evaluated for a 2-month history of recurrent melena. He has had recurrent 2 - or 3-day periods of black, tarry stool followed by normal stool for the next week. His most recent black stool was yesterday. During this time, he has developed anemia and required transfusions of a total of eight units of blood. He has not had chest pain, abdominal pain, nausea or vomiting, or bleeding. The patient's medical history includes hypertension and mild chronic obstructive pulmonary disease; his medications are enalapril, albuterol by metered-dose inhaler, and aspirin.

On physical examination, the temperature is 37.0 °C (98.6 °F), the blood pressure is 132/74 mm Hg, the pulse rate is 84/min, and the respiration rate is 12/min; the BMI is 26.5. There is no scleral icterus and no abdominal distention or tenderness; bowel sounds are normal and there is no organomegaly. Rectal examination reveals black, tarry stool that is positive for occult blood. Laboratory studies reveal hemoglobin of 8.6 g/dL (86 g/L) with a mean corpuscular volume of 80 fL; leukocyte count, platelet count, prothrombin time, activated partial thromboplastin time, and INR are normal. Esophagogastroduodenoscopy on two occasions and a colonoscopy fail to identify a bleeding source.

Which of the following is the most appropriate next step in the evaluation of this patient?

(A) CT angiography

(B) Double-balloon enteroscopy

(C) Intraoperative endoscopy

(D) Small-bowel barium examination

(E) Wireless capsule endoscopy

Item 61

A 40-year-old man undergoes a pre-employment physical examination and mentions that he has a 10-year history of heartburn and regurgitation that are not associated with dysphagia or weight loss and that are well-controlled with once-daily omeprazole therapy. He has stopped the omeprazole before, but his symptoms return. He has never had an endoscopic examination. His father was diagnosed with esophageal cancer at age 62 years, and the patient agrees to undergo screening for Barrett esophagus. He is otherwise healthy, and physical examination and laboratory evaluation are normal.

Esophagogastroduodenoscopy reveals a small hiatal hernia but no features of Barrett esophagus. In addition, eight 2- to 4-mm polyps are detected in the body and fundus of the stomach; the polyps are uniform in appearance, and biopsy specimen of one of the polyps reveals a fundic gland polyp.

Which of the following is the most appropriate next step in the evaluation of this patient?

(A) Colonoscopy

(B) Endoscopic ultrasonography

(C) *Helicobacter pylori* serum antibody testing

(D) Repeat endoscopy with removal of all polyps

(E) No further testing

Item 62

A 35-year-old woman in her second trimester of pregnancy is evaluated for liver cysts detected on ultrasonography of the abdomen. She has had a normal pregnancy and has no abdominal pain, jaundice, fever, or weight loss. Her only medications are a multivitamin and folic acid.

On physical examination, the temperature is 36.1 °C (97.0 °F), the blood pressure is 105/70 mm Hg, the pulse rate is 90/min, and the respiration rate is 14/min. The right lower lobe of the liver is palpable two finger breadths below the costal margin. Laboratory tests, including liver chemistry tests, are normal. Ultrasonography shows four 2- to 4-cm fluid-filled cysts with no internal masses or debris.

Which of the following is the most appropriate diagnostic evaluation?

(A) Aspiration of the cysts after delivery

(B) Measurement of serum α-fetoprotein and carcinoembryonic antigen

(C) MRI of the liver

(D) No further evaluation

Item 63

A 45-year-old man is evaluated 6 months after undergoing liver transplantation for hepatitis C virus–related cirrhosis. The infection had never been treated and the patient was viremic at the time of transplantation. His medications are tacrolimus, mycophenolate, trimethoprim-sulfamethoxazole, and ursodeoxycholic acid.

On physical examination, the patient is afebrile; the blood pressure is 100/78 mm Hg, the pulse rate is 65/min, and the respiration rate is 12/min. The BMI is 26. There is a healed midline abdominal incision but no ascites, lower extremity edema, or jaundice.

Laboratory studies:

Bilirubin (total)	1.4 mg/dL (23.9 µmol/L)
Bilirubin (direct)	0.9 mg/dL (15.4 µmol/L)
Aspartate aminotransferase	75 U/L
Alanine aminotransferase	95 U/L
Albumin	3.7 g/dL (37 g/L)
Hepatitis C virus RNA	>500,000 U/mL
Genotype	1A
Hepatitis A total antibody	Positive

Ultrasonography of the liver shows patent vessels, no bile duct dilatation, and normal echotexture.

Which of the following is the most appropriate management of this patient?

(A) Discontinue mycophenolate
(B) Pegylated interferon and ribavirin therapy
(C) Liver biopsy
(D) Observation; reevaluation in 3 months

Item 64

A 76-year-old man is evaluated in the emergency department after having passed a large amount of red and maroon blood per rectum. After this episode, the patient felt dizzy and stumbled but did not lose consciousness or injure himself. In the ambulance on the way to the emergency department, he passed more blood, and the blood pressure was 100/60 mm Hg and the pulse rate was 110/min. He has not had abdominal pain, nausea, vomiting, fever, or weight loss. He had a colonoscopy 1 year ago that showed a benign polyp and diverticulosis. His medical history includes hypertension and hypercholesterolemia, and his medications are hydrochlorothiazide, lisinopril, simvastatin, and aspirin.

On physical examination, the patient is pale; the blood pressure is 105/65 mm Hg and the pulse rate is 100/min. Abdominal examination is normal; there is dried blood in the perianal area, and rectal examination reveals normal tone but fresh blood on the examination glove. Laboratory studies reveal hemoglobin 10.1 g/dL (101 g/L) and normal biochemical studies, including blood urea nitrogen. Leukocyte count is 5600/µL (5.6 × 10⁹/L) and platelet count is 348,000/µL (348 × 10⁹/L); prothrombin time and activated partial thromboplastin time are normal.

Which of the following is the most appropriate next step in the management of this patient?

(A) Colonoscopy
(B) Esophagogastroduodenoscopy
(C) Intravenous access
(D) Placement of a nasogastric tube with lavage
(E) Technetium-labeled red blood cell scan

Item 65

A 34-year-old man is evaluated as a new patient. He is asymptomatic and has no significant medical history, but he is concerned about his risk for colon cancer. His 59-year-old mother had two adenomatous polyps detected at the age of 52 years. She has had surveillance colonoscopy every 3 years since then and has had two additional polyps detected. His father has no history of colon polyps, and there is no family history of colorectal cancer.

On physical examination, vital signs are normal; BMI is 21.5; the rest of the physical examination is normal. Laboratory results are all within normal limits.

Which of the following is the most appropriate screening strategy for this patient?

(A) Colonoscopy at age 40 years
(B) Colonoscopy at age 42 years
(C) Colonoscopy at age 50 years
(D) Fecal occult blood testing at age 40 years
(E) Fecal occult blood testing at age 50 years

Item 66

A 25-year-old woman is brought to the emergency department by her husband for yellowing of the eyes and increasing confusion and somnolence. The patient is 30 weeks' pregnant and just returned from visiting her parents in Africa. She has been previously healthy and takes only prenatal vitamins. Previously a social drinker, she stopped consuming alcohol entirely at the onset of her pregnancy.

On physical examination, the temperature is 37.2 °C (99.0 °F), the blood pressure is 90/40 mm Hg, the pulse rate is 100/min, and the respiration rate is 12/min; the BMI is 20. Examination reveals a gravid uterus and asterixis.

Laboratory studies:

Hemoglobin	14 g/dL (140 g/L)
Leukocyte count	15,000/µL (15 × 10⁹/L)
Platelet count	450,000/µL (450 × 10⁹/L)
INR	4.7
Bilirubin (total)	12.0 mg/dL (205.2 µmol/L)
Bilirubin (direct)	9.0 mg/dL (153.9 µmol/L)
Aspartate aminotransferase	3000 U/L
Alanine aminotransferase	2870 U/L
Alkaline phosphatase	400 U/L
Albumin	2.3 g/dL (23 g/L)
Ammonia	120 µg/dL (70.4 µmol/L)

Hepatitis A virus (IgM)	Negative
Hepatitis B surface antigen (IgG and IgM)	Negative
Hepatitis B virus DNA (PCR)	Negative
Hepatitis C virus antibody	Negative
Antinuclear antibody	Negative
Anti–smooth muscle antibody	Negative
Antimitochondrial antibody	Negative
Alcohol screen	Negative
Herpes simplex virus (PCR)	Negative

The peripheral blood smear is normal. Ultrasonography of the abdomen shows a small liver, no ductal dilatation, and no varices.

Which of the following is the most likely cause of this patient's fulminant hepatic failure?

(A) Acute autoimmune hepatitis
(B) Acute alcoholic hepatitis
(C) HELLP syndrome
(D) Hepatitis E virus infection

Item 67

A 51-year-old man is evaluated for a 6-month history of nausea, bloating, and diarrhea. He typically has nausea and bloating within an hour after eating and then has an explosive bowel movement; during the episode he is tachycardic. He feels reasonably well between episodes and at night. The episodes are worst in the morning even though he consumes only coffee and a breakfast drink. High-fat foods are better tolerated and do not seem to provoke symptoms. He has no abdominal pain, vomiting, or weight loss. His medical history includes a distal gastrectomy 9 months ago for a perforated NSAID-induced peptic ulcer. He has no other medical problems and takes no medications.

On physical examination, the BMI is 24 and vital signs are normal. He has hyperactive bowel sounds. The heart, lungs, and abdomen are normal. Laboratory studies, including complete blood count and routine biochemistry tests, are normal. Esophagogastroduodenoscopy shows changes of a distal gastrectomy with a widely patent anastomosis. The mucosa is normal throughout, and biopsy specimens and aspirates of the small bowel are normal.

Which of the following is the most likely diagnosis?

(A) Carcinoid syndrome
(B) Chronic mesenteric ischemia
(C) Dumping syndrome
(D) Gastrinoma
(E) Irritable bowel syndrome

Item 68

A 65-year-old woman is evaluated for a 6-month history of watery, nonbloody diarrhea; she has from 3 to 20 bowel movements a day. She also has abdominal cramps, bloating,

and occasional fecal incontinence and has lost 2.2 kg (5 lb) since the beginning of the episode. She had been previously healthy. She has not traveled recently or used antibiotics.

On physical examination, the temperature is 37.2 °C (99.0 °F), the blood pressure is 118/82 mm Hg, the pulse rate is 76/min, and the respiration rate is 14/min. The heart rate is regular and the chest is clear. The abdomen is soft with slight distention.

Which of the following is the most likely diagnosis?

(A) *Clostridium difficile* colitis
(B) Microscopic colitis
(C) Tropical sprue
(D) Ulcerative colitis

Item 69

A 20-year-old woman is evaluated in the emergency department for a 2-week history of malaise, fatigue, and mild jaundice. The patient has no significant medical history, but she uses injection drugs. She drinks alcohol socially.

On physical examination, the temperature is 37.8 °C (100.0 °F), the blood pressure is 128/70 mm Hg, the pulse rate is 100/min, and the respiration rate is 16/min. Examination reveals slight scleral icterus, needle puncture marks in the antecubital fossae, and hepatomegaly; there is no splenomegaly, cutaneous angiomata, ascites, or asterixis.

Laboratory studies:

Bilirubin (total)	4.6 mg/dL (78.7 µmol/L)
Aspartate aminotransferase	580 U/L
Alanine aminotransferase	750 U/L
Alkaline phosphatase	145 U/L
Albumin	4.2 g/dL (42 g/L)
Hepatitis B surface antigen	Negative
Hepatitis B core antibody (IgG and IgM)	Negative
Hepatitis C virus antibody	Negative
Hepatitis A virus antibody (IgG and IgM)	Negative
Drug and alcohol screens	Negative

Ultrasonography shows hepatomegaly.

In addition to screening for HIV infection, which of the following is the most appropriate next diagnostic test?

(A) Hepatitis B virus DNA
(B) Hepatitis C virus RNA
(C) Liver biopsy
(D) MRI of the liver

Item 70

A 63-year-old woman is evaluated for heartburn, sour regurgitation, and substernal chest pain, symptoms that have occurred several times a week for the past 5 years. She does not have fever, nausea, vomiting, or weight loss. The patient has a history of hypertension, and her medications include an angiotensin receptor blocker and hydrochlorothiazide.

On physical examination, vital signs are normal; BMI is 28.5. The abdomen is soft without tenderness or distention; bowel sounds are normal.

Which of the following is the most appropriate management of this patient?

(A) Ambulatory esophageal pH monitoring
(B) Esophageal manometry
(C) Esophagogastroduodenoscopy
(D) Oral calcium channel blocker therapy

Item 71

A 68-year-old man is evaluated in the emergency department for a 6-hour history of nausea and vomiting, with some bright red emesis. For the past 2 hours he has felt lightheaded and weak.

On physical examination, the temperature is 37.0 °C (98.6 °F), the blood pressure is 88/51 mm Hg, the pulse rate is 114/min, and the respiration rate is 18/min. Nasogastric aspiration shows a mixture of coffee grounds and dark blood. The abdomen is not tender, and bowel sounds are normal. Laboratory studies reveal hemoglobin of 9.4 g/dL (94 g/L); all other tests are normal. Omeprazole therapy is begun. After volume repletion with saline and transfusion of two units of packed erythrocytes, esophagogastroduodenoscopy is performed and reveals a duodenal ulcer with a small visible vessel.

Which of the following is the best management option for this patient?

(A) Endoscopic therapy
(B) Immediate surgical intervention
(C) Observation
(D) Octreotide infusion
(E) Ranitidine infusion

Item 72

A 52-year-old man is evaluated for a 5-month history of three to four loose, bloody stools a day with mild urgency, abdominal cramping, and fatigue. He has not lost weight during this episode. The patient is a former cigarette smoker but quit smoking 18 months ago. He is otherwise healthy.

On physical examination, vital signs are normal. There is mild lower abdominal tenderness without rebound or guarding; there are no palpable abdominal masses. Examination of the rectum shows gross blood. Laboratory studies reveal hemoglobin 12.9 g/dL (129 g/L) with a mean corpuscular volume of 78 fL. Stool culture is negative. Colonoscopy shows continuous mild erythema and loss of vascular pattern from the rectum to the proximal sigmoid colon; the rest of the colon and terminal ileum are normal. Biopsy specimens from the abnormal mucosa show cryptitis, crypt abscesses, and distortion of crypt architecture.

Which of the following would be the most appropriate therapy for this patient?

(A) Azathioprine
(B) Ciprofloxacin
(C) Metronidazole
(D) Infliximab
(E) Mesalamine

Item 73

A 34-year-old woman is evaluated for a 6-month history of nausea and vomiting. The symptoms were initially mild but have become progressively severe, and she now has daily symptoms that are exacerbated by eating. She has early satiety and postprandial bloating; she vomits partially digested food a few hours after eating. She has mild epigastric burning but no other features of abdominal pain. She has lost 6.8 kg (15 lb) since the beginning of this episode; her most recent menses was 1 week ago. The patient's medical history includes endometriosis and migraine, and her only medication is as-needed ibuprofen. Her mother has scleroderma and her father has type 2 diabetes mellitus.

On physical examination, the patient is thin (BMI 20); the abdomen is distended with a succussion splash and mild epigastric tenderness; there are no palpable abdominal masses or hepatosplenomegaly. Laboratory studies, including liver enzymes and fasting blood glucose, are normal.

Which of the following is the most appropriate next step in the evaluation of this patient?

(A) Biliary ultrasonography
(B) Esophagogastroduodenoscopy
(C) Gastric scintigraphy
(D) Measurement of anticentromere and anti-scl-70 antibodies
(E) Oral glucose tolerance test

Item 74

A 37-year-old woman is evaluated for a 4-month history of recurrent bloody stool described as bright red blood on the outside of the stool and on the toilet paper. She does not have blood mixed in the stool. She has no pain on defecation, and no diarrhea, constipation, fever, or chills. She has been taking a fiber supplement for the past month without effect. The patient is otherwise healthy and takes no medications. There is no family history of colon cancer.

On physical examination, vital signs are normal; BMI is 19.5. Abdominal and rectal examinations are normal; stool is positive for occult blood. Laboratory studies, including complete blood count, are normal.

Which of the following is the most appropriate next step in the management of this patient?

(A) Colonoscopy now
(B) Continued high-fiber diet
(C) Flexible sigmoidoscopy
(D) Oral prednisone therapy

Item 75

A 28-year-old woman who is 30 weeks pregnant is evaluated for a 2-week history of pruritus and scleral icterus. It is her first pregnancy, and she has no significant medical history; she does not drink alcohol and takes only a prenatal vitamin.

On physical examination, the patient is afebrile; the blood pressure is 100/70 mm Hg, the pulse rate is 72/min, and the respiration rate is 15/min. Examination reveals a gravid uterus, mild scleral icterus, and linear excoriations on the skin; there is no ascites or lower extremity edema.

Laboratory studies:

Hemoglobin	13.4 g/dL (134 g/L)
Platelet count	275,000/µL (275 × 10⁹/L)
Bilirubin (total)	4.2 mg/dL (71.8 µmol/L)
Bilirubin (direct)	2.3 mg/dL (39.3 µmol/L)
Aspartate aminotransferase	44 U/L
Alanine aminotransferase	38 U/L
Alkaline phosphatase	180 U/L
Lactate dehydrogenase	82 U/L
INR	1.0
Hepatitis B surface antigen	Negative
Hepatitis B surface antibody	Positive
Hepatitis C virus antibody	Negative
Hepatitis A virus antibody (IgG)	Positive
Antinuclear antibody	Negative
Anti–smooth muscle antibody	Negative

Ultrasonography of the liver is normal.

Which of the following is the most likely diagnosis?

(A) Acute fatty liver of pregnancy
(B) Acute hepatitis A infection
(C) Cholestasis of pregnancy
(D) HELLP syndrome

Item 76

A 42-year-old man is evaluated in the hospital for a 1-year history of postprandial abdominal pain that radiates to the back and that is worse after eating and is associated with nausea. He has not had vomiting, weight loss, or change in bowel habits. The patient has had at least five alcohol-containing drinks a day for 20 years; he has reduced his intake in the past year because of continued abdominal pain.

On physical examination, vital signs are normal; BMI is 24. There is mild epigastric tenderness with no guarding or rebound and normal bowel sounds. Laboratory studies reveal normal complete blood count, fasting glucose, and liver chemistry tests; amylase is 221 U/L and lipase 472 U/L. Radiography, ultrasonography, and CT scan of the abdomen are normal, as is esophagogastroduodenoscopy.

Which of the following is the most appropriate next step in the evaluation of this patient?

(A) Biliary scintigraphy
(B) Colonoscopy
(C) Endoscopic retrograde cholangiopancreatography
(D) Measurement of stool elastase

Item 77

A 62-year-old woman with a 10-year history of gastroesophageal reflux symptoms undergoes screening esophagogastroduodenoscopy. Salmon-colored mucosa is seen in the distal 7 cm of esophagus. A biopsy of the abnormal esophageal mucosa shows intestinal metaplasia with goblet cells. The patient is asymptomatic, and her only medication is omeprazole, 40 mg/d.

Which of the following is the most appropriate management for this patient?

(A) Endoscopic/histologic surveillance
(B) No further endoscopic evaluation
(C) Surgical esophagectomy
(D) Test and treat for *Helicobacter pylori*

Item 78

A 55-year-old man is evaluated for a 3-month history of five or six bowel movements a day. The patient was diagnosed with pancolitis 25 years ago. He has had severe attacks in the past necessitating corticosteroid therapy. His disease had been maintained on therapy with azathioprine and mesalamine, and he is contemplating a change in his regimen to an anti-tumor necrosis factor-α agent. His most recent surveillance colonoscopy was 18 months ago, and before instituting the change, he undergoes another colonoscopy. He is otherwise healthy, and his only medications are the azathioprine, 150 mg/d, and mesalamine, 4.8 g/d.

On physical examination, vital signs are normal; there is mild lower abdominal tenderness, but the rest of the examination and the results of laboratory studies are normal. Colonoscopy shows numerous pseudopolyps and moderate to severe active inflammation in the left colon, with a transition to normal appearing mucosa at the splenic flexure. Biopsy specimen from the sigmoid colon shows high-grade dysplasia; a specimen from the descending colon shows low-grade dysplasia.

Which of the following is the most appropriate management for this patient?

(A) Annual surveillance colonoscopy with multiple biopsies
(B) Hemicolectomy with colorectal anastomosis
(C) Therapy with infliximab
(D) Total proctocolectomy

Item 79

A 64-year-old woman is evaluated in the emergency department for a 3-week history of postprandial right upper quadrant abdominal pain that has become increasingly intense. The pain is now constant and radiates to her right shoulder and is accompanied by fever, nausea, and vomiting. The patient has a history of type 2 diabetes mellitus and obesity, and her medications are metformin, glimepiride, and aspirin.

On physical examination, the patient is uncomfortable; the temperature is 38.3 °C (101.0 °F), the blood pressure is 110/65 mm Hg, the pulse rate is 110/min, and the respiration rate is 20/min. The BMI is 42. There is pain on palpation in the right upper quadrant of the abdomen with a Murphy sign. There is no rebound or tenderness or jaundice.

Laboratory studies:

Leukocyte count	16,000/μL (16 × 10⁹/L) with 20% band forms
Bilirubin (total)	2.0 mg/dL (34.2 μmol/L)
Aspartate aminotransferase	40 U/L
Alanine aminotransferase	120 U/L
Alkaline phosphatase	120 U/L
Amylase	58 U/L
Lipase	36 U/L

Ultrasonography shows pericholecystic fluid with echogenic stones in the gallbladder. The wall of the gallbladder is thickened (6 mm), and there is no dilatation of the bile ducts.

In addition to antibiotics, which of the following is the most appropriate management for this patient?

(A) CT scan of the abdomen
(B) Endoscopic retrograde cholangiopancreatography
(C) Cholecystectomy
(D) Magnetic resonance cholangiopancreatography

Item 80

A 47-year-old woman is evaluated in the emergency department for 3 days of abdominal pain and distention; she has not had a bowel movement during that time. The patient has early satiety and decreased appetite; she has had nausea and vomited once. She has had similar symptoms previously. The patient has a history of systemic sclerosis. Her medications include nifedipine for Raynaud phenomenon and omeprazole for gastroesophageal reflux disease.

On physical examination, pulse rate is 92/min; other vital signs are normal. The abdomen is distended with hypoactive bowel sounds and tympany. There is no succussion splash. There are no abdominal masses or organomegaly. Laboratory studies reveal hemoglobin 12.1 g/dL (121 g/L); serum thyroid-stimulating hormone, amylase, and liver chemistry tests are normal. Plain radiograph of the abdomen shows dilated loops of small bowel. After bowel decompression with a nasogastric tube and bowel rest, upper and lower gastrointestinal radiographic series shows no obstructive lesions.

Which of the following is the most likely diagnosis?

(A) Chronic intestinal pseudo-obstruction
(B) Colonic inertia
(C) Gastroparesis
(D) Small-bowel obstruction

Item 81

A 63-year-old man is evaluated for a 3-month history of a 9-kg (20-lb) weight loss and 1 month of painless jaundice and decreased appetite. The patient was diagnosed with ulcerative colitis at age 21 years and underwent a colectomy with ileostomy. He was diagnosed with primary sclerosing cholangitis 2 years ago.

On physical examination, the patient is thin and cachectic; he is afebrile. The blood pressure is 130/75 mm Hg, the pulse rate is 80/min, and the respiration rate is 14/min; the BMI is 22. Examination reveals scleral icterus, but no ascites or right upper quadrant tenderness on deep palpation; Murphy sign was not elicited.

Laboratory studies:

Hemoglobin	14.5 g/dL (145 g/L)
Leukocyte count	3400/μL (3.4 × 10⁹/L) with normal differential
Platelet count	225,000/μL (225 × 10⁹/L)
Bilirubin (total)	8.0 mg/dL (136.8 μmol/L)
Bilirubin (direct)	3.6 mg/dL (61.56 μmol/L)
Aspartate aminotransferase	120 U/L
Alanine aminotransferase	145 U/L
Alkaline phosphatase	456 U/L
CA 19-9	1200 U/mL (1200 kU/L)
α-Fetoprotein	9.0 ng/mL (9.0 μ/L)

Magnetic resonance cholangiopancreatography shows dilated intrahepatic bile ducts with new irregular strictures at the common hepatic duct with a periductal irregular mass surrounding the stricture; the pancreatic duct has a normal caliber. The gallbladder appears normal without edema or wall thickening.

Which of the following is the most likely diagnosis?

(A) Acute cholecystitis
(B) Cholangiocarcinoma
(C) Choledocholithiasis
(D) Progressive primary sclerosing cholangitis

Item 82

A 47-year-old man is evaluated in the emergency department for 7 days of odynophagia with epigastric pain, nausea and vomiting, diarrhea, and low-grade fever; he has lost 4.5 kg (10 lb) during the episode. The patient received a kidney transplant 6 months ago for hypertensive kidney disease; his medications are atenolol, prednisone, tacrolimus, and mycophenolate mofetil. He has no other medical problems and denies any HIV risk factors.

On physical examination, the temperature is 38.0 °C (100.8 °F), the blood pressure is 148/94 mm Hg, the pulse rate is 90/min, and the respiration rate is 22/min. Esophagogastroduodenoscopy shows a 2.5-cm esophageal ulcer with raised borders. The rest of the esophagus appears normal. Biopsy specimen from the base of the ulcer shows intense inflammatory infiltrates with granulation tissue associated with occlusion body cells.

Which of the following is the most likely diagnosis?

(A) *Candida albicans* esophagitis

(B) Cytomegalovirus esophagitis

(C) HIV esophagitis

(D) Pill-induced esophageal ulcer

Item 83

A 67-year-old woman is evaluated for a 2-month history of epigastric discomfort, a burning sensation that does not radiate and is not associated with eating. She has had episodic mild nausea and intermittent bloating but no acid regurgitation, heartburn, dysphagia, or odynophagia. She has one bowel movement of well-formed stool a day, and her weight is stable. The patient has a history of osteopenia and gallstone pancreatitis for which she had a cholecystectomy; her medications include calcium and vitamin D supplements. Her mother had gastric cancer.

On physical examination, vital signs are normal. There is mild epigastric tenderness, normal bowel sounds with no bruits, no rebound or guarding, and no hepatomegaly or lymphadenopathy. Complete blood count and serum chemistry tests, including liver enzymes, amylase, and lipase, are normal.

Which of the following is the most appropriate management of this patient?

(A) Endoscopic retrograde cholangiopancreatography

(B) Esophagogastroduodenoscopy

(C) *Helicobacter pylori* stool antigen assay

(D) Nortriptyline at bedtime

(E) Proton pump inhibitor empiric trial

Item 84

A 42-year-old woman is evaluated in the emergency department for the acute onset of epigastric pain that radiates to the back and is associated with nausea and vomiting. The patient had previously been healthy and has no history of alcohol or tobacco use. Her only medication is an oral contraceptive pill.

On physical examination, the temperature is 37.2 °C (99 °F), the blood pressure is 158/90 mm Hg, the pulse rate is 101/min, and the respiration rate is 20/min. There is no scleral icterus or jaundice. The abdomen is distended with mid-epigastric tenderness without rebound or guarding and with hypoactive bowel sounds.

Laboratory studies:

Leukocyte count	13,500/µL (13.5×10^9/L)
Aspartate aminotransferase	131 U/L
Alanine aminotransferase	567 U/L
Bilirubin (total)	1.1 mg/dL (18.8 µmol/L)
Amylase	824 U/L
Lipase	1432 U/L

Radiography of the abdomen shows mild ileus.

Which of the following is the most appropriate next step in the evaluation of this patient?

(A) CT scan of the abdomen and pelvis

(B) Endoscopic retrograde cholangiopancreatography

(C) Esophagogastroduodenoscopy

(D) Ultrasonography of the abdomen

Item 85

A 57-year-old man is evaluated for elevated aminotransferase concentrations detected on evaluation for fatigue. The patient has a history of osteoarthritis, type 1 diabetes mellitus, and hypertension, and his medications are ibuprofen, glargine and lispro insulins, lisinopril, simvastatin, and low-dose aspirin. The patient does not use illicit drugs, alcohol, or tobacco; he has never had a blood transfusion. His mother died of heart failure and a maternal aunt died of cirrhosis of unknown cause.

On physical examination, the patient is afebrile; the blood pressure is 135/81 mm Hg, the pulse rate is 53/min, and the respiration rate is 14/min. The BMI is 27. Cardiopulmonary examination is normal; there are no stigmata of chronic liver disease.

Laboratory studies:

Hemoglobin	14 g/dL (140 g/L)
Glucose (fasting)	145 mg/dL (8.0 mmol/L)
Bilirubin (total)	1.2 mg/dL (20.5 µmol/L)
Bilirubin (direct)	0.4 mg/dL (6.8 µmol/L)
Aspartate aminotransferase	75 U/L
Alanine aminotransferase	88 U/L
Alkaline phosphatase	120 U/L
Albumin	4.2 g/dL (42 g/L)
Ferritin	1267 ng/mL (1267 mg/L)
Transferrin saturation	75%

Serologic tests for viral hepatitis, antinuclear antibody, anti–smooth muscle antibody, and antimitochondrial antibody are negative. Chest radiography and electrocardiography are normal.

Which of the following is the most appropriate next step in the management for this patient?

(A) Deferoxamine therapy

(B) Genetic testing for mutations of the *HFE* gene

(C) MRI of the abdomen

(D) Phlebotomy

Item 86

A 35-year-old man is evaluated in the emergency department for the acute onset of abdominal pain and nausea; he does not have diarrhea or other changes in bowel habits. The patient has a 17-year history of Crohn disease, which was managed with long-term corticosteroid therapy until he began therapy with azathioprine 4 months ago; his disease has been stable since that time until the current episode. He takes no other medications.

On physical examination, the temperature is 37.0 °C (98.5 °F), the blood pressure is 108/76 mm Hg, the pulse rate is 110/min, and the respiration rate is 19/min. There is no scleral icterus. There is mild epigastric tenderness, but the rest of the examination is normal. Right upper quadrant abdominal ultrasonography is normal.

Laboratory studies:

Hemoglobin	17.2 g/dL (172 g/L)
Leukocyte count	4500/μL (4.5 × 10⁹/L)
Aspartate aminotransferase	20 U/L
Alanine aminotransferase	22 U/L
Bilirubin (total)	0.9 mg/dL (15.4 μmol/L)
Amylase	1500 U/L
Lipase	1630 U/L

Which of the following is the most likely diagnosis?

(A) Azathioprine-induced pancreatitis
(B) Crohn disease flare
(C) Gallstone pancreatitis
(D) *Helicobacter pylori*–associated gastritis
(E) Peptic ulcer disease

Item 87

A 68-year-old woman is evaluated after surgical resection for colon cancer. Three months ago, the patient presented with abdominal pain and rectal bleeding; colonoscopy revealed a mass in the mid-sigmoid colon, obstructing the lumen and preventing passage of the colonoscope. A left hemicolectomy was done, and she was found to have stage IIA disease. She has recovered well from surgery. Her medical history also includes coronary artery disease and hypercholesterolemia, and her medications are metoprolol, atorvastatin, and aspirin.

On physical examination, vital signs are normal; BMI is 23.5. She has a well-healed abdominal scar; the abdomen is not tender and there is no organomegaly. The chest is clear. Laboratory results, including complete blood count, are normal; she had a normal serum carcinoembryonic antigen (CEA) level before surgery. Preoperative CT scan of the abdomen showed no lymphadenopathy or liver masses.

In addition to CEA testing in 3 months, which of the following is the most appropriate management for this patient?

(A) Colonoscopy now and again in 1 year
(B) Colonoscopy in 3 years
(C) CT scan in 3 and 12 months
(D) Positron emission tomography scan now
(E) Proctoscopy now

Item 88

A 72-year-old man is evaluated in the hospital for 6 weeks of progressive dysphagia, initially for solid foods and now for both solid foods and liquids. He has had a 6.8-kg (15-lb) weight loss during this episode. He has not had fever, chills, sweats, nausea, or vomiting. The patient has hypertension, which is controlled with amlodipine therapy. He also takes a daily aspirin.

On physical examination, he appears ill and is thin (BMI 19); vital signs are normal. Laboratory findings include hemoglobin of 10.3 g/dL (103 g/L), mean corpuscular volume 88 fL, creatinine 1.5 mg/dL (114.5 μmol/L), and sodium 133 meq/L (133 mmol/L). CT scan shows a right lower lobe pulmonary infiltrate, thickening of the lower esophagus, multiple enhancing hepatic lesions, and celiac lymphadenopathy. Esophagogastroduodenoscopy shows a circumferential mass in the lower esophagus; the endoscope can pass through the mass. Biopsy specimen of the mass shows adenocarcinoma.

Which of the following is the most appropriate management for this patient?

(A) Esophagectomy
(B) Esophagectomy with hepatic wedge resection
(C) Neoadjuvant chemotherapy
(D) Palliative self-expanding metal stent

Item 89

A 42-year-old woman is evaluated in the emergency department for lower chest pain and dyspnea that awoke her suddenly from sleep. The pain is moderately severe and does not radiate. The patient had laparoscopic Roux-en-Y gastric bypass for morbid obesity 10 days ago and was discharged from the hospital 5 days ago. She has had mild nausea and an average of five bowel movements a day since surgery. She also has a history of reflux esophagitis and hypertension; her medications include a multivitamin with iron, calcium, vitamin D, thiamine, vitamin B₁₂, pantoprazole, metoprolol, and prochlorperazine.

On physical examination, the patient appears to be in mild distress; she is afebrile, the blood pressure is 105/70 mm Hg, the pulse rate is 110/min, and the respiration rate is 22/min. The oxygen saturation is 88% with the patient breathing ambient air, and the BMI is 48. Cardiac examination shows regular tachycardia. The lungs are clear bilaterally. Abdominal examination shows several small, mildly tender surgical incisions with no surrounding erythema; there is no guarding or rebound, and bowel sounds are normal. Laboratory studies reveal a normal complete blood count, normal cardiac enzymes, and normal serum lactate. Electrocardiography shows sinus tachycardia without ST changes. Chest radiograph shows linear atelectasis at the lung bases. Abdominal radiograph shows a small amount of intraperitoneal air, which is unchanged from postoperative radiographs, and a normal bowel gas pattern.

Which of the following is the most likely diagnosis?

(A) Bowel obstruction
(B) Gastrojejunostomy leak
(C) Gastroesophageal reflux
(D) Myocardial infarction
(E) Pulmonary embolism

Item 90

A 30-year-old man is evaluated in the emergency department for a 3-week history of malaise, fatigue, and jaundice. The patient is an injection drug user and was diagnosed with chronic hepatitis B virus infection 4 years ago. He drinks beer occasionally and does not use any medications, including over-the-counter medications.

On physical examination, the temperature is 36.1 °C (97.0 °F), the blood pressure is 120/65 mm Hg, the pulse rate is 100/min, and the respiration rate is 16/min. Abdominal examination reveals mild tenderness to palpation in the right upper quadrant.

Laboratory studies:

INR	1.2
Bilirubin (total)	3.5 mg/dL (59.9 µmol/L)
Bilirubin (direct)	1.8 mg/dL (30.8 µmol/L)
Aspartate aminotransferase	1100 U/L
Alanine aminotransferase	1450 U/L
Hepatitis B surface antigen	Positive
Hepatitis B core antibody (IgG)	Positive
Hepatitis B core antibody (IgM)	Negative
Hepatitis B virus DNA	Negative
Hepatitis C virus antibody	Negative
Acetaminophen	Negative

Ultrasonography shows heterogeneous hepatic echotexture with no masses.

Which of the following is the most likely diagnosis?

(A) Acute alcoholic hepatitis
(B) Hepatitis delta virus superinfection
(C) Hepatocellular carcinoma
(D) Reactivated hepatitis B virus infection

Item 91

A 57-year-old woman with cirrhosis is evaluated for worsening ascites and abdominal discomfort. The patient has hepatitis C virus infection, which failed to respond to antiviral therapy. She has been followed with regular cross-sectional imaging. Her medications are furosemide, spironolactone, nadolol, lactulose, and acetaminophen.

On physical examination, the patient is afebrile; the blood pressure is 90/50 mm Hg, the pulse rate is 80/min, and the respiration rate is 14/min. The BMI is 26. Examination reveals scleral icterus, a firm palpable liver edge, bulging flanks with shifting dullness, spider angiomata, caput medusae, and 2+ lower extremity edema. Palpation does not elicit Murphy sign, and there is no guarding, rebound, or peritoneal signs.

Laboratory studies

Hemoglobin	16.4 g/dL (164 g/L)
Platelet count	45,000/µL (45 × 10⁹/L)
INR	1.7
Creatinine	1.4 mg/dL (123.76 µmol/L)
Bilirubin (total)	1.8 mg/dL (30.78 µmol/L)
Bilirubin (direct)	0.9 mg/dL (15.39 µmol/L)
Aspartate aminotransferase	67 U/L
Alanine aminotransferase	45 U/L
Alkaline phosphatase	120 U/L
Albumin	2.6 g/dL (26 g/L)
α-Fetoprotein	200 ng/mL (200 µg/L)
Amylase	75 U/L
Lipase	58 U/L

MRI of the abdomen shows patent hepatic vessels, cirrhosis, and a new 4.2-cm enhancing mass in the right hepatic lobe. There is no tumor thrombus, and CT scan of the chest shows no pulmonary nodules.

Which of the following is the most appropriate management for this patient?

(A) Biopsy of the liver mass
(B) Evaluation for liver transplantation
(C) Resection of the liver mass
(D) Systemic chemotherapy

Item 92

A 67-year-old woman is evaluated for a 9-month history of postprandial abdominal pain. The pain is diffuse but slightly more epigastric and periumbilical. She has not had heartburn, nausea, vomiting, or a change in bowel movements. She avoids eating to minimize episodes of pain and has lost 9 kg (20 lb). The patient had a myocardial infarction 2 years ago and underwent carotid endarterectomy 5 years ago. She has a 30-pack-year smoking history and still smokes. Her medications are simvastatin, lisinopril, metoprolol, and aspirin.

On physical examination, the blood pressure is 140/90 mm Hg; other vital signs are normal. BMI is 20. There is an epigastric bruit but no abdominal tenderness, masses, or organomegaly. Laboratory studies reveal hemoglobin 13.5 g/dL (135 g/L); amylase, metabolic profile, and liver chemistry tests are normal. Abdominal ultrasonography, CT scan of the abdomen and pelvis, and esophagogastroduodenoscopy are normal. The patient had a normal colonoscopy one and a half years ago.

Which of the following is the most appropriate next step in the evaluation of this patient?

(A) Colonoscopy
(B) Gastric emptying study
(C) Magnetic resonance angiography of the abdomen
(D) Small-bowel radiographic series

Item 93

A 38-year-old man is evaluated for a 2-month history of progressive mid-epigastric pain that is worse after eating, postprandial nausea, and a 4.6-kg (10 lb) weight loss.

The patient has a 5-year history of chronic pancreatitis and has six alcohol-containing drinks a day. His medications are amitriptyline, oral morphine, and pancreatic enzyme supplements.

On physical examination, the patient is thin (BMI 20) and appears to be in mild distress. There is epigastric tenderness without rebound or guarding. The liver is slightly enlarged, but there are no palpable masses. Laboratory studies reveal a normal complete blood count and serum amylase of 175 U/L and lipase of 333 U/L. CT scan of the abdomen and pelvis shows multiple pancreatic calcifications, a calcified stone in the head of the pancreas within the main pancreatic duct, as well as dilation of the duct in the body and tail of the gland.

In addition to alcohol cessation, which of the following is the most appropriate management for this patient?

(A) Celiac nerve block
(B) Endoscopic retrograde cholangiopancreatography with removal of stones
(C) Increasing the dose of pancreatic enzymes
(D) Pancreatoduodenectomy

Item 94

A 50-year-old man is evaluated after having had his first screening colonoscopy. The colonoscopy revealed a 12-mm polyp in the sigmoid colon and a 7-mm polyp in the transverse colon; both polyps were tubular adenomas. He has no personal or family history of inflammatory bowel disease, colon polyps, or colon cancer. The patient is healthy and takes no medications. On physical examination, vital signs are normal; BMI is 25.5.

When should the next colonoscopy be scheduled for this patient?

(A) 1 year
(B) 3 years
(C) 5 years
(D) 10 years

Item 95

A 29-year-old woman is evaluated for a 6-week history of bright red blood per rectum along with mucoid stool and tenesmus. She has two or three bowel movements a day. The patient is otherwise healthy and takes no medications; her parents and two siblings are alive and well.

On physical examination, the temperature is 36.8 °C (98.0 °F), the blood pressure is 110/76 mm Hg, the pulse rate is 76/min, and the respiration rate is 12/min. There is no scleral icterus. The abdomen is soft and not tender or distended with normal bowel sounds. Rectal examination reveals red blood in the rectal vault with normal rectal tone and no palpable masses. Laboratory studies, including serum C-reactive protein and erythrocyte sedimentation rate, are normal. Ileocolonoscopy shows mild to moderate erythema from the anal verge to 10 cm; the rest of the colon and terminal ileum are normal. Biopsy specimens show mildly active chronic colitis in the rectum.

Which of the following is the most appropriate therapy for this patient?

(A) Azathioprine
(B) Infliximab
(C) Mesalamine (topical)
(D) Metronidazole
(E) Prednisone

Item 96

A 45-year-old man is evaluated for a 6-month history of recurrent ascites refractory to salt restriction and diuretic therapy. He is managed with serial large-volume paracentesis. The patient has a history of hepatitis C, and cirrhosis was detected on liver biopsy 5 years ago. The patient's medications are spironolactone and furosemide.

On physical examination, the patient is afebrile; the blood pressure is 85/60 mm Hg, the pulse rate is 80/min, and the respiration rate is 16/min. The BMI is 26. Examination reveals jaundice, cutaneous angiomata, cachexia, large-volume ascites, edema, and asterixis. The abdomen is not tender to palpation and a liver edge is not palpable.

Laboratory studies:

INR	3.5
Creatinine	1.4 mg/dL (106.8 μmol/L)
Bilirubin (total)	6.5 mg/dL (111.2 μmol/L)
Aspartate aminotransferase	49 U/L
Alanine aminotransferase	50 U/L
Albumin	2.4 g/dL (24 g/L)
α-Fetoprotein	10 ng/mL (10 μg/L)

The serum creatinine has been stable for the past 4 months and he continues to make approximately 800 mL of urine daily. Serum electrolytes are normal. Ultrasonography shows a nodular liver without space-occupying lesions and massive ascites.

Which of the following is the most appropriate next step in the management of this patient?

(A) Hemodialysis
(B) Liver transplantation
(C) Peritoneovenous shunt
(D) Transjugular intrahepatic portosystemic shunt (TIPS)

Item 97

A 32-year-old woman is evaluated in the hospital. She was hospitalized 2 days ago because of nausea, vomiting, and dehydration as a result of documented gastroparesis secondary to long-standing, difficult-to-control type 1 diabetes mellitus. Her symptoms had been controlled with oral erythromycin therapy, but the therapy became ineffective with time. She recently began taking metoclopramide, which controlled the nausea and vomiting but caused tardive dyskinesia, and the therapy was stopped. Oral antiemetic therapy has not prevented vomiting, and modifying her diet by eating multiple, small-volume, low-residue meals or limiting her diet to liquid supplements only has not been effective. Over the past 3 months, she has lost 5.8 kg (15 lb) and been hospitalized four times. In addition to type 1 diabetes mellitus, her medical history includes erosive esophagitis, and her medications include insulin glargine and insulin lispro and pantoprazole.

On admission she was given intravenous fluids, and her volume status improved over 2 days. On physical examination, she is afebrile, the blood pressure is 105/68 mm Hg with no orthostatic changes, and the pulse rate is 88/min; the BMI is 21. The patient has intermittent dystonic movements of the mouth; the mucous membranes are moist, skin turgor is intact, and abdominal examination is normal. Laboratory studies reveal a plasma glucose of 160 mg/dL (8.88 mmol/L); all other studies, including complete blood count, serum creatinine, liver chemistry tests, thyroid-stimulating hormone, calcium, tissue transglutaminase, and cortisol, and spot urine for microalbumin, are normal.

Which of the following is the most appropriate next step in the management of this patient?

(A) Metoclopramide at a reduced dose
(B) Nasojejunal feeding trial
(C) Percutaneous gastrostomy tube placement
(D) Total parenteral nutrition

Item 98

A 70-year-old man is evaluated for an 8-year history of elevated liver enzyme concentrations without jaundice, ascites, encephalopathy or hospitalizations for complications of cirrhosis or portal hypertension. The medical history also includes type 2 diabetes mellitus, hyperlipidemia, and obesity, and his medications include metformin, glyburide, rosiglitazone, hydrochlorothiazide, metoprolol, simvastatin, aspirin, and fish oil capsules; he does not drink alcohol.

On physical examination, the temperature is 36.0 °C (97.0 °F), the blood pressure is 130/80 mm Hg, the pulse rate is 70/min, and the respiration rate is 14/min; the BMI is 30. Examination reveals hepatomegaly but no jaundice, ascites, edema, splenomegaly, or asterixis.

Laboratory studies:

Glucose (fasting)	101 mg/dL (5.6 mmol/L)
Hemoglobin A_{1c}	6%
Bilirubin (total)	1.4 mg/dL (23.9 μmol/L)
Aspartate aminotransferase	80 U/L
Alanine aminotransferase	150 U/L
Alkaline phosphatase	200 U/L
Albumin	4.0 g/dL (40 g/L)
Cholesterol (total)	140 mg/dL (3.63 mmol/L)
HDL cholesterol	50 mg/dL (1.3 mmol/L)
Triglycerides	100 mg/dL (1.13 mmol/L)
Ferritin	255 ng/mL (255 mg/L)
Transferrin saturation	30%

Ultrasonography shows fatty infiltration.

Which of the following is the most appropriate next step in management for this patient?

(A) Gemfibrozil therapy
(B) Insulin therapy
(C) Liver biopsy
(D) MRI of the abdomen
(E) Observation

Item 99

A 63-year-old man is evaluated for a 2-day history of left lower quadrant abdominal pain. The pain is constant and is not relieved by a bowel movement or by positional changes. The patient is slightly nauseated and has no appetite but is not vomiting. He has never had a similar episode. The patient's medical history includes hypertension, and his only medication is hydrochlorothiazide.

On physical examination, the temperature is 38.0 °C (101.1 °F), the blood pressure is 125/85 mm Hg, the pulse rate is 95/min, and the respiration rate is 14/min. There is fullness and tenderness of the left lower quadrant with no rebound or guarding; bowel sounds are decreased. Rectal examination is normal; examination of stool for occult blood is negative. Leukocyte count is 14,000/μL (14×10^9/L); all other laboratory results are normal. A plain abdominal radiograph is unremarkable, and a chest radiograph shows no free air beneath the diaphragms.

Which of the following is the most appropriate next step in the evaluation of this patient?

(A) Barium enema
(B) Colonoscopy
(C) Contrast-enhanced CT scan of the abdomen and pelvis
(D) Small-bowel radiographic series

Item 100

A 65-year-old woman is evaluated 1 week after having had an esophagogastroduodenoscopy for persistent abdominal pain. The procedure showed a 1-cm, clean-based ulcer in the duodenal bulb and scattered antral erosions. Biopsy specimens from the stomach showed nonspecific gastritis but no evidence of *Helicobacter pylori* infection. Serum antibody testing for *H. pylori* was also negative. Proton pump inhibitor therapy was started, and the patient's symptoms were alleviated. The patient has a history of mild osteoarthritis and osteoporosis, and her medications include a nonprescription analgesic for arthritis and a calcium supplement, vitamin D, and alendronate.

On physical examination, vital signs are normal. The abdominal examination reveals no tenderness, hepatomegaly, or palpable masses. Complete blood count is normal.

Which of the following is the most appropriate next step in the management of this patient?

(A) Measure serum gastrin
(B) Perform fecal antigen test for *Helicobacter pylori*
(C) Repeat esophagogastroduodenoscopy with biopsy of the ulcer
(D) Review the nonprescription arthritis analgesic
(E) Stop alendronate therapy

Item 101

A 26-year-old woman is evaluated in the emergency department for progressive odynophagia of 3 days' duration. The patient has a 6-year history of limited systemic sclerosis characterized by skin sclerosis limited to the fingers with early contractures, Raynaud phenomenon, and gastric dysmotility and gastroesophageal reflux disease. Her medications include nicardipine, omeprazole, erythromycin, acetaminophen and NSAIDs as needed. Prednisone, 5 mg/d, was recently started to treat increasingly painful fingers.

On physical examination, the patient appears anxious and uncomfortable. The temperature is 37.0 °C (98.6 °F), the blood pressure is 132/88 mm Hg, the pulse rate is 80/min, and the respiration rate is 22/min. She has skin tightening and cutaneous telangiectasia involving the proximal and distal digits. Cardiopulmonary examination is normal and the abdomen has active bowel sounds and is soft to palpation.

Which of the following is the most likely diagnosis?

(A) Barrett esophagus
(B) Candidal esophagitis
(C) Esophageal stricture
(D) Herpetic esophagitis
(E) Pill-induced esophagitis

Item 102

A 35-year-old woman is evaluated for a 6-month history of right upper quadrant abdominal pain that has slowly increased in intensity and is worse on deep inspiration. The patient is otherwise well, and her only medication is an oral contraceptive pill that she has taken for 15 years. She drinks alcohol socially but has no history of heavy alcohol use, injection drug use, or blood transfusion.

On physical examination, vital signs are normal; BMI is 26. There is slight hepatomegaly with mild discomfort on deep palpation in the right upper quadrant and mid-epigastrium. There is no jaundice or ascites. The lungs are clear. Complete blood count and serum biochemistry studies, including aminotransferases, bilirubin, and α-fetoprotein, are normal. Ultrasonography shows a solitary hyperechoic 9-cm lesion in the right lobe of the liver. CT scan shows a well-demarcated lesion with peripheral enhancement after injection of intravenous contrast; there is no central scar. Liver biopsy specimen reveals sheets of hepatocytes, with no bile ducts or Kupffer cells.

Which of the following is the most likely diagnosis?

(A) Focal nodular hyperplasia
(B) Hepatic adenoma
(C) Hepatocellular carcinoma
(D) Simple hepatic cyst

Item 103

A 41-year-old woman with type 1 diabetes mellitus is evaluated for a 5-year history of large-volume, nonbloody diarrhea that occurs several times a day, sometimes waking her at night; the diarrhea is associated with significant bloating and gas but no abdominal pain. The stool is not oily, and she has not lost weight. The patient's diabetes is complicated by peripheral neuropathy and diabetic nephropathy; she also has hypothyroidism. Her medications are insulin

lispro and insulin glargine, levothyroxine, lisinopril, duloxetine, and pregabalin.

On physical examination, vital signs are normal; abdominal examination is normal. Laboratory studies reveal fasting plasma glucose 125 mg/dL (6.94 mmol/L), hemoglobin A$_{1c}$ 8.7%, and creatinine 1.6 mg/dL (122 μmol/L). Complete blood count, thyroid-stimulating hormone, and other routine laboratory tests are normal; serologic tests for tissue transglutaminase and antiendomysial antibodies are negative. Breath test for bacterial overgrowth is negative; colonoscopy is macroscopically normal; biopsy specimens are also normal. Esophagogastroduodenoscopy with small-bowel biopsy is also normal.

In addition to improved control of the diabetes, which of the following is the most appropriate next step in the management of this patient?

(A) Antibiotic therapy
(B) Diphenoxylate/atropine
(C) Gluten-free diet
(D) Octreotide

Item 104

A 75-year-old woman is evaluated in the emergency department for the acute onset of passage of bright red blood per rectum. This morning she had crampy abdominal pain and had two episodes of diarrhea after which she passed bright red blood. The patient has a history of hypertension and coronary artery disease, and her medications are aspirin, ramipril, metoprolol, and simvastatin. She is otherwise healthy and has not traveled recently or taken antibiotics. She had a colonoscopy 6 months ago, which was normal.

On physical examination, the patient is not in acute distress; the temperature is 36.8 °C (98.0 °F), the blood pressure is 130/80 mm Hg, the pulse rate is 70/min, and the respiration rate is 14/min. The heart and lungs are normal. The abdomen is soft with tenderness in the left lower quadrant without rebound or guarding. Rectal examination shows the presence of bright red blood. Laboratory studies reveal hemoglobin 11.9 g/dL (119 g/L), leukocyte count 8400/μL (8.4 × 10^9/L), and platelet count 246,000/μL (246 × 10^9/L). Serum electrolytes, glucose, creatinine, and urea nitrogen are normal. CT scan of the abdomen and pelvis shows segmental thickening in the sigmoid colon.

Which of the following is the most likely diagnosis?

(A) Crohn disease
(B) Cytomegalovirus colitis
(C) Irritable bowel syndrome
(D) Ischemic colitis
(E) Peptic ulcer disease

Item 105

An 81-year-old woman is evaluated for a 3-month history of abdominal and back pain. She also has anorexia and has lost 11.4 kg (25 lb). For the past 2 weeks she has had progressive pruritus and a yellow tint to her skin.

On physical examination, the patient appears ill; the temperature is 37.2 °C (99 °F), the blood pressure is 104/62 mm Hg, the pulse rate is 98/min, and the respiration rate is 16/min. There is scleral icterus, jaundiced skin, and generalized abdominal tenderness. Laboratory studies reveal a leukocyte count of 13,200/µL (13.2 × 10^9/L), total bilirubin 12.4 mg/dL (212 µmol/L), alkaline phosphatase 748 U/L, and CA 19-9 822 U/L. CT scan shows a 3.2-cm lesion in the head of the pancreas with dilation of the pancreatic and bile ducts and multiple lesions throughout the liver that are consistent with metastases. Endoscopic ultrasonography biopsy specimen of the mass is positive for adenocarcinoma.

Which of the following is the most appropriate next step in the management of this patient?

(A) Biopsy of a liver lesion
(B) Placement of a metal biliary stent
(C) Radiation to the pancreas and liver lesions
(D) Surgical resection of the pancreatic lesion and adjuvant chemotherapy

Item 106

A 62-year-old woman with a 10-year history of Barrett esophagus is evaluated after an esophagogastroduodenoscopy performed as part of a Barrett esophagus surveillance program. The biopsy specimen from the endoscopy showed high-grade dysplasia; the diagnosis was confirmed on subsequent biopsy 3 months later. No cancer is present. The patient is asymptomatic, and her only medication is omeprazole, 40 mg/d.

On physical examination, the patient appears healthy with normal vital signs. Cardiopulmonary examination is normal. The abdomen is soft and is not tender or distended; there is no hepatosplenomegaly. CT scan of the chest, abdomen, and pelvis shows no masses or lymphadenopathy.

Which of the following is the most appropriate management for this patient?

(A) Combined chemotherapy and radiation therapy
(B) Endoscopic mucosal resection
(C) Esophagectomy
(D) Photodynamic therapy
(E) Repeat biopsy in 3 months

Item 107

A 57-year-old woman is evaluated in the emergency department for acute left lower quadrant pain, an episode of nonbloody diarrhea, and mild nausea without vomiting that began 1 day ago; her temperature at the time was 38.1 °C (100.6 °F). She has been able to eat and maintain her hydration with oral fluids. She had been previously healthy and has no significant medical history.

On physical examination, the temperature is 38.1 °C (100.6 °F), the blood pressure is 115/76 mm Hg, the pulse rate is 98/min, and the respiration rate is 14/min. There is tenderness of the left lower quadrant with no rebound, guarding, or palpable masses. Leukocyte count is 14,900/µL (14.9 × 10^9/L); all other laboratory results are normal. Contrast-enhanced CT scan of the abdomen and pelvis shows diverticula of the sigmoid colon with pericolic fatty infiltration and thickening of the bowel wall consistent with diverticulitis; there is no abscess, obstruction, or fistula.

Which of the following is the most appropriate next step in the management of this patient?

(A) Flexible sigmoidoscopy
(B) Oral ciprofloxacin and metronidazole therapy
(C) Oral cephalexin therapy
(D) Surgical resection

Item 108

A 58-year-old man is evaluated for a 3-month history of epigastric pain. The pain varies in intensity and is not aggravated by eating; it is not associated with nausea, vomiting, bloating, or weight loss. He started pantoprazole therapy 1 month ago without relief. The patient has a history of resolved peptic ulcer 3 years ago and osteoarthritis of the hands and knees, and his medications are ibuprofen as needed for arthritic pain and pantoprazole.

On physical examination, vital signs are normal. There is mild epigastric tenderness, normal bowel sounds, and no hepatomegaly or lymphadenopathy. Complete blood count and serum chemistry tests, including liver enzymes, are normal. Esophagogastroduodenoscopy shows mild erythema and a few superficial erosions throughout the distal stomach and a 1-cm pedunculated polyp in the antrum of the stomach that is biopsied but not removed. Biopsy specimens of the erythematous gastric mucosa show chronic active gastritis and the presence of *Helicobacter pylori*; specimens of the polyp show a tubular adenoma with low-grade dysplasia. Eradication therapy for *H. pylori* is begun.

Which of the following is the most appropriate additional management of this patient?

(A) Endoscopic ultrasonography
(B) Esophagogastroduodenoscopy with polypectomy now
(C) Esophagogastroduodenoscopy in 3 years
(D) Surgical resection
(E) No further intervention

Item 109

A 55-year-old woman is evaluated for a 4-month history of progressive fatigue and pruritus. She is otherwise healthy and takes no medications.

On physical examination, vital signs are normal; BMI is 25. Examination reveals mild hepatomegaly and excoriations of the skin. There is no jaundice, rash, or skin eruption.

Laboratory studies:

Bilirubin (total)	1.5 mg/dL (25.6 μmol/L)
Aspartate aminotransferase	60 U/L
Alanine aminotransferase	75 U/L
Alkaline phosphatase	470 U/L
Albumin	4.0 g/dL (40 g/L)
Hepatitis C virus antibody	Negative
Hepatitis B surface antigen	Negative

Ultrasonography of the abdomen is normal with no bile duct dilatation.

Which of the following is the most appropriate next step in the diagnosis of this patient?

(A) α_1-Antitrypsin phenotype
(B) Liver biopsy
(C) Measurement of serum antimitochondrial antibody
(D) Serum protein electrophoresis

Item 110

A 44-year-old man is evaluated in the hospital for 3-day history of five or six watery stools a day 3 months after surgical resection of the small bowel. The patient was recently diagnosed with a desmoid tumor involving the right transverse colon and ileum, and the tumor was resected, requiring removal of the proximal colon and 80 cm of distal ileum. The remaining small bowel was anastomosed to the mid-transverse colon. Vital signs and physical examination are normal.

Which of the following is the most appropriate therapy for this patient?

(A) Antibiotics
(B) Cholestyramine
(C) Prednisone
(D) Tincture of opium

Answers and Critiques

Item 1   Answer: B

Educational Objective: Treat persistent *Helicobacter pylori* infection.

This patient has persistent *Helicobacter pylori* infection despite initial therapy with a proton pump inhibitor, clarithromycin, and metronidazole, an appropriate regimen for this patient with penicillin allergy. The most likely reason for failure of treatment in most patients is either noncompliance with therapy or antibiotic resistance; antibiotic resistance (probably to clarithromycin) is a likely cause of treatment failure in this patient. Therefore, an additional treatment regimen, one that does not contain clarithromycin, needs to be given. In the United States, bismuth-based quadruple therapy is indicated in a patient whose infection has failed to respond to proton pump inhibitor–based triple therapy. Levofloxacin-based triple therapy is also used in patients with persistent infection, but this regimen has not been validated in the United States.

Regimens containing amoxicillin would not be indicated in this patient with penicillin allergy. Therapy with the same regimen that failed initially to eradicate the organism because of likely antibiotic resistance would not be appropriate. *H. pylori* is naturally resistant to trimethoprim, and the regimen of trimethroprim–sulfamethoxazole and erythromycin is not an approved regimen for eradication of the organism.

> **KEY POINT**
> - **Bismuth-based quadruple therapy should be considered in a patient in whom initial proton pump inhibitor–based triple therapy has failed to eradicate *Helicobacter pylori*.**

Bibliography

Vakil N, Megraud F. Eradication therapy for Helicobacter pylori. Gastroenterology. 2007;133(3):985-1001. [PMID: 17854602]

Item 2   Answer: D

Educational Objective: Evaluate drug-induced liver injury.

This patient has drug-induced liver injury secondary to trimethoprim-sulfamethoxazole therapy. Antibiotics are common causes of drug-induced liver injury, which can cause either an elevation in the aminotransferases or, as in this patient, a cholestatic form of liver injury. Some drugs have their own particular fingerprint of injury. For example, acetaminophen causes a predominant hepatocellular injury, whereas trimethoprim-sulfamethoxazole often produces a cholestatic form characterized by an alkaline phosphatase level more than twice normal. If a mixed pattern injury occurs in combination with an elevated alkaline phosphatase level, the patient is at increased risk of progressive liver injury. Phenytoin is an example of a drug that characteristically produces a mixed pattern. Drug-induced liver injury is often difficult to diagnose because there is no gold standard for diagnosis. Some drugs causing hepatic injury may be associated with the more familiar hypersensitivity syndrome characterized by fever, rash, and peripheral eosinophilia, but many drug reactions are characterized only by hepatic injury. Therefore, it is often a diagnosis of exclusion of other causes of liver injury in the presence of a potential offending agent taken within a recent period of time, usually weeks. Most patients can be monitored conservatively because discontinuation of the offending drug usually leads to eventual recovery, which can, however, take months. It is important to monitor for signs of progressive liver injury by monitoring prothrombin time and clinical status of the patient.

Cholecystectomy is incorrect because the patient has no radiographic evidence to suggest cholecystitis, her gallbladder is normal on imaging, she has no Murphy sign, gallstones, leukocytosis, or anything else to suggest cholecystitis. Endoscopic retrograde cholangiopancreatography (ERCP) is not correct because the patient has no clinical or radiographic suggestion of choledocholithiasis. Proceeding to ERCP in the absence of clinical suspicion is unlikely to be effective and places the patient at up to a 5% risk of post-ERCP pancreatitis. Liver biopsy is incorrect because there is a good clinical suspicion that the patient has drug-induced liver injury. If, however, her condition does not improve or if the diagnosis were less clear, then biopsy may be correct. Another time when liver biopsy might be appropriate is in the patient with hepatocellular injury who may have autoimmune hepatitis, which could respond to corticosteroid therapy.

> **KEY POINT**
> - **Liver test elevations in the setting of a recently started medication should raise the suspicion of a possible drug induced liver injury.**

Bibliography

Lee WM. Drug-induced hepatotoxicity. N Engl J Med. 2003;349(5): 474-485. [PMID: 12890847]

Item 3   Answer: D

Educational Objective: Treat ulcerative colitis.

5-Aminosalicylates (5-ASA) are the first-line therapy for ulcerative colitis, and remission can often be induced and maintained with a 5-ASA only. When 5-ASA therapy is not effective initially or patients develop a flare while in remission on 5-ASAs, often a short course of corticosteroids is required to induce or re-induce remission. However, corticosteroids are not effective as maintenance therapy and have many potential side effects, including hyperglycemia, osteoporosis, hypertension, mood instability, acne, infection, and osteonecrosis. Although some patients may maintain remission with continued 5-ASA therapy after corticosteroid taper, other patients become corticosteroid-dependent or -resistant, as did this patient, and therapy with an immunomodulator such as 6-mercaptopurine or azathioprine should be started. These agents are nucleotide analogues that interfere with DNA synthesis and induce apoptosis. Therapy with these agents may be required for up to 3 months before providing clinical benefit, and therefore, they are generally started with corticosteroids, which are then tapered.

Because corticosteroids are not effective maintenance therapy, simply increasing the dose of prednisone without adding an immunomodulator would not be appropriate in this patient. The addition of another 5-ASA, such as olsalazine, will not provide any greater benefit. Antibiotic therapy has not been shown to be effective in the treatment of ulcerative colitis, and the patient's stool was negative for *Clostridium difficile*. Budesonide is a nonsystemic corticosteroid that is useful in the induction of remission in patients with ulcerative colitis disease involving the terminal ileum and right colon, but would not be of added benefit in this patient with pan-ulcerative colitis.

KEY POINT

- Patients with ulcerative colitis who become corticosteroid-dependent should be started on therapy with an immunomodulator, such as azathioprine or 6-mercaptopurine with a steroid taper.

Bibliography

Baumgart DC, Sandborn WJ. Inflammatory bowel disease: clinical aspects and established and evolving therapies. Lancet. 2007;369 (9573):1641-1657. [PMID: 17499606]

Item 4   Answer: C

Educational Objective: Manage colon cancer risk in a patient with inflammatory bowel disease.

This patient has pancolitis of 8 years' duration. The inflammation involves the ileum and proximal colon. The colon cancer risk in patients with ulcerative colitis or Crohn disease reaches a significant level after 8 years of inflammation; the annual cancer risk is estimated to be 1% to 2% per year after 8 years. The cancer risk is slightly delayed for patients with inflammation limited to the distal colon. The recommendation is to initiate a surveillance program with colonoscopy 8 years after onset of her disease, with follow-up colonoscopy every 1 to 2 years thereafter. Biopsies are performed in four-quadrant fashion throughout the entire colon.

The patient's disease is reasonably well controlled on her current dose of mesalamine, and treatment with mesalamine does not in itself prevent colon cancer. There is no recommendation for standard screening for small-bowel carcinoma in the setting of ulcerative colitis or Crohn disease, and therefore, capsule endoscopy is not indicated. Flexible sigmoidoscopy would not reach the at-risk colonic mucosa in the proximal colon beyond the reach of the sigmoidoscope.

KEY POINT

- Patients with inflammatory bowel disease should initiate screening for colorectal cancer after 8 years of duration of disease.

Bibliography

Levin B, Lieberman DA, McFarland B, et al. Screening and surveillance for the early detection of colorectal cancer and adenomatous polyps, 2008: a joint guideline from the American Cancer Society, the US Multi-Society Task Force on Colorectal Cancer, and the American College of Radiology. Gastroenterology. 2008;134(5): 1570-1595. [PMID: 18384785]

Item 5   Answer: C

Educational Objective: Diagnose gastrinoma.

Gastrinoma is a neuroendocrine tumor that secretes the hormone gastrin, which in turn results in hypersecretion of acid. Gastrinoma should be suspected when ulcers are present in a patient who has a negative test for *Helicobacter pylori* and who does not take NSAIDs. The initial test when gastrinoma is suspected is measurement of serum gastrin; a gastrin concentration of 1000 pg/mL (1000 ng/L) or greater is highly suggestive of a gastrinoma, but gastrinoma may be present with gastrin levels as low as 150 to 200 pg/mL (150 to 200 ng/L).

After the diagnosis of gastrinoma is made by detecting hypergastrinemia, various tests are used to localize the tumor and to evaluate for metastases. CT scan of the abdomen and pelvis is often the first test but may miss small pancreatic gastrinomas. Endoscopic ultrasonography is the most sensitive test for pancreatic endocrine tumors, including gastrinoma, but may miss tumors that are not localized within the pancreas. Somatostatin receptor scintigraphy is the most sensitive procedure for identifying the primary gastrinoma and detecting whether metastatic disease is present.

KEY POINT

- The first step in the evaluation of suspected gastrinoma is measurement of serum gastrin; serum gastrin concentration greater than 1000 pg/mL (1000 ng/L) is highly suggestive of gastrinoma.

Bibliography

Modlin IM, Oberg K, Chung DC, et al. Gastroenteropancreatic neuroendocrine tumours. Lancet Oncol. 2008;9(1):61-72. [PMID: 18177818]

Item 6   Answer: A

Educational Objective: Diagnose gastroesophageal reflux disease.

This patient's clinical presentation is highly suggestive of gastroesophageal reflux disease (GERD). The typical symptoms of pyrosis, along with obesity, make the pretest probability of GERD high, although the lack of response to proton pump inhibitor therapy argues against the diagnosis. In patients with a high pretest probability of GERD who fail to respond to a therapeutic trial, ambulatory esophageal pH monitoring is most useful. Ambulatory pH monitoring employs a narrow-gauge cannula placed transnasally into the distal esophagus. Simultaneous pH measurement is made by several detectors. An endoscopically placed ambulatory monitor is becoming more commonly used. Abnormal esophageal acid exposure is determined by the percentage of time that esophageal pH is less than 4.0, esophageal acid exposure time, number of reflux episodes, mean duration and number of reflux episodes, and longest duration of reflux. The patient can record time of meals, episodes of reflux symptoms or pain, supine position, and other parameters to correlate symptoms to actual abnormal esophageal acid exposure.

Barium esophagography is a useful initial test in the evaluation of oropharyngeal reflux and to determine the presence of strictures but is less useful in determining significant episodes of gastroesophageal reflux or their relationship to symptoms. CT scan of the chest is performed in cases of dysphagia to investigate potential masses in the region of the gastric cardia. Esophageal manometry is useful in esophageal motility disorders such as diffuse esophageal spasm, achalasia, and hypotonic motility disorders. Newer techniques of esophageal function include esophageal impedance monitoring, which provides information on esophageal bolus transit as opposed to manometry's ability to detect esophageal contractile activity.

KEY POINT

- In patients with a high pretest probability of gastroesophageal reflux disease who fail to respond to a therapeutic trial of a proton pump inhibitor, ambulatory esophageal pH monitoring is most useful.

Bibliography

Bredenoord AJ, Tutuian R, Smout AJ, Castell DO. Technology review: Esophageal impedance monitoring. Am J Gastroenterol. 2007;102(1):187-194. [PMID: 17100961]

Item 7   Answer: A

Educational Objective: Manage a bleeding ulcer of the small bowel.

Ulceration of the ileum may occur as a result of infection, inflammation, or neoplasia. Medication-induced injury of the small bowel is a well-recognized complication of NSAID therapy; and discontinuing the medication results in ulcer healing and cessation of bleeding. Mild NSAID-induced gastrointestinal side effects include abdominal pain, nausea, constipation, diarrhea, and dyspepsia; major complications include ulcers, bleeding, perforation, and the attendant morbidity and morality. After NSAID therapy is discontinued, no further investigation is warranted if the patient's bleeding ceases. Alternatively, ongoing blood loss or symptoms referable to the ulcer warrants further evaluation which may include directed biopsy and/or resection. The information from the capsule study regarding location of the bleeding site would direct the enteroscopy, which could be performed using the double-balloon technique to reach the site of injury.

Although estrogen/progesterone therapy and octreotide therapy may be useful for management of bleeding from enteric angiodysplasia, these therapies would not aid in ulcer healing. Mesenteric angiography would not identify an ulcer that is not actively bleeding and therefore would not be indicated in this patient.

KEY POINT

- NSAID-induced injury to the bowel is a relatively common cause of small-bowel ulceration and may present with obscure gastrointestinal bleeding.

Bibliography

Goldstein JL, Eisen GM, Lewis B, Gralnek IM, Zlotnick S, Fort JG. Video capsule endoscopy to prospectively assess small bowel injury with celecoxib, naproxen plus omeprazole, and placebo. Clin Gastroenterol Hepatol. 2005;3(2):133-141. [PMID: 15704047]

Item 8   Answer: D

Educational Objective: Evaluate dyspepsia.

This patient has new-onset uninvestigated dyspepsia. In a patient younger than 55 years without alarm features, the recommendation is to "test and treat" for *Helicobacter pylori* infection. The *H. pylori* stool antigen test detects active infection and therefore can be used in the initial diagnosis as well as for eradication testing.

An abdominal ultrasonography can be used in the evaluation of presumed biliary colic or chronic mesenteric ischemia (the latter if Doppler evaluation is additionally performed). The likelihood of biliary disease in this patient who is post-cholecystectomy and who has normal serum chemistry tests is low. Chronic mesenteric ischemia is also very unlikely because her pain does not increase with eating, and she has not lost weight, has no known risk factors for atherosclerosis, and has no abdominal bruits. An esophagogastroduodenoscopy is not needed given her age and lack of alarm features, but the procedure could be considered if her symptoms persist after *H. pylori* treatment. Gastric scintigraphy is used in the evaluation of gastroparesis and should only be performed after mechanical obstruction has been ruled out with upper endoscopy or barium radiography. The patient's predominant symptom is pain and she has not vomited or had early satiety, and therefore, dyspepsia is more likely than gastroparesis. Although this patient has had several abdominal surgeries putting her at risk for a small-bowel obstruction from adhesions, the fact that her pain does not worsen with eating, she has not vomited, has maintained normal bowel movements, and has normal bowel sounds make obstruction unlikely; therefore, a small-bowel radiograph would be unnecessary at this point.

KEY POINT

- In patients younger than 55 years who have new-onset dyspepsia without alarm symptoms, a "test and treat" approach for *Helicobacter pylori* is recommended.

Bibliography

Talley NJ, Vakil NB, Moayyedi P. American Gastroenterological Association Technical Review on the Evaluation of Dyspepsia. Gastroenterology. 2005;129(5):1756-1780. [PMID: 16285971]

Item 9   Answer: B
Educational Objective: Diagnose autoimmune hepatitis.

This patient has autoimmune hepatitis, a disorder that occurs most commonly in girls and young women. Like this patient with hypothyroidism, many affected patients have other autoimmune disorders and a family history of autoimmunity. These patients usually present with vague symptoms. Fatigue, which occurs in 85% of patients, is the most common presenting symptom, followed by jaundice (46%), anorexia (30%), myalgias (30%), and diarrhea. On physical examination, 78% of patients have an enlarged liver. Others have a normal examination despite the presence of advanced disease. The results of liver chemistry tests can be quite elevated, with aminotransferase concentrations into the thousands, but typically less than 500 IU at presentation, with elevated bilirubin, often with near-normal alkaline phosphatase. Autoimmune serologic tests, specifically antinuclear antibodies, anti–smooth muscle antibodies, and antibody to liver/kidney microsome type 1 (anti-LKM1), may be positive but are not detected in up to 25% of patients. Antibody levels are not prognostic of the disease course.

Primary biliary cirrhosis is a chronic progressive cholestatic liver disease of unknown cause. It is an autoimmune disorder that occurs predominantly in women (80% to 90% of cases) between 40 and 60 years of age. The diagnostic triad associated with primary biliary cirrhosis includes a cholestatic liver profile, positive antimitochondrial antibody titers, and compatible histologic findings on liver biopsy. Serum alkaline phosphatase level is usually elevated ten times or more above normal. The patient's near normal

alkaline phosphatase concentration and negative antimitochondrial antibody essentially rule out primary biliary cirrhosis. Although drug-induced liver injury can cause similar liver test abnormalities, the patient has not taken any new medications recently, making this diagnosis unlikely. She has no pain to suggest cholecystitis. Primary sclerosing cholangitis is a chronic cholestatic liver disease of unknown cause that is characterized by progressive bile duct destruction and may lead to secondary biliary cirrhosis. Laboratory findings include a cholestatic liver profile, with serum alkaline phosphatase levels three to five times greater than normal and mild hyperbilirubinemia. This patient's alkaline phosphatase level is minimally elevated making primary sclerosing cholangitis unlikely.

KEY POINT

- Laboratory findings in patients with autoimmune hepatitis include elevated serum aminotransferase values, hypergammaglobulinemia, mild hyperbilirubinemia, elevated serum alkaline phosphatase values, and the presence of autoantibodies.

Bibliography

Krawitt EL. Autoimmune hepatitis. N Engl J Med. 2006;354(1):54-66. [PMID: 16394302]

Item 10   Answer: B
Educational Objective: Manage *Clostridium difficile* colitis.

This patient likely has *Clostridium difficile* antibiotic-associated colitis complicating his underlying inflammatory bowel disease. *C. difficile* is an anaerobic gram-positive rod that produces two toxins, both capable of damaging the mucosa of the colon and causing pseudomembranous colitis. Infectious diarrhea associated with *C. difficile* has emerged as a major public health concern and can be seen in patients with underlying inflammatory bowel disease. Whenever a patient with inflammatory bowel disease presents with a new flair, stool studies, including *C. difficile* toxin assay, should be done. This patient's recent history of antibiotic use greatly increases his risk of *C. difficile* infection. The fever, orthostasis, leukocytosis, and abdominal tenderness in the setting of chronic immunosuppression are all signs that he needs to be hospitalized for further investigations (for example, CT scan to rule out toxic megacolon) and to start empiric therapy. Optimal therapy is orally administered metronidazole or vancomycin and should be initiated promptly for severely ill patients.

It would be unwise to increase his immunosuppression either by adding prednisone or increasing the azathioprine in the setting of possible infection. There is no role for evaluation of the small bowel mucosa with a small-bowel series in order to diagnose small-bowel inflammation.

- Infectious causes should be considered in exacerbations of diarrhea in patients with inflammatory bowel disease.

Bibliography

Monaghan T, Boswell T, Mahida YR. Recent advances in *Clostridium difficile*–associated disease. Gut. 2008;57(6):850-60. [PMID: 18252748]

Item 11   Answer: A
Educational Objective: Manage severe acute pancreatitis.

This patient has moderate to severe acute pancreatitis and after 5 days remains febrile, continues to be in pain, and cannot take in any oral nutrition. The patient will likely have an extended period before being able to take in oral nutrition. Two routes are available for providing nutrition in patients with severe acute pancreatitis: enteral nutrition and parenteral nutrition. Enteral nutrition is provided through a feeding tube ideally placed past the ligament of Treitz so as not to stimulate the pancreas. Parenteral nutrition is provided through a large peripheral or central intravenous line. Enteral nutrition is preferred over parenteral nutrition because of its lower complication rate, especially a lower infection rate. A meta-analysis of six studies with 263 participants compared enteral nutrition with total parenteral nutrition. Enteral nutrition was associated with a significantly lower incidence of infections, reduced surgical interventions to control complications of pancreatitis, and a reduced length of hospital stay. In another randomized, controlled trial, enteral nutrition showed a trend towards faster attenuation of inflammation, with fewer septic complications, and also was a dominant therapy in terms of cost-effectiveness.

Imipenem therapy is only helpful in acute pancreatitis when there is evidence of pancreatic necrosis. Pancreatic necrosis is diagnosed by a contrast-enhanced CT scan that shows nonenhancing pancreatic tissue. In patients with noninfected pancreatic necrosis, antibiotics may decrease the incidence of sepsis, systemic complications (for example, respiratory failure), and local complications (for example, infected pancreatic necrosis or pancreatic abscess). Randomized, prospective trials have shown no benefit from antibiotic use in acute pancreatitis of mild to moderate severity but may lead to development of nosocomial infections with resistant pathogens. Similarly pancreatic débridement is recommended only in patients with pancreatitis and infected pancreatic necrosis.

- Enteral feeding is the preferred route of providing nutrition in patients with severe acute pancreatitis.

Bibliography

Marik PE, Zaloga GP. Meta-analysis of parenteral nutrition versus enteral nutrition in patients with acute pancreatitis. BMJ. 2004;328(7453):1407. [PMID: 15175229]

Item 12   Answer: D
Educational Objective: Diagnose slow-transit constipation.

Functional constipation is a common complaint. To make the diagnosis, there should not be any secondary causes such as an underlying metabolic or neurologic disease, mechanical obstruction, or drug effect. The disorder is characterized by the presence of two of the following Rome III criteria for functional constipation (for at least 3 months): straining during ≥25% of defecations; lumpy or hard stools ≥25% of defecations; sensation of incomplete evacuation for ≥25% of defecations; sensation of anorectal obstruction/ blockage for ≥25% of defecations; manual maneuvers to facilitate ≥25% of defecations; and less than three defecations per week. Patients should not meet the Rome criteria for irritable bowel syndrome, which consist of recurrent abdominal pain or discomfort at least 3 days a month in past 3 months associated with two or more of the following: improvement with defecation; onset associated with change in frequency of stool; and onset associated with change in form (appearance) of stool. Patients with functional constipation should also not have alternating loose stools and constipation. There are two types of functional constipation: slow-transit (colonic inertia) and dyssynergic. This patient has slow-transit functional constipation. Affected patients have prolonged transit of radiopaque markers through the proximal colon, which is likely the result of an abnormality in the enteric nerve plexus.

In dyssynergic functional constipation or pelvic floor dysfunction (also known as outlet delay), transit time through the colon is normal but rectal expulsion of radiopaque markers is impaired, often resulting from the loss of the coordinated relaxation (or paradoxical contraction) of the puborectalis muscle and external anal sphincter. A radiopaque marker study therefore helps to differentiate these two types of functional constipation. Anorectal manometry can also help distinguish the two types, but a simpler diagnostic maneuver is having the patient mimic a bowel movement and attempt to expel the examiner's inserted finger; if the patient cannot do so, dyssynergia rather than slow transit is present. This patient does not meet criteria for irritable bowel syndrome. There is no underlying disease or radiographic evidence in this patient to support the diagnosis of chronic pseudo-obstruction.

- In a radiopaque marker study, patients with slow-transit functional constipation have prolonged transit of markers through the proximal colon, whereas patients with dyssynergic functional constipation have normal transit time but impaired rectal expulsion of the markers.

Bibliography

Longstreth GF, Thompson WG, Chey WD, Houghton LA, Mearin F, Spiller RC. Functional bowel disorders. Gastroenterology. 2006; 130(5):1480-1491. [PMID: 16678561]

Item 13   Answer: B

Educational Objective: Manage upper gastro-intestinal bleeding.

The first step in the management of acute variceal hemorrhage is the restoration of the intravascular volume using a large bore peripheral intravenous line or a central line. Packed erythrocytes are used as need to replace blood loss and clotting factors are replaced as needed. Platelet transfusions may be indicated if values fall below 50,000/µL (50 × 10^9/L). In addition, this patient should undergo urgent esophagogastroduodenoscopy and band ligation of esophageal varices. Clinical studies have shown that sclerotherapy was superior to balloon tamponade alone, vasopressin alone, and a combination of vasopressin and balloon tamponade in controlling active variceal hemorrhage, preventing early rebleeding, and improving survival in patients with esophageal and gastroesophageal varices. Band ligation has been shown to be as effective as sclerotherapy for preventing early rebleeding. Therapy should also be started with intravenous octreotide, which reduces portal venous blood inflow through inhibition of the release of vasodilatory hormones and is more effective for controlling bleeding than placebo; however, its ultimate effect on survival is unknown. Bacterial infections are present in a sizable percentage of hospitalized patients with variceal bleeding and are associated with a high mortality rate. Clinical trials have demonstrated that the use of prophylactic antibiotics in these patients results in a reduction in infectious complications and possibly mortality.

Arteriography is not first-line therapy in patients with a variceal bleed from venous portal hypertension. Arteriography is reserved for patients with a presumed arterial source of bleeding as can be seen in peptic ulcer disease or tumors anywhere along the gastrointestinal tract. In such cases, arteriography can be used to identify and embolize the specific vessel involved. This method is usually reserved for cases in which the patient is actively bleeding and either endoscopic therapy has failed to stop the bleeding or the presence of active bleeding interferes with identification of the bleeding site and the patient is unstable. Mesocaval shunt is a surgical shunt that decompresses the portal system by diverting portal venous flow into the inferior vena cava, thus bypassing the liver. This type of shunt is rarely used for acute variceal bleeding as it carries a high intraoperative risk in an acutely decompensated patient with underlying liver disease and coagulopathy. Intravenous nadolol is not appropriate because this patient is hypotensive and needs endoscopic intervention rather than medical

therapy. Lastly, transjugular intrahepatic portosystemic shunting (TIPS) should not be used without first performing an upper endoscopy with esophageal band ligation. Many variceal bleeds can be controlled with endoscopic therapy alone, obviating the need for urgent TIPS which can have significant comorbidities including hepatic decompensation, bleeding complications, or resultant encephalopathy.

KEY POINT

- **Antibiotics, endoscopic variceal band ligation, and intravenous octreotide are the first-line therapies for acute esophageal variceal bleeding.**

Bibliography

Garcia-Tsao, G, Sanyal, AJ, Grace, ND, Carey W; Practice Guidelines Committee of the American Association for the Study of Liver Diseases; Practice Parameters Committee of the American College of Gastroenterology. Prevention and management of gastroesophageal varices and variceal hemorrhage in cirrhosis [erratum in Hepatology. 2007;46(6):2052]. Hepatology. 2007;46(3):922-938. [PMID: 17879356]

Item 14   Answer: C

Educational Objective: Evaluate for *Helicobacter pylori* infection in a patient with mucosa-associated lymphoid tissue (MALT) lymphoma.

This patient has a mucosa-associated lymphoid tissue (MALT) lymphoma, a low-grade B-cell lymphoma arising from the mucosal lymphoid tissue of the gastrointestinal tract. Half of MALT lymphomas are indolent, and most are located within the stomach. MALT lymphomas are thought to arise from clonal lymphocyte expansion in patients with chronic active gastritis secondary to *Helicobacter pylori* infection; eradication therapy for *H. pylori* infection alone results in lymphoma regression in up to 80% of affected patients; therefore, testing for *H. pylori* by stool antigen test is indicated in this patient.

Patients with HIV infection are at increased risk for Burkitt lymphoma, which can occur in the gastrointestinal tract; however, these tumors tend to be large and are usually located in the terminal ileum or rectum rather than the stomach and are not associated with chronic active gastritis. Patients with MALT lymphoma who have increased extent of disease as evidenced by ulceration, invasion through the gastric wall, or lymphadenopathy, which were not present in this case, are more likely to require standard chemotherapy for lymphoma. Although intestinal lymphoma is a malignant complication of celiac disease, this form of lymphoma is of T-cell origin (also known as enteropathy-associated T-cell lymphoma), and therefore, measurement of serum tissue transglutaminase antibody is not necessary. Surgical resection would not be required in a patient with early-stage MALToma who may fully respond to *H. pylori* eradication alone.

KEY POINT

- Patients with mucosa-associated lymphoid tissue (MALT) lymphoma should be tested for *Helicobacter pylori* infection.

Bibliography

Chey WD, Wong BC; Practice Parameters Committee of the American College of Gastroenterology. American College of Gastroenterology guideline on the management of Helicobacter pylori infection. Am J Gastroenterol. 2007;102(8):1808-1825. [PMID: 17608775]

Item 15   Answer: A
Educational Objective: Diagnose achalasia.

The patient's history is typical for achalasia, an uncommon but important primary motility disorder of the esophagus. The barium study and endoscopic appearance described are typical for achalasia, but the diagnosis is confirmed manometrically with esophageal motility studies. The manometric diagnosis of achalasia usually includes an elevated lower esophageal sphincter pressure, failure of the lower esophageal sphincter to relax with swallowing, and diminished or absent peristalsis of the esophageal body.

Diffuse esophageal spasm typically presents with noncardiac chest pain. The diagnosis of diffuse esophageal spasm is made manometrically by the finding of more than 20% of swallows having simultaneous contractions in the distal esophagus. Peptic stricture would present with dysphagia, but would typically show a longer, non-tapered stricture on barium esophagography. Furthermore, peptic strictures seldom present with megaesophagus, as seen in this patient. Scleroderma esophagus leads to loss of esophageal motility and often severe reflux or distal esophageal strictures, not a dilated esophagus.

Treatment of achalasia is usually pneumatic dilatation of the esophagus or surgical myomectomy, the latter of which can be done laparoscopically. Pneumatic dilatation, even in experienced hands, is associated with a 5% to 10% risk of esophageal perforation. Botulinum toxin injection can afford relief of achalasia in patients who are not considered candidates for endoscopic or surgical interventions.

KEY POINT

- Achalasia is a primary motility disorder of the esophagus and requires manometric diagnosis.

Bibliography

Pohl D, Tutuian R. Achalasia: an overview of diagnosis and treatment. J Gastrointestin Liver Dis. 2007;16(3):297-303. [PMID: 17925926]

Item 16   Answer: D
Educational Objective: Diagnose extraintestinal manifestations of Crohn disease.

The prevalence of extraintestinal manifestations in patients with inflammatory bowel disease ranges from 21% to 40%. In most large studies, the prevalence is higher in Crohn disease than in ulcerative colitis. The right colon and transverse colon can abut the right psoas muscle, and the transmural inflammation of Crohn disease can lead to extension into the surrounding tissues and abscess formation. In this patient, who has a history of stricturing disease with fistula formation, it is likely that the fever, pain, and limp are complications of penetrating disease.

Peripheral and axial musculoskeletal syndromes occur in approximately 30% of patients with inflammatory bowel disease and are considered part of the seronegative spondyloarthropathies. The course of peripheral arthritis tends to parallel the activity of the bowel disease. Isolated hip involvement would be an unusual extra-colonic manifestation of Crohn disease and it would not explain this patient's physical examination findings.

Patients with inflammatory bowel disease are at increased risk for developing osteoporosis, secondary to the disease process itself and the medications commonly used for treatment (such as corticosteroids). The fracture risk in such patients is 40% greater than that of the general population. All patients with inflammatory bowel disease older than 65 years with a history of corticosteroid use for more than 3 months should undergo bone mineral density scan. Furthermore, both short- and long-term corticosteroid therapy is associated with avascular necrosis of the femoral head. However, this patient has not taken corticosteroids for 25 years, and neither steroid-related avascular necrosis nor osteoporosis is likely and cannot account for her fever and flank pain.

KEY POINT

- The inflammation in Crohn disease is transmural and can extend into any adjacent structure, including muscle.

Bibliography

Su CG, Judge TA, Lichtenstein GR. Extraintestinal manifestations of inflammatory bowel disease. Gastroenterol Clin North Am. 2002;31(1):307-327. [PMID: 12122740]

Item 17   Answer: A
Educational Objective: Manage new-onset ascites.

This patient should have a diagnostic paracentesis to confirm the etiology of the ascites and to rule out spontaneous bacterial peritonitis (SBP). All patients who present with ascites should have a diagnostic paracentesis to categorize the ascites as secondary to portal hypertension or to other causes. This patient should have a small amount of fluid sampled for cell count with differential. An absolute polymorphonuclear cell count greater than 250/mL is indicative of SBP. Also total protein should be measured as well as albumin to calculate the serum albumin to ascites gradient (SAAG). An SAAG greater than 1.1 is consistent with portal hypertension; an SAAG less than 1.1 can occur in patients with malignant ascites. Patients do not always have symptoms suggestive of SBP such as fever, abdominal pain, or leukocytosis; therefore, their absence should not preclude a paracentesis to rule out SBP. In addition this patient has an elevated serum creatinine, which poses the possibility of hepatorenal syndrome for which SBP is a significant risk. Therefore, it is important to determine whether she has SBP.

Furosemide and spironolactone therapy is not indicated in the setting of an elevated serum creatinine and possible hepatorenal syndrome, because diuresis can precipitate worsening hemodynamic status or renal failure. Ceftriaxone and albumin are appropriate therapy for spontaneous bacterial peritonitis but are not indicated unless a diagnostic paracentesis can confirm the diagnosis. TIPS is not first-line therapy for new-onset ascites.

KEY POINT

- An ascitic fluid absolute polymorphonuclear cell count greater than 250/mL is indicative of spontaneous bacterial peritonitis.

Bibliography

Moore KP, Wong F, Gines P, et al. The management of ascites in cirrhosis: report in the consensus conference of the International Ascites Club. Hepatology. 2003;38(1):258-266. [PMID: 12830009]

Item 18   Answer: B

Educational Objective: Treat immunomodulator-refractory Crohn disease.

The patient's Crohn disease had been well controlled on therapy with the immunomodulator azathioprine but is no longer responding; the small-joint arthritis may also be a complication of azathioprine. The next agent that should be used is the biologic agent infliximab an anti-tumor necrosis factor-α inhibitor. This potent biologic agent can bring the disease into remission quickly while sparing the effects of systemic corticosteroids. However, there is an increased risk of lymphoma and solid tumors associated with infliximab therapy. Recently it has been reported that combined infliximab and azathioprine is associated with an increased risk of hepatosplenic T-cell lymphoma in pediatric patients. Therefore, combination therapy is not preferred in patients who are receiving fixed-interval infliximab (every 8 weeks). Azathioprine dosage should be

tapered and therapy with this agent eventually discontinued. Early use of infliximab has been shown to be more effective than conventional management with corticosteroids for induction of remission.

Corticosteroids are not used as maintenance therapy in Crohn disease primarily because of their numerous short- and long-term complications. The patient's disease has now failed to respond to the steroid-sparing immunomodulator, and there is no role for corticosteroids. Calcineurin inhibitors have not been shown to be efficacious in Crohn disease. Mesalamines are not effective in immunomodulator-refractory Crohn disease.

KEY POINT

- Patients whose Crohn disease becomes refractory to immunomodulator therapy should be given anti-tumor necrosis factor-α inhibitor therapy.

Bibliography

D'Haens G, Baert F, van Assche G, et al; Belgian Inflammatory Bowel Disease Research Group; North-Holland Gut Club. Early combined immunosuppression or conventional management in patients with newly diagnosed Crohn's disease: an open randomised trial. Lancet. 2008;371(9613):660-667. [PMID: 18295023]

Item 19   Answer: D

Educational Objective: Treat diffuse esophageal spasm.

This patient has chest pain resulting from diffuse esophageal spasm. Although the diagnosis can be suggested by clinical presentation and the distinctive appearance of the esophagus on barium study, the disorder can only be diagnosed on manometry characterized by the finding of more than 20% of swallows having simultaneous contractions in the distal esophagus. Although the treatment for diffuse esophageal spasm is not clearly defined or the subject of general expert agreement, it is clear that many cases result from uncontrolled gastroesophageal reflux. Consequently, an empiric trial of acid suppression is usually recommended as the first therapeutic maneuver.

Oral anticholinergic agents have had limited success in this disorder, and their use is associated with frequent side effects. The more aggressive options of esophageal dilatation and surgical intervention have been proposed in case reports but have not been shown to be generally useful. Such approaches are reserved for patients with severe symptoms refractory to medical therapy.

KEY POINT

- Diffuse esophageal spasm is frequently related to gastroesophageal reflux; empiric therapy with acid suppression is the recommended first therapeutic intervention.

Bibliography

Dogan I, Mittal RK. Esophageal motor disorders: recent advances. Curr Opin Gastroenterol. 2006;22(4):417-422. [PMID: 16760760]

Item 20   Answer: E

Educational Objective: Diagnose small intestinal bacterial overgrowth as a complication of bariatric surgery.

Patients who undergo bariatric surgery are at risk for specific early and late complications of the procedure; small intestinal bacterial overgrowth is a late complication that can manifest with bloating, diarrhea, and features of malabsorption. Having segments of small bowel excluded from the usual stream of gastric acid, bile, and proteolytic enzymes, which all act to decrease excess bacterial growth in the small bowel, is a risk factor for bacterial overgrowth. The diarrhea in bacterial overgrowth can be from deconjugation of bile salts from the intestinal bacteria leading to fat malabsorption as well as from decreased disaccharidase levels leading to carbohydrate malabsorption. Other clues in this patient include the macrocytic anemia, with a low serum vitamin B_{12} level (bacteria bind and consume vitamin B_{12} and cleave it from intrinsic factor) and an elevated serum folate level (intestinal bacteria synthesize folate). Even though the patient is taking oral vitamin B_{12} replacement, his level is still low, suggesting inadequate replacement versus excessive loss. Culture of the small intestine or breath testing can be done to substantiate the diagnosis; alternatively, an empiric trial of antibiotic therapy could be considered.

Although celiac disease should be considered in any patient with diarrhea and features of malabsorption, the negative serologic studies and negative small-bowel biopsy rule out the diagnosis. Irritable bowel syndrome should not cause nocturnal stools, weight loss, and vitamin derangements. Crohn disease is possible given the patient's symptoms and family history of inflammatory bowel disease, but the negative endoscopic, histologic, and radiographic findings make this disorder unlikely. The patient has young children in diapers who attend a daycare center, and, therefore, giardiasis is in the differential diagnosis; however, stool ova and parasite testing on three occasions has been negative, with the yield for repeated testing close to 90%.

KEY POINT

- Small intestinal bacterial overgrowth is a late complication of bariatric surgery and should be considered in patients presenting with diarrhea, bloating, and features of malabsorption after such surgery.

Bibliography

Decker GA, Swain JM, Crowell MD, Scolapio JS. Gastrointestinal and nutritional complications after bariatric surgery. Am J Gastroenterol. 2007;102(11):2571-2580. [PMID: 17640325]

Item 21   Answer: E

Educational Objective: Diagnose ulcerative colitis.

This patient has mild to moderate left-sided ulcerative colitis based on his clinical presentation and endoscopic and histologic findings. His ex-smoking status, microcytic anemia, and the presence of arthritis, which is the most common extraintestinal manifestation of inflammatory bowel disease, further support the diagnosis. While many colitides can have overlapping clinical, endoscopic, and even histologic features, there are important differences to consider. Microscopic colitis presents with nonbloody diarrhea, and colonoscopy shows normal mucosa macroscopically and histology shows either increased intraepithelial lymphocytes (lymphocytic colitis) or an increased submucosal collagen layer (collagenous colitis). Bleeding is less often a feature of Crohn colitis, and endoscopic inflammatory changes are patchy and generally spare the rectum; histologic features, however, may be indistinguishable from those of ulcerative colitis. Infectious colitis usually presents with more acute symptoms, and chronic changes such as crypt architecture distortion are absent. Ischemic colitis also generally has a more acute course and spares the rectum because of the dual blood supply to this region.

KEY POINT

- Chronic histologic changes such as crypt architectural distortion are key distinguishing features of ulcerative colitis as compared to other causes of colitis, such as infection.

Bibliography

Baumgart DC, Sandborn WJ. Inflammatory bowel disease: clinical aspects and established and evolving therapies. Lancet. 2007; 369(9573):1641-1657. [PMID: 17499606]

Item 22   Answer: A

Educational Objective: Diagnose pancreatic necrosis.

Pancreatic necrosis should be suspected in a patient with severe acute pancreatitis whose condition is not improving or is worsening after 5 days or more of treatment. Pancreatic necrosis on CT scan can be identified as unenhanced areas of the pancreas. Neither endoscopic retrograde cholangiopancreatography nor endoscopic ultrasonography can detect the presence of pancreatic necrosis in the setting of acute pancreatitis. Stool chymotrypsin can be measured when chronic pancreatitis is suspected to help evaluate for decreased pancreatic function.

Pancreatic necrosis is the most important predictor of poor outcome in acute pancreatitis. Patients who develop pancreatic necrosis should be given antibiotic prophylaxis, usually with imipenem. The necrosis should be sampled for the presence of infection, and if infection is present, surgical débridement is recommended.

KEY POINT

- CT scan of the abdomen with intravenous contrast is the most sensitive test to diagnose pancreatic necrosis.

Bibliography

Hughes SJ, Papachristou GI, Federle MP, Lee KK. Necrotizing pancreatitis. Gastroenterol Clin North Am. 2007;36(2):313-323. [PMID: 17533081]

Item 23   Answer: B

Educational Objective: Manage severe alcoholic hepatitis.

This patient has severe alcoholic hepatitis. Excessive alcohol intake may cause liver disease directly or may increase the risk of an unfavorable outcome in patients with pre-existing liver disease. This patient with chronic alcohol abuse has a history of recent heavy alcohol use, elevated serum aspartate aminotransferase (AST) and alanine aminotransferase values (usually greater than 300 U/L) and a serum aspartate aminotransferase concentration that is greater than the alanine aminotransferase concentration in roughly a 2 to 1 ratio, elevated alkaline phosphatase concentration, jaundice, coagulopathy, and encephalopathy. Moreover, other causes of acute and chronic liver disease have been excluded. The severity of the presentation and poor prognosis are underscored by the presence of the very high serum bilirubin concentration, coagulopathy, and encephalopathy.

The mortality risk in this setting is calculated by the discriminant function as follows: (4.6 × [prothrombin time − control prothrombin time]) + serum bilirubin. A discriminant function score of greater than 32 identifies patients with a 50% mortality rate within 30 days and has been used to identify patients who have a survival benefit from corticosteroid therapy. In addition, nutrition therapy has been shown to improve survival in severely malnourished hospitalized alcoholic patients.

The presentation of alcoholic hepatitis may resemble infection because of the fever and leukocytosis; however, this patient's chest radiograph and blood and urine cultures were negative. In the absence of active bleeding, fresh frozen plasma is not indicated. Although many patients with alcoholic hepatitis recover with appropriate therapy, it would be inappropriate to offer liver transplantation to an alcoholic patient who is not involved in rehabilitation counseling. Some transplant programs require abstinence of at least 6 months. This not only confirms a commitment to abstaining from alcohol but also allows

time for improvement of the alcoholic hepatitis to the point that transplantation may not be needed. Antibiotic therapy has no role in alcoholic hepatitis. Fresh frozen plasma is not a priority in a patient with alcoholic hepatitis and a coagulopathy unless active bleeding is present.

KEY POINT

- Patients with severe alcoholic hepatitis, as defined by a discriminant function score of 32 or more, benefit from corticosteroid therapy.

Bibliography

Rambaldi A, Saconato HH, Christensen E, Thorlund K, Wetterslev J, Gluud C. Systematic review: glucocorticosteroids for alcoholic hepatitis—a Cochrane Hepato-Biliary Group systematic review with meta-analyses and trial sequential analyses of randomized clinical trials. Aliment Pharmacol Ther. 2008;27(12):1167-1178. [PMID: 18363896]

Item 24   Answer: C

Educational Objective: Evaluate a patient with recurrent blood loss.

This patient presents with obscure overt bleeding in that blood loss is clinically apparent because of the maroon stool, but the source is not identified despite endoscopic investigation. The most appropriate next test would be to repeat upper endoscopy. Studies have shown that between one third and two thirds of sources of obscure upper gastrointestinal bleeding are found within the reach of the upper endoscope on repeat endoscopy. The missed lesions are most often bleeding erosions associated with hiatus hernia, gastroduodenal angiodysplasia, Dieulafoy lesions, gastric antral vascular ectasias, and peptic ulcers. Moreover, endoscopy offers therapeutic options if a lesion is found in addition to establishing a diagnosis.

A colonoscopy is less likely to be helpful because the blood detected on nasogastric lavage suggests an upper gastrointestinal source. Wireless capsule endoscopy may be helpful if a repeat upper endoscopy is normal to assess the remainder of the small bowel; however, in contrast to endoscopy, capsule endoscopy does not offer therapeutic options. A radiolabeled red blood cell scan would not be the next test of choice; the results are nonspecific and would delay diagnosis and therapy that could be delivered more rapidly with endoscopy. In double-balloon enteroscopy, deep intubation of the small bowel is achieved by using a two-balloon technique to anchor the endoscope and assist in advancement. The procedure is lengthy and requires prolonged sedation, although it offers diagnostic and therapeutic capabilities. This test is reserved until a more proximal source of bleeding has been excluded and wireless capsule endoscopy has been performed. The capsule would direct whether the double-balloon enteroscope is to be introduced via the mouth (for jejunal abnormalities) or anus (ileal abnormalities).

- Repeat upper endoscopy in a patient with obscure upper gastrointestinal bleeding will identify a bleeding source in a significant proportion of patients.

Bibliography

Lin S, Rockey DC. Obscure gastrointestinal bleeding. Gastroenterol Clin North Am. 2005;34(4):679-698. [PMID: 16303577]

Item 25   Answer: D

Educational Objective: Manage diarrhea secondary to chronic pancreatitis.

The patient has chronic pancreatitis, which results from alcohol use in approximately 70% of adult cases, and most such patients have consumed more than 150 g/d of alcohol over 6 to 12 years. He also has concomitant alcoholic liver disease. Although the use of pancreatic enzyme supplementation for pain relief has had mixed results in patients with alcohol-related chronic pancreatitis, its use for control of the steatorrhea that results from pancreatic insufficiency is well established. This patient's diarrhea will likely resolve by this intervention.

Fiber will bulk-up the stool but will not address the malabsorptive cause of diarrhea. Cholestyramine will bind bile salts, which is not the patient's primary problem. Loperamide will slow down gut motility but he will continue to have fat malabsorption without pancreatic enzyme replacement.

- The treatment of pancreatic insufficiency is enzyme replacement therapy.

Bibliography

Nair RJ, Lawler L, Miller MR. Chronic Pancreatitis Am Fam Physician. 2007;76(11):1679-1688. [PMID: 18092710]

Item 26   Answer: B

Educational Objective: Treat achalasia in a patient who is not a candidate for endoscopic or surgical therapy.

This patient's history is typical for achalasia, an uncommon but important primary motility disorder of the esophagus. Although endoscopic evaluation is required to investigate the possibility of a mass lesion leading to partial esophageal obstruction, the diagnosis of achalasia is made manometrically using esophageal motility studies. The manometric diagnosis usually includes an elevated lower esophageal sphincter resting pressure, failure of the lower esophageal sphincter to relax with swallowing, and diminished or absent peristalsis of the esophageal body. Radiologic findings of note in achalasia include a "bird's beak" abnormality of the distal esophagus, widening of the esophagus, and

less commonly, megaesophagus with an air/fluid level. CT of the chest can be employed to differentiate achalasia from pseudoachalasia, the latter mimicking the true motility disorder but caused by a mass lesion at the distal esophagus or gastric cardia.

Treatment of achalasia is usually pneumatic dilatation of the esophagus or surgical myomectomy, the latter of which can be done laparoscopically. Pneumatic dilatation, even in experienced hands, is associated with a 5% to 10% risk of esophageal perforation. Botulinum toxin injection can afford relief of achalasia in patients like this one who because of age or comorbidities are not candidates for endoscopic or surgical intervention. Botulinum toxin inhibits the release of acetylcholine from nerve endings and has been used successfully for decades to treat certain spastic disorders of skeletal muscle such as blepharospasm and torticollis. Anticholinergic therapy is not indicated for achalasia.

- Botulinum toxin injection can afford relief of achalasia in patients who because of age or comorbidities are not candidates for endoscopic or surgical intervention.

Bibliography

Pohl D, Tutuian R. Achalasia: an overview of diagnosis and treatment. J Gastrointestin Liver Dis. 2007;16(3):297-303. [PMID: 17925926]

Item 27   Answer: C

Educational Objective: Manage NSAID-induced gastric injury in a patient who requires long-term NSAID therapy.

This patient has gastric erosions and ulcerations consistent with NSAID-induced gastropathy, which would account for her iron-deficiency anemia. In most patients with NSAID-induced gastric injury, discontinuation of the NSAID in addition to starting proton pump inhibitor therapy, would be reasonable, but in certain patients (like this one who requires NSAID therapy for her rheumatoid arthritis), the best option is to start proton pump inhibitor therapy, which has been found to heal peptic ulcerations whether or not NSAID therapy is ongoing. In such patients, reducing the dose of the NSAID versus switching to either a selective COX-2 inhibitor, such as celecoxib, or an NSAID with a safer side effect profile, such as nabumetone, etodolac, or meloxicam, should be considered. This patient did not receive sufficient pain relief with celecoxib and she is already taking nabumetone; therefore, simply adding a proton pump inhibitor is indicated.

Although high-dose H_2-receptor antagonists such as famotidine are thought to be helpful in preventing ulcers, these agents have not been first-line therapy since the advent of proton pump inhibitors because they are not as effective. Misoprostol can reduce NSAID-related ulcers, but it has a dose-related side effect of diarrhea and would therefore not be indicated in this patient with diarrhea-predominant irritable bowel syndrome. Sucralfate has been used for ulcer prophylaxis, but there is no good evidence for its use in patients with long-term NSAID use and current ulcers.

KEY POINT

- **Proton pump inhibitors are the drugs of choice in NSAID-induced gastric injury whether or not NSAID therapy is discontinued.**

Bibliography

Scheiman JM. Prevention of NSAID-induced ulcers. Curr Treat Options Gastroenterol. 2008;11(2):125-134. [PMID: 18321440]

Item 28   Answer: D
Educational Objective: Manage hepatic abscess.

This patient requires percutaneous drainage of the hepatic lesion, which is likely an abscess. He has a history of recurrent diverticulitis, which does not appear to have been adequately treated in the past. He now has fever, right upper quadrant pain, and a large fluid-filled lesion in his liver. The clinical manifestations of pyogenic liver abscess usually include fever and right upper quadrant abdominal pain. Most pyogenic liver abscesses are due to biliary tract infection. Intra-abdominal infection may result in liver abscesses from seeding via the portal vein, whereas systemic bacteremia may cause abscesses from seeding via the hepatic artery. Abscesses resulting from an intra-abdominal infection are frequently due to anaerobic organisms, and many liver abscesses are polymicrobial. Percutaneous aspiration is recommended for diagnosis and subsequent treatment of a suspected pyogenic liver abscess. Antibiotics may be started even before aspiration and should not interfere with culture results. Parenteral antibiotic therapy to cover enteric gram-negative bacilli, anaerobes, and enterococci is recommended until culture results are available. Antibiotics specific for the causative organisms are then started and are continued for 4 to 6 weeks. Oral agents can be instituted after the abscess is drained and the patient is afebrile.

Lobectomy is not required in this patient because in most cases, a hepatic abscess can be managed with the combination of antibiotics and percutaneous drainage. Endoscopic retrograde cholangiopancreatography (ERCP) would not be appropriate because there is no evidence that this patient has cholangitis or obstructive jaundice. Although he has abnormal liver chemistry tests, these can be explained by the presence of the large abscess rather than biliary disease, especially because the CT scan does not show any evidence of ductal dilatation to suggest obstructive jaundice or cholangitis, which might require ERCP. MRI with gadolinium is not appropriate because the diagnosis can be made on the information provided, and no further confirmatory imaging is needed. The patient needs to be treated, and antibiotics and percutaneous drainage are required at this time.

KEY POINT

- **Hepatic abscess is usually managed with percutaneous drainage of the lesion and intravenous antibiotics.**

Bibliography

Yu SC, Ho SS, Lau WY, et al. Treatment of pyogenic liver abscess: prospective randomized comparison of catheter drainage and needle aspiration. Hepatology. 2004;39(4):932-938. [PMID: 15057896]

Item 29   Answer: B
Educational Objective: Manage gallstone pancreatitis.

This patient has a classic presentation of acute pancreatitis with the acute onset of epigastric abdominal pain, nausea, and vomiting associated with markedly elevated pancreatic enzymes. The presence of stones in the gallbladder, a dilated bile duct, and elevated aminotransferase levels highly suggest gallstones as the cause of pancreatitis. The scleral icterus, jaundice, and elevated bilirubin level suggest continuing bile duct obstruction. Abdominal ultrasonography has a sensitivity of only 50% to 75% for choledocholithiasis, and a common duct stone should be suspected in the correct clinical situation even when ultrasonography does not show a stone.

Endoscopic retrograde cholangiopancreatography (ERCP) with sphincterotomy and stone removal is the most appropriate procedure in patients with acute gallstone pancreatitis and with imaging and biochemical evidence of biliary obstruction from a common duct stone. The procedure can document the diagnosis of choledocholithiasis and remove the gallstones, which lessens the morbidity and mortality due to biliary sepsis.

CT scan will likely show evidence of acute pancreatitis and magnetic resonance cholangiopancreatography (MRCP) will show pancreatitis and the presence of a common duct stone, with sensitivities for CT being approximately 75% for stones and MRCP having sensitivities ranging from 80% to 100% as compared with ERCP for the diagnosis of choledocholithiasis. Biliary scintigraphy may show obstruction of the cystic or common bile duct but will not determine the cause. However, CT, biliary scintigraphy, and MRCP will not be therapeutic for bile duct stones.

KEY POINT

- **In patients with gallstone pancreatitis and evidence of biliary obstruction, endoscopic retrograde cholangiopancreatography and stone removal reduces morbidity and mortality by reducing the risk of biliary sepsis.**

Bibliography

Ayub K, Imada R, Slavin J. Endoscopic retrograde cholangiopancreatography in gallstone-associated acute pancreatitis. Cochrane Database Syst Rev. 2004;(4):CD003630. [PMID: 15495060]

Item 30   Answer: A

Educational Objective: Manage acute mesenteric ischemia.

This patient most likely has acute mesenteric ischemia, a potentially fatal condition that typically affects elderly patients. The disorder may result from embolic or thrombotic occlusions of the splanchnic vessels or may be nonocclusive. Superior mesenteric artery embolism is the most common cause, accounting for approximately 50% of cases and usually developing from ventricular or left atrial thrombi in patients with atrial fibrillation. This patient's age, recent myocardial infarction, atrial fibrillation, history of discontinuing anticoagulation, and hypotension are all significant risk factors for this condition. His low-grade fever, hypotension, sudden onset of severe abdominal pain out-of-proportion to physical examination findings, as well as his elevated leukocyte count all support the diagnosis. CT arteriography is a sensitive test for acute mesenteric ischemia; the procedure can evaluate the mesenteric vessels and also assess for signs of bowel ischemia and rule out other potential causes of acute onset abdominal pain, such as perforation or obstruction. Surgical consultation should be done simultaneously because if the results of CT arteriography support the diagnosis of acute mesenteric ischemia, the patient may need emergent surgery. Traditional angiography is the gold standard for diagnosis of acute mesenteric ischemia and can also offer therapeutic options such as the use of vasodilators as well as balloon dilation and stent placement. Surgery is required for patients with peritoneal signs and/or evidence of bowel necrosis on imaging. Surgical interventions include peritoneal lavage, resection of necrotic and perforated bowel, thrombolectomy, patch angioplasty, endarterectomy, and bypass procedures. Successful thrombolytic therapy in stable patients without peritoneal signs has been reported.

Colonoscopy would not be appropriate for this patient, because it does not evaluate the mesenteric vessels or the small intestine, only the mucosa of the colon. Intravenous famotidine therapy for possible dyspepsia would also not be appropriate in this patient with a potentially life-threatening condition. Likewise, although the patient may be somewhat constipated, giving him lactulose only is not correct.

KEY POINT

- **CT angiography is the most sensitive diagnostic test for acute mesenteric ischemia.**

Bibliography
Kozuch PL, Brandt LJ. Review article: diagnosis and management of mesenteric ischaemia with an emphasis on pharmacotherapy. Aliment Pharmacol Ther. 2005;21(3):201-215. [PMID: 15691294]

Item 31   Answer: C

Educational Objective: Manage interferon-induced autoimmune hepatitis.

This patient is experiencing a flare of autoimmune hepatitis precipitated by interferon therapy. Such a flare can occur in patients with quiescent autoimmune hepatitis or as new-onset disease induced by interferon therapy. Other autoimmune diseases can develop or be exacerbated during interferon therapy, including rheumatoid arthritis, sarcoidosis, dermatitis, and type 1 diabetes mellitus. Accordingly, interferon therapy should be used cautiously in patients with autoimmune disease and is contraindicated in patients with pre-existing autoimmune hepatitis. This patient has worsening liver disease as well as established hypothyroidism; therefore, the interferon and ribavirin therapy should be discontinued and the patient monitored closely. If the autoimmune hepatitis does not stabilize, treatment for this disorder will have to be considered. This patient should not be rechallenged with hepatitis C therapy because it is likely to cause worsening liver disease.

Decreasing the dosage of the interferon and ribavirin is not an option, because the autoimmune response is not dose-related. Although some patients receiving therapy for hepatitis C experience a flare of hepatitis before clearing the virus, this patient has persistent viral replication, and given the newly positive antinuclear antibody and anti–smooth muscle antibody test results suggestive of autoimmune hepatitis and personal and family history of autoimmune disorders, therapy should be discontinued to avoid worsening hepatic decompensation.

KEY POINT

- **Interferon therapy can precipitate autoimmune hepatitis, and therapy should be discontinued in affected patients.**

Bibliography
Conrad B. Potential mechanisms of interferon-alpha induced autoimmunity. Autoimmunity. 2003;36(8):519-523. [PMID: 14984029]

Item 32   Answer: D

Educational Objective: Manage diarrhea-predominant irritable bowel syndrome.

This patient presents with symptoms that meet the Rome III criteria for irritable bowel syndrome (IBS). The Rome criteria were developed to establish consensus guidelines for diagnosis of functional bowel disorders. Criteria for IBS are symptoms of recurrent abdominal pain or discomfort and a marked change in bowel habit for at least 6 months, with symptoms experienced on at least 3 days a month for at least 3 months. Two or more of the following must also apply: (1) pain is relieved by a bowel movement; (2) onset of pain is related to a change in frequency of stool; and/or (3) onset of pain is related to a change in the appearance of stool. IBS is the most common gastrointestinal condition diagnosed in the United States. It is characterized by chronic abdominal pain and altered bowel habits in the absence of any organic cause.

In this otherwise healthy young woman, reassurance that she has a chronic but not a life-threatening disease with recommendation of a high-fiber diet should be the initial therapy. CT enteroscopy or colonoscopy would be premature at this point given the absence of alarm symptoms: fever, weight loss, blood in stool, abnormal physical examination, family history of inflammatory bowel disease or colon cancer, or pain or diarrhea that awakens/interferes with sleep.

This patient does not have evidence of malabsorption, anemia, or weight loss to suggest a diagnosis of celiac disease; therefore, an empiric gluten-free diet would be inappropriate.

KEY POINT

- Irritable bowel syndrome is a diagnosis of exclusion but in the absence of alarm symptoms, invasive work up is not necessary

Bibliography
Drossman DA. The functional gastrointestinal disorders and the Rome III process. Gastroenterology. 2006;130(5):1377-1390. [PMID: 16678553]

Item 33   Answer: C
Educational Objective: Treat eosinophilic esophagitis.

Eosinophilic esophagitis is characterized by eosinophilic infiltration of the esophageal mucosa. Clinically, the disease most commonly presents with dysphagia or food impaction in atopic men in their third to fourth decades of life. For many years considered a pediatric disorder, the disease (or at least its recognition) appears to be rapidly increasing in adults. Diagnosis is suggested from clinical context, supported by endoscopic findings of mucosal furrowing or raised white specks (thought to represent eosinophilic microabscesses), and confirmed by histologic examination of the esophageal mucosa.

Besides disimpaction of a food bolus, initial treatment is medical because of concerns about mucosal friability and esophageal perforation in the setting of dilatation. Swallowed topical corticosteroids (fluticasone propionate or beclomethasone) have been shown to produce clinical remission in up to 50% of adults. Proton pump inhibitors do not appear to be effective. Case reports citing the efficacy of leukotriene receptor antagonists have yet to be confirmed in randomized trials.

KEY POINT

- Swallowed liquid corticosteroids are the first-line therapy for eosinophilic esophagitis.

Bibliography
Furuta GT, Liacouras CA, Collins MH, et al.; First International Gastrointestinal Eosinophil Research Symposium (FIGERS)

Subcommittees. Eosinophilic esophagitis in children and adults: a systematic review and consensus recommendations for diagnosis and treatment. Gastroenterology. 2007;133(4):1342-1363. [PMID: 17919504]

Item 34   Answer: B
Educational Objective: Manage localized adenocarcinoma of the pancreas.

At the time of diagnosis, about 80% to 85% of pancreatic cancers are unresectable because of distant metastases or invasion or encasement of the major blood vessels. Treatment of pancreatic cancer that has not metastasized nor spread to the local vasculature is surgical resection, with distal pancreatectomy being the preferred procedure for lesions of the pancreatic body. Evaluation of whether the tumor is resectable pre-operatively is performed with a combination of helical CT of the abdomen and endoscopic ultrasonography. Even with surgery and complete resection of the tumor, the 5-year survival rate is only 10% to 30%.

Concurrent radiation therapy and chemotherapy alone delays disease progression and may improve survival in patients with localized unresectable pancreatic cancer but will not provide a cure in patients with localized resectable pancreatic cancer. Pancreatic enzymes are used in patients with chronic pancreatitis or after pancreatic surgery to treat pancreatic malabsorption. In this otherwise healthy patient with a localized lesion and a potential for curative resection, palliative care is not indicated.

KEY POINT

- Surgery is the only treatment that provides a potential cure in patients with localized pancreatic cancer, with a 5-year survival rate of 10% to 30%.

Bibliography
Ujiki MB, Talamonti MS. Guidelines for the surgical management of pancreatic adenocarcinoma. Semin Oncol. 2007;34(4):311-20. [PMID: 17674959]

Item 35   Answer: B
Educational Objective: Diagnose vitamin D deficiency after bariatric surgery.

Patients who have bariatric surgery are at risk for various vitamin deficiencies. After such surgery, most patients require ongoing therapy with a multivitamin containing iron, along with vitamin B_{12}, calcium, and vitamin D. Other requirements include folic acid and vitamin A, which are often adequately replaced through the use of a multivitamin, although additional supplementation may be required. In addition, thiamine should be given for the first 6 postoperative months. This patient is taking calcium and vitamin D supplementation, but over-the-counter vitamin D supplementation may not be of sufficient quantity to sustain the requirements in this patient. Her diffuse musculoskeletal discomfort and elevated serum alkaline phosphatase are likely the result of vitamin D deficiency, with resultant osteomalacia, and, therefore, serum 25-hydroxyvitamin D should be measured.

Anti–smooth muscle antibody is a serologic marker of autoimmune hepatitis; although this disorder may produce abnormal liver chemistry studies, it usually is considered a hepatitic condition with predominant elevation of the aminotransferases rather than cholestasis. Serum creatine kinase may be a reasonable test in a patient who has myalgias while taking a statin, but this patient's musculoskeletal pain began months after she stopped taking the drug. Although thyroid dysregulation can cause both myalgias and abnormal liver chemistry results, the patient's thyroid-stimulating hormone and thyroxine levels are within normal limits while she is taking thyroid hormone replacement; therefore, further thyroid function testing is unnecessary. Ultrasonography of the liver would be the next best step in a patient who has serum chemistry results indicative of cholestasis, but with alkaline phosphatase being the only test elevated and without clinical features of biliary disease, nonhepatic causes of an elevated alkaline phosphatase need to be considered.

KEY POINT

- **Nutritional deficiencies are common after bariatric surgery, and patients typically need ongoing supplementation with iron, vitamin B$_{12}$, calcium, and vitamin D.**

Bibliography

Decker GA, Swain JM, Crowell MD and Scolapio JS. Gastrointestinal and nutritional complications after bariatric surgery. Am J Gastroenterol. 2007;102(11):2571-80. [PMID: 17640325]

Item 36   Answer: D

Educational Objective: Evaluate a patient with a potential familial colorectal cancer syndrome.

This patient has a family history that meets the Amsterdam criteria for hereditary nonpolyposis colorectal cancer (HNPCC). He should be referred to a genetic counselor to review the family history and be able to address the many issues that surround genetic testing and the implications for both the patient and his family members.

The best approach to test for HNPCC in this case and confirm the diagnosis would be to obtain tumor tissue from the patient's mother and test it for microsatellite instability. If the test is positive, a blood test can be done in the patient's mother in an attempt to find a germline mutation in the mismatch repair genes, and if identified, the patient may be tested to determine whether he is a carrier of that mutation. A negative blood test in the mother does not exclude the diagnosis of HNPCC. Screening for colon cancer in HNPCC should be initiated between age 20 and 25 years and requires a complete colonoscopy because cancers frequently occur in the ascending colon.

Genetic testing for colon cancer syndromes should be performed under the guidance of a genetic counselor. The counselor is skilled at appropriate data collection, pedigree analysis, and pre- and posttest counseling. Flexible sigmoidoscopy may identify polyposis for patients with familial adenomatous polyposis; however, it is inadequate screening for other hereditary colorectal cancer syndromes, such as attenuated familial adenomatous polyposis and HNPCC.

KEY POINT

- **Initial genetic testing for colon cancer syndromes is most effective in a patient with cancer rather than in an unaffected family member.**

Bibliography

Lindor NM. Recognition of genetic syndromes in families with suspected hereditary colon cancer syndromes. Clin Gastro Hep. 2004;2(5):366-375. [PMID: 15118973]

Item 37   Answer: C

Educational Objective: Recognize and manage focal nodular hyperplasia.

This young woman has focal nodular hyperplasia, the most common nonmalignant hepatic tumor that is not of vascular origin. This tumor occurs more commonly in women and usually causes no symptoms unless it is very large, in which case an affected patient may experience discomfort from mass effect on nearby organs. The tumors are caused by aberrant blood supply to an area of the liver and classically are differentiated by the appearance of a central scar.

Unlike adenomas, focal nodular neoplastic tumors are not estrogen-sensitive, and therefore, the patient does not need to discontinue oral birth control. In addition, these tumors do not have a malignant potential and do not need to be resected unless they are large and exert mass effect on other organs or cause focal ductal dilatation. This patient, therefore, does not need to be referred for resection. Because this lesion is radiographically consistent with focal nodular hyperplasia rather than hepatocellular cancer, the patient does not have to be referred for evaluation for liver transplantation. Focal nodular hyperplasia is usually stable and uncomplicated, and therefore, no immediate management is required for this patient.

KEY POINT

- **Focal nodular hyperplasia is the most common nonmalignant hepatic tumor not of vascular origin and is usually stable and uncomplicated requiring no immediate management.**

Bibliography

Bioulac-Sage P, Balabaud C, Bedossa P, et al; Laennec and Elves groups. Pathological diagnosis of liver cell adenoma and focal nodular hyperplasia: Bordeaux update. J Hepatol. 2007;46(3):521-527. [PMID: 17239484]

Item 38   Answer: D

Educational Objective: Manage constipation-predominant irritable bowel syndrome.

This patient has irritable bowel syndrome. As a young woman, she fits the demographic profile, and she also meets the Rome III criteria, with abdominal pain relieved by defecation and a change in bowel habits. The most recent formal criteria are the Rome II criteria, which require the presence of at least two of three symptoms occurring for 3 months (not necessarily consecutive) during a 12-month period. These symptoms include pain relieved with defecation, onset associated with change in stool frequency, or onset associated with change in the consistency of the stool. In clinical practice, these criteria have a positive predictive value of 98%. Importantly, she has no alarm indicators, including older age, male sex, nocturnal awakening, rectal bleeding, weight loss, or family history of colon cancer. In the absence of alarm symptoms, additional tests have a diagnostic yield of 2% or less. Furthermore, laboratory studies indicate no anemia or thyroid deficiency. Irritable bowel syndrome is a clinical diagnosis, and there are no laboratory, radiographic, or endoscopic findings that aid in diagnosis. Additional evaluation is not only unnecessary and expensive but also potentially harmful, especially when invasive procedures are ordered; additionally, confidence in the diagnosis is undermined when serial testing is ordered. The patient should be reassured that although this problem is annoying and inconvenient, it is not life-threatening. The patient has constipation-predominant irritable bowel syndrome, and her symptoms will likely be alleviated if she has more frequent and satisfying bowel movements. Because fiber supplementation has not been helpful, a nonabsorbed osmotic laxative such as polyethylene glycol will likely provide her significant relief.

There is no indication for the patient to undergo a CT scan or colonoscopy. Oral contraceptives are not typically associated with the syndrome, and she began taking the medication after the onset of her symptoms.

KEY POINT

- Irritable bowel syndrome is a clinical diagnosis that can be made confidently when patients meet the Rome III criteria and do not have alarm indicators.

Bibliography

Agrawal A, Whorwell PJ. Irritable bowel syndrome: diagnosis and management. BMJ. 2006;332(7536):280-283. [PMID: 16455728]

Item 39   Answer: D

Educational Objective: Evaluate a young patient with obscure gastrointestinal bleeding.

In a young patient, the next best test of the options provided to identify a source of bleeding would be a technetium-99m (^{99m}Tc) pertechnetate scan (Meckel scan) to identify the presence of Meckel diverticulum. Meckel diverticulum is the most common congenital anomaly of the gastrointestinal track and is located near the ileocecal valve. It often contains heterotopic gastric mucosa that ulcerates and bleeds. Technetium-99m (^{99m}Tc) pertechnetate has an affinity for the gastric mucose, and the Meckel scan identifies the heterotopic mucosa. Bleeding from a Meckel diverticulum is common in children but is an uncommon cause of blood loss in adults.

CT scan does not provide a luminal view of the intestine and is not likely to identify a bleeding source in this patient. Mesenteric angiography is not the appropriate next step because the patient does not have active, ongoing, brisk bleeding that would be detected and treated with angiography. A small-bowel barium study would not be a good choice; it obscures endoscopic visualization, has poor sensitivity for identifying sources of blood loss, and does not offer therapeutic options.

KEY POINT

- Bleeding from a Meckel diverticulum may be a source of obscure bleeding in young patients.

Bibliography

Lin S, Rockey DC. Obscure gastrointestinal bleeding. Gastroenterol Clin North Am. 2005;34(4):679-698. [PMID: 16303577]

Item 40   Answer: D

Educational Objective: Evaluate dysphagia.

The diagnosis and management of swallowing difficulties depend initially on determining whether the patient's symptoms are characteristic of either oropharyngeal dysphagia or esophageal dysphagia. The cornerstone of this determination is the medical history. In this patient, the immediate onset of symptoms with the initiation of a swallow, the difficulty swallowing liquids, and the cough associated with the swallowing difficulty make oropharyngeal, or transfer, dysphagia more likely than esophageal dysphagia. Videofluoroscopy, which allows real-time radiographic analysis of swallowing function, is the most sensitive test for oropharyngeal dysphagia. The procedure can show abnormal movement of a bolus, such as aspiration, pooling in pharyngeal recesses, movement of anatomic structures, muscle activities throughout the area, and oral and pharyngeal transit times. Common causes of oropharyngeal dysphagia are stroke, Parkinson disease, amyotrophic lateral sclerosis, myasthenia gravis, and muscular dystrophy.

Ambulatory esophageal pH monitoring is the most accurate technique to diagnose gastroesophageal reflux disease but is not the study of choice for evaluation of oropharyngeal dysphagia. CT scan of chest and abdomen can be an important adjunct to the evaluation of patients with esophageal dysphagia, because extraluminal causes of obstruction can be detected by cross-sectional imaging. Esophageal manometry is used in the diagnostic evaluation of patients with motility disorders of the esophagus. Although patients with such disorders may present with dysphagia of both solids and liquids, the immediate onset of symptoms with swallowing makes oropharyngeal dysphagia more likely.

KEY POINT

- In patients with dysphagia, immediate onset of symptoms with initiation of a swallow, difficulty swallowing liquids, and cough associated with the swallowing difficulty are characteristic of oropharyngeal rather than esophageal dysphagia.

Bibliography

Lind CD. Dysphagia: evaluation and treatment. Gastroenterol Clin North Am. 2003;32(2):553-575. [PMID: 12858606]

Item 41   Answer: B

Educational Objective: Evaluate for eradication of *Helicobacter pylori* infection.

Although testing for eradication of *Helicobacter pylori* is not cost-effective or practical in most cases, in this patient with a history of significant gastrointestinal bleeding from *H. pylori* infection requiring hospitalization and transfusion, eradication testing would be important to prevent future complications. In addition to patients with *H. pylori*-associated ulcers, eradication testing should be considered in patients with previous early-stage gastric cancer, *H. pylori*-related MALT lymphoma, or persistent dyspepsia after a test-and-treat approach. The father's history of gastric cancer would be another compelling reason to evaluate for eradication of the organism in this patient. Urea breath testing is a noninvasive test for evaluation of *H. pylori* eradication, but the sensitivity of the test can be markedly reduced in patients taking a proton pump inhibitor or recent antibiotics, and therefore, waiting to perform this test in 4 to 8 weeks after recent discontinuation of omeprazole would be recommended rather than testing now, which may lead to false negative results.

Although serum antibody testing is widely available and has good negative predictive value, it is not recommended after therapy because sustained antibody titers cannot easily distinguish between active and treated infection. Because this patient had a duodenal rather than gastric ulcer, a follow-up esophagogastroduodenoscopy to assess for healing and rule out malignancy is not required; in addition, repeating the procedure to evaluate for *H. pylori* eradication would not be a cost-effective testing method and would only be recommended if additional histopathologic evaluation were needed, for example, if dysplasia had been found initially. To do no further testing would not be recommended in this patient with a significant *H. pylori*-associated ulcer bleed.

KEY POINT

- The two noninvasive tests for determining *Helicobacter pylori* eradication are the stool antigen test and the urea breath test; the sensitivity of breath testing is adversely affected by recent therapy with a proton pump inhibitor or antibiotic.

Bibliography

Chey WD, Wong BC; Practice Parameters Committee of the American College of Gastroenterology. American College of Gastroenterology guideline on the management of *Helicobacter pylori* infection. Am J Gastroenterol. 2007;102(8):1808-1825. [PMID: 17608775]

Item 42   Answer: B

Educational Objective: Diagnose chronic pancreatitis.

This patient has chronic pancreatitis secondary to alcohol abuse, which has resulted in malabsorption. The three classic findings in chronic pancreatitis are abdominal pain that is usually mid-epigastric, postprandial diarrhea, and diabetes mellitus secondary to pancreatic endocrine insufficiency. Malabsorption occurs in patients with chronic pancreatitis when approximately 80% of the pancreas is destroyed. Malabsorption presents with diarrhea and steatorrhea, weight loss, and deficiencies of fat-soluble vitamins because the damaged pancreatic gland is no longer producing the pancreatic exocrine enzymes to absorb food. Patients with a typical presentation may not need additional testing. However, most patients with chronic pancreatitis have only nonspecific abdominal pain and require diagnostic radiographic imaging studies. The presence of pancreatic calcifications on radiographs confirms the diagnosis. Plain films of the abdomen will show pancreatic calcifications in approximately 30% of patients. Most patients, however, require abdominal CT scans, which are able to detect pancreatic calcification in up to 90% of patients. CT scanning can also exclude other causes of pain. Radiographic evidence of pancreatic ductal dilation, pseudocysts, or mass lesions may also help identify the cause of pain and determine the type of therapy.

Antiendomysial antibodies are a marker for celiac disease, which is unlikely in this patient with an evident history of pancreatic malabsorption. Although colonoscopy is indicated as a screening tool for average risk asymptomatic patients beginning at the age of 50 years and for patients with a change in bowel habits and weight loss, this patient's history suggests pancreatic malabsorption and colonoscopy is less likely than abdominal CT scan to confirm the diagnosis. Stool studies are appropriate for determining the cause of an acute infectious diarrhea, but this patient has had diarrhea for 8 months and infectious diarrhea is not usually associated with such a degree of weight loss.

Answers and Critiques

KEY POINT

- Patients with chronic pancreatitis present with abdominal pain and in more severe cases with malabsorption and endocrine insufficiency.

Bibliography

Witt H, Apte MV, Keim V, Wilson JS. Chronic pancreatitis: challenges and advances in pathogenesis, genetics, diagnosis, and therapy. Gastroenterology. 2007;132(4):1557-1573. [PMID: 17466744]

Item 43   Answer: B

Educational Objective: Manage fulminant liver failure.

The markedly elevated aminotransferase levels, positive hepatitis B surface antigen, and IgM antibody to hepatitis B core antigen establish the diagnosis of acute hepatitis B. Patients at greatest risk for exposure to hepatitis B virus (HBV) infection are those with a history of multiple sexual partners and injection drug users. The course of HBV infection depends mainly on the age at which a patient is exposed. Most patients who are first exposed as adults develop flu-like symptoms with malaise, nausea, vomiting, and diarrhea with associated jaundice. Children on the other hand most often do not develop symptoms after exposure to HBV. Despite the presentation of an acute infection, most adult patients will clear their infection after a few months. Therefore, most patients can be monitored as outpatients and treated for symptoms only. However, about 5% patients develop acute progressive hepatitis B with hepatic decompensation and need urgent liver transplantation. These patients tend to have an elevated INR and a rising bilirubin level and may develop encephalopathy, a marker of fulminant hepatic failure. This subgroup of patients needs to be recognized, admitted to the hospital, and started on antiviral therapy. Telbivudine, lamivudine, adefovir, and entecavir are acceptable options. Transplantation evaluation should be pursued. Transplantation should be performed when a poor outcome is anticipated but before the patient develops uncontrolled sepsis or prolonged periods of increased intracranial pressure that would preclude recovery even if a functioning liver is transplanted. In the United States, patients with fulminant hepatic failure are given highest priority for transplantation and often receive a transplanted liver within 1 week of evaluation.

Interferon should be avoided in patients with acute hepatitis B and particularly in fulminant hepatic failure due to hepatitis B because of the increased risk of hepatic necroinflammation. The patient has no evidence of ductal dilatation on ultrasonography, and therefore, there is a low yield and high risk to proceed with endoscopic retrograde cholangiopancreatography. Corticosteroids have been studied as a treatment for fulminant hepatic failure and have been found to be not effective. In addition, corticosteroid use is associated with an increased risk for infectious complications.

KEY POINT

- About 5% patients with acute hepatitis B virus infection develop acute progressive hepatitis B with fulminant hepatic decompensation and need urgent liver transplantation.

Bibliography

Terrault N, Roche B, Samuel D. Management of the hepatitis B virus in the liver transplantation setting: a European and an American perspective. Liver Transpl. 2005; 11(7):716-732. [PMID: 15973718]

Item 44   Answer: A

Educational Objective: Evaluate chronic hepatitis C virus infection.

This patient presented with asymptomatic elevation of hepatic biochemical tests; further testing demonstrated the presence of hepatitis C virus infection and signs of cirrhosis (splenomegaly, nodular liver contour, thrombocytopenia). Variceal hemorrhage occurs in 25% to 40% of patients with cirrhosis, and since mortality from variceal bleeding is high, screening for varices is a high priority task in all patients with newly discovered cirrhosis. Esophagogastroduodenoscopy is the next best management option to exclude the presence of esophageal varices. Depending on the size and appearance of the varices and the patient's Child-Pugh grade, prophylactic treatment may be indicated.

Patients with hepatitis C may be candidates for treatment with pegylated interferon and ribavirin; however, in this patient, cirrhosis and its potential complications must be assessed before therapy is begun. Moreover, treatment efficacy is lower in patients with cirrhosis than in patients without cirrhosis. Liver transplantation is the treatment of choice for suitable candidates with end-stage liver disease, fulminant hepatic failure, and certain metabolic disorders. Although the patient appears to have cirrhosis, there is no ascites, jaundice, or hepatic dysfunction that is severe enough to warrant consideration of transplantation. Treatment is recommended for all patients with chronic hepatitis B who have abnormal serum alanine aminotransferase values, HBV DNA levels >10^5 copies/mL, and liver biopsy findings of active disease. The oral agents lamivudine, adefovir, and entecavir are safe and well tolerated and may improve liver function in patients with decompensated hepatitis B. However, there is no indication that this patient has hepatitis B and therapy with lamivudine is not indicated.

KEY POINT

- Variceal hemorrhage occurs in 25% to 40% of patients with cirrhosis; upper endoscopy is indicated in patients with newly diagnosed cirrhosis.

136

Bibliography

Khaderi S, Barnes D. Preventing a first episode of esophageal variceal hemorrhage. Cleve Clin J Med. 2008;75(3):235-244. [PMID: 18383932]

Item 45   Answer: A

Educational Objective: Diagnose asymptomatic celiac disease.

Celiac disease is a small-bowel disorder characterized by mucosal inflammation, villous atrophy, and crypt hyperplasia, which occur on exposure to gluten. The disease is rather common, affecting nearly 1% (1/133 persons) of the population. Although many affected patients have diarrhea and steatorrhea, as well as bloating, abdominal pain, and malabsorption of vitamins and minerals, other patients are asymptomatic at diagnosis. Such patients may be found to have anemia or osteoporosis as part of routine health maintenance testing. Still others present with neurologic symptoms, dermatitis herpetiformis, or elevated concentrations of liver enzymes. The elevated alanine aminotransferase in this patient should normalize with a gluten-free diet if he has celiac disease. The patient's elevated alkaline phosphatase concentration is likely the result of increased bone turnover as a result of vitamin D and calcium malabsorption. Celiac disease is one of the most common causes of osteoporosis in men. Measurement of serum anti-tissue transglutaminase antibodies has a sensitivity and specificity of approximately 90% for celiac disease.

α_1-Antitrypsin deficiency affects approximately 1 in 1600 persons, and although measurement of α_1-antitrypsin is an appropriate test in the work-up of abnormal liver function tests, it is not the next best test because of the low prevalence of the disease compared to celiac disease, and it cannot explain the patient's anemia. The patient admits to social use of alcohol, and this is to be strictly avoided in the setting of liver disease. Unless the patient was actively drinking alcohol around the time of the testing, measuring the blood alcohol would not be helpful. Furthermore, in alcoholic liver disease, the aspartate aminotransferase concentration is usually greater than the alanine aminotransferase. Liver biopsy would be an extreme measure to take as a result of a mildly abnormal set of liver chemistry tests and is not indicated as an initial step.

KEY POINT

- Measurement of serum anti-tissue transglutaminase antibodies has a sensitivity and specificity of approximately 90% for celiac disease.

Bibliography

Green PH, Cellier C. Celiac Disease. N Engl J Med. 2007;357 (17):1731-1743. [PMID: 17960014]

Item 46   Answer: D

Educational Objective: Manage acute gastrointestinal bleeding that does not respond to endoscopic therapy.

Most cases of upper gastrointestinal bleeding can be effectively treated with medical and endoscopic therapy. The most common need for surgical treatment in such bleeding is failure of the bleeding to respond to endoscopic treatment. Surgical consultation should also be considered in patients who rebleed, in patients who require a large number of transfusions, and for large ulcers of the lesser curve of the stomach or posterior wall of the duodenum.

The diagnosis of bleeding from a gastric ulcer has already been made in this patient, and therefore no further diagnostic modalities such as a bleeding scan are required. Some studies have suggested the use of intravenous octreotide in the use of peptic ulcer bleeding, but no data supports its effectiveness after endoscopic therapy fails. In patients with *Helicobacter pylori*, eradication prevents ulcer recurrence but has no effect on the outcome of patients with acute upper gastrointestinal bleeding. However, all patients with bleeding peptic ulcers should receive high-dose proton pump inhibitor therapy. A meta-analysis showed that adjuvant high-dose proton pump inhibitor therapy following endoscopic hemostasis for ulcers at high risk of rebleeding reduces rebleeding, surgery, and mortality.

KEY POINT

- Surgical treatment of upper gastrointestinal bleeding should be considered when endoscopic therapy fails.

Bibliography

Martin RF. Surgical management of ulcer disease. Surg Clin North Am. 2005;85(5):907-929. [PMID: 16139028]

Item 47   Answer: B

Educational Objective: Manage hepatic encephalopathy.

This patient has severe encephalopathy manifested by worsening somnolence. The patient began manifesting signs of increasing encephalopathy days prior to the admission, when his wife noticed that he was becoming more agitated and slurring his speech. Encephalopathy progresses from subtle findings, such as reversal of the sleep-wake cycle or mild mental status changes, to irritability, confusion, slurred speech, and ultimately coma if not recognized and treated. There can be multiple inciting causes of encephalopathy in patients with cirrhosis, including dehydration, infection (especially spontaneous bacterial peritonitis), diet indiscretions, gastrointestinal bleeding, and medications. This patient likely became worse with the development of the urinary tract infection.

The best course of management is to treat the infection and to discontinue the diuretics and increase the lactulose to respond to the encephalopathy. The dose of lactulose should be titrated to achieve two to three soft stools per day with a pH below 6.0. Approximately 70% to 80% of patients with hepatic encephalopathy improve on lactulose therapy, and treatment is usually well tolerated.

Corticosteroids have no role in the reversal of hepatic encephalopathy. Although albumin therapy is often instituted in patients hospitalized with infections, especially spontaneous bacterial peritonitis and associated dehydration, it is not a primary treatment of encephalopathy. Transjugular intrahepatic portosystemic shunt (TIPS) is also not appropriate because placement of TIPS is likely to precipitate worsening hepatic encephalopathy as more blood is bypassed through the shunt rather than processed by the liver.

KEY POINT

- First-line therapy for hepatic encephalopathy is lactulose.

Bibliography

Kalaitzakis E, Bjornsson E. Lactulose treatment for hepatic encephalopathy, gastrointestinal symptoms, and health-related quality of life. Hepatology. 2007;46(3):949-950. [PMID: 17879365]

Item 48   Answer: A

Educational Objective: Manage gastric adenocarcinoma.

In a patient with a newly diagnosed gastric adenocarcinoma, the most important next step in staging would be to evaluate for metastatic disease. CT scan of the abdomen would assess for distant metastases, which would be concerning in this patient with profound weight loss and hepatomegaly. If no distant metastases are detected on initial staging, then endoscopic ultrasonography would be a helpful next test, because it can assess depth of invasion, whereas CT cannot accurately assess depth of early lesions. However, ultrasonography is less sensitive at determining metastatic disease, which is why it is not considered the initial test of choice for staging, especially considering most symptomatic patients such as this one have advanced disease at presentation.

Testing for *Helicobacter pylori* and eradication of the organism if present are recommended in patients with early-stage gastric cancer but would not be of benefit in someone with advanced disease. Positron emission tomography (PET) scanning should be considered preoperatively to follow-up suspicious but indeterminate lesions on CT imaging, but it is not recommended as the initial step in staging.

KEY POINT

- CT imaging is the next step after esophagogastroduodenoscopy in the staging of newly diagnosed gastric adenocarcinoma to evaluate for metastatic disease.

Bibliography

Brancato S, Miner TJ. Surgical management of gastric cancer: review and consideration for total care of the gastric cancer patient. Curr Treat Options Gastroenterol. 2008;11(2):109-118. [PMID: 18321438]

Item 49   Answer: D

Educational Objective: Manage acalculous cholecystitis.

This patient has evidence of cholecystitis on imaging, with gallbladder wall edema and the presence of pericholecystic fluid. However, she does not have any evidence of either cholelithiasis or choledocholithiasis. Therefore, the patient has acalculous cholecystitis. The clinical presentation of acalculous cholecystitis is variable. In critically ill patients, the only clues may be fever, leukocytosis, or nonspecific abdominal pain. In other patients, it may present similarly to calculous cholecystitis with right upper quadrant pain, fever, and right upper quadrant tenderness and a positive Murphy sign. Patients at risk for acalculous cholecystitis are those who are ill in the hospital with comorbidities, requiring long-term parenteral nutrition. These patients may be too ill for cholecystectomy and, therefore, require percutaneous drainage of the gallbladder until they are stable enough to undergo definitive therapy with surgery.

Without intervention acalculous cholecystitis has a mortality rate of 10% to 50%, and, therefore, this patient cannot continue to be observed with ongoing antibiotic therapy. The patient does not have any evidence of choledocholithiasis as the cause of her pain or cholecystitis, and, therefore, endoscopic retrograde cholangiopancreatography will not be therapeutic and places the patient at increased risk of complications or worsening pancreatitis. Although antifungal therapy should be considered in patients with necrotizing pancreatitis whose condition deteriorates clinically on antibiotic therapy, this patient's pancreatitis is stable and not the cause of the current change in her status.

KEY POINT

- Definitive therapy for acalculous cholecystitis is cholecystectomy; percutaneous cholecystostomy may be necessary in critically ill patients who cannot undergo cholecystectomy.

Bibliography

Batey A, Khan MA. Acalculous cholecystitis. Clin Gastroenterol Hepatol. 2007;5(3):e8. [PMID: 17218165]

Item 50   Answer: B

Educational Objective: Manage a mass lesion of the distal esophagus.

This patient presents with classic symptoms of achalasia: relatively short history of dysphagia, dilated esophagus, "bird's beak" abnormality on barium study, and typical manometric criteria for the diagnosis. However, in the presence of a mass lesion of the distal esophagus, the diagnosis of pseudoachalasia must be considered. Pseudoachalasia, also known as secondary achalasia, is not a primary motility disorder of the esophagus; rather it is a result of obstruction or neuronal infiltration at the gastroesophageal junction. The lesion is often neoplastic. Differentiation of pseudoachalasia from true achalasia can be problematic. Patients with pseudoachalasia tend to be older than patients with achalasia, have a shorter duration of symptoms, and have greater weight loss. Neither barium esophagography nor esophageal manometry can distinguish between primary and secondary achalasia. In this case, a history of lymphoma and the presence of a submusosal lesion require further evaluation. Endoscopic ultrasonography will allow delineation of the depth and invasiveness of the lesion, as well as permit transluminal needle biopsy of the mass.

Repeat mucosal biopsy is unlikely to be of sufficient depth to make a tissue diagnosis. Surgical exploration is not necessary to retrieve an adequate histologic sample of the lesion. Pneumatic dilatation and botulinum toxin injection are reserved for patients with primary achalasia, not pseudoachalasia, which frequently responds to treatment of the underlying disorder.

KEY POINT

- Patients with pseudoachalasia tend to be older than patients with achalasia, have a shorter duration of symptoms, and have greater weight loss.

Bibliography

Pohl D, Tutuian R. Achalasia: an overview of diagnosis and treatment. J Gastrointestin Liver Dis. 2007;16(3):297-303. [PMID: 17925926]

Item 51 Answer: B

Educational Objective: Manage a patient with probable hereditary nonpolyposis colorectal cancer.

This patient's family history meets the Amsterdam II clinical criteria for hereditary nonpolyposis colorectal cancer (HNPCC), which use the 3-2-1 rule: three relatives with an HNPCC-associated cancer, two generations affected, one person diagnosed before age 50 years. She should therefore be considered to be at risk for cancers associated with the disorder despite the negative genetic tests. The patient was tested negative for germline mutations *MLH1* and *MSH2*, but because there is no information whether a mutation had been identified in an affected member (her father, sister, or uncle), it is not clear whether the test represents a true negative in which case she is not at risk for HNPCC or if the test is uninformative. A genetic test for HNPCC must be interpreted along with consideration for the clinical and genetic data within the kindred. The strong family history of HNPCC-associated cancers suggests that the patient remains at risk for HNPCC, and she should be treated as if she is affected. Recommendations included colonoscopy

every 1 to 2 years from age 20 to 25 years and surveillance for gynecologic malignancy every 1 to 2 years from age 30 years. Abdominal CT scan is not part of the consensus screening guideline for HNPCC.

Breast cancer is not associated with HNPCC. False-negative germline testing is very rare and repeating the blood testing is not indicated.

KEY POINT

- Management of hereditary nonpolyposis colorectal cancer (HNPCC) requires regular testing for colon cancer and HNPCC-associated cancers starting at an early age.

Bibliography

Syngal S, Bandipalliam P, Boland CR. Surveillance of patients at high risk for colorectal cancer. Med Clin North Am. 2005;89(1):61-84. [PMID: 15527809]

Item 52 Answer: D

Educational Objective: Manage hepatorenal syndrome.

This patient has the hepatorenal syndrome. The diagnosis is made in the absence of other causes of renal disease in the setting of advanced liver disease. Other causes of renal failure should be excluded by performing a careful history and physical examination, obtaining basic laboratory tests, and ruling out an infectious process (especially spontaneous bacterial peritonitis). Failure to improve following withdrawal of diuretics and administration of 1–1.5 L of normal saline is indicative of the hepatorenal syndrome. Renal replacement therapy is indicated for patients with clinically significant volume overload or severe electrolyte abnormalities. There are two basic forms of the syndrome: type 1, which is what this patient has, is rapidly progressive over a course of 1 to 2 weeks; type 2 more commonly occurs in the outpatient setting in patients who also have diuretic-resistant ascites. Type 1, however, leads to rapidly progressive renal dysfunction and oliguria ultimately necessitating the initiation of supportive dialysis.

The hepatorenal syndrome is purely a reflection of advanced liver disease caused by severe renal vascular vasoconstriction in the setting of profound splanchnic vasodilation. The syndrome is not due to intrinsic renal disease and reverses with liver transplantation. Therefore, this patient should proceed with liver transplant alone, and the kidney function will return after liver function is restored.

A peritoneovenous shunt drains peritoneal fluid from the peritoneum into the internal jugular vein and has been used both for the treatment of refractory ascites and the hepatorenal syndrome. Insertion of a peritoneovenous shunt has been shown to modestly improve the creatinine concentration but not survival. Furthermore, shunting is associated with the risk of complications and cannot be recommended for this patient. Angiotensin-converting enzyme (ACE) inhibitors such as lisinopril have been used in the treatment of hepatorenal syndrome without success. In addition, this class of drugs can induce hypotension and reduce the glomerular filtration rate. Angiotensin-converting enzyme inhibitors cannot be recommended for the treatment of hepatorenal syndrome.

KEY POINT

- **The hepatorenal syndrome resolves with liver transplantation.**

Bibliography

Arroyo V, Fernandez J, Ginès P. Pathogenesis and treatment of hepatorenal syndrome. Semin Liver Dis. 2008;28(1):81-95. [PMID: 18293279]

Item 53   Answer: A

Educational Objective: Evaluate pancreatic cancer.

Patients with pancreatic cancer present most commonly with epigastric pain, weight loss, and in 70% of cases in which the tumor is in the head of the pancreas, with obstructive jaundice. Diagnosis is most frequently made by CT scan of the abdomen. However, smaller tumors may be missed by CT scan. Endoscopic ultrasonography is more sensitive than CT for tumors 2 cm or less. Endoscopic ultrasonography can also provide nodal and vascular staging and if desired can provide tissue through fine-needle aspiration.

Angiography is no longer used for the diagnosis or staging of pancreatic cancer. Surgical exploration in suspected pancreatic cancer would be performed as an attempt at curative resection and would not be performed until the diagnosis of a pancreatic mass is established and the tumor is properly staged.

Diagnostic procedures to confirm candidacy for exploratory laparotomy in patients with potentially resectable pancreatic cancer include diagnostic imaging with helical CT scans, endoscopic ultrasonography, and diagnostic laparoscopy. Although serum concentrations of CA 19-9, a Lewis blood group–related mucin, are frequently elevated in patients with this disease, this tumor marker's role has not been proved in the diagnosis or management of pancreatic cancer.

KEY POINT

- **Endoscopic ultrasonography is used commonly to diagnose pancreatic cancer, particularly in tumors of less than 2 cm.**

Bibliography

Boujaoude J. Role of endoscopic ultrasound in diagnosis and therapy of pancreatic adenocarcinoma. World J Gastroenterol. 2007;13 (27):3662-3666. [PMID: 17659723]

Item 54   Answer: D

Educational Objective: Manage postoperative ileus.

This patient has a postoperative ileus. An ileus is a functional, as opposed to mechanical, gut obstruction that occurs when the normal bowel motility is inhibited. Metabolic derangements, medications such as narcotic analgesics and anticholinergic agents, and infection may exacerbate or contribute to the development of an ileus. The pathogenesis of a postoperative ileus likely relates to impaired gut electrical, neurologic, and hormonal activity; inflammatory mediators; and a dysmotility effect from anesthesia. Patients have difficulty tolerating oral intake and may complain of bloating, abdominal pain, and lack of flatus and stool passage; abdominal distention, normal or decreased bowel sounds, and diffuse mild tenderness may be observed on physical examination. An abdominal plain film generally shows air throughout the intestine but may be confused with mechanical small-bowel obstruction because air-fluid levels and minimal colonic gas may also be seen; therefore, CT and barium studies may help distinguish these entities. Management of an ileus is generally supportive, including the discontinuation of any medications such as narcotics and calcium channel blockers that may further slow gut motility and correction of electrolyte and other metabolic abnormalities.

Although nasogastric tubes may be appropriate for a small-bowel obstruction, they are generally not efficacious in managing an ileus except to provide symptomatic relief from emesis. Rectal tubes are used to decompress the colon but would not be helpful in treating an ileus. Studies of metoclopramide therapy in this setting have not shown accelerated postoperative gastrointestinal recovery.

KEY POINT

- **Ileus is a functional obstruction of the bowel that commonly complicates the postoperative period; treatment is generally supportive, including the discontinuation of medications that slow gut motility and correction of electrolyte abnormalities.**

Bibliography

Luckey A, Livingston E, Tache Y. Mechanisms and treatment of postoperative ileus. Arch Surg. 2003;138(2):206-214. [PMID: 12578422]

Item 55   Answer: D

Educational Objective: Manage noncardiac chest pain caused by gastroesophageal reflux disease.

Esophageal disease is the most common cause of noncardiac chest pain. This patient's lack of signs and symptoms referring to the heart and her previous normal stress test make cardiac disease very unlikely. Because noncardiac chest pain is often associated with gastroesophageal reflux disease, it is reasonable in this patient to attempt empiric acid suppression therapy with a proton pump inhibitor.

Ambulatory esophageal pH monitoring can be used if the patient's condition does not respond to empiric therapy or if the patient has atypical symptoms. A history consistent with diffuse esophageal spasm or achalasia might require esophageal manometry as a first test, but it should also be reserved for patients who do not respond to empiric therapy. Esophagogastroduodenoscopy is indicated in patients with long-standing reflux disease to screen for Barrett esophagus or in patients with such alarm symptoms as gastrointestinal bleeding, weight loss, or fever. Repeating the stress test would not be indicated before a trial of a proton pump inhibitor in this patient with likely reflux disease.

KEY POINT

- Empiric proton pump inhibitor therapy is the first step in management of esophageal noncardiac chest pain.

Bibliography

Dore MP, Pedroni A, Pes GM, et al. Effect of antisecretory therapy on atypical symptoms in gastroesophageal reflux disease. Dig Dis Sci. 2007;52(2):463-468. [PMID: 17211695]

Item 56   Answer: B
Educational Objective: Evaluate gastroparesis.

This patient has the typical clinical features of delayed gastric emptying after an episode of infectious gastroenteritis. The abrupt onset of this syndrome makes postviral gastroparesis likely, especially because mechanical obstruction has been excluded. The test of choice to substantiate the diagnosis of gastroparesis is a 4-hour gastric scintigraphy of a solid meal.

In the absence of abdominal pain and with normal liver chemistry studies, the utility of biliary ultrasonography would be low in the evaluation of her symptoms. Although central nervous system lesions should always be considered in a patient with nausea and vomiting of unknown cause, the presence of her early satiety, bloating, and retained gastric contents makes central nervous system pathology unlikely, and, therefore, MRI of the head would not be indicated. Patients with cyclical vomiting syndrome or bulimia may benefit from biofeedback training, but neither condition is likely in this patient. Patients with cyclical vomiting tend to have discrete periods of intense vomiting, often feeling well between episodes, whereas patients with bulimia are unlikely to present for an evaluation of vomiting and do not have an abrupt onset as in this patient. Even though this patient likely has postviral gastroparesis, stool cultures for a viral infection would not be helpful because the acute viral infection has resolved.

KEY POINT

- Four-hour gastric scintigraphy of a solid meal is the test of choice for establishing the diagnosis of gastroparesis.

Bibliography

Parkman HP, Hasler WL, Fisher RS; American Gastroenterological Association. American Gastroenterological Association Technical Review on the Diagnosis and Treatment of Gastroparesis. Gastroenterology. 2004;127(5):1592-1622. [PMID: 15521026]

Item 57   Answer: D
Educational Objective: Treat primary biliary cirrhosis.

This patient has early-stage primary biliary cirrhosis, and the most appropriate therapy is ursodeoxycholic acid. Primary biliary cirrhosis is a chronic progressive cholestatic liver disease of unknown cause. This disorder is overwhelmingly a disease of women (>90%) older than 30 years. The most common symptom is persistent fatigue, which occurs in as many as 80% of patients. Either localized or general pruritus frequently develops. The pruritus often begins in the perineal area or on the palmar and plantar surfaces and is typically worse at night or in a warm environment. Jaundice and abdominal pain may also develop. However, many patients may be asymptomatic at presentation. An antimitochondrial antibody titer of ≥1:40 is the serologic hallmark for the presence of primary biliary cirrhosis and occurs in 90% to 95% of patients. However, the titer does not appear to correlate with the severity or progression of the clinical disease. Treatment with ursodeoxycholic acid improves the biochemical profile, reduces pruritus, decreases progression to cirrhosis, and delays the need for liver transplantation if begun at an early stage of disease. The data are more conflicting for later stages of disease. Therapy is usually continued indefinitely.

Alendronate may be appropriate for patients with primary biliary cirrhosis and osteoporosis, but this patient has normal bone mineral density and is taking adequate calcium and vitamin D replacement. Hormone replacement therapy is no longer regarded as the mainstay of therapy for osteoporosis. In the Women's Health Initiative, the use of conjugated estrogens and medroxyprogesterone in postmenopausal women increased the risk of cardiovascular disease, invasive breast cancer, stroke, deep venous thrombosis, and pulmonary embolism. The patient reports no menopausal symptoms that might be an indication for short term use of estrogen replacement therapy. The patient has no indications of liver failure, and therefore liver transplantation is not indicated.

KEY POINT

- Ursodeoxycholic acid therapy is indicated for early-stage primary biliary cirrhosis and may reduce the rate of liver transplantation and prolong survival in affected patients.

Bibliography

Corpechot C, Carrat F, Bahr A, Chrétien Y, Poupon RE, Poupon R. The effect of ursodeoxycholic acid therapy on the natural course of primary biliary cirrhosis. Gastroenterology. 2005;128(2):297-303. [PMID: 15685541]

Item 58   Answer: D

Educational Objective: Diagnose primary sclerosing cholangitis.

This patient likely has primary sclerosing cholangitis, a chronic cholestatic liver disease associated with inflammatory bowel disease and characterized by fibrosis, inflammation, and stricturing of the biliary tree. Up to 85% of affected patients have underlying inflammatory bowel disease, but <5% of patients with inflammatory bowel disease have primary sclerosing cholangitis. The disorder is more common in patients with ulcerative colitis than with Crohn disease. Most patients are diagnosed while asymptomatic with abnormal results on liver biochemistry tests, but jaundice and pruritus can occur in patients with advanced disease. The diagnosis is usually made by endoscopic retrograde cholangiopancreatography, which is especially useful in advanced disease where histologic samples can be taken to rule out cholangiocarcinoma and stents can be placed if there is a dominant stricture. Magnetic resonance cholangiopancreatography can also be used.

Autoimmune hepatitis, which is more common in women than in men, may have a cholestatic picture as in this patient, but it is often associated with other autoimmune disorders, such as hemolytic anemia, idiopathic thrombocytopenic purpura, type 1 diabetes mellitus, thyroiditis, and celiac disease. Laboratory findings in patients with autoimmune hepatitis include elevated serum aminotransferase values, hypergammaglobulinemia, mild hyperbilirubinemia, elevated serum alkaline phosphatase values, and the presence of autoantibodies. Serum gamma globulin values ≥1.5 times the upper limit of normal are common. This patient's gamma globulin level is not elevated (estimated by subtracting the albumin concentration from the total protein), making autoimmune hepatitis unlikely.

Patients with acute hepatitis C are usually asymptomatic and therefore rarely present clinically, but 60% to 85% of persons who acquire acute hepatitis C develop chronic infection. The cholestatic picture in the absence of other signs of advanced liver disease is inconsistent with hepatitis C cirrhosis. Hepatitis A can present acutely with fulminant liver failure, but the concentrations of the aminotransferases would be much higher, usually greater than 500 U/L.

KEY POINT

- Patients with acute hepatitis have a marked elevation of aminotransferases, whereas patients with primary sclerosing cholangitis have a cholestatic pattern.

Bibliography

Broomé U, Bergquist A. Primary sclerosing cholangitis, inflammatory bowel disease, and colon cancer. Semin Liver Dis. 2006;26(1):31-41. [PMID: 16496231]

Item 59   Answer: B

Educational Objective: Manage a patient at average risk for colon cancer.

This patient is at average risk for colorectal cancer; this population includes persons with no personal or family history of colon adenoma or cancer and who do not have a condition that predisposes them to cancer, such as inflammatory bowel disease. Screening for colorectal cancer is cost effective and well tolerated; it also saves lives. Screening is feasible because the 10 to 15 years needed for a polyp to develop into cancer are sufficient time to detect and remove an adenoma. Screening in the average-risk population should be started at age 50 years; there are various effective screening strategies in average-risk patients, with surveillance intervals depending upon chosen strategy. Endoscopic screening of the distal colon with flexible sigmoidoscopy decreases colon cancer diagnoses in the screened colonic segment and decreases colorectal cancer–related mortality by 45%. Colonoscopy reduces the incidence of colorectal cancer by 76% to 90% when compared with control populations. Advanced adenomas (≥1 cm in diameter, villous histology, high-grade dysplasia or cancer) are detected three times more often by sigmoidoscopy than by fecal occult blood testing.

Annual fecal occult blood testing is an option but requires that two samples be collected from each of three spontaneously passed stools. Digital examination to retrieve a sample is not an acceptable substitute. Flexible sigmoidoscopy in combination with fecal occult blood testing in 5-year intervals would be an option as well. Double-contrast barium enema is no longer considered to be a primary method of colorectal cancer screening by the U.S. Preventive Services Task Force. If double-contrast barium enema must be used for technical or anatomical reasons, the correct screening interval is 5 to 10 years.

KEY POINT

- Screening for colorectal cancer in the average-risk population should be started at age 50 years.

Bibliography

Levin B, Lieberman DA, McFarland B, et al. Screening and surveillance for the early detection of colorectal cancer and adenomatous polyps, 2008: a joint guideline from the American Cancer Society, the US Multi-Society Task Force on Colorectal Cancer, and the American College of Radiology. Gastroenterology. 2008;134(5): 1570-1595. [PMID: 18384785]

Item 60   Answer: E

Educational Objective: Manage a patient with bleeding of the small bowel.

This patient has obscure, overt gastrointestinal blood loss accompanied by anemia requiring blood transfusion. The most likely source of bleeding in this older patient is angiodysplasia from the small bowel, as endoscopy on two occasions as well as colonoscopy were nondiagnostic, and the melenic stool suggests a proximal gastrointestinal bleeding source. The next test would be a wireless capsule endoscopy.

Double-balloon enteroscopy is an option in this patient but only after the capsule endoscopy has identified a potential bleeding source. The capsule study may direct a peroral or transanal route for the double-balloon enteroscopy, which can then be used for diagnosis and to treat a bleeding source. CT angiography and small-bowel barium radiography are insensitive for detecting sources of bleeding and therefore not likely to assist in the management of the patient. Intraoperative endoscopy would allow a detailed assessment of the bowel but should be reserved until after less invasive options have been carried out to avoid the morbidity and mortality resulting from surgery.

KEY POINT

- Wireless capsule endoscopy is the preferred test to identify a bleeding source following a negative evaluation with upper endoscopy and colonoscopy.

Bibliography

Lewis BS. Obscure GI bleeding in the world of capsule endoscopy, push, and double balloon enteroscopies. Gastrointest Endoscopy. 2007;66(3 Suppl):S66-68. [PMID: 17709036]

Item 61   Answer: E

Educational Objective: Manage fundic gland polyps.

Fundic gland polyps, the most common form of gastric polyps, are small (1 to 5 mm in diameter), multiple (often <10), located in the body and fundus of the stomach, and convey no known cancer risk. The endoscopic description of this patient's polyps is classic for fundic gland polyps, with histologic confirmation of the diagnosis. In this setting, no further testing is recommended.

Fundic gland polyps may occur more frequently in patients with familial adenomatous polyposis syndrome, in which case fundic gland polyps are often found in greater numbers, with higher risk of dysplasia, yet low cancer risk. Unless this patient had a known family history of familial adenomatous polyposis or had an unusually high number of polyps with or without dysplasia, colonoscopy would not be recommended simply because of the presence of the polyps. Gastric hyperplastic polyps often occur in the setting of chronic active gastritis and may regress with eradication of

Helicobacter pylori; however, fundic gland polyps are not related to *H. pylori* infection and testing for the organism is not recommended in this setting. Testing for *H. pylori* is also not indicated in this patient because his symptoms are controlled with omeprazole. Although only one of the polyps was sampled, repeating the endoscopy to remove other polyps is not necessary because of the uniformity of the polyps on visual inspection and the fact that they convey no defined cancer risk. Endoscopic ultrasonography is similarly not required because these lesions have no defined risk for invasiveness.

KEY POINT

- Fundic gland polyps convey no defined cancer risk and require no follow-up.

Bibliography

Burt RW. Gastric fundic gland polyps. Gastroenterology. 2003;125 (5):1462-1469. [PMID: 14598262]

Item 62   Answer: D

Educational Objective: Manage liver cysts in a pregnant patient.

No further diagnostic tests are required in this asymptomatic patient with cystic liver lesions; the ultrasonographic findings show the cysts to have the characteristics of simple cysts (hypoechoic; no solid component) and no features of more concerning lesions such as cystadenoma or cystadenocarcinoma (for example, thickened irregular walls) or metastasis (necrotic center). Simple cysts are the most common benign mass of the liver and are characterized as cystic formations containing clear fluid that do not communicate with the intrahepatic biliary tree; few cysts enlarge or cause symptoms. Simple cysts are not estrogen sensitive and have no relation to the pregnancy. Subsequent use of oral contraceptives would be acceptable. Clinical features combined with the ultrasonographic findings are usually sufficient to distinguish simple cysts from liver abscess, necrotic malignant tumor, hemangioma, and hamartoma.

The lack of symptoms attributable to the cysts and the ultrasonographic features are sufficient to feel confident about the diagnosis. Therefore, further imaging, aspiration, or measurement of tumor markers is not needed.

KEY POINT

- Simple liver cysts are cystic formations that containing clear fluid; few simple cysts enlarge or cause symptoms.

Bibliography

Regev A, Reddy KR, Berho M, et al. Large cystic lesions of the liver in adults: A 15-year experience in a tertiary center. J Am Coll Surg. 2001;193(1):36-45. [PMID: 11442252]

Item 63   Answer: C

Educational Objective: Manage recurrent hepatitis C after liver transplantation.

This patient has abnormal liver chemistry tests after receiving a liver transplant for hepatitis C virus (HCV)-related cirrhosis, and a liver biopsy is indicated to distinguish between rejection and recurrent HCV infection. HCV is known to recur in the transplanted liver almost immediately after surgery if the patient was viremic at the time of transplant. As a result, some degree of inflammation is to be expected and in some patients early histologic injury as the HCV establishes itself in the new liver. In a small percentage of patients, the HCV can recur very quickly and aggressively a few months after liver transplantation, a condition termed rapidly recurring cholestatic hepatitis C, which carries a poor prognosis. Fortunately, most patients have a much more benign course, with approximately 30% still developing recurrent cirrhosis within 5 to 10 years after transplantation. Identifying those patients who show histologic injury in the liver graft and initiating therapy in these patients is important. Therefore, this patient should undergo a liver biopsy to assess histology and also to rule out other causes of post-transplantation abnormal liver chemistry tests, such as acute cellular rejection, which would clearly be managed quite differently from recurrent HCV infection. Pegylated interferon and ribavirin are effective in clearing the virus in about 30% to 40% of patients with post-transplant hepatitis C and are indicated for patients with progressive histologic changes. Prophylactic treatment has not yet been shown to be effective.

Because liver chemistry tests after transplantation are expected to be normal, conservative management with observation is not appropriate, and since this patient may have either recurrent HCV or rejection as a cause of his liver test abnormalities, it is incorrect to simply discontinue mycophenolate or start anti-HCV therapy with pegylated interferon and ribavirin without a histologic diagnosis.

KEY POINT

- Evaluation of abnormal liver test results after liver transplantation often requires a liver biopsy especially to differentiate between recurrent hepatitis C virus infection and rejection.

Bibliography

Carrión JA, Navasa M, García-Retortillo M, et al. Efficacy of antiviral therapy on hepatitis C recurrence after liver transplantation: a randomized controlled study. Gastroenterology. 2007;132(5):1746-1756. [PMID: 17484872]

Item 64   Answer: C

Educational Objective: Manage a diverticular bleed.

The likely source of gastrointestinal bleeding in this patient is lower, with diverticulosis and vascular ectasia being most likely. Although a brisk upper gastrointestinal bleeding source is possible, generally an elevated blood urea nitrogen level and symptoms referable to the upper gastrointestinal tract would be seen. The patient's recent colonoscopy and lack of other symptoms and large-volume bleeding make a neoplasm unlikely. Colonic ischemia generally presents with abdominal pain and only a small amount of bleeding. Regardless of the source of bleeding at this point in the emergency department, however, the first rule of management is to achieve hemodynamic stability. This patient is volume-depleted and not hemodynamically stable. Therefore, the most appropriate next step is to ensure proper intravenous access, generally via two large-bore peripheral catheters or a central line for volume repletion with crystalloid fluids and blood products as necessary.

A nasogastric tube may be considered after volume resuscitation if an upper gastrointestinal bleeding source were suspected, but given his lack of upper gastrointestinal symptoms and normal blood urea nitrogen concentration, this is unlikely. Further, if an upper gastrointestinal source were highly suspected, an esophagogastroduodenoscopy should be performed regardless of the lavage results, which have a high false-negative rate. Although a colonoscopy is the diagnostic test of choice to evaluate for diverticular bleeding, vascular ectasias, neoplasms, internal hemorrhoids, and other possible sources of lower gastrointestinal bleeding, again this should not occur before volume resuscitation. A bleeding scan would be indicated only if endoscopic evaluation is not revealing and the patient continues to bleed. Up to 90% of diverticular bleeding resolves spontaneously. If a bleeding diverticulum is detected on colonoscopy, it can be treated with epinephrine injection and/or thermal coagulation.

KEY POINT

- Diverticular bleeding is one of the most common sources of lower gastrointestinal bleeding, but diagnosis and therapy via colonoscopy are secondary to volume resuscitation and achieving hemodynamic stability.

Bibliography

Bogardus ST Jr. What do we know about diverticular disease? A brief overview. J Clin Gastroentero. 2006;40(7 Suppl 3):S108-111. [PMID: 16885691]

Item 65   Answer: A

Educational Objective: Manage a patient with a family history of colonic polyps.

Persons with a first-degree relative with a history of colonic adenoma or cancer have a 2- to 4-fold increased risk for colorectal cancer. This risk is modified by the age of onset of neoplasia in the affected relative. The current recommendation is that anyone with a first-degree relative with colon cancer or with an adenoma diagnosed before age 60 years should initiate screening at an earlier age than the general population and follow a shortened surveillance interval. Screening with colonoscopy is initiated at age 40 years or 10 years younger than the earliest diagnosis in the affected relative, whichever comes first. The recommended surveillance modality and interval is colonoscopy every 3 to 5 years.

Surveillance colonoscopy is recommended rather than other modalities because it offers a structural assessment of the colon in its entirety and provides a means to find and to remove polyps throughout the colon in this population at increased risk of polyp and cancer development. Fecal occult blood testing is a recommended screening modality in the average-risk population but not in patients at increased risk.

KEY POINT

- Patients with a family history of colon cancer or adenoma should undergo a screening protocol at age 40 years or 10 years younger than the earliest diagnosis in the affected relative and with a shortened surveillance interval compared with those at average risk of colorectal cancer.

Bibliography

Davila RE, Rajan E, Baron TH, et al; Standards of Practice Committee, American Society for Gastrointestinal Endoscopy. Standards of Practice Committee, American Society for Gastrointestinal. ASGE guideline: colorectal cancer screening and surveillance [erratum in Gastrointest Endosc. 2006;63(6):892]. Gastrointest Endosc. 2006;63(4):546-57. [PMID: 16564851]

Item 66   Answer: D

Educational Objective: Diagnose hepatitis E virus infection.

This young pregnant woman has clinical and biochemical evidence of fulminant hepatic failure, which is the rapid development of severe acute liver injury with impaired synthetic function and encephalopathy in a previously normal person or a patient with well-compensated liver disease. She is encephalopathic and has profound coagulopathy with an INR greater than 4.0. Her elevated ammonia level is also a poor prognostic indicator.

Her recent travel to Africa and the fact that she is pregnant should raise suspicion for acquisition of acute hepatitis E virus infection. Hepatitis E virus causes large outbreaks of acute hepatitis in underdeveloped countries. Clinically, hepatitis E is similar to hepatitis A. Hepatitis E is usually self-limited, and chronic infection does not occur. However, patients exposed to this virus especially in the pregnant state or in the presence of chronic advanced liver disease are at risk for developing fulminant hepatic failure. Unfortunately, there is no direct therapy and treatment is supportive care; in this patient management would include delivery of fetus and evaluation for liver transplantation if possible.

Although autoimmune hepatitis and the HELLP syndrome (hemolysis, elevated liver enzymes, low platelets) can both lead to acute liver failure, the patient's platelet count is elevated and she does not have evidence of hemolytic anemia and has a normal peripheral blood smear and therefore, does not meet the criteria for HELLP syndrome. In addition, she does not have associated clinical evidence of pre-eclampsia (hypertension and proteinuria after 20 weeks of gestation) or eclampsia (preeclampsia and seizures) often seen with the HELLP syndrome. Although autoimmune hepatitis is a possibility, she has no history of previous liver disease or abnormal liver chemistry tests, and it would be unlikely to see a flare of autoimmune hepatitis in the pregnant state when the immune system is often suppressed by pregnancy. The clinical presentation of patients with alcoholic hepatitis ranges from being asymptomatic to developing jaundice, fever, and findings consistent with portal hypertension. Serum aspartate aminotransferase (AST) and alanine aminotransferase (ALT) values are less than 300 U/L, and the AST:ALT ratio is usually greater than 2. Mild to moderate serum alkaline phosphatase elevations are common. The lack of alcohol intake and the marked elevations of the aminotransferase levels with an AST:ALT ratio that is less than 2 excludes alcoholic hepatitis as the cause of her fulminant hepatic failure.

KEY POINT

- Pregnant patients and those with chronic advanced liver disease who become infected with hepatitis E virus are at risk for fulminant hepatic failure.

Bibliography

Patra S, Kumar A, Trivedi SS, Puri M, Sarin SK. Maternal and fetal outcomes in pregnant women with acute hepatitis E virus infection. Ann Intern Med. 2007;147(1):28-33. [PMID: 17606958]

Item 67   Answer: C

Educational Objective: Diagnose dumping syndrome.

This patient has recently undergone a distal gastrectomy and now has classic features of early dumping syndrome. Patients with early dumping syndrome often have diarrhea, nausea, bloating, and tachycardia that occur within 30 minutes of eating as a result of hyperosmolar substances being rapidly emptied into the small bowel in the absence of the pylorus; therefore, carbohydrates and liquid nutrient drinks are often poorly tolerated as this case demonstrates. Late dumping syndrome occurs 1 to 3 hours after a meal and is characterized by neuroglycopenic symptoms.

Although carcinoid syndrome can be associated with diarrhea, flushing, and tachycardia, the diarrhea is often secretory in nature and continuous, including nocturnal episodes, unlike the features in this patient, which seem to be osmotically driven. Patients with chronic mesenteric ischemia also tend to have postprandial symptoms, but abdominal pain is often the predominant feature associated with weight loss secondary to fear of eating (sitophobia), neither of which was present in this patient. A gastrinoma should be considered in a patient with recurrent or complicated peptic ulcer disease that cannot be explained by NSAID use (as in this patient) or *Helicobacter pylori* infection. Patients with a gastrinoma usually have diarrhea secondary to fat malabsorption because the low pH from excess acid production inactivates pancreatic lipase. This patient notes his symptoms are actually better on a higher-fat diet, which would be more compatible with dumping syndrome because the food will have a longer phase of gastric digestion given that ingested fat can slow gastric emptying. Although irritable bowel syndrome is common in the general population, other diagnoses need to be considered first in this middle-aged man with new-onset symptoms following a surgical procedure.

KEY POINT

- Early dumping syndrome is associated with nausea, bloating, diarrhea, and tachycardia that often occur within 30 minutes after a meal.

Bibliography

Scholmerich J. Postgastrectomy syndromes-diagnosis and treatment. Best Pract Res Clin Gastroenterol. 2004;18(5):917-933. [PMID: 15494286]

Item 68   Answer: B

Educational Objective: Diagnose microscopic colitis.

This patient most likely has microscopic colitis, which is characterized by chronic watery diarrhea without bleeding. There are two types of microscopic colitis: collagenous colitis and lymphocytic colitis. The average age of onset for collagenous colitis is in the sixth decade of life and it tends to affect more women than men. The average age of onset for lymphocytic colitis is in the seventh decade of life, and women seem to be affected slightly more often than men. The cause of microscopic colitis is unknown. One theory is that the use of NSAIDs may contribute to the development of the disorder. Another theory is that it is caused by an autoimmune response. Colonoscopy in affected patients is grossly normal; to make a diagnosis, several biopsies must be taken from the colon. In collagenous colitis, biopsy specimens show more than normal amounts of collagen beneath the lining of the colon. In lymphocytic colitis, the specimen may also show an increased number of lymphocytes. Loperamide, diphenoxylate, and bismuth subsalicylate, either alone or in combination, are effective and well-tolerated when used as initial therapy.

Ulcerative colitis is characterized by bloody diarrhea associated with rectal discomfort, which the patient does not have. Fever, weight loss, tachycardia, dehydration, and significant abdominal tenderness or rebound indicate more severe disease. The patient has not taken any antibiotics and does not have other established risk factors for *Clostridium difficile* colitis, including recent hospitalization, advanced

age, and severe illness. She has not traveled out of the country recently, and therefore, is not at risk for tropical sprue.

KEY POINT

- Microscopic colitis is characterized by chronic watery diarrhea without bleeding; the diagnosis must be made by histologic examination of colonoscopic biopsy specimens.

Bibliography

Fernández-Bañares F, Salas A, Esteve M, Espinós J, Forné M, Viver JM. Collagenous and lymphocytic colitis. evaluation of clinical and histological features, response to treatment, and long-term follow-up. Am J Gastroenterol. 2003;98(2):340-347. [PMID: 12591052]

Item 69   Answer: B

Educational Objective: Evaluate acute hepatitis C virus infection.

The patient has signs of an acute hepatitis, including elevated liver test results with concurrent fatigue, malaise, and jaundice, and a recent exposure putting her at risk for viral hepatitis (injection drug use). Acute hepatitis C virus (HCV) infection may occur as a result of injection drug use, and although most infected persons do not develop a clinically apparent acute hepatitis, approximately 20% develop an acute infectious episode. Infected patients may remain seronegative for longer than 8 weeks, and therefore, in this clinical setting with a possibility of recent HCV infection, the most appropriate test would be measurement of HCV RNA. HCV RNA can be measured by PCR-based methods or signal amplification technologies. Hepatitis B virus (HBV) DNA should be measured only if the patient is positive for hepatitis B surface antigen (HBsAg).

HBsAg appears in serum 1 to 10 weeks after an acute exposure to hepatitis B virus and is present in the blood prior to the onset of symptoms or liver aminotransferase elevation. IgM anti-HBc can be the only serologic evidence of HBV infection during the period between the disappearance of HBsAg and the appearance of anti-HBs. Since the serologic tests for HBV are negative in this symptomatic person with elevated liver chemistry tests, there is no value in measuring HBV DNA. Acute hepatitis C is associated with characteristic histopathologic features including steatosis, lymphoid aggregates, and bile duct damage. However, these findings are not specific for HCV and similar findings are associated with acute HBV infection. Liver biopsy in this setting will not lead to a specific diagnosis without complementary serologic testing. MRI of the liver will detail hepatic morphology but will not contribute any more to the diagnosis than the ultrasonography.

KEY POINT

- In possible acute hepatitis C virus infection in seronegative patients, the most sensitive diagnostic test is measurement of hepatitis C viral RNA.

Bibliography

Strader DB, Wright T, Thomas DL, Seef LB; American Association for the Study of Liver Diseases. Diagnosis, management, and treatment of hepatitis C [erratum in Hepatology. 2004;40(1):269]. Hepatology. 2004;39(4):1147-1171. [PMID: 15057920]

Item 70   Answer: C

Educational Objective: Evaluate a patient with long-standing gastroesophageal reflux disease.

Long-standing gastroesophageal reflux is associated with risk for Barrett esophagus, a premalignant condition. Barrett esophagus is diagnosed endoscopically: the presence of columnar-appearing mucosa in the distal esophagus suggests the disorder, and it is confirmed histologically by detection of specialized intestinal epithelium. The presence of Barrett esophagus increases the risk for esophageal adenocarcinoma by approximately 30- to 100-fold. Endoscopic and histologic surveillance of patients with Barrett esophagus for dysplastic changes is recommended, although the frequency of surveillance is controversial.

Ambulatory pH monitoring is the most sensitive procedure for detection of increased esophageal acid exposure, but such a finding would be expected in this patient from the history alone. Esophageal manometry is useful in elucidating the cause of noncardiac chest pain or esophageal dysphagia. An oral calcium channel blocker may be prescribed in spastic motility disorders of the esophagus, but this patient's symptoms are typical of gastroesophageal reflux disease.

KEY POINT

- **Long-standing symptoms of gastroesophageal reflux disease should prompt an esophagogastroduodenoscopy to evaluate for Barrett esophagus.**

Bibliography

Konda VJ, Ross AS, Ferguson MK, et al. Is the risk of concomitant invasive esophageal cancer in high-grade dysplasia in Barrett's esophagus overestimated? Clin Gastroenterol Hepatol. 2008;6 (2):159-164. [PMID: 18096439]

Item 71   Answer: A

Educational Objective: Recognize risks of rebleeding in a patient with upper gastrointestinal bleeding.

Upper endoscopy should be performed at the time of an upper gastrointestinal bleed after appropriate volume resuscitation to provide a diagnosis as to the cause of bleeding, provide a prognosis, and perform endoscopic guided therapy if required. An ulcer with a visible vessel has an approximately 50% risk of rebleeding if not treated endoscopically. These ulcers can be effectively treated with injection therapy, thermal coagulation via endoscopic probes, or mechanical modalities such as endoclips. Clean-based ulcers rebleed in less than 5% of cases and do not require endoscopic therapy.

Prospective trials have shown a 5% to 10% rebleeding rate for endoscopic hemostasis. In these patients, endoscopic therapy may be repeated if the patient remains hemodynamically stable and if the endoscopist thinks that the bleeding lesion is amenable to endoscopic therapy. If repeat endoscopy is unsuccessful or the bleeding vessel is inaccessible or too large, surgical consultation should be obtained. However, in this case endoscopic intervention is the first management choice for an accessible and small visible vessel.

Intravenous omeprazole has been shown to reduce the risk of recurrent upper gastrointestinal bleeding in peptic ulcers after endoscopic hemostasis. Oral omeprazole also may decrease rebleeding. A meta-analysis showed that adjuvant high-dose proton pump inhibitor therapy following endoscopic hemostasis for ulcers at high risk of rebleeding reduces rebleeding, surgery, and mortality. Octreotide may have a marginal benefit by decreasing the rate of nonvariceal bleeding but is inferior to intravenous proton pump inhibitors. Ranitidine is inferior to proton pump inhibitors as an adjunct to endoscopic therapy.

KEY POINT

- **An ulcer with a visible vessel as a cause of upper gastrointestinal bleeding has an approximately 50% risk of rebleeding if not treated endoscopically.**

Bibliography

DiMaio CJ, Stevens PD. Nonvariceal upper gastrointestinal bleeding. Gastrointest Endosc Clin N Am. 2007;17(2):253-272. [PMID: 17556147]

Item 72   Answer: E

Educational Objective: Treat ulcerative colitis.

This patient has mild left-sided ulcerative colitis based on his clinical presentation and laboratory, endoscopic, and histologic findings. His ex-smoking status further supports this diagnosis. Mesalamine, a 5-aminosalicylate (5-ASA), is an effective agent to induce and maintain remission in this setting, and in mild cases, may be the only medication necessary. Its safety profile is excellent.

Azathioprine, an immunomodulator, may require 2 to 3 months to have a therapeutic effect and is generally reserved for patients who require corticosteroids for a short period of time and then transition to this medication. Antibiotics, including both metronidazole and ciprofloxacin, have not been shown to be effective in ulcerative colitis. The role of infliximab, a chimeric antibody against tumor necrosis factor-α, in ulcerative colitis is evolving; in patients with severe disease or who do not respond to corticosteroid therapy for remission, infliximab may be effective, but it would not be an appropriate first-line medication in mild ulcerative colitis.

- First-line therapy for induction and maintenance of remission in mild to moderate ulcerative colitis is mesalamine or another 5-aminosalicylate agent.

Bibliography

Baumgart DC, Sandborn WJ. Inflammatory bowel disease: clinical aspects and established and evolving therapies. Lancet. 2007; 369(9573):1641-1657. [PMID: 17499606]

Item 73   Answer: B

Educational Objective: Evaluate delayed gastric emptying.

This patient has clinical and examination findings suggestive of delayed gastric emptying, but it is not possible to distinguish mechanical obstruction from gastroparesis from the history and examination alone. The patient takes ibuprofen regularly, and, therefore, peptic ulceration causing gastric outlet obstruction needs to be considered; an esophagogastroduodenoscopy would be the next step to exclude mechanical obstruction. If the initial evaluation is negative for obstruction, gastric scintigraphy would be a reasonable test to evaluate for gastroparesis.

Biliary ultrasonography could be considered if abdominal pain were a prominent feature of the clinical presentation, although her symptoms are not compatible with biliary colic and it would not explain the historical or examination features of delayed gastric emptying. After gastroparesis has been established based on an abnormal scintigraphic study, an evaluation to determine an underlying cause may include screening for diabetes mellitus and serologic tests to detect an underlying autoimmune rheumatologic condition, which may be reasonable given her family history; however, these tests would not be recommended as the next step in this patient's evaluation.

- The initial step in the evaluation of delayed gastric emptying is esophagogastroduodenoscopy to rule out mechanical obstruction as a cause of symptoms.

Bibliography

Parkman HP, Hasler WL, Fisher RS; American Gastroenterological Association. American Gastroenterological Association Technical Review on the Diagnosis and Treatment of Gastroparesis. Gastroenterology. 2004;127(5):1592-1622. [PMID: 15521026]

Item 74   Answer: C

Educational Objective: Evaluate a patient with hematochezia.

The strongest clinical predictor of colonic neoplasia is the presence of blood in the stool. The likelihood of identifying colon polyps or cancer increases with age, and therefore, a patient younger than 40 years with bleeding should undergo flexible sigmoidoscopy as the first step in evaluation. The likelihood of proximal colonic neoplasia is low in this setting and, therefore, the risks associated with complete colonoscopy are not warranted.

Oral prednisone would not be indicated. A high fiber diet may be helpful for treatment for benign anorectal sources of bleeding; however, further evaluation to exclude neoplasia is indicated because of the multiple occurrences of bleeding.

- Patients at low risk of colonic neoplasia may undergo evaluation for hematochezia with flexible sigmoidoscopy rather than colonoscopy.

Bibliography

Lewis JD, Shih CE, Blecker D. Endoscopy for hematochezia in patients under 50 years of age. Dig Dis Sci. 2001;46(12):2660-2665. [PMID: 11768257]

Item 75   Answer: C

Educational Objective: Diagnose cholestasis of pregnancy.

This patient has cholestasis of pregnancy, the most common and most benign pregnancy-related liver disorder. It often presents in the second or third trimester of pregnancy and is associated with pruritus and mild elevation of the bilirubin level with or without a mild elevation of the aminotransferase levels. The total bilirubin rarely exceeds 10 mg/dL (171 μmol/L). The absence of other potentially dangerous pregnancy-related liver diseases needs to be confirmed. Treatment consists of ursodeoxycholic acid, which usually controls the symptoms. Although considered benign, this disorder can be associated with increased risk of fetal distress and preterm delivery; therefore, management should involve an experienced obstetrician.

Acute fatty liver of pregnancy usually occurs during the third trimester of pregnancy; it can be associated with high aminotransferase levels, increased bilirubin level, and evidence of fat on liver ultrasonography. Fetal mortality is high in the absence of delivery. The patient does not have evidence of acute hepatitis A, which often presents with very high aminotransferase levels (usually greater than 500 U/L) in a patient with likely exposure to the virus. The presence of the positive total hepatitis A virus antibody signifies a resolved infection. The HELLP syndrome is incorrect because the diagnostic criteria of this disorder—hemolytic anemia, significantly elevated aminotransferase levels, and thrombocytopenia—are not present. HELLP, a serious pregnancy-related disease also occurs during the third trimester and up to 48 hours postpartum. It is part of the spectrum of eclampsia or pre-eclampsia and should be considered in a pregnant patient who presents with hypertension, proteinuria, and acute liver disease. There is no treatment; therefore, prompt recognition along with urgent delivery of the fetus is the best therapy and often curative. If the disorder is not recognized and treated, the morbidity and the mortality rate of fetus and mother are significant.

KEY POINT

• Cholestasis of pregnancy, the most common and most benign pregnancy-related liver disorder, often presents in the second or third trimester of pregnancy and is associated with pruritus and mild elevation of the bilirubin level with or without a mild elevation of the aminotransferase levels.

Bibliography

Riely, CA. Liver disease in the pregnant patients. Am J Gastroenterol. 1999;94(7):1728-1732. [PMID: 10406228]

Item 76   Answer: C
Educational Objective: Diagnose chronic pancreatitis.

Establishing the diagnosis of chronic pancreatitis in a patient with early disease can be difficult. No blood or stool tests are currently available for the accurate diagnosis of early chronic pancreatitis. This patient's pain is most likely secondary to chronic pancreatitis with minimally elevated pancreatic enzymes and a history of harmful drinking. The patient has no evidence of exocrine or endocrine insufficiency and thus likely has early chronic pancreatitis. Normal liver enzymes, normal upper endoscopy, and a normal abdominal ultrasonography and CT scan of the abdomen make biliary causes and peptic ulcer disease less likely the cause of pain.

Endoscopic retrograde cholangiopancreatography (ERCP) has a sensitivity of nearly 95% for chronic pancreatitis and can show ductal dilation, strictures, and irregularity in both the main duct and its side branches. CT scan of the abdomen has a sensitivity of up to 90% for diagnosing chronic pancreatitis and should be ordered with thin cuts of the pancreas to improve sensitivity. Endoscopic ultrasonography may also be used to diagnose chronic pancreatitis with sensitivities equal to ERCP for moderate and advanced chronic pancreatitis but with lower sensitivity and specificity for mild and early chronic pancreatitis. Magnetic resonance cholangiopancreatography does not have sensitivities or specificities that match ERCP in the diagnosis of chronic pancreatitis at this time and cannot be routinely recommended. Biliary scintigraphy is used to diagnose acute cholecystitis and does not have a role in diagnosing chronic pancreatitis. Stool elastase can be abnormal in patients with more advanced chronic pancreatitis, particularly those who have malabsorption. However, stool elastase has poor sensitivity in patients with early chronic pancreatitis. Colonoscopy has a low yield in patients with upper abdominal pain.

KEY POINT

• Endoscopic retrograde cholangiopancreatography is the most sensitive imaging test for chronic pancreatitis.

Bibliography

Kamisawa T, Matsukawa M. Possibility of diagnosing early-stage chronic pancreatitis by endoscopic retrograde pancreatography. J Gastroenterol. 2007;42 Suppl 17:103-107. [PMID: 17238037]

Item 77   Answer: A
Educational Objective: Recognize the need for endoscopic and histologic surveillance in Barrett esophagus.

Adenocarcinoma of the esophagus is one of the most rapidly increasing cancers in the United States. Because this malignancy often arises from metaplastic esophageal mucosa (Barrett esophagus), endoscopic surveillance is recommended for patients with Barrett esophagus. Although the details of when to begin surveillance and the frequency are not clear, the confirmed finding of high-grade dysplasia requires surgical removal or endoscopic ablation of the abnormal mucosa.

In this case, long-standing reflux led to endoscopic evaluation. The "salmon-colored" columnar mucosa typical of Barrett esophagus was noted in the distal esophagus; metaplastic changes were confirmed by biopsy. In the absence of dysplasia, surgical esophagectomy is not indicated. *Helicobacter pylori* infection has not been implicated in the pathogenesis of Barrett esophagus. In fact, epidemiologic evidence points to a potential protective effect of *H. pylori* regarding development of Barrett esophagus.

KEY POINT

• Endoscopic surveillance is recommended for patients with Barrett esophagus.

Bibliography

Wani S, Sharma P. The rationale for screening and surveillance of Barrett's metaplasia. Best Pract Res Clin Gastroenterol. 2006;20 (5):829-842. [PMID: 16997164]

Item 78   Answer: D
Educational Objective: Manage a patient with ulcerative colitis and dysplasia.

This patient has had intensive medical therapy including azathioprine, an immunomodulator, and occasional corticosteroid therapy. His disease is now active despite his compliance with an intensive medical regimen. His medical options are limited, and infliximab would be the next best choice of nonsurgical therapy. However, the presence of multifocal dysplasia (with one being high-grade) precludes any option other than colectomy. A total proctocolectomy is the only acceptable option for this patient. Between 25%

and 40% of patients with ulcerative colitis eventually require surgery for dysplasia, cancer, or medically refractory disease.

In order to achieve a 90% sensitivity for the detection of dysplasia on surveillance colonoscopy, 33 biopsy specimens must be taken; the number increases to 56 specimens for a 95% sensitivity. However, in this patient high-grade dysplasia has already been established, and therefore further surveillance is unnecessary.

Although the active disease and areas of dysplasia do not appear to affect the more proximal colon, a segmental colectomy, although appropriate for sporadic colorectal carcinoma, is not appropriate in ulcerative colitis. The inflammatory activity will recur in the remaining colon, and the cancer risk persists throughout the colon, particularly in this patient who has had severe pancolitis in the past.

KEY POINT

- High-grade dysplasia detected at a surveillance colonoscopy for ulcerative colitis necessitates total proctocolectomy.

Bibliography

Ullman T, Croog V, Harpaz N, Sachar D, Itzkowitz S. Progression of flat low-grade dysplasia to advanced neoplasia in patients with ulcerative colitis. Gastroenterology. 2003;125(5):1311-1319. [PMID: 14598247]

Item 79 Answer: C

Educational Objective: Manage acute cholecystitis.

The patient likely has acute cholecystitis; she has a history of biliary colic, including pain that radiates to the right shoulder, a Murphy sign elicited on examination, fever, leukocytosis, mild bilirubin and aminotransferase elevation, gallstones and pericholecystic fluid, and thickening of the gallbladder wall on ultrasonography. When ultrasonography reveals gallstones and a positive ultrasonographic Murphy sign, the positive predictive value for acute cholecystitis is 92%. When the patient has the additional findings of gallstones and gallbladder wall thickening (≥3 mm), the positive predictive value is 95% for acute cholecystitis. Ultrasonography can be less sensitive in patients with ascites, hypoalbuminemia, hepatitis, obesity, and heart failure. Surgical cholecystectomy is advisable once gallstones lead to such complications as acute cholecystitis. Early cholecystectomy is associated with a shorter recovery period and fewer complications, such as gangrene and empyema of the gallbladder. While definitive evidence regarding the use of antibiotics in acute cholecystitis is lacking, it would seem prudent to consider using antibiotics in toxic-appearing patients.

Endoscopic retrograde cholangiopancreatography would be indicated if there were evidence of bile duct obstruction, which is not present on ultrasonography in this case. Abdominal CT scan would not be useful in this case; it can be useful when complications of acute cholecystitis (such as emphysematous cholecystitis or gallbladder

perforation) are suspected. The presence of a sepsis would suggest the diagnosis of gallbladder gangrene and perforation usually occurs after the development of gangrene. MRCP could confirm bile duct obstruction, if it were suspected on ultrasonography.

KEY POINT

- The classic findings of acute cholecystitis on ultrasonography are pericholecystic fluid and a thickened gallbladder wall of 3 to 4 mm, and ultrasonographic Murphy sign further confirms the diagnosis.

Bibliography

Ahmed A, Cheung RC, Keeffe EB. Management of gallstones and their complications. Am Fam Physician. 2000;61(6):1673-1680,1687-1688. [PMID: 10750875]

Item 80 Answer: A

Educational Objective: Diagnose chronic intestinal pseudo-obstruction.

This patient has chronic intestinal pseudo-obstruction (CIPO), which is characterized by chronic or recurrent episodes of abdominal pain, distention, nausea, vomiting, and obstipation; also, in this patient abdominal imaging showing distended loops of small bowel supports the diagnosis. Systemic sclerosis, a connective tissue disorder, has been associated with CIPO. Other causes include neuropathic disorders such as amyloidosis, diabetes mellitus, and paraneoplastic syndromes. A hereditary cause is recognized as well. Gastrointestinal manometry may be used to confirm the diagnosis, but this test is available only at academic institutions with motility centers; full-thickness small-bowel biopsy can demonstrate neuronal loss and degenerative features as well as inflammatory enteric neuropathies, histologic features that may be seen in CIPO. Treatment of CIPO is generally supportive, with initial decompression of bowel via nasogastric tube and bowel rest. Medications that decrease intestinal motility (for example, narcotics, calcium channel blockers) should be reduced to the minimum necessary. In this patient's case, nitroglycerin paste might be substituted for nifedipine to manage the Raynaud phenomenon. An oral diet should be adhered to as tolerated; if gastroparesis coexists, medications that increase gastric motility such as metoclopramide may be used. Low-dose octreotide may improve motor activity of the small bowel, and antibiotics may be used when concomitant bacterial overgrowth is present. Laxatives may be used in cases with associated constipation.

Colonic inertia often occurs concomitantly with CIPO, but in this patient, dilated loops of small bowel, rather than colon, are present. Although gastroparesis can also present with similar symptoms and/or coexist with CIPO, it is generally not an acute presentation, nor would patients stop having bowel movements or have distended loops of small bowel on radiography, although gastric distention may occur. Mechanical obstruction needs to be excluded as signs and symptoms are often very similar, and plain abdominal films can appear similar in these two diagnoses. In this patient, imaging studies did not show any obstructive lesion or mass.

> **KEY POINT**
>
> - Chronic intestinal pseudo-obstruction is characterized by chronic or recurrent episodes of abdominal pain, distention, nausea, vomiting and obstipation; the disorder may be due to myopathic causes (such as scleroderma) or neuropathic causes (such as amyloidosis, diabetes mellitus, and paraneoplastic syndromes).

Bibliography

Antonucci A, Fronzoni L, Cogliandro L, et al. Chronic intestinal pseudo-obstruction. World J Gastroenterol. 2008;14(19):2953-2961. [PMID: 18494042]

Item 81   Answer: B

Educational Objective: Diagnose cholangiocarcinoma.

Primary sclerosing cholangitis is a chronic cholestatic liver disease of unknown cause that is characterized by progressive bile duct destruction and may lead to secondary biliary cirrhosis. Up to 80% of patients with primary sclerosing cholangitis have an inflammatory bowel disease (most often ulcerative colitis), although less than 5% develop primary sclerosing cholangitis. Patients with primary sclerosing cholangitis are at risk for developing cholangiocarcinoma (lifetime prevalence of 10% to 30%). Patients with advanced primary sclerosing cholangitis and cirrhosis are also at risk for developing hepatocellular carcinoma. This patient has a history of primary sclerosing cholangitis and now presents with onset of painless jaundice and weight loss, which should raise the suspicion for cholangiocarcinoma. The detection of an irregular stricture in the hepatic duct further raises concern that a malignancy has developed. Additional pertinent findings are the elevated CA 19-9 level, which although not specific to cholangiocarcinoma, in the correct clinical setting is helpful in raising the likelihood of the diagnosis.

The patient has no findings suggesting acute cholecystitis on physical examination, the leukocyte count is normal, and on imaging the gallbladder appears normal without any wall thickening or edema, which would be expected findings in a patient with acute cholecystitis. Furthermore, biliary ductal dilatation would be uncommon in cholecystitis. Choledocholithiasis usually presents with biliary colic in the absence of weight loss. The lack of cholelithiasis, which does not entirely exclude this diagnosis, in the presence of the other clinical findings makes it less likely. Furthermore, a filling defect in the ducts would be expected rather than an irregular stricture, which makes malignancy more likely. Progressive primary sclerosing cholangitis,

although possible given the patient's disease, should not exclude the more likely diagnosis of cholangiocarcinoma in this patient who now presents with painless jaundice, weight loss, an irregular new stricture, and a very elevated CA 19-9.

> **KEY POINT**
>
> - Patients with primary sclerosing cholangitis are at risk for developing cholangiocarcinoma (lifetime prevalence of 10% to 30%).

Bibliography

Siqueira E, Schoen RE, Silverman W, et al. Detecting cholangiocarcinoma in patients with primary sclerosing cholangitis [erratum in Gastrointest Endosc. 2002;56(4):612]. Gastrointest Endosc. 2002;56(1):40-47. [PMID: 12085033]

Item 82   Answer: B

Educational Objective: Diagnose cytomegalovirus esophagitis in an immunosuppressed patient.

The sudden onset of odynophagia should raise suspicion for inflammatory conditions of the esophagus. In the absence of risk factors for caustic, radiation-induced, or pill-induced esophageal injury, infectious esophagitis is frequently the diagnosis, especially in immunosuppressed patients. In the absence of oral thrush and endoscopically visible esophageal plaques, candidal infection is less likely than cytomegalovirus-induced ulcerations. The viral cytopathic effect seen on microscopy confirms the diagnosis. Furthermore, candidal esophagitis is more likely to present with dysphagia rather than odynophagia.

Primary HIV ulcers can be visibly indistinguishable from cytomegalovirus ulcers, but the lack of HIV infection risk factors and the characteristic histologic findings make such a diagnosis unlikely in this case.

> **KEY POINT**
>
> - Sudden-onset odynophagia in an immunosuppressed patient suggests infectious esophagitis.

Bibliography

Pace F, Pallotta S, Antinori S. Nongastroesophageal reflux disease-related infectious, inflammatory and injurious disorders of the esophagus. Curr Opin Gastroenterol. 2007;23(4):446-451. [PMID: 17545784]

Item 83   Answer: B

Educational Objective: Evaluate dyspepsia in a patient with alarm features.

This patient has new-onset dyspepsia, and although she does not have any worrisome clinical features, the new onset of symptoms at her age and her mother's history of gastric cancer constitute alarm features, and therefore, further evaluation with esophagogastroduodenoscopy is warranted. Alarm features associated with dyspepsia include the following: age greater than 55 years with new-onset symptoms, family history of gastric cancer, weight loss, gastrointestinal bleeding, dysphagia, odynophagia, iron-deficiency anemia, vomiting, or abnormal examination findings.

Although pancreatic disease, such as adenocarcinoma of the pancreas, may present with similar clinical symptoms, evaluation with endoscopic retrograde cholangiopancreatography would not precede upper endoscopy or cross-sectional imaging, especially because of the increased invasiveness of this test. If the patient had not had any alarm features, testing for *Helicobacter pylori* and treating if positive would be recommended. In this patient with dyspepsia and alarm features, it would be inappropriate to simply diagnose functional dyspepsia or treat her with a neuromodulating agent before a fuller evaluation. An empiric trial with a proton pump inhibitor would be reasonable in a patient with features suggestive of gastroesophageal reflux, but should not replace further evaluation in this elderly patient with new symptoms.

KEY POINT

- Alarm features associated with dyspepsia include age greater than 55 years with new-onset symptoms, family history of gastric cancer, weight loss, gastrointestinal bleeding, dysphagia, odynophagia, iron-deficiency anemia, vomiting, and abnormal examination findings.

Bibliography

Talley NJ, Vakil NB, Moayyedi P. American Gastroenterological Association Technical Review on the Evaluation of Dyspepsia. Gastroenterology. 2005;129(5):1756-80. [PMID: 16285971]

Item 84   Answer: D

Educational Objective: Evaluate acute pancreatitis.

The diagnosis of pancreatitis relies heavily on the serum amylase and lipase, which are elevated in 75% to 90% of patients. Serum lipase is more specific and stays elevated longer than amylase. The two most common causes of acute pancreatitis in the United States are alcohol and gallstones. In this patient who does not consume alcohol, gallstones are the most likely cause of acute pancreatitis as shown by the pattern of liver enzymes. Abdominal ultrasonography is the most sensitive test for detecting the presence of gallstones and ductal dilation, which can provide indirect evidence for the presence of a retained common duct stone. Ultrasonography has no risk, is widely available, and is relatively inexpensive.

CT scan is less sensitive than ultrasonography for the detection of cholelithiasis. CT with contrast is indicated in patients with moderate or severe pancreatitis or those who do not improve clinically within 48 to 72 hours, to confirm the diagnosis, to exclude other intra-abdominal processes, to grade the severity of pancreatitis, and to diagnose local complications such as pancreatic necrosis, pseudocyst, or

abscess. Magnetic resonance cholangiopancreatography is used if there is a contraindication to intravenous radiocontrast. Endoscopic retrograde cholangiopancreatography (ERCP) is the most sensitive test for choledocholithiasis and can provide direct treatment by removing common duct stones. ERCP is indicated in patients with persisting pancreatitis, persistent elevation of aminotransferase levels, or dilated bile ducts suggesting the presence of retained bile duct stones. Stone extraction with biliary sphincterotomy improves the outcome, prevents further attacks of acute biliary pancreatitis, and reduces pancreatitis-related complications. However, in this patient there is not enough evidence yet that a common duct stone is still present to perform this more invasive test before ultrasonography. Upper endoscopy will not aid in determining the cause of acute pancreatitis.

KEY POINT

- The most common cause of acute pancreatitis in the United States is gallstones, which are diagnosed with abdominal ultrasonography.

Bibliography

Frossard JL, Steer ML, Pastor CM. Acute pancreatitis. Lancet. 2008;371(9607):143-152. [PMID: 18191686]

Item 85   Answer: B

Educational Objective: Evaluate hereditary hemochromatosis.

Although the classic description of hereditary hemochromatosis includes the findings of cirrhosis, type 1 diabetes mellitus, and skin hyperpigmentation ("bronze diabetes"), it is now uncommon for patients to present with this triad because of earlier detection of the disease. The most common presenting symptoms today are fatigue, impotence, and destructive arthropathy, characteristically of the second and third metacarpophalangeal joints. However, many patients are asymptomatic and are diagnosed after abnormal results are noted during routine laboratory testing. Patients who have abnormal liver chemistry tests and an abnormal transferrin saturation should be screened for hereditary hemochromatosis, an autosomal recessive disorder in which mutations in the *HFE* gene cause increased intestinal absorption of iron; the disorder is a common genetic disorder especially in the white population. The genetic mutation is located on chromosome 6 and is most commonly associated with the C282Y homozygous state or the compound heterozygote C282Y/H63D. This patient not only has elevated transferrin saturation but a serum ferritin greater than 1000 ng/mL (1000 mg/L) which has been shown to be predictive of advanced liver fibrosis in patients with hereditary hemochromatosis. Furthermore, he has diabetes mellitus and arthritis. In addition, his family history is also suggestive of the diagnosis.

Generally, a transferrin saturation of greater than 55% in a man and greater than 50% in a woman should raise suspicion for the disorder. Identifying an affected patient is also important for family members who then should be screened for the disorder as well, generally starting with a simple transferrin saturation and evaluating further those in whom an elevated saturation is found. Identifying patients before they develop disease is important because it can generally be managed with therapeutic phlebotomy until iron stores are depleted.

Therapy with deferoxamine, an iron chelator, is indicated only for patients who cannot tolerate phlebotomy, such as those with significant anemia. Iron chelation therapy is significantly less effective at removing iron than is phlebotomy and must be administered by subcutaneous or intravenous infusion. MRI is not diagnostic for hemochromatosis.

KEY POINT

- Patients who have abnormal liver chemistry tests and an abnormal transferrin saturation should be screened for hereditary hemochromatosis.

Bibliography

Tavill AS; American Association for the Study of Liver Diseases; American College of Gastroenterology; American Gastroenterological Association. Diagnosis and Management of Hemochromatosis. AASLD Practice Guideline. Hepatology. 2001;33(5):1321-1328. [PMID: 11343262]

Item 86   Answer: A
Educational Objective: Diagnose azathioprine-induced pancreatitis.

In patients with Crohn disease, not every episode of acute abdominal pain is related to the underlying inflammatory bowel disease. Patients with the disease who are refractory to or dependent on corticosteroids are a challenging problem. Since surgery for Crohn disease is associated with a high rate of recurrence, medical therapy with immunomodulators, such as 6-mercaptopurine and azathioprine, and biologic agents, such as infliximab and adalimumab, remain important therapies for the disorder. However, idiosyncratic pancreatitis may occur in up to 2% of patients treated with azathioprine, and the drug must be discontinued and not restarted in affected patients. The patient's symptoms, relatively benign abdominal examination, and the markedly increased concentrations of pancreatic enzymes make pancreatitis the most likely diagnosis.

The patient does not have an increase in the frequency of bowel movements, and therefore, a Crohn disease flair is unlikely and cannot explain the elevated serum amylase and lipase concentrations. The patient's normal aminotransferase and bilirubin concentrations make gallstone pancreatitis unlikely. The patient's markedly increased amylase and lipase concentrations make peptic ulcer disease and *Helicobacter pylori*-associated gastritis unlikely.

KEY POINT

- Azathioprine can cause pancreatitis in about 2% of patients taking the drug; the drug should be discontinued and not resumed if pancreatitis occurs.

Bibliography

Trividi CD, Pitchumoni CS. Drug-induced pancreatitis: an update. J Clin Gastroenterol. 2005;39(8):709-16. [PMID: 16082282]

Item 87   Answer: A
Educational Objective: Manage a patient after resection for colon cancer.

Patients diagnosed with colon cancer require a complete survey of the colon. The complete survey is usually done during the initial colonoscopy; however when a complete colonoscopy cannot be done preoperatively, it should be done postoperatively to determine whether synchronous lesions are present. Surveillance colonoscopy is then performed at 1, 3, and 5 years. Serum carcinoembryonic antigen (CEA) is usually measured every 3 months postoperatively, and CT scan is obtained at 1 year. Three meta-analyses showed increased survival with intensive follow-up after surgical resection for colorectal cancer. Recommendations from the American Society of Clinical Oncology suggest history and physical exams every 3 to 6 months for 3 years and then every 6 months for the next 2 years, CEA testing every 3 months for at least 3 years after diagnosis, and CT scans yearly for 3 years.

FDG-PET may provide information regarding distant spread of disease, but it is not currently recommended as part of a routine surveillance program. Proctosigmoidoscopy surveillance is indicated for rectal cancers but not for more proximal lesions.

KEY POINT

- Surveillance with colonoscopy, serial measurement of serum carcinoembryonic antigen, and CT scan is indicated in patients who have undergone curative resection for colon cancer.

Bibliography

Desch CE, Benson AB 3rd, Somerfield MR, et al; American Society of Clinical Oncology. Colorectal Cancer Surveillance: 2005 Update of an American Society of Clinical Oncology Practice Guideline [erratum in J Clin Oncol. 2006;24(7):1224]. J Clin Oncol. 2005; 23(33):8512-8519. [PMID: 16260687]

Item 88   Answer: D
Educational Objective: Treat advanced esophageal carcinoma.

This patient has advanced esophageal adenocarcinoma. Although clinical trials have shown survival benefit with aggressive therapy in early-stage esophageal adenocarcinoma, the management options in advanced disease are largely palliative. Patients with advanced stages of esophageal cancer or those that are poor candidates for surgery can be offered stenting as a palliative treatment for dysphagia. Stenting can also be used for palliation of patients with postoperative tumor recurrence. Both plastic and metal stents can be used for palliation of obstructing esophageal adenocarcinoma, although complications are more frequent with plastic stents.

In this case, the patient presents with very advanced disease, including hepatic metastases. Esophagectomy is a highly morbid procedure, which will offer no survival advantage to this individual. Hepatic wedge resection is not indicated in such advanced disease.

KEY POINT

- Endoscopic stenting therapy in advanced esophageal carcinoma can provide significant improvements in quality of life.

Bibliography

Ginsberg GG. Palliation of malignant esophageal dysphagia: would you like plastic or metal? Am J Gastroenterol. 2007;102(12):2678-2679. [PMID: 18042103]

Item 89   Answer: E

Educational Objective: Diagnose pulmonary embolism as an early complication of bariatric surgery.

Pulmonary embolism is a potential early complication (within the first 30 days) of bariatric surgery, and although infrequent, it accounts for 50% of all deaths in such patients. In this patient who recently underwent bariatric surgery and who presents emergently with chest pain, dyspnea, tachycardia, tachypnea, and hypoxemia, pulmonary embolism is the most likely cause, and immediate evaluation and management are important.

A postoperative bowel obstruction may occur secondary to internal hernias or adhesions, and patients with obstruction often present with nausea, pain, and abdominal distention. This patient has had stable nausea since surgery but has normal bowel sounds, is having bowel movements, and has normal abdominal imaging, making obstruction less likely. A patient with an anastomotic leak may also present with tachycardia and pain, but it is often associated with fever and leukocytosis, neither of which this patient has. Some intraperitoneal air would not be uncommon after a recent surgery, but comparison with past films, as in this case, should always be considered. Gastroesophageal reflux is a common cause of noncardiac chest pain, but would not explain the patient's tachycardia, tachypnea, and hypoxemia. Although myocardial infarction needs to be considered in any patient presenting with chest pain, the normal cardiac enzymes and lack of ischemic changes on electrocardiography make myocardial infarction unlikely.

KEY POINT

- Pulmonary embolism is an infrequent early complication after bariatric surgery, but it accounts for 50% of deaths in these patients.

Bibliography

Nguyen NT, Wilson SE. Complications of antiobesity surgery. Nat Clin Pract Gastroenterol Hepatol. 2007;4(3):138-147. [PMID: 17339851]

Item 90   Answer: B

Educational Objective: Diagnose hepatitis delta virus infection.

This patient likely has a superimposed hepatitis delta virus (HDV) infection, which is most common among injection drug users. HDV is a defective virus that requires the presence of hepatitis B virus (HBV) to exist. The outer lipoprotein envelope of the hepatitis D virus is made of the surface antigen of the HBV (HBsAg). Therefore, detectable hepatitis B surface antigen is necessary for the diagnosis of HDV infection. Two major patterns of serologic response may be seen depending upon the type of infection. In acute HBV/HDV D coinfection, the presence of IgM antibody to hepatitis B core antigen (anti-HBc IgM) is present. This simultaneous infection is clinically indistinguishable from acute HBV infection, although it may be more severe and is associated with a higher prevalence of acute liver failure. In acute HDV superinfection, the IgM antibody to hepatitis B core antigen is negative but the IgG antibody is positive. This type of infection may present clinically as either an apparent worsening of a previously established chronic HBV infection or an acute infection of viral hepatitis in a person with previously unrecognized chronic HBV infection. In this situation, the superimposed HDV infection suppresses hepatitis B replication and the HBV DNA level becomes undetectable. The reason for the suppression of HBV virus replication is unknown. Patients with HDV superinfection may be at greater risk for progression to cirrhosis. This patient's clinical presentation of an acute worsening of a chronic hepatitis B infection is most compatible with a superinfection with HDV. It is possible to diagnose HDV infection by using total anti-HDV antibodies, which would be the next diagnostic step for this patient; IgM and IgG can be detected by enzyme immunoassay or radioimmunoassay.

Acute alcoholic hepatitis is unlikely given the lack of a history of alcohol ingestion and the degree of elevation and pattern of the aminotransferases. In alcohol injury, the aspartate aminotransferase concentration tends to be higher than the alanine aminotransferase but rarely greater than 300 U/L. Ultrasonography did not show a space-occupying liver lesion, and therefore, hepatocellular carcinoma is unlikely. Furthermore, hepatocellular carcinoma is associated with cirrhosis, which is not present in this patient.

Reactivation of hepatitis B can occur, but in this case the anti-HB core IgM and DNA should be positive.

KEY POINT

- Chronic carriers of hepatitis B are susceptible to superinfection with hepatitis delta virus, which is a defective virus that requires the presence of hepatitis B virus to exist.

Bibliography

Fattovich G, Giustina G, Christensen E, et al. Influence of hepatitis delta virus infection on morbidity and mortality in compensated cirrhosis type B. The European Concerted Action on Viral Hepatitis (Eurohep). Gut. 2000;46(3):420-426. [PMID: 10673308]

Item 91   Answer: B

Educational Objective: Manage hepatocellular carcinoma.

This patient has radiographic evidence of cirrhosis with recent worsening hepatic decompensation manifested by worsening of ascites. Patients who develop hepatocellular carcinoma can, like this patient, present with new hepatic decompensation. The hemoglobin concentration is also elevated, a finding that can be a paraneoplastic manifestation of hepatocellular carcinoma. Furthermore, the findings on MRI are consistent with hepatocellular carcinoma in a patient with underlying cirrhosis. The patient has a single hepatocellular carcinoma in the absence of vascular involvement or extrahepatic spread; the stage of the tumor (T2) is within the Milan criteria for transplantation. Therefore, the next best management option is evaluation for liver transplantation.

When the imaging suggests hepatocellular carcinoma and there is either an elevation of the serum α-fetoprotein concentration or another image finding suggestive of hepatocellular carcinoma, diagnostic biopsy is not necessary, and there is a small but real risk for tumor seeding with biopsy of this lesion. Hepatic resection is reserved for a select group of patients with hepatocellular carcinoma. Such patients need to have stable disease with good hepatic reserve. Thus hepatic resection is often limited either to patients without underlying cirrhosis or patients who have stable cirrhosis but no evidence of portal hypertension or hepatic dysfunction, which would lead to hepatic decompensation and increased patient morbidity after resection. Although systemic chemotherapy may be considered for patients who have extensive tumors who do not meet the Milan criteria, the preferred therapy in this patient is transplantation rather than systemic chemotherapy.

KEY POINT

- Liver transplantation has become the primary treatment of choice for many patients with cirrhosis and hepatocellular carcinoma.

Bibliography

Bruix J, Sherman M; Practice Guidelines Committee, American Association for the Study of Liver Diseases. Management of Hepatocellular Carcinoma. Hepatology. 2005;42(5):1208-1236. [PMID: 16250051]

Item 92   Answer: C

Educational Objective: Evaluate chronic mesenteric ischemia.

This patient has classic signs and symptoms of chronic mesenteric ischemia: postprandial abdominal pain associated with sitophobia (fear of eating) and weight loss in the setting of vascular disease and a history of smoking. The clinical history is an essential part of the diagnosis of the disorder. Other possible causes of her abdominal pain have been evaluated, including biliary disease, peptic ulcer disease, pancreatitis, and malignancy, by the ultrasonography, upper endoscopy, CT scan, and laboratory tests. Although the gold standard for evaluating stenoses of the mesenteric vessels is traditional angiography, CT or magnetic resonance angiography both have high sensitivity in the diagnosis of chronic mesenteric ischemia. Two vessels are involved in 90% of affected patients, and 50% have significant stenosis of all three vessels (celiac artery, superior mesenteric artery, inferior mesenteric artery). Doppler ultrasonography may also be useful in evaluating these vessels.

Although colonoscopy would be indicated in this patient to screen for colon cancer if she had not had one within the last 10 years, this test should not be prioritized at this time. Colonoscopy is normal in chronic mesenteric ischemia as it does not involve the colon. A small bowel series would not be helpful in this setting because it evaluates only the lumen and not the vasculature of the small intestine. A gastric emptying study measures the half-time for the stomach to empty its contents and can be helpful in diagnosing gastroparesis; although the symptoms of gastroparesis and chronic mesenteric ischemia overlap, given the patient's history of vascular disease and extreme weight loss as well as the importance of timely diagnosis to avoid a superimposed life-threatening acute ischemic event, a gastric emptying study would not be the most appropriate next test.

KEY POINT

- Magnetic resonance arteriography is a highly sensitive test to diagnose chronic mesenteric ischemia.

Bibliography

Brandt LJ, Boley SJ. AGA technical review on intestinal ischemia. American Gastrointestinal Association. Gastroenterology. 2000;118 (5):954-968. [PMID: 10784596]

Item 93   Answer: B

Educational Objective: Treat chronic pancreatitis with pancreatic duct stones.

Patients with chronic pancreatitis must avoid alcohol. Patients who continue to drink alcohol have an increase in painful attacks and mortality. Pain in chronic pancreatitis results from chronic inflammation, chronic noxious stimulation of the nerves to the pancreas, and increased pancreatic intraductal pressure secondary to pancreatic duct stones, calcifications, or strictures. Large stones in the pancreatic duct can be crushed with extracorporeal shock wave lithotripsy; endoscopic retrograde cholangiopancreatography can then remove the stones and place stents in pancreatic duct strictures to decrease pancreatic duct pressure. Studies have documented symptom improvement in 11% to 75% of patients and resolution of stricture in 10% to 50%.

A surgical pancreatoduodenectomy (Whipple procedure) can be performed to relieve pain but is effective only in patients who have disease limited to the head of the pancreas and who have failed to respond to medical and endoscopic therapy. A surgical procedure to divert the pancreatic duct into the small intestine has been used widely in the treatment of patients with a chronic pancreatitis and a dilated pancreatic duct and is effective in many patients. The procedure involves removing pancreatic tissue that overlies the ductal system in the head of the pancreas. A less invasive procedure is preferred to surgical intervention as the next management step.

Celiac nerve block has been used to treat chronic pancreatitis pain but is considered by many experts to be an unproved therapy. Even in patients who respond, pain returns in 2 to 6 months and significant procedural complications have been reported. Furthermore, it would not be the first procedure of choice in a patient with a pancreatic ductal stone and evidence of obstruction. Pancreatic enzyme supplements are not consistently effective for pain control in chronic pancreatitis.

KEY POINT

- **Endoscopic treatment of pain in chronic pancreatitis is performed by removing pancreatic duct stones and placing stents in pancreatic duct strictures to decrease pancreatic duct pressure.**

Bibliography

Maydeo A, Soehendra N, Reddy N, Bhandari S. Endotherapy for chronic pancreatitis with intracanalar stones. 2007;39(7):653-658. [PMID: 17516288]

Item 94   Answer: B

Educational Objective: Evaluate a patient with a history of adenomatous colonic polyps.

This patient has had two adenomas identified on colonoscopy. The largest adenoma is greater than 1 cm in diameter and therefore requires a repeat colonoscopy in 3 years. Predictors for recurrent advanced adenoma on surveillance examinations include the presence of large polyps (>1 cm), more than three adenomas, villous histology, and adenoma with advanced dysplasia.

If only one or two adenomas are detected, and they are less than 1 cm in diameter, 5-year colonoscopic surveillance is appropriate. If an initial colonoscopy were normal or reveals only hyperplastic polyps in a patient with no family history of colon cancer, a 10-year interval would be appropriate.

KEY POINT

- **Patients who had high-risk colon polyps (three or more adenomas, high-grade dysplasia, villous features, or >1 cm in size) should have a repeat colonoscopy in 3 years, whereas those who had lower risk polyps (one or two <1-cm tubular adenomas with no high-grade dysplasia) can wait 5 to 10 years, and those who had only hyperplastic polyps can wait 10 years.**

Bibliography

Winawer SJ, Zauber AG, Fletcher RH, et al. Guidelines for colonoscopy surveillance after polypectomy: a consensus update by the US Multi-Society Task Force on Colorectal Cancer and the American Cancer Society. CA Cancer J Clin. 2006;56(3):143-159. [PMID: 16737947]

Item 95   Answer: C

Educational Objective: Treat ulcerative proctitis.

Ulcerative colitis can be classified by both extent and severity of disease, and treatment is guided by both factors. This patient has mild to moderate ulcerative proctitis, with disease limited to the distal rectum. Therefore, the best treatment would be local therapy with suppositories or enemas. Options include cortisone foam and mesalamine or corticosteroid suppositories for proctitis and hydrocortisone or mesalamine enemas for left-sided colitis. Topical mesalamine is more effective than topical corticosteroids, and almost half of the dose of topical corticosteroids may be absorbed systemically, leading to adverse long-term side effects. Maintenance of remission can be achieved with topical mesalamine.

Oral 5-aminosalicylates, including sulfasalazine, mesalamine, balsalazide, and olsalazine, are appropriate for distal disease that does not respond to topical therapy or for mild to moderate pancolitis. Oral prednisone is used when symptoms do not respond to 5-aminosalicylates. Because prednisone and other corticosteroids have many acute and chronic toxic effects that are dose- and duration-dependent, the lowest effective dose should be given for the shortest time. Azathioprine or 6-mercaptopurine (6-MP) may be used for patients who have incomplete disease remission while on corticosteroids. However, because both agents have delayed onset of action, concomitant administration of either azathioprine or 6-MP together with a 3- to 4-month course of prednisone is often necessary. The patient's mild and limited disease makes oral immunosuppressive therapy such as prednisone or azathioprine inappropriate.

Controlled trials have not demonstrated a consistent benefit of antibiotic therapy in the treatment of ulcerative colitis. There is probably a role for antibiotics in the treatment of fulminant colitis to treat or prevent a life-threatening infection but not in this patient with mild to moderate disease.

KEY POINT

- Topical therapy with corticosteroids or mesalamine is appropriate for distal ulcerative colitis.

Bibliography

Safdi M, DeMicco M, Sninsky C, et al. A double-blind comparison of oral versus rectal mesalamine versus combination therapy in the treatment of distal ulcerative colitis. Am J Gastroenterol. 1997;92(10):1867-1871. [PMID: 9382054]

Item 96   Answer: B

Educational Objective: Manage diuretic-refractory ascites and end-stage liver failure.

The patient has diuretic-resistant ascites, which portends a poor survival. Diuretic-resistant ascites is a common indication for liver transplantation and constitutes a reason to refer the patient for transplant evaluation. True refractory ascites is uncommon and can be managed with serial large-volume paracentesis or transjugular intrahepatic portosystemic shunt (TIPS). Randomized trials suggest that both therapeutic procedures are effective in controlling refractory ascites, although TIPS may be associated with a higher complication rate and increased risk for encephalopathy, and patients with poorly compensated liver disease may experience further decompensation after the procedure. The Practice Guidelines Committee of the American Association for the Study of Liver Diseases state that although TIPS will decrease the need for repeated large-volume paracentesis in patients with refractory ascites associated with cirrhosis, it should be used only in those patients who are intolerant of repeated large-volume paracentesis. Patients undergoing paracentesis of more than 5 L of ascitic fluid should be given intravenous albumin at the time of fluid removal in order to prevent post-paracentesis circulatory dysfunction.

Peritoneovenous shunt is rarely used because of an appreciable rate of complications and the lack of evidence that it prolongs patient survival, which may be several years in patients with normal or near normal hepatic and renal function tests but less than 6 weeks in patients with the hepatorenal syndrome. Although diuretic-resistant ascites is present, the patient has a stable serum creatinine, electrolytes are normal, he is not anuric and therefore, dialysis is not indicated.

KEY POINT

- Diuretic-resistant ascites is a common and important indication for referral for liver transplantation.

Bibliography

Steinman TI, Becker BN, Frost AE, et al. Guidelines for the referral and management of patient's eligible for solid organ transplantation. Transplantation. 2001;71(9):1189-1204. [PMID: 11397947]

Item 97   Answer: B

Educational Objective: Manage gastroparesis.

This patient with gastroparesis has had weight loss, dehydration, and recurrent hospital admissions, and diet modification and pharmacologic therapy have failed to control her symptoms. Because she cannot meet her nutritional needs, a nasojejunal feeding trial would be recommended to provide enteral nutrition support beyond the stomach. If such a feeding trial is successful, a more permanent feeding jejunostomy with or without a venting gastrostomy could be considered.

Because she developed tardive dyskinesia while taking metoclopramide, restarting the drug, even at a reduced dose, would not be appropriate. Placing a percutaneous gastrostomy tube and feeding into the stomach will likely offer no additional clinical benefit because the patient did not tolerate liquid supplements by mouth; therefore, feeding beyond the stomach into the jejunum would be recommended. Although total parenteral nutrition may be needed in some patients with gastroparesis, it has long-term risks and is, therefore, reserved for patients who cannot tolerate enteral feeding.

KEY POINT

- In patients with gastroparesis who fail to meet nutritional needs, alternative modalities for enteral feeding need to be considered.

Bibliography

Camilleri M. Diabetic gastroparesis [erratum in N Engl J Med. 2007;357(4):427]. N Engl J Med. 2007;356(8):820-829. [PMID: 17314341]

Item 98   Answer: C

Educational Objective: Evaluate nonalcoholic steatohepatitis.

Nonalcoholic fatty liver disease includes nonalcoholic steatohepatitis (NASH) and steatosis (fatty degeneration). Liver biopsy would differentiate between the two disorders. NASH, the most likely finding in this patient, generally occurs in obese patients with dyslipidemia and diabetes mellitus or glucose intolerance. This patient has the metabolic syndrome with persistently elevated liver chemistry tests despite adequate management of the diabetes and lipid disorder that are components of the syndrome. However, he remains obese. The patient's evaluation excludes viral hepatitis, space-occupying lesions, and hemochromatosis, and the remaining possibilities include NASH and drug-induced liver injury. The liver biopsy specimen would likely show features of NASH, which include macrovesicular steatosis, ballooning degeneration, and lobular inflammation. Also, the presence of fibrosis would further identify this patient as being potentially at risk for progressive fibrosis attributable to NASH. Treatment of NASH depends on the cause. Drugs known to be associated with NASH should be discontinued. If this is not possible, the dose should be reduced. Weight loss is the cornerstone of treatment for patients with obesity, diabetes mellitus, and dyslipidemia.

The patient's metabolic syndrome is adequately controlled, and therefore, therapy with insulin or a fibric acid derivative is not necessary and has not been shown to affect NASH. Because the only abnormality shown on ultrasonography is fatty infiltration, MRI would add little to the patient's evaluation.

KEY POINT

- Patients with metabolic syndrome and persistently elevated liver enzyme concentrations, despite adequate treatment of its components, should undergo liver biopsy.

Bibliography

Brunt EM. Nonalcoholic steatohepatitis: definition and pathology. Semin Liver Dis. 2001;21(1):3-16. [PMID: 11296695]

Item 99   Answer: C

Educational Objective: Evaluate diverticulitis.

This patient's left lower quadrant pain, fever, and elevated leukocyte count are classic symptoms and signs of diverticulitis. The most sensitive imaging modality to confirm this diagnosis as well as evaluate for any complications such as perforation, abscess, obstruction, and fistula is a contrast-enhanced CT scan of the abdomen and pelvis. A number of prospective investigations have reported a sensitivity of 69% to 95% and specificity of 75% to 100% for CT scan in acute diverticulitis. The presence of severe disease found on CT scan was prognostically very useful by accurately predicting failure of medical treatment and risk of secondary complications.

Colonoscopy is generally avoided during an episode of acute diverticulitis for concern of increased risk of perforation with air insufflation; furthermore, colonoscopy would miss the extraluminal complications. A small-bowel series evaluates the small intestine, which is not affected in diverticulitis. Before the availability of CT scanning, barium enema was used to diagnose diverticulitis, but it is more cumbersome for both the patient and radiologist and like colonoscopy, presents a risk for perforation.

KEY POINT

- The best imaging modality to confirm suspected diverticulitis and evaluate for extraluminal complications is a contrast-enhanced CT scan.

Bibliography

Bogardus ST Jr. What do we know about diverticular disease? A brief overview. J Clin Gastroenterol. 2006;40 Suppl 3:S108-111. [PMID: 16885691]

Item 100   Answer: D

Educational Objective: Evaluate peptic ulcer disease.

The two most common causes of peptic ulcer disease are NSAIDs and *Helicobacter pylori* infection, which account for more than 90% of cases. This patient has a history of arthritis for which she takes an over-the-counter analgesic, and therefore, inadvertent use of NSAIDs, which are widely available without a prescription and are often used in arthritis as analgesics, needs to be considered; many patients who take such nonprescription medications are unaware that they are taking NSAIDs.

H. pylori infection has been ruled out in this patient by the negative histology for the organism as well as negative serum antibody testing; therefore, no further testing for *H. pylori* is needed. Measuring serum gastrin should be considered in a patient in whom there is a suspicion of an acid hypersecretion state, such as a gastrinoma (Zollinger-Ellison syndrome), clinical features of which include multiple peptic ulcers, ulcers in unusual locations, severe esophagitis, or fat malabsorption, none of which this patient has.

Malignancy always needs to be considered in a patient with a gastric ulcer; therefore, biopsies of the ulcer and follow-up endoscopy to ensure ulcer healing would be recommended. However, this patient has a duodenal ulcer, which is much less likely to represent a malignancy, and biopsy of the ulcer or follow-up endoscopy to assess for healing is not needed. Alendronate therapy for osteoporosis has been associated with esophagitis and rare cases of gastric or duodenal ulcers; however stopping alendronate without considering the more common causes of peptic ulcer disease would not be appropriate at this time.

KEY POINT

- In patients with peptic ulcers, nonprescription medications should be reviewed to determine whether NSAIDs are being inadvertently used.

Bibliography

Gupta S, McQuaid K. Management of nonsteroidal, anti-inflammatory, drug-associated dyspepsia. Gastroenterology. 2005;129(5): 1711-1719. [PMID: 16285968]

Item 101   Answer: E

Educational Objective: Diagnose systemic sclerosis-associated pill-induced esophagitis.

Systemic sclerosis is a multisystem autoimmune disease characterized by microvascular injury with resultant fibrosis of skin and various internal organs, including the distal esophagus. In this case, the rather abrupt onset of odynophagia suggests focal ulceration of the esophagus, possibly related to one of her medications. Patients with systemic sclerosis often develop pill-induced esophagitis due to stasis in the distal esophagus.

Dysphagia is more frequently caused by dysmotility and gastroesophageal reflux, although peptic strictures occur in up to 29% of patients with Barrett esophagus. Although both fungal and viral esophagitis can present with odynophagia in immunosuppressed patients, the patient's prednisone therapy is probably not of sufficient amount and duration to predispose to these conditions. However, a diagnostic upper endoscopy may be indicated. Pill esophagitis will be much more likely in this patient. Barrett esophagus is usually asymptomatic and is detected on screening endoscopic evaluation. Esophageal stricture, although relatively common in patients with scleroderma, generally presents with dysphagia, not odynophagia.

KEY POINT

- Systemic sclerosis-induced esophageal dysmotility can result in dysphagia, stricture, and increased risk for pill-induced esophagitis.

Bibliography

Ebert EC. Esophageal disease in scleroderma. J Clin Gastroenterol. 2006;40(9):769-775. [PMID: 17016130]

Item 102   Answer: B

Educational Objective: Diagnose hepatic adenoma.

This patient likely has hepatic adenoma, which is associated with oral contraceptive use and occurs most commonly in women between the ages of 20 and 45 years. These lesions are usually solitary and occur most frequently in the right lobe. Diagnosis of hepatic adenoma depends on a lesion occurring in the proper clinical setting, with imaging showing a hyperechoic lesion on ultrasonography and peripheral arterial enhancement on a contrast-enhanced CT scan. MRI shows hyperintensity on both T1- and T2-weighted images. Surgical resection should be considered for patients with symptomatic hepatic adenomas.

The absence of a central scar makes focal nodular hyperplasia less likely than adenoma, although only one third of focal nodular hyperplastic lesions have a central scar. The lack of bile ducts and Kupffer cells on the biopsy specimen would effectively exclude focal nodular hyperplasia, in which such findings are prominent. The solid nature of the lesion on imaging excludes the diagnosis of simple hepatic cyst. The MRI in hepatocellular carcinoma usually shows high intensity on T2-weighted imaging and low intensity on T1-weighted images. Biopsy is generally not needed to make the diagnosis. In addition, the normal serum α-fetoprotein concentration, absence of cirrhosis, and biopsy findings make hepatocellular carcinoma highly unlikely.

KEY POINT

- Hepatic adenomas show a hyperechoic lesion on ultrasonography and peripheral arterial enhancement on a contrast-enhanced CT scan.

Bibliography

Grazioli L, Federle MP, Brancatelli G, Ichikawa T, Olivetti L, Blachar A. Hepatic adenomas: Imaging and pathologic findings. Radiographics. 2001;21(4):877-892. [PMID: 11452062]

Item 103   Answer: B

Educational Objective: Manage diarrhea in diabetic autonomic dysmotility.

This patient has chronic diarrhea in the setting of suboptimally-controlled type 1 diabetes mellitus with end-organ disease and likely has autonomic dysfunction that affects her gastrointestinal motility. Dysmotility associated with diabetes can manifest with either diarrhea or constipation; the diarrhea may be painless, nocturnal, and quite severe. In general, treatment should be supportive. Therefore, in addition to repairing fluid, electrolyte, and nutritional deficiencies and attempting to achieve tight glycemic control, diphenoxylate/atropine therapy is the most appropriate therapy for this patient. The patient has already been tested for small-intestine bacterial overgrowth, which may be superimposed upon dysmotility syndromes, but given that the breath test was negative, antibiotic therapy is unnecessary.

Although celiac disease, an immune-mediated sensitivity to gluten and other related proteins in wheat, rye, and barley, is commonly associated with other autoimmune disease such as diabetes mellitus and autoimmune thyroiditis, the patient has already been screened for this condition with serologic testing (anti-tissue transglutaminase and antiendomysial antibodies) and small-bowel biopsy. Therefore, having the patient start a gluten-free diet would not be appropriate. Octreotide, a somatostatin analogue, has been used to treat diarrhea related to diabetic-associated autonomic dysmotility, but the evidence of its efficacy is equivocal and treatment may be complicated by recurrent episodes of hypoglycemia that may be related to reduced secretion of counterregulatory hormones; therefore, octreotide would not be first-line therapy.

KEY POINT

- Diabetic autonomic dysmotility may manifest as constipation or diarrhea and is usually seen in the setting of other end-organ disease; treatment is generally supportive.

Bibliography

Longstreth GF, Thompson WG, Chey WD, Houghton LA, Mearin F, Spiller RC. Functional bowel disorders [erratum in Gastroenterology. 2006;131(2):688]. Gastroenterology. 2006;130(5):1480-1491. [PMID: 16678561]

Item 104   Answer: D

Educational Objective: Diagnose ischemic colitis.

This patient likely has ischemic colitis, the most frequent form of ischemia of the gastrointestinal tract. This type of ischemia usually affects the elderly with atherosclerotic disease, and in most cases is transient and resolves with conservative management. Patients with acute colonic ischemia usually present with rapid onset of abdominal pain and tenderness over the affected bowel. Rectal bleeding or bloody diarrhea usually develops within 24 hours of the onset of abdominal pain. The typical finding on CT scan is thickening of the bowel wall in a segmental pattern, which is not specific for ischemia and can be seen in infectious colitis and Crohn disease. The finding of patchy segmental ulcerations on colonoscopy in a patient with a compatible history establishes the diagnosis. Colonic ischemia is usually the result of a sudden and usually temporary reduction in blood flow that is insufficient to meet the metabolic demands of discrete regions of the colon but usually develops insidiously without a specific cause being identified. Colonic strictures are a rare complication.

The patient's acute onset of symptoms with bloody diarrhea is not consistent with Crohn disease. Patients with Crohn disease commonly present with a chronic history of abdominal pain, diarrhea, and weight loss. Disease involving the small intestine often causes nonbloody diarrhea, whereas hematochezia is more likely when the colon is involved. Cytomegalovirus colitis usually occurs in immunosuppressed patients, and peptic ulcer disease could present with bright red blood but only in the setting of a large and rapid bleed and could not explain the findings on the CT scan. Irritable bowel syndrome is a diagnosis of exclusion and does not present with rectal bleeding and the changes noted on the CT scan. Segmental thickening suggests a regional disorder rather than a systemic disorder.

KEY POINT

- Ischemic colitis presents most commonly in elderly patients with atherosclerotic vascular disease with crampy abdominal pain and bloody stool, and in most cases is self-limited.

Bibliography

American Gastroenterological Association Medical Position Statement: guidelines on intestinal ischemia [erratum in Gastroenterology. 2000;119(1):280-281]. Gastroenterology. 2000;118(5):951-953. [PMID: 10784595]

Item 105   Answer: B

Educational Objective: Manage metastatic pancreatic cancer.

Up to 85% of patients with pancreatic cancer present with advanced disease that cannot be surgically resected. Resection is also contraindicated in patients with metastatic disease. Overall survival of patients with metastatic pancreatic cancer is 6 months or less with treatment aimed at palliation with pain control, relief of biliary obstruction with endoscopic stenting, relief of duodenal obstruction if present, and usually chemotherapy.

In patients with biopsy-proven pancreatic cancer, markedly elevated tumor marker CA 19-9, and characteristic liver lesions on CT, an additional biopsy of the liver is not needed. Radiation therapy does not affect outcome in patients with metastatic disease of the pancreas. Radiation therapy may have a role in locally advanced disease but has little role in palliation of metastatic disease or the pain associated with pancreatic cancer.

KEY POINT

- Quality of life is significantly improved in patients undergoing palliative biliary decompression for pancreatic cancer.

Bibliography

Wisinski KB, Wahl AO, Small W Jr, Benson AB 3rd. Inoperable pancreatic cancer: standard of care. Oncology (Williston Park). 2007;21(13):1558-1564. [PMID: 18179046]

Item 106   Answer: C

Educational Objective: Manage high-grade esophageal dysplasia in a patient with Barrett esophagus.

The rationale for surveillance in patients with Barrett esophagus is that removal of premalignant lesions or in situ malignancies results in superior outcome to treatment of more advanced lesions. Esophagectomy is the procedure of choice to remove all diseased tissue, despite the rigors of the procedure. Resections performed for confirmed high-grade dysplasia have been shown to contain adenocarcinoma in up to 50% of cases. Less invasive approaches, such as ablative therapies and endoscopic mucosal resection, have shown promise, but esophagectomy is still considered the optimal procedure for long-term, disease-free survival.

Endoscopic mucosal resection used in selected patients with mass lesions and without radiographic evidence of lymphatic spread has been associated with excellent 5-year survival rates, but when such lesions arise in the setting of high-grade dysplasia, ablative therapies must accompany the treatment strategy. Photodynamic therapy is an ablative technique that showed early promise in the endoscopic treatment of high-grade dysplasia, but the procedure is associated with an unacceptable incidence of esophageal strictures and has largely been abandoned. Radiofrequency ablation of dysplastic tissue allows therapy of the mucosa with a shallower zone of tissue injury and results in a lower incidence of esophageal stricture. Long-term results for this approach are not yet available. Combined chemotherapy and radiation therapy is a palliative approach used only in patients with unresectable disease. Repeat endoscopy with biopsy is insufficiently aggressive in this patient with confirmed high-grade dysplasia arising in Barrett esophagus.

KEY POINT

- Esophagectomy is the procedure with the highest likelihood of long-term cancer-free survival in patients with Barrett esophagus and high-grade-dysplasia.

Bibliography

Schembre DB, Huang JL, Lin OS, Cantone N, Low DE. Treatment of Barrett's esophagus with early neoplasia: a comparison of endoscopic therapy and esophagectomy. Gastrointest Endosc. 2008;67 (4):595-601. [PMID: 18279860]

Item 107 Answer: B

Educational Objective: Treat diverticulitis.

This patient has uncomplicated diverticulitis; her left lower quadrant pain, fever, and leukocytosis all suggest the diagnosis, and the CT findings confirm it. Uncomplicated mild diverticulitis can be treated in the outpatient setting using broad-spectrum antibiotics such as ciprofloxacin and metronidazole for 7 to 10 days and a soft diet. Patients who are unable to maintain oral intake require hospitalization. As symptoms improve, a full diet can be resumed. The role of diet in preventing recurrence is not well documented, although patients are often asked to follow a high-fiber diet. Four to eight weeks after resolution, patients should undergo evaluation of the colon to exclude other disorders that may mimic diverticulitis, such as a malignancy.

A first-generation cephalosporin, such as cephalexin, is not appropriate because it has poor coverage of many gram-negative aerobic and anaerobic bacteria. A flexible sigmoidoscopy would not provide any additional useful information and may actually be harmful as perforation risk is likely higher in the setting of acute inflammation.

This patient has mild nausea with no vomiting and is able to eat and maintain oral hydration. If she should deteriorate and not tolerate oral feedings, the patient should be given intravenous fluids and parenteral pain control as needed, as well as intravenous antibiotics. Surgical consultation for sigmoid resection would not be appropriate at this time but may be indicated if she develops recurrent episodes of diverticulitis or a complication such as fistula, obstruction, or abscess.

KEY POINT

- Uncomplicated diverticulitis is treated with antibiotics to cover gram-negative and anaerobic bacteria, such as a fluoroquinolone and metronidazole.

Bibliography

Petruzziello L, Iacopini F, Bulajic M, Shah S, Costamagna G. Review article: uncomplicated diverticular disease of the colon. Aliment Pharmacol Ther. 2006;23(10):1379-1391. [PMID: 16669953]

Item 108 Answer: B

Educational Objective: Manage a gastric adenomatous polyp.

This patient has an adenomatous gastric polyp, a lesion that is most commonly detected in the antrum and, as in this patient, can occur in the setting of chronic gastritis. Like colonic adenomatous polyps, gastric adenomas can have varying degrees of dysplasia and risk of malignant transformation if not removed; therefore, since this patient's polyp was biopsied but not removed, endoscopic polypectomy would be recommended.

Because of the risk of malignant transformation if the polyp is not removed, doing no further testing would not be recommended. Similarly, there is no reason to delay repeating the esophagogastroduodenoscopy for 3 years, which may allow the polyp to grow, develop a higher degree of dysplasia, and possibly transform into a malignant lesion. Endoscopic ultrasonography is indicated for the evaluation of submucosal lesions, and because this patient's lesion is pedunculated, on the mucosal surface (rather than submucosal), and has no endoscopic or histologic features of malignancy, endoscopic ultrasonography is not indicated. Surgical resection would be indicated only if the lesion could not be removed endoscopically or of if there were evidence of malignancy on histologic assessment of the excised polyp.

KEY POINT

- Endoscopic polypectomy is the treatment of choice for most gastric adenomatous polyps.

Bibliography

Hirota WK, Zuckerman MJ, Adler DG, et al; Standards of Practice Committee, American Society for Gastrointestinal Endoscopy. ASGE guidelines: the role of endoscopy in the surveillance of premalignant conditions of the upper GI tract. Gastrointest Endosc. 2006;63(4):570-580. [PMID: 16564854]

Item 109 Answer: C

Educational Objective: Diagnose primary biliary cirrhosis.

This patient likely has primary biliary cirrhosis, and measurement of antimitochondrial antibody is a highly sensitive and specific test for the disorder; more than 95% of patients with primary biliary cirrhosis have antimitochondrial antibodies and the false positive rate is approximately 2%. Fatigue, pruritus, an elevated alkaline phosphatase concentration, and the presence of these antibodies strongly suggest this diagnosis and are unusual in other liver disorders, such as acute and chronic hepatitis and alcoholic liver disease. Although fatigue and pruritus used to be the most common presenting symptoms of primary biliary cirrhosis, the disease is now more widely recognized and many patients are diagnosed at earlier stages when they are asymptomatic. Imaging tests should be obtained in patients with chronic cholestasis to exclude extrahepatic bile duct obstruction or other biliary tree abnormalities (i.e., sclerosing cholangitis) in patients with a history of colitis.

If the antimitochondrial antibody is positive, liver biopsy is useful to provide evidence that would stage the disease and rule out drug toxicity or other liver disorders that may cause cholestasis similar to that associated with primary biliary cirrhosis. α_1-Antitrypsin deficiency would present with abnormal aminotransferase concentrations, not with a cholestatic picture. A serum protein electrophoresis may demonstrate elevation in serum IgM, but would not be diagnostic of primary biliary cirrhosis.

KEY POINT

- Fatigue, pruritus, an elevated alkaline phosphatase concentration, and the presence of antimitochondrial antibodies strongly suggest the diagnosis of primary biliary cirrhosis and are unusual in other liver disorders.

Bibliography

Talwalkar JA, Lindor KD. Primary biliary cirrhosis. Lancet. 2003;362(9377):53-61. [PMID: 12853201]

Item 110   Answer: B

Educational Objective: Treat bile salt–induced diarrhea.

The primary mechanism of secretory diarrhea in this patient is an increased luminal concentration of bile salts. He had his ileocecal valve and 80 cm of terminal ileum removed, which are the most important locations for bile salt reabsorption for enterohepatic circulation. The liver can compensate for the loss of bile salts when less than 100 cm of ileum has been resected but excessive presentation of bile salts in the colon can cause a secretory diarrhea. Cholestyramine will act as a binder and help prevent these bile salts from directly stimulating the colon. Lack of improvement following therapy with cholestyramine suggests an alternative diagnosis.

There is no role for immunosuppressive therapy in this patient in the absence of a confirmed diagnosis of inflammatory bowel disease. Without evidence of an infection, it is not reasonable to start empiric antibiotic therapy. There were no blind pouches created during the surgery, and therefore it is unlikely that the diarrhea is caused by small intestinal bacterial overgrowth. Tincture of opium will slow intestinal motility but will not address the underlying problem of bile salt-induced enteropathy.

KEY POINT

- Cholestyramine is a treatment for bile salt–induced diarrhea.

Bibliography

Robb BW, Matthews JB. Bile salt diarrhea. Curr Gastroenterol Rep. 2005;7(5):379-383. [PMID: 16168236]

Index

Note: Page numbers followed by f and t denote figures and tables, respectively. Test questions are indicated by a Q.